FROM THE LAND OF SHADOW

NATION OF NATIONS:
IMMIGRANT HISTORY AS AMERICAN HISTORY
General Editors: Rachel Buff, Matthew Jacobson, and Werner Sollors

Beyond the Shadow of Camptown: Korean Military Brides in America
Ji-Yeon Yuh

Feeling Italian: The Art of Ethnicity in America
Thomas J. Ferraro

Constructing Black Selves: Caribbean American Narratives and the Second Generation
Lisa D. McGill

Transnational Adoption: A Cultural Economy of Race, Gender, and Kinship
Sara K. Dorow

Immigration and American Popular Culture: An Introduction
Jeffrey Melnick and Rachel Rubin

From Arrival to Incorporation: Migrants to the U.S. in a Global Era
Edited by Elliott R. Barkan, Hasia Diner, and Alan M. Kraut

Migrant Imaginaries: Latino Cultural Politics in the U.S.-Mexico Borderlands
Alicia Schmidt Camacho

The Force of Domesticity: Filipina Migrants and Globalization
Rhacel Salazar Parreñas

Immigrant Rights in the Shadows of Citizenship
Edited by Rachel Ida Buff

Rough Writing: Ethnic Authorship in Theodore Roosevelt's America
Aviva F. Taubenfeld

The Third Asiatic Invasion: Empire and Migration in Filipino America, 1898–1946
Rick Baldoz

Race for Citizenship: Black Orientalism and Asian Uplift from Pre-Emancipation to Neoliberal America
Helen Heran Jun

From the Land of Shadows

*War, Revolution, and the Making
of the Cambodian Diaspora*

Khatharya Um

NEW YORK UNIVERSITY PRESS

New York and London

NEW YORK UNIVERSITY PRESS
New York and London
www.nyupress.org
© 2015 by New York University
All rights reserved

Library of Congress Cataloging-in-Publication Data
Um, Khatharya.
From the land of shadows : war, revolution, and the making of the Cambodian diaspora
/ Khatharya Um. ISBN 978-1-4798-0473-3 (cloth : acid-free paper) -- ISBN 978-1-4798-
5823-1 (paperback : acid-free paper)
1. Cambodia--Politics and government--1975-1979. 2. Political violence--Cam-
bodia--History--20th century. 3. Genocide--Cambodia--History--20th century. 4.
Totalitarianism--Social aspects--Cambodia--History--20th century. 5. Cambodians-
-Migrations--History--20th century. 6. Cambodian Americans--Social conditions. 7.
Refugees--United States--Social conditions. 8. Cambodian Americans--Interviews. 9.
Cambodians--France--Interviews. 10. Victims of state-sponsored terrorism--Cambodia-
-Interviews. I. Title.
DS554.8.U46 2015
959.604'2--dc23
2015016214

New York University Press books are printed on acid-free paper, and their binding materials
are chosen for strength and durability.
We strive to use environmentally responsible suppliers and materials to the greatest extent
possible in publishing our books.

Manufactured in the United States of America

10 9 8 7 6 5 4 3 2 1

Also available as an ebook

To my parents,

who taught me that no war, revolution, or exile

can take away one's dignity.

That is humanity's ultimate triumph.

CONTENTS

ACKNOWLEDGMENTS

This project is more than a book. It is a life journey where one is defined by each and every encounter. As in life, it is not possible to pinpoint and acknowledge them all. I am deeply grateful for the mentorship that Chalmers Johnson, Douglas Pike, and Samuel Popkin gave me through the early years of my academic career. I owe profound intellectual debts to the Asian American Studies scholars whose works have informed my thinking about empire, race, refuge, and refugees, and to the Cambodia scholars, for deepening my understanding of Cambodian history and society, particularly David Chandler and Ben Kiernan, who reached out to me when I was just a budding graduate student, and to all the Cambodians who opened their doors and hearts to me, not as a researcher but as a Khmer. I am grateful for the encouragement and helpful comments from the anonymous reviewers and from Gordon Chang, and for the enthusiasm that Eric Zinner and Alicia Nadkarni at New York University Press expressed about the project.

An undertaking of this nature would not be possible without the love and support from colleagues, friends, and family: Elaine Kim, my mentor and lifeline, without whom I would never have found my way to Asian American Studies or through the many hurdles since; Sau-ling Wong, with her bottomless generosity of spirit, who humanizes the space of the academy; Jane Singh, my co-conspirator in our many plans to change the world; Boreth Ly, for the gift of laughter; and above all, my husband, my compass on this journey with its many dark tunnels. As for the young ones in the family, the impetus for this endeavor, our history is you, and yours.

HISTORICAL TIMELINE

1863–1953 French protectorate period. With the exception of Japan's brief occupation in 1945, French control extended throughout the period.

November 1953 Independence from France

1955–1970 Sangkum period (also referred to as the Sihanouk period)

July 1954 Signing of the Geneva Accords, which stipulated the withdrawal of all foreign troops. Many Khmer communist leaders left for Hanoi with the departing Vietnamese communist troops.

1963 Rejection of American aid

1967 Peasant uprising in Samlaut

1969 Beginning of Operation Menu and intensified U.S. bombing of Cambodia

March 18, 1970 Right-wing coup that deposed Sihanouk and abolished the monarchy

1970–1975 Khmer Republic period

May 1, 1970 Joint U.S.–South Vietnamese incursion into Cambodia

June 1970 Withdrawal of U.S. ground troops from Cambodia

1970–1973 Saturated bombing of Cambodia

April 17, 1975 Khmer Rouge seizure of Phnom Penh

1975–1979 Democratic Kampuchea period

1979–1988 Vietnamese invasion and occupation of Cambodia Establishment of the People's Republic of Kampuchea (PRK)

1979 Beginning of resistance against Vietnamese occupation

1982 Formation of the Coalition Government of Democratic Kampuchea between royalist, republican, and Khmer Rouge political factions.

Trial in absentia of Pol Pot, Ieng Sary, and Khieu Samphan

1988   Withdrawal of Vietnamese communist forces from
       Cambodia

1989   Renaming of PRK to the State of Cambodia

       Reintroduction of Buddhism and private property

1991   Signing of the Comprehensive Political Settlement of the
       Cambodia Conflict, also known as the Paris Peace
       Accords

1992–1993   Deployment of United Nations forces and establishment of
       the UN Transitional Authority for Cambodia (UNTAC)

1992   Repatriation of Cambodians from Thai border camps

1993   UN-monitored and -endorsed national elections

       Formation of a coalition government, consisting of
       communist (CPP) and noncommunist groups

1997   CPP-led coup against its noncommunist allies

1998   Pol Pot's death

1999   Arrest of Kaing Guek Eav (also known as Duch), head of
       the Tuol Sleng (S-21) extermination center

2003   Agreement to form the Extraordinary Chambers in the
       Courts of Cambodia for the Khmer Rouge tribunal

2007   Duch charged with crimes against humanity and war crimes

2010   Duch sentenced to thirty-five years in prison and later given
       a life sentence

2011   Beginning of the trials of Nuon Chea, Ieng Sary, Ieng
       Thirith, and Khieu Samphan

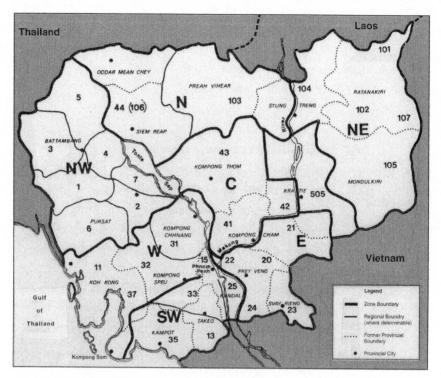

Administrative map of Democratic Kampuchea, 1975–1979. Source: Yale Cambodian Genocide Program.

Introduction

This voice from the grave urges itself on our hearing. For . . .
the life-and-death discourse of the twenty-first century is un-
ambiguously the discourse of fanaticism and intolerance.
—Wole Soyinka[1]

The funeral procession carrying King Norodom Suramarit made its way in reverse circumambulation, as deemed by royal custom, toward Veal Men, the sacred ground at the center of the capital. High-ranking officials in white court attire (*sampot chang kben* and *av kot*) moved silently along the float of golden *neak*[2] upon which was placed the gilded urn. Atop the royal elephants sat members of the court ballet in full regalia.[3] No one who beheld this ritualized event in 1960 could deny the sense of continuity that it imparted despite the paradoxical sense of finality that it connoted. Certainly, no one reflecting upon that moment could have envisioned that less than ten years later, Cambodia's age-old monarchy would be abolished and the country engulfed in a fratricidal war that paved the way for a revolution so radical in its transformative vision that it left in its wake an indelible genocidal imprint. As the "dominoes" fell to communist forces that fateful spring of 1975—first Phnom Penh, then Saigon, and finally Vientiane—the promise of postwar peace and prosperity gave way to the horrors of forced labor camps, mass graves, flight, and exile. For Cambodia, the Khmer Rouge march into Phnom Penh on April 17 marked the beginning of a spiraling descent into one of the nation's darkest eras. The "oasis of peace" that was Cambodia in the 1960s became the killing fields of the 1970s, its tranquility replaced by the silence of the death of almost a quarter of its people.

Even in a century of mass atrocities, the Cambodian experience under the Khmer Rouge (1975–1979) stands out as one of the most extreme and traumatic instances in human history. What emerged in the aftermath of this genocidal encounter was a nation fractured by death and dispersal. In less than four years, almost two million of the country's estimated seven million people had perished from hard labor, disease, starvation, execution, and "disappearances," leaving in the wake of the regime's collapse in 1979 a population comprised mostly of women and children. Another 600,000 Cambodians fled their ancestral homeland,[4] of which over 100,000 found refuge in America.

The Cambodian nation, now bifurcated by dispersal, bears the indelible stain of auto-genocide[5] that continues to register in the Cambodian culture, institutions, and psyche both in Cambodia and in diaspora. While scholars and jurists debate whether or not the term "genocide" could and should be applied to what took place in Democratic Kampuchea (DK),[6] there can be no disputing the magnitude of human loss under the Khmer Rouge, or the irreparable tear that it has left on the Khmer nation, at least for the survivor generation if not beyond. The ancient practice of generational deracination—*samlab muy pouch*, which literally translates as the killing of the seed (*genos*)—reared its contemporaneous head in the mass killings of Democratic Kampuchea. For Cambodians, it is this notion of *geno-cide*, in the simplest and most literal terms, that resonates.

It has been said of Cambodia that "it rarely happens that a historian can look back over the recent past of any contemporary society with the feeling that a curtain has been rung down on a play, and that what happened up to that time may be studied without regard to what is going on at present, or what may happen in the future."[7] As it is with Africa in the Western imaginary,[8] the various preconceptions and myths[9] that enveloped prerevolutionary Cambodia had kept this small Buddhist kingdom suspended in antiquity, frozen in time, and fixed in the imaginary of the outside world. The scenes captured in the displays at the Exposition Coloniale in France in 1906 have held the colonial gaze and that of successive generations in a mesmerized rapture: "In these fantasies, Cambodia would always be a beautiful and graceful country, veiled in mysterious exoticism of divine kingship and dancing *apsaras*."[10] Fixing the gaze on the ruins of antiquity makes it possible to disregard the ruins of empire. Orientalism, to borrow from Said,[11] thus conspires with the instinctually human temptation to regard horrific political developments such as those of Democratic Kampuchea as an eruption of the irrational, an undisciplined nation running amok. The absolute secrecy and virtual autarky that shrouded the country after 1975 reinforced this view of the Khmer Rouge period as historically compartmentalized, an aberration unmoored to the country's historical continuum. Even Khmers speak suggestively of their experiences of the *samay a-Pot* (Pol Pot era) as being ahistorical, often with the refrain *khmer yoeung men del sos* (never before for us Khmers). For Cambodian diasporas, the disconnect is made even more emphatic by exile.

While historical instances of mass atrocity do reveal features and patterns that transcend narrow cultural or historical frames, we cannot fully understand genocidal violence without locating it within the sociohistorical contexts that produced it. Underscoring the importance of contextualization, Mark Levene posits that "blaming 'mad' or 'evil' regimes alone for genocide will not suffice if this fails to take heed of the circumstances in which those regimes arise."[12] While culture informs survivors' understanding of the genocidal experience, Khmer Rouge extremism was not lodged in any cultural disposition to violence, despite the temptation to fix our gaze on the cultural script. Rather, it was embedded in the sociohistorical conditions from which the movement emerged that not only informed the desire for totalistic change but also accounted for the trajectories toward radical solutions and the permissibility of unbridled violence. Though it may have been catapulted to power by external forces and drawn inspiration from larger intellectual traditions, the Khmer Rouge regime was shaped by both the movement's own political histories and those of the nation, and by the circumstances under which the Pol Potist faction conspired and battled its way against both foes and allies internally and externally to total power in 1975.

Of the weightiness of the past, Marx wrote, "Men make their own history, but . . . they do not make it under circumstances chosen by themselves, but under circumstances directly encountered, given and transmitted from the past."[13] Despite the seemingly apocalyptic break that Democratic Kampuchea connotes, no change, no matter how much it may have been desired, is ever so total and no severance ever so complete that it nullifies the historical preface. The vanguards of the Khmer Rouge revolution were, after all, historical subjects, and even in their rejection of it, the past informed and shaped their vision of the alternative. Flawed as it was, the Khmer Rouge did have a vision of change that they pursued with blind resoluteness, one that was not incubated in isolation but within the "ruins and ruination"[14] of empire. If the compounded traumas of colonization, territorial loss, and betrayal fostered an intense longing for national revival, communism presented itself, at least to a committed core of Khmer communists, as the vehicle for change. From under the rubble of imperial debris,[15] and against a post-independence montage of entrenchment, disenchantment, and decay, Khmer Rouge utopia, as an emanation of "postcolonial politics of resentment,"[16] was deemed possible only through the annihilation of the old order.

Of the conflagration that consumed Cambodia, Michael Vickery wrote, "The war did not begin suddenly in 1970, and the conflict which seemed to explode at that time proceeded naturally from trends in the country's political history over the preceding 25 years."[17] I posit that the analytic gaze needs to be cast even further back, into the nation's colonized past, for the political and ideological struggles enacted on the political stage in the two decades following independence reflected not just new power dynamics but colonial legacies. As Derek Walcott asserts, "The rot remains with us, [though] the men are gone."[18] Of this provocative reflection on imperial ruination, Ann Stoler asks, "What does it corrode, from what interior spaces does it take hold?"[19] Emerging from almost a century of colonization, postcolonial Cambodia, not unlike many newly independent countries that emerged on the international scene in the 1950s–1960s, reflected both promise and disillusionment. In fundamental aspects, the growth and eventual radicalization of the Cambodian Left, then largely unseen by external observers, were a response to the persistent entrenchment and stagnancy of the old order, a "counterpoint to the dominant theme of Cambodia's modern history."[20] Ironically, what Milton Osborne describes as "the failure of open politics to provide stable government"[21] ultimately brought about one of the world's most closed and opaque regimes of all times.

Internal developments alone cannot account for the Khmer Rouge victory in Cambodia. From the initial formation of the communist movement in colonial Cambodia to the Khmer Rouge seizure of power and the regime's eventual collapse, the history of Cambodian communism was shaped by different imperial formations that spanned three "Indochina Wars," of which the destruction levied upon Cambodia during the "Vietnam War" (a geographically bounded reference that invisibilizes this very destruction) was but one chapter. That the previously insipid Khmer communist movement was able to acquire political momentum only with the exportation, by both the Americans and the Vietnamese communists, of the Vietnam War into Cambodia had significant implications both for the Khmer Rouge victory and for the genocidal consequences. These early years of subjugation and betrayal seeded the uncompromising political culture that came to govern both the internal workings of the Khmer communist organization and its interactions with the outside world. These relational histories[22] infuse density and texture into Southeast Asia as an analytic terrain that is often vacated of local histories, interests, and power relationships by the preoccupation with East-West conflicts, and complicate the discourse of war and empire with attention to the plurality of imperial formations. The implicated roles of externalities also curtail the explanatory power of the term "auto-genocide" with the implied self-infliction of the historical injury, despite its usefulness in distinguishing the Cambodian experience from other genocidal moments in history. They also inform our understanding of the Cambodian diasporic community, including the copresence of refugee gratitude and ambivalence toward the America that connotes both abandonment and rescue.

Locating the extremism of Democratic Kampuchea within this larger and longer historical frame is to build upon Ann Stoler's contention that ruins are not just found but also made.[23] Ruins also beget new ruins, as the vision of hopeful alternatives that fed Khmer Rouge utopian aspiration gave way to genocidal ruination and the remains that it bequeaths. Genocide does more than wound the nation physically. It also injures it metaphysically, and tears asunder the normative fabric that gives coherence and cohesion to the social order. Like colonialism, which Achebe describes as having "put a knife on the things that held us together, and we have fallen apart,"[24] genocide engendered "not a temporary disturbance" but "a once and for all alteration of . . . society."[25] In the Cambodian experience, this wounding encounter is made even more injurious by the self-implicating nature of auto-genocide and the ever-present absence of disappearances and mass graves, the implications of which are profoundly different from many other instances of state-sponsored terror.

In the diaspora, this historical trauma, which registers its presence in the refugee body, the fractured families, and the destabilized institutions, is made even more acute by what is, for most, not only a forced severance from their homeland but also permanent exile. As the body moves, where does memory live? If memory is spatially constituted, as Halbwachs and Nora have argued, then the diaspora is one site where individual and collective memory is incubated, enhanced, edited, and transmitted. In its travel across space and time, memory takes on different forms, manifesting traces of transgenerational haunting in the silence that continues to envelop the Cambodian family. Silence thus becomes an analytic site for culturally informed reflection and theorizing about despair and resistance, reconciliation and healing.

Be it in Cambodia or in the diaspora, it is also in the gaps and interstices that survivors' resilience and agency reveal themselves, not in loud registers but in the daily acts of living and repair. For many in the diaspora, rebuilding lives and community means weaving meaning and continuity from fragments and disorder, and transnationally re-stitching relational fabrics that have been frayed by time, distance, and politics. This process is compelled as much by their past experiences in Asia as by their present encounters in diaspora. As Sau-ling Wong reminds us, this "perpetual turning of [the] gaze towards the lost homeland" is a poignant critique both of the assumed linearity in immigration discourse and of American triumphalism.[26] In that sense, the national and the transnational are not just complementary, but mutually constitutive. Though not without disillusion or ambivalence, "return," in its multifarious forms, is for many a reparative act, a step toward reconciliation, not in the sense of forgiveness and healing, but perhaps of transcendence.

From the Land of Shadows is an analysis of revolutionary violence and the effects of the "spiral transgressions"[27] of politics and state power on individuals and social systems, and specifically an analysis of the causes and consequences of the Cambodian genocide and of the post-genocide struggle of Cambodians to make meaning of this historical trauma and to move forward. The study is thus an interrogation not only of revolutionary violence, but also of the ways both survivors and successive generations, individually and collectively, understand and work through this experience long after the genocide, including how exile mediates remembering and reconnections with the ancestral homeland. The book argues that explanations for Khmer Rouge extremism are to be found in various intersections—between ideology and structure, internalities and externalities, continuity and rupture. The genesis of the violent and tragic syllogism was in the spaces of contradiction, specifically in the unlikely contexts from which the Khmer Rouge were catapulted to power and which accounted in large part for their utopian ambitions and self-consuming paranoia. In their millenarian pursuit, violence emerged as paramount both in the enforcement of policy and in the response to the failure of policy, as a purposively deployed coercive implement of change and an unintended consequence of the irrational stress levied upon the system by unrealizable ambitions, excess zeal, and corrosive fear.

The pathology of power—genocidal and implosive—in turn leaves deep and enduring traces on the Cambodian individual, community, and nation that defy temporality. This history casts its shadow over the present and, in many families, even transgenerationally. In essence, this study echoes and recasts the provocative questions that Mimi Nguyen raised in her study of war, refugees, and the "gift of freedom": "How do people live with debt? How can debt disturb our sense of history or inform our critique?"[28] In this discussion of refugees, the notion of debt is that which defines their relationality not only with America but also with the dead and the disappeared, a debt in both instances accrued through the granting not just of freedom but also of life. The quest for and discourse about justice and accountability necessarily exceed legal and juridical premises that currently prevail, provoking in the process an interrogation of the assumption that justice, reconciliation, and healing are necessarily causally connected and mutually reinforcing.

*

With its sociohistorical and multidisciplinary approach, and an analytic multifocality that spans Southeast Asia and Southeast Asian America and that moves between past, present, and future, the book provides a richly historicized and holistic context necessary for understanding the complexity of diasporic lives and the sequelae of trauma that remains neither fully present nor fully absent, as Derrida contends, in refugee lives and homes.[29] It builds upon, complements, and enriches the discourse about war, genocide, displacement, and reconstitution. With its concerns and approaches, it also pushes against many disciplinary boundaries, particularly the intellectual binary between Asian Studies and Asian American Studies. For Asian Studies, which has been and remains fixed in its gaze on Asia, diasporas are outside the geographical and cultural frame of "authenticity," hence beyond its intellectual concerns. This disciplinary boundedness largely confines studies of the Cambodian genocide to a certain geographical framework, namely, Cambodia/Asia. Scholarship on the Cambodian genocide is also challenged by the tension embedded in area studies as a product of the Cold War, that is now called upon as a discipline to address the remains of that war. Despite these shortcomings, those interested in historicizing the Cambodian American experience are limited to texts in area studies, mostly history and anthropology, for the contextualization needed to understand the trauma, liminality, and resilience of the diasporic community.

Asian American Studies, on the other hand, notwithstanding its increased orientation toward transnationalism and diasporas, remains, for political and other reasons, primarily U.S.-focused, despite the fact that Asian American lives have always defied national boundaries. Where transnational concerns have emerged, they remain largely moored to the exigencies of economic migration, which continues to dominate migration studies in the United States. The preoccupations and opportunities afforded through flexible citizenship,[30] for one, however, are not necessarily those of liminal citizenship that refugees represent. Moreover, for the politically displaced, the exigencies and features of transnationality extend beyond the prevailing concerns with economic remittance to include the many forms of reconnection and repair, for the imperative is less about gain than regain. Through their reengagement, refugees remind us that they are not just those "who fought and lost" but those who in fact "lost out and fought."[31]

The widening of the intellectual lens of this study is by no means an abandonment of, or even a shifting away from, the Asian American genealogy. Rather, it is a step, necessary and critical, toward making more holistic, textured, and nuanced the scholarly rendering of Asian American lives. It is not possible to discuss the Cambodian diaspora without referencing the historical tragedies that make transnationality not just a strand but *the* strand in Cambodian American discourse. Whereas many existing works on Cambodian Americans address war and genocide as historical background, this study uses pre-migration history not simply as a temporal preface for community formation in the United States, but as fundamentally linked to the prevailing challenges facing Cambodian Americans. In its emphasis on the continuum of experience, it focuses not just on the "there" and the "here," but how the "there" informs the "here." History is neither just a prelude to nor just a cause of migration, but threads through and informs post-migration experiences in the diaspora. Critical issues such as citizenship and transnational belonging cannot be disentangled from the histories that produce the liminality and bifocality of the Cambodian American reality.

By embedding the Cambodian diaspora not only in the genocidal chapter of Cambodia's history but also within the entangled histories of the wars in Southeast Asia, the book threads global politics with local manifestations, and the brutalizing logic of empire with the ravages on local lives. In critical ways, the Southeast Asian refugee figure, the scattered human debris of a failed U.S. imperial project, disrupts classical immigration narratives into which refugee discourse in the United States has long been collapsed. Taking the analysis of migration and resettlement beyond the customary framing of push-pull forces, exit-resettlement, and the paradigmatic binary of assimilation and alienation, it looks at the textured lives of refugees and of the generations that grew up or were born in the diaspora as they struggle to reconcile with this vexed history and negotiate between remembering and forgetting, between the intrusive past and the seemingly elusive future, between the "here" and the "there." In the everyday, the hyphen in "Asian-American" is blurred, and connects as much as it separates.

Such density of refugee experiences, however, is often obscured in the dominant discourse about Cambodian Americans. Though refugee studies as a field is invested in understanding (and intervening in) the conditions and processes that engender mass displacement, the form that it has taken in the United States, prompted in no small way by the Southeast Asian resettlement, is largely centered on the refugee body —the concerns for shelter, food, health, and mental health. As Malkki points out, extant scholarship on refugees often fails to locate the problem "first in the political oppression or violence that produces 'massive territorial displacements of people.'"[32] Often labeled "a crisis," refugee resettlement is a "situation" to be managed, and the refugee figure, to be rescued, rehabilitated, salvaged. This premise provides for little consideration not only of the larger contexts of their displacement and re-emplacement, but moreover, of how the former informs and even collides with the latter. Discourse about trauma, for instance, though a topic of research and policy interests, is largely relegated to mental health professionals and approached as individual pathology rather than a historicized collective phenomenon. It also omits reflections about the ways historical subjects navigate and negotiate "macro forces with micro strategies," including how survivors have lived with, transmitted, and even transformed their history of victimization into that of resilience and fortitude.

By extension, other than Cathy Schlund-Vials's book on Cambodian American artistic production and a few other studies of the "1.5" generation,[33] we know little of the ways young Cambodians, particularly those of the post-genocide generations, receive and make meaning of this history that is filtered down to them. With the exception of the Killing Fields Memorial in Chicago, the absence of public commemorative sites for Cambodians in the diaspora relegates acts of mourning and remembrance associated with this historical experience to other realms, often "below the thresholds at which visibility begins," as Michel de Certeau would have it, less legible from the outside. As a result, the different and multiple registers of agency that refugees and refugee communities exhibit, including their political and philanthropic lives, often presumed to be absent in immigrant communities, are unnoted. It is thus not sufficient to merely reposition our scholarly inquiry "in the 'Third World frame' . . . that acknowledges the link to empire,"[34] as Yên Lê Espiritu rightly proposes; we must also illuminate the ways refugees negotiate and, in many instances, defy the ruinations of empire at and from the center of empire.

In its multilevel and multifaceted analysis, this study places theories and concepts drawn from the corpus of work on comparative revolutions, totalitarianism, diaspora, transnationalism, and memory works in conversation with survivor narratives culled from ethnographic research and over 250 interviews with a cross-section of survivors and their children between the ages of sixteen and eighty-two, which I conducted in Khmer and English, mostly in the United States, but also in France and Cambodia. The multi- and trans-locality of the interviews strengthens and deepens the analysis. Of the interviews, approximately

200 were of first-generation survivors, of which 150 were randomly selected. Data on "1.8-generation"[35] and second-generation Cambodians
came from structured questionnaires and "circles of conversation" conducted in key Cambodian communities in the United States in 2012
and 2013.

Contrary to the depiction of Cambodian refugees as "wealthy, urban,
educated and often of military backgrounds [whose] experience of the
revolution does not match those of workers and peasants,"[36] the respondents came from diverse socioeconomic and regional backgrounds, and
included factory workers, small subsistence farmers, and landless and
illiterate peasants, as well urbane professionals, high-ranking officials,
former students, and rank-and-file soldiers. If they can be said to be
"privileged," it is in the fact that they had survived and, in some cases,
had left, a particularity that was balanced by information gathered on
individuals who remained in Cambodia. In the same vein, whatever
concerns may be engendered by the significant representation of refugees from northwestern Cambodia is mitigated by the fact that their
life histories reflect multiple displacements from different parts of Cambodia prior to and during the Khmer Rouge era; for many, the Northwest was simply the last region to which they were relocated prior to
their cross-border flight. To further countenance criticisms of refugee
bias,[37] I note that the interviews were conducted after their exit from
the refugee camps, thus allowing for geographical and temporal distance
from the trauma source, but not so long after as to be compromised by
forgetfulness.

Additional information and insights were culled from "conversational
narratives" that emerged organically from years of living in and working
with Cambodian diasporic communities and, as such, are enhanced by
longitudinal perspectives. Unless cited, all quotes throughout the book
are from all these various encounters. Materials from French, Khmer,
and English-language archives at Aix-en-Provence, Washington, DC,
Maryland, Berkeley, and the Documentation Center of Cambodia, along
with the corpus of secondary materials on Cambodia and Cambodian
diasporas, provide supplemental information and contextualization.
The findings are further enriched by my own experiences as a Cambodian refugee and native Khmer speaker who has lost virtually all of her
family to the genocide.

Seeking History

Almost twenty years after the Khmer Rouge fateful march into Phnom Penh, I made my first trip back to Cambodia. Tottering through a slow recovery, the country still bore the pockmarks of its recent trauma. Shadows loomed everywhere—over old buildings that stood frozen in time despite new ownership; in the outline of neighborhoods where shards of their former identities still protruded through the seams of a new sociopolitical cartography; and in the ingrained fear that continues to grip a generation battered to near extinction. In the faces that I had searched in vain for signs of recognition, there were lingering shadows of innocence robbed and childhoods denied, of lives that could have been. It was only at the killing grounds of Choeung Ek, when I looked down at fragments scattered throughout and, after a stunned moment, recognized them to be pieces of human remains, that I confronted the magnitude of the loss and the profound, incomprehensible nature of what had taken place in this country that was once home. A torn piece of pale blue cotton with a long-faded label bearing the word "Arrow" was the only remnant of a life that refused oblivion. The mental image that it conjured of a civil servant, dressed in his crisp short-sleeve dress shirt of a brand so popular during that time, walking toward a future that he could not have suspected would end in a shallow mass grave, was surreal in its ordinariness.

Even in a century that had seen two world wars, nuclear attacks on populated cities, two major revolutions that changed the world, and countless armed conflicts, the Cambodian experience stands out both for its own particular features and as a metaphor for the afflictions of the modern age. As William Shawcross opined,

> Cambodia has an importance beyond itself, because there in its fragile heart paraded, throughout the 1970s, many of the most frightful beasts that now stalk the world. Brutal civil war, superpower intervention carelessly conducted from afar, nationalism exaggerated into paranoid racism, fanatical and vengeful revolution, invasion, starvation and back to unobserved civil war without end.[38]

Here on the parched killing fields, hidden behind verdant rice fields that deceived with the illusion of normalcy, the survivors' stories take on a poignant realism that is possible only when one steps beyond the elegant confines of theory. What *did* happen here? What was the Khmer Rouge trying to do? What accounted for the erosion of moral and other restraints that allowed wanton killings to go undeterred? How does this historical injury imprint itself on the Cambodian person and on the nation? How, if at all, can a nation heal from such extreme injury? These are the questions that set me on a quest for answers to both the causes *and* consequences of the Khmer Rouge regime of terror.

When I first embarked on this study, scholarship on the Khmer Rouge was just emerging. In the United States, newly admitted Cambodian refugees were just settling into their new lives, finding refuge, for the most part, in America's inner-city housing complexes. The trauma of revolution, flight, and exile was compounded by the challenges of rebuilding lives in a foreign and not always embracing country. California cities such as East Oakland and Long Beach were sites of multiple encounters. An area known as "Cambodian Village" in Oakland, where many of the interviews took place, was actually only a square of dilapidated concrete buildings with iron bars on the windows, overlooking a dusty quad where, on any given morning, one could see Hmong women in their colorful clothing walk around with their babies strapped on their backs, while a Khmer woman in her sarong swept the small concrete landing where her entrepreneurial husband had set up a one-stool barbershop in front of the family's cramped apartment. The sound of mortar and pestle and aromatic scent of lemongrass conveyed a feel of a Southeast Asia compressed, transplanted, and reinvented. It was also in these places that refugees, inserted into an already volatile context, were often reminded of their vulnerability as newcomers. Many had not wanted to be here, and were fast realizing that they were not wanted here.

Distanced from the source of trauma but unable to free themselves from the haunting past, refugees responded to the compulsion to bear witness:

> I have lived to see the world turned upside down [*kalab phen dey*]. I have lost everything—my family, my youth, my home, my country. These memories are all that I have left. Those things that happened to us—they are like shadows that follow us always. We have to ask ourselves how is it that such savagery can still exist today.

The experiences they sought to recount, however, could only be snapshots of the realities of Democratic Kampuchea, for most had little information beyond their own immediate experiences of what transpired elsewhere in the country. Survivors' accounts were also punctuated by the constant relocation to which they were subjected, and by the strategic survival imperative of not seeing, not hearing, and not asking. They too wanted to understand.

Against the weight of an uncertain present and a shadowing past, and torn between the desire to forget and the pressure to remember, between the fear of speaking and the need to speak, refugees struggled to give form and meaning to their experiences in a country where few were willing to listen. America then was enveloped simultaneously in the post-Vietnam amnesia of the Right and the self-vindication (and later self-defensiveness) of the Left. Neither side saw refugees as much more than pieces in the political game, as either a living condemnation of a brutal communist regime, collaborators implicated in an imperialist war, or mere opportunists seeking to capitalize on international compassion for the chance to migrate. With post-Vietnam economic retraction and high unemployment, most Americans simply saw them as an unwanted social burden.

In academia, developments in Democratic Kampuchea, especially when they could no longer be denied, provoked scholarly and, to no small extent, ideological debates about Cambodian communism and the postcolonial environment that engendered such virulent response. To a far lesser extent, these events compelled soul-searching among Western academics. The extremism of the Khmer Rouge regime was a staggering reminder that totalitarianism can emanate from all ends of the ideological spectrum, committed by left-wing as well as right-wing dictatorships. This reality was disconcerting to many who had held on to the optimism of the revolutionary promise. For the Asian American movement that was catalyzed to activism by the U.S. wars in Asia, the genocide and mass refugee exodus that followed the long-awaited peace disturbed fundamental assumptions.

In this fraught context, the scholarship that was produced over the last four decades has nonetheless contributed much to our understanding of Cambodian society, politics, and history, especially of the Khmer communist movement, of which little was known prior to 1975. Even works that have since been invalidated by historical developments were instructive of the politico-intellectual environment of the time. Invaluable as they are to the scholarly world, the theorizing, debates, and questions that preoccupy academics (such as how accurate the body counts are, or whether these experiences constitute genocide or a "rupture") have little significance for survivors who are struggling to make sense of the incomprehensible experiences that ravaged their lives. If anything, such discourse often acts as a silencing force. As one survivor simply and poignantly asked, "Why [do they] correct my memory?"[39]

With memory works, recall inevitably involves filters, biases, and the instinct to fill in memory gaps, largely out of the human desire for structure and order. Already present in any probing into such painful histories, these tendencies are particularly accentuated by the nature of auto-genocidal violence. For researchers, the challenge is to wade through these pitfalls of remembering and recounting and to grasp what Schama terms the "chaotic authenticity" of survivor narratives. Engaging this history means moving into the dark areas of abject loss and liminality, the full extent of which can only be understood not by simply observing and analyzing but by living and feeling it. In the community, distrust further compromises discourse, a challenge that Linda Tuhiwai Smith poignantly documented in her seminal work on research and indigenous peoples. Paradoxically, survivors may speak more readily about their experiences with non-Cambodians; what they share, however, may be more superficial or oblique such that the meaning is lost in the cultural translation. Among Cambodians, once long-withheld trust is established, there are nuances and textures to the stories that are conveyed and understood within the cultural framework, that need no translation, and that elsewhere are easily overlooked.

Written from many intersections and interstices of Asia-America, past-present, continuity-rupture, macro-micro, theories-narratives, public-private, collective-personal, this study emerges from the conviction that the theorizing about and understanding of a nation's collective histories of war and genocide must be grounded in accountings of individual histories, and that the complexity of these issues and experiences can be captured only through prismatic and multidisciplinary lenses that allow "ordinary people's constructions of their life histories, with their internal silences and mythologies" to surface.[40] Studies of nations, communities, and lives cannot be approached in binary terms—war/ peace, homeland/host land, refugees/citizens, victims/warriors, trauma- tized/whole—but in the complexities, layers, and copresence of all these defining markers. It is about simultaneity and interstitiality—the "space between," a feeling of belonging to many worlds, or to none.

This book is thus about foregrounding the survivor-refugees as expe- riencing subjects and the integrity of the experiences as they were lived, remembered, and articulated without the mediation of linguistic and cultural translation, as countermemory and counternarratives to state rhetoric and externally imposed recounting. It is to rewrite the indi- vidual, the human, back where necropolitics had sought to vacate, and to ground macro discussion of political forces and global machinations in the micro details and nuances of real lives, for to echo Schama, revo- lutions must be read not just as "a march of abstractions and ideologies but as a human event of complicated and often tragic outcomes."[41] This "re-storying," as Achebe points out, is not simply a balancing of narra- tives but also a balancing of power, namely, the power to describe, to narrate, and to legitimate. As the first scholarly book that approaches these entangled subjects as such written by a Cambodian refugee and scholar with deep and wide connections to the communities both in the diaspora and in Cambodia, it also pries open the intellectual space that has been a monopoly of Western academics. For many of us born of this experience and in exile, it means struggling from beneath the weight of history to write this history, in a language that is not one's own, and in a country that is not one's home.

This book is, thus, a step toward re-centering that which has here- tofore remained on the margins, to redress the position of multifold invisibilization that Cambodians occupy—that is, to move Cambodia from the "sideshow" of U.S. history and Cambodians from the periph- ery of American public and intellectual life. The invisibility of Cambo- dia, in essence, has translated into the invisibility of Cambodians in the United States. If Americans lost during the covert wars in Cambodia were the "missing in action," Cambodians, to borrow from Helen Zia, are the "missing in history."[42] Despite the rapid growth of the South- east Asian communities in the United States, very little is taught in the schools about these chapters of American history or about the Cam- bodian American experience. Just as Vietnam became a war and not a country, so it is that the magnitude of the Cambodian genocide often renders "un-visible" the Cambodian figure. It is, however, a double-layered invisibility. The terror that rained over Cambodia in the form of carpet bombings was overshadowed by the reign of terror that ensued. If Cambodia and Cambodians surface in American public consciousness, it is often only as an ahistoricized genocidal "apparition." If the Cambodian refugee figure, in many instances, destabilizes the image of the "good refugee," it is replaced by that of the "saved." Beyond survival, can this liberatory narrative itself be salvaged in the face of enduring poverty and criminalized raciality, or is it simply replaced with disregard? It is this absent space for remembering and acknowledgment that Nguyen-Vo Thu Huong invokes when she writes that "refugees occupy the position of self-mourners because no one else mourns us."[43] Read as such, mourning, that "constant tracing of traces,"[44] is not submission but a refusal to submit.

By extension, similar to the ways the pan–Asian American framework masks internal differentiation, the pan–Southeast Asian American rubric obscures the more vulnerable communities. With neither the numerical strength of Vietnamese Americans nor the political cachet of Hmong Americans, Cambodians are peripheral despite the not insignificant size of the community. While Cambodian American educational data and mental health statistics are often used to highlight achievement gaps and disparities and argue for resources to assist refugees, very few programs are for or run by Cambodian Americans. In academe and related enterprises, Southeast Asian American studies is often made synonymous with Vietnamese American studies. If Southeast Asians in the United States are politically and otherwise peripheral, as Yên Lê Espiritu rightfully asserts, Cambodians hover on the margin of that periphery. In contrast to scholarship on Vietnamese Americans, who, as Espiritu also observed, are objects "of intense scholarly interest," and "over documented" as compared to other immigrant groups, scholarship on Cambodian Americans is especially scant, and that *by* Cambodian Americans even more so. Much of the scholarship dates back to the "refugee era" of the 1980s; over the last four decades, only a handful of book-length studies specifically written about Cambodian Americans have appeared. Works by Jeremy Hein, Aihwa Ong, Nancy Smith-Hefner, Sucheng Chan, Susan Needham, and Karen Quintiliani are foundational in their dedication to the Cambodian American experience. Though not without historical context, most focus on the Cambodian resettlement experiences in the United States and are based on one community, locale, or region. Significantly, though Cambodian survivors have been the subject of research and source of information for researchers, published works by Cambodian Americans are essentially limited to a handful of memoirs and a novel, most produced in the last fifteen years and authored by child survivors now in their adulthood. Heartwrenchingly poignant, they generally provide little in the way of overarching analysis.

It is in these multiple and intersecting contexts that I deploy the concept of "shadows." Like the traditional *lakhon sbek* (shadow puppet performance), the internal workings of the Khmer Rouge movement and of Democratic Kampuchea were veiled, mysterious. With unseen forces manipulating people's lives and thoughts, and being themselves manipulated, the internecine power struggles were reminiscent of the epic battles of the Ramayana, fought in the abstract in a realm beyond the mundane. In the world of the Khmer Rouge, humanity lost its way as individuals were subjugated to the uncompromising exaction of obedience. Humans became puppets, moving in fear of thoughts and hope, and like Mbembe's rendering of the slave, "the perfect figure of a shadow."[45] Shadows are also the genocidal remains, a spectral register of loss, real and symbolic, that casts its presence trans-temporally, in forms distorted by space and time. Shadow also references the war fought as a "sideshow" veiled from the public gaze, the anonymity of the refugee mass, and the marginality of the Cambodian refugee figure, the invisible legacy of an unseen war.

Consisting of seven chapters, *From the Land of Shadows* is organized into three parts, and bookended with an introduction and an epilogue. Part 1 focuses on the question of state power and the necropolitics[46] of Democratic Kampuchea, drawing on survivors' accounts to describe life-and-death conditions under the Khmer Rouge. Interweaving analysis with narratives, it maps the political vicissitudes in Democratic Kampuchea as they relate to the emergence of terror and hunger as paramount disciplinary technologies. It also underscores human resilience and agency in the ways that ordinary people navigated, negotiated, resisted, and survived extraordinary conditions.

Part 2 argues for the importance of situating Khmer Rouge extremism within the larger historical context from which the movement emerged and gained power. It posits that Cambodia's colonial and postcolonial history and prewar society created forces and conditions that both deterred and advanced Khmer communist success. The thick description of prewar Cambodian society not only illuminates revolutionary dynamics in Cambodia but also provides an important *entrée* into the sociocultural world of the majority of Cambodian refugees in the diaspora, and a rare context for understanding the nature and scope of the dislocations that predated the "refugee era." In positioning violence within the historical frame, this section traces the roots of many features of Democratic Kampuchea—namely, the deeply felt anxiety about national survival, nativistic impulse, suspicion of and disdain for cities and intellectuals, and destructive self-reliance—to the experiences of colonization and betrayal. Rather than looking at the Khmer Rouge terror regime as an eruption of the irrational, it analyzes the purposive nature of revolutionary violence, providing both structural and ideological explanations for its emergence as a policy instrument by linking it to the twin imperatives of ensuring regime survival and radically transforming Cambodian society.

Part 3 examines the legacies of historical trauma as it registers in Cambodian families and communities, and the individual and collective struggle of survivors to emerge from social death. It looks at the self-implicating nature of auto-genocidal violence, the particular nature of the wounds and void engendered by disappearances and mass graves, and ramifications for reconciliation and healing. It places analytic focus on the tense relationship between speech and silence, remembering and forgetting, both as extensions of trauma and as acts of agency and resistance. It also looks at the different forms that memory, mourning, and memorialization take in the aftermath of this traumatic encounter, and examines the longing for reconnection and the different facets and layers of transnationality that manifest in the Cambodian American community. With the ancestral homeland, for many, connoting both solace and pain, it also reflects on the ambivalence that inhabits the spaces of disconnection and reconnection, and examines the ways memory travels across time, space, and generations. Given the implication of America in these tragedies, the book unpacks and problematizes notions of citizenship, belonging, and return, and provides a critical analysis of the complex relationship among diasporas, the sending and the receiving countries.

The epilogue opens with the trial of Kaing Guek Eav, alias Duch, head of the Tuol Sleng extermination center, as a jumping-off point for reflections about one of the most painful encounters of modern history, about justice and healing, and about what the Cambodian experience illuminates of the darker side of modernity. As Todorov posits, "The remedy must not consist in merely remembering the evil. . . . We have to go a step farther and ask ourselves about the reasons that gave rise to the evil."[47] The nature of the scholarly enterprise makes it easy and tempting to engage these intellectually, politically, and humanly important issues at a certain level of abstraction and with a certain and perhaps even necessary degree of disengagement. How to do this without losing sight of the fact that behind the statistics are real individuals is a challenge, rendered even more acute for those who live this history and in whom this history continues to live. To honor the stories and the memories of both the dead and the survivors is one small way of restoring humanity to those the system had sought to deny.

Though colossal and extreme, the Cambodian tragedy is not an aberration. Perhaps what is most disconcerting about this history is not its extraordinariness, but how short is the line between "extra-" and "ordinary." Mass displacement, statelessness, and refugees are features of modernity, conditions that reveal both the vulnerability of the modern age and the resiliency of history's battered subjects. Just as there is no singular cause of the extremism of Democratic Kampuchea or a singular response to such extreme injury, perhaps there can never be a fully satisfactory answer to the profound questions about, or complete understanding of, such experience. Man's inherent and seemingly limitless capacity to inflict harm onto his own, as well as the nobility of the human spirit that shines in the face of adversity, has been and perhaps will remain beyond our ability to intellectualize. We owe it to those who are no longer here to continue to ask and to acknowledge nonetheless.

The bones cannot find peace until the truth they hold in themselves has been revealed.
—*Youk Chhang*

PART I

Life and Death under the Khmer Rouge

The Prisoner

His eyes grow accustomed to the darkness of the room. The presences that his mind, dulled from extreme hunger and fatigue, has sensed earlier are human forms stretched out on the floor . . . twisted forms, some semi-naked, angling for comfort in this condensed pack of humanity. He tries to mentally feel his shackled legs. They are attached to a long wooden manacle, with an iron bar that was slid through to secure them. A picture flashes through his mind: "These are not humans!" They are like trey chhae, *those smoked fish that his father used to take to the town's market at the end of the fishing season, brittle and held together by a wooden stick pierced through their mouths [*chakac trey chhae*]. Some part of his mind laughs at the drollness of this mental image. One cannot say the Revolution has not achieved anything; even the shackles have been communalized.[1]*

The Revolution has indeed changed its face. When he was a little boy, there were many months when his father would leave his family for the jungle. It was the time of the Issarak,[2] the anticolonial resistance. He could still hear his father's voice—low and pensive through the dim of the evening light—telling him that, in those days, there were only three principles that a revolutionary had to remember: to treat each other as equals, to assist one's comrades in times of need, and to believe in one's ability to achieve one's goals. The movement has since been injected with new blood, and those ideals are long buried under secrecy, deception, and a revolutionary absolutism that justifies all. In the twilight of his years, his father could no longer discern that simple but binding spirit in the young village boys who came to urge his re-involvement with the movement. They spoke a different revolutionary language, of "class struggle," of Khmers killing Khmers. He recalled his father softly uttering, "Others are painting our face." The nocturnal visits became more frequent, and the appeal more insistent. When he finally left, it was without a word, without ceremony. By then, the nightly visits of persuasion had acquired a hard edge.

Now he understands. In the pitch darkness of his cell, he sees things ever more clearly. Ideological rhetoric aside, Khmer hands are indeed taking Khmer lives. Many of the old faces, names, and heroic intentions have been consumed by the dust of history, made to "disappear" by a party whose paranoia has led it to view its own history as the ultimate con-tradiction. The Padevat (revolution) could easily be termed pak-devat[3] *(factionalism)—internecine, self-consuming, with roots that extended all the way to the genesis of the movement. The history of the party is a history of betrayal—betrayal by outsiders, betrayal by each other.*

In the darkness of the makeshift prison, past and present weave a seam-less reality. His mind, dulled with pain and confusion, gropes for reason, his lifeline out of the abyss. Somewhere in the recesses of the past lies the explanation for all this seeming irrationality. This is no madness, but a chartable course of the nation's hopes and disenchantment; of myths and wounding reality; of blinding faith and betrayal; of utopian ideas and dystopia.

Somewhere down the corridor, a door slams, jerking him back to reality. A woman's voice whimpers in the dark.

1

Violence in Utopia

And the black crows drop the lovea fruits all throughout the land. . . . Blood will flow until it reaches the belly of the elephant before peace would return. . . . During that cursed era, the people will be so driven by hunger and deprivation that they would run behind a dog, fighting over a grain of rice, stuck to its tail. . . . There will be houses but no people to live in them, roads but no one to walk on them.
—*Puth Tomney (Predictions of Puth)*[1]

He greeted my question about the Khmer Rouge era with a sigh, and with an unsteady gait that contrasted with his sinewy body, honed by years of toil, moved toward the altar that filled a corner of the prayer hall, a dimly lit converted carport of a well-worn bungalow that now serves as a place of worship. In his late seventies, widowed and childless from the genocide, Lok Ta (grandfather)[2] Tip found whatever solace and meaning he could in this room, shielded from the disorder and cacophony of a life dislocated and estranged in America's inner city. Lighting an incense, he uttered the stanza from the *Puth Tomney*, an ancient prophecy that, though few can recall it in its entirety, has been worked into the Khmer understanding of their own history. When life became reduced to an infernal existence, as it did for many who lived through *samay a-pot* (the Pol Pot era), some turned to these oracles for the meaning that eluded them. Even those looking cursorily at Democratic Kampuchea could discern a poignant resonance in the prophetic words uttered centuries ago, in the hunger so abject that it dehumanized and the loss measured by the emptiness of homes and villages. The Khmer Rouge *khaek khmao* (black crows) had indeed sown their ideological *lovea* in their promise of a new order, so tantalizing amidst the decadence and decay of the ancien régime. Like the fruit, enticing on the outside but filled with gnats, Khmer communism was exposed in its deceptiveness by the bloody hand of the revolution.

In a world where "gourds sink and shards float"[3] (*khlok lich, ambeng andet*), in that seeming inversion of the natural order that defied human comprehension, the unreal reality of their experiences perhaps could be grasped only with the elemental fatalism of myths and prophecies. In times of flux, there is solace in the belief that even the most seemingly irrational experiences have been foretold. To those desperately grasping for meaning and order, these prophecies lend coherence to an uncertain world. Above all, they provided hope: "The reign of the *thmils* [infidels, nonbelievers] would last only seven years, seven months and seven days." For many survivors, it was the belief in the inevitability of things that comforted them when reason failed, and it was the belief in the impermanence of things that sustained them through nearly four years of infernal existence.

The first stories that filtered out of Democratic Kampuchea stunned the world. Upon the Khmer Rouge seizure of power in April 1975, the country, led by a faceless leadership known only as "Angkar" (the Organization), was sealed off from outside scrutiny by a virtual autarky that was pried open only by the arrival of refugees at the Thai-Cambodian border. The gruesome tales they brought out with them only reinforced the impression of an "otherworldliness" that heretofore had been widely associated only with the Jewish Holocaust. Skeletal human beings, physically and psychically ravaged by starvation and terror, bore witness to some of the most unspeakable of human experiences. Horror became disbelief. Many in the West who supported the Khmer Rouge readily dismissed accounts of mass atrocities as a campaign by governments already implicated in past deception to discredit revolutionary Kampuchea. The denial that sprang from the visceral human need to avert our gaze from horror acquired an intellectual rationale with the appearance of "inconsistencies" in survivors' accounts that were readily held up as self-serving "exaggerations and wholesale falsehood"[4] fabricated by refugees accused of being on the payroll of the CIA[5] or motivated by their desire for asylum.[6] The thin whispers of truth were silenced. Of the complicity of the West, Francois Bizot wrote, "What oppresses me more still than the unclosed eyes of the dead . . . is the way the West applauded the Khmer Rouge. . . . The ovation was so frenzied as to drown out the protracted wailing of the millions being massacred."[7] If, as Terrence Des Pres asserts, "the worst torment is not being able to speak,"[8] a greater tragedy is not to be believed, for where in the former there is always hope for voice, in the latter, the whole experience is nullified.

It has since been established that developments in Democratic Kampuchea were far more complex than previously thought, and that both the descriptions of and the explanations for what transpired in 1975–1979 were far from uniform or simplistic. Areal and temporal variations were features of the chaotic reality of Democratic Kampuchea. Rather than fabrications and half-truths, inconsistencies and even contradictions in survivor accounts reflected not just the constraints of the traumatic experience that kept their "eyes fixed to the ground by every single minute's needs"[9] and of traumatic recall,[10] but also the prevailing structural and political conditions engendered by the existence of disparate power centers and the sanguinary push by the Pol Potist-dominated Party Center to consolidate its totalistic control.[11] Following the seizure of power in 1975, Democratic Kampuchea was divided into seven administrative zones[12]—the Northwest, North, Northeast, East, Southwest, West, and Center, and two "special regions" of Kratie and Siemreap, which were later consolidated into six zones in 1977. These zones conformed not to prewar provincial borders but to Khmer Rouge wartime divisions, representing not only different administrative jurisdictions but also disparate and previously quasi-autonomous power bases. Differences among the Khmer Rouge groups were discernible during the evacuation of Phnom Penh in the information given to cadres, in the level of brutality with which the evacuations were carried out, and in the early administration of the zones.[13]

That the lack of uniformity could not be attributed to the chaos of the moment was underscored by the fact that it continued to register over time. Differences in the way policies were implemented, particularly with regard to the treatment of urban evacuees and presumed "class enemies," were discernible from one area to another, and from one period to another within the same locale. In some places, mass relocation was conducted immediately after Khmer Rouge forces entered the area, markets and commerce were disallowed, and money largely ceased to have any value. There, traditional social practices were also banned and communal eating enforced soon thereafter. In some villages, Buddhist monks were forcibly defrocked and assigned tasks that violated Buddhist precepts; some were conscripted into military units.[14] In those areas, policies regulating movement and activities were strictly enforced, while executions and disappearances began almost immediately. In certain locales, reprisals targeted only high-ranking individuals, while elsewhere they were also directed at rank-and-file soldiers and their families.

At the other extreme were places where population relocation was delayed, markets continued to function longer, communal eating was introduced much later, and religious and cultural activities, elsewhere considered "arcane traditionalism," were tolerated. Surviving refugees recalled that in parts of the East, Buddhist monks were permitted to remain in the temples and preside over weddings and other traditional celebrations until 1976. Similarly, in the West, a former worker at a coffee plantation in Pailin noted that traditional ceremonies were still performed openly in his area as late as 1977,[15] while nuns reportedly were allowed to reside at the local monastery in Boeung Reng until early 1976. In those comparatively benign areas, treatment of "class enemies" was relatively tempered, hunger never reached starvation level, and work quotas, though exacting, were manageable largely because of better food rations, and in some instances because urban relocatees were given time to ease into their new situation. With more lax surveillance and investigation, evacuees with "tainted" biographies could hide their background and elude Angkar's terror web. Those whose identities were exposed were subjected to punitive sentences, including hard labor, but not necessarily executed. Many returning elites and intellectuals were sent to reeducation camps to "shed" (*chamrous*) their individualism and class consciousness rather than being summarily killed. In some cities, including Phnom Penh and Battambang, workers were retained at local factories, and others were brought back from the countryside, at least temporarily, to train new recruits.

Variations registered not only among locales and different segments of the population, but also temporally, largely coinciding with the internal strife that erupted soon after victory. As the Party Center,[16] also known simply as the "Center," aggressively moved to consolidate its control, arrests and purges not only of the leadership but often of entire networks intensified. The deployment of cadres from other zones into the area often resulted in changes in local conditions, in some cases for better and, in other cases, for worse.

For the most part, because of repeated relocation, individual experiences under the Khmer Rouge rarely fall into any one extreme, and were not constant. At any given time, one's experience depended on a number of factors, such as class, age, and gender, when and where one was resettled, the nature of the leadership who had discretionary power over life and death, and above all, one's sociopolitical classification. In Democratic Kampuchea, the class structure of the ancien régime was replaced by a new social order[17] that differentiated among those officially classified as having full rights, candidates, and depositees,[18] or more simply between base peasants (*mulathan*)[19] or "old people" (*neak chas*), and *neak chaleas* (relocatees) or "new people" (*neak thmey*).[20] While the Khmer Rouge professed to have done away with classism (*vannak niyum*), these sociopolitical categories in fact constituted a new social hierarchy, with base peasants at the zenith of the structure of power and privilege, with rights and access to resources not available to the "new" people. Of this new social reality, Locard observed, "In fact, this Marxist language was nothing but a cover to describe a reality, which in practice, had its origins in ancient Southeast Asian traditions: the victor had the right to make an entire people his prisoners, and to reduce them to some sort of slavery."[21] Like the war captives of ancient Cambodia, the "new people" were, in the eyes of the victorious regime, disfranchised *chhleuy*,[22] stripped, as Giorgio Agamben contends, to "bare life,"[23] stripped not just of their rights but of their humanity, to be exploited and discarded at will. Unlike chattel slaves, who could at least count on their economic worth to ensure survival, the majority of the "new people" had no such buffer in the necropolitical world[24] of Democratic Kampuchea, where, to evoke Hannah Arendt, they had no right to have rights. Whereas Foucault's panopticon is delimited by the bounded space, what survivors term *kouk ot chanchaing* (prison without walls) into which the entire country was transformed mirrors Achille Mbembe's "death world," in which social existence was defined by the "absolute power of the negative" and where the disposability of the "new people" was encoded in the Khmer Rouge's oft-repeated admonition, "A single *yothea* [cadre] was worth ten thousand of you. So if you were to die and there was only one *yothea* left, it would still be all right." Embedded in Mbembe's concept of necropower is this very notion of dispensability that moves the discussion of sovereign power beyond the Foucaultian concern with the subjugation of the individual to disciplinary apparati to the "subjugation of life to the power of death," where terror was made manifest in what Nordstrom terms "the hegemony of violence in the minutia of everyday life."[25] It is thus that Tony Barta asserts that, rather than focusing on genocidal intent, we will find it more instructive to look at relations of destruction,[26] which allows for the understanding of genocidal outcomes without the conceptual and juridical encumbrance of intentionality.

As with mass atrocities elsewhere, Democratic Kampuchea evokes the question of how such a regime was able to implement its extremist policies and impose its totalistic control over the populace despite its political and numerical weakness. As with other totalitarian regimes, different technologies of control shored up state power in Democratic Kampuchea. Abrupt and repeated population relocation uprooted individuals from their support system. Sociality was further disrupted as individuals were subjected to the architecture of coercion and panoptic surveillance of communal living and gender- and age-based work units, and to a new regulatory reality governing social relations. Where previously social interactions between non-kin men and women were prescribed, the Khmer Rouge made "immoral conduct" (*khos selathor*), often defined as unauthorized interactions, a capital crime. Where arranged marriage was once the purview of parents and elders, "red weddings,"[27] forced marriages imposed by the state and conducted en masse, epitomized Angkar's ultimate appropriation of parental and kinship rights. Through state control over every aspect of social life, and manipulation of language and loyalty, violence not only unmakes the family but ultimately destroys relationality. Huot, a factory worker, spoke of the state-regulated conjugal visits. "It was no longer as if we were a family," he said, "with thoughts and respect for each other. It was as if we were allowed visits to a mating partner and not our wives. The destruction was at the core of the Khmer family. We no longer related to each other the same way, . . . no longer humans with dignity but like mating animals."

The abolishment of critical institutions such as Buddhism and the family struck not only at the very fabric of Khmer society, but also at the core of the Khmer identity. With the individual atomized, the system worked through hunger and fear to destroy the human spirit (*bambak sbat*) and extract unquestioning compliance. While the institutionalization of communal eating prevented the stockpiling of provisions, chronic hunger with its debilitating and disorienting effects not only suppressed the will and ability to resist, but also allowed the system to purchase complicity. This was especially true of children, many of whom became malleable instruments of the terroristic state. In this "necro-world," to build upon Achille Mbembe, in which the only "choice" is between life and death, the "technologies of destruction have become more tactile, more anatomical and sensorial."[28] As a result, terror that reinforced hunger, deprivation, and despair in the destruction of the self was also multisensory as people were deliberately subjected to the sight, sound, and smell of brutalization and death. With their paralyzing and disorienting effects, executions and disappearances were not simply retributive but also disciplinary. Unlike violence, terror provides no possibility for behavior modification, thereby leaving the victim feeling perpetually disoriented and helpless: "With hunger you can scrounge around for something to eat—roots, leaves, barks, insects; but with the killing, you don't know where to run." Bereft of hope, many submitted to cowering subservience.

Life and Death under the Khmer Rouge: The Biopolitics of Terror

It was an uninhabitable place, and we had nothing. But there were a lot of small crabs, at least when we first got there. It was as if tevada[29] had sent them to feed us. Then later on, there was no more. Even the land could no longer help us.
—*Cambodian refugee-survivor*

With starvation and execution as a gauge, survivors' descriptions of the different zones in Democratic Kampuchea range from *men sov ey-te* (not too bad) to *probak men ten* (really difficult) or *chea kanleng slab* (the place of death).[30] One of the factors accounting for the disparities was the objective condition. Areas with high starvation and illness-related death were often remote tracts in malaria-infested forest regions, inhospitable in general but particularly deadly for urban evacuees unfamiliar with the area and unaccustomed to the harsh environment. The Northwest, for instance, is a region of intrinsic diversity, comprising both rich fertile land and inhospitable terrain. Impacted by larger resettlement of evacuees than other parts of the country, the zone came to be associated with some of the early and greatest instances of deprivation and brutality. In the ultimate confrontation with social abandonment, survivors described many of the new settlements as places where they were "discarded to die" (kravat chaol oy slab), where famine, draconian discipline, and illness, especially malaria, exacted their toll. Left without adequate provisions, tools, or seeds to sustain themselves, many of the "new" people, especially from the cities, perished soon after arrival. At Veal Vong, for example, one-third of the population reportedly died within months of their relocation.[31] Starvation often set in before the first harvest, only to escalate after the crops were requisitioned by the state or after the settlers were forcibly relocated from the area following the harvest. At a cooperative in Ang Romich, an estimated 30 percent of the villagers perished from starvation by 1976, less than a year after the communist takeover.[32]

Similarly, high death rates in the West were in desolate and parched areas. Rith, a student who was sent on a work detail to Veal Krabei Prey, recalled that there was only "sour water" (toeuk chour) in that area and each person was allotted only one small cup of drinking water per day. In Kompong Chhnang, few workers could finish digging the daily requisite of three cubic meters because of the soil composition. As these workers were often segregated from base peasants and cut off from any prospect of bartering, and, as in Kompong Tram, given only ang-kor sraley,[33] starvation was widespread by the end of 1975. Culture and gender conflate in tragic ways, as many women perished because they relinquished their meager, life-sustaining ration to their loved ones, or because they were killed for stealing food for their children or dying parents. Pech, a surviving orphan, remembered her mother's sacrifice: "Our legs were already swollen and we could not walk, but my mother would give her rations and whatever she had to my father, who had become ill. She said that he had to labor much harder and would not survive if he had nothing to eat. She fell ill and died."

In addition to intrinsic characteristics, political and economic histories also determined areal conditions. Just as some places were inherently inhospitable, others were more benign because of their strategic locations, revolutionary history, and natural fecundity. While Phnom

Penh was in an economic stranglehold in the final years of the war, Battambang and Koh Kong with their vital cross-border economies remained robust, and hence had better food stockpiles than most of the country at the time of the Republic's collapse in 1975.[34] As a result, in some areas of the Northwest such as Mongkol Borei, a region known as the country's rice basket, food conditions remained relatively favorable longer than in other parts of the country. Tragically, the reputed bountifulness of the Northwest accounted for the Center's high requisitioned quota and expectation that the zone would produce 30 percent of the country's annual yield, making the zone one of the harshest areas.[35] Survivors recalled rice grains being trucked away in burlap sacks with Chinese writing, and being told that the harvests had to be shared with other villages.[36]

In the same vein, the purported orderliness of the Southwest and the East can be attributed to their long revolutionary histories as the bedrock of anticolonial and, subsequently, Khmer communist insurgency. During the war in 1970–1975, eighteen Khmer Rouge bases were located in the Southwest. With effective control over the area, they were able to introduce the cooperative system as early as mid-1973.[37] Thus, while other zones had to implement collectivization in the post-victory period with perilous inexperience, unconsolidated power, and fragile administrative and political infrastructure, the Southwestern leadership had the confidence that came with political security, the experience garnered from their early experimentation with rural reform, and relatively undisrupted administrative infrastructure to manage the challenges that elsewhere contributed to massive death and deprivation very early on. As a result, at least in the early months, life in the Southwest according to refugee accounts appeared to be among the least disrupted. The political confidence of local leaders also translated into reportedly less punitive policies and less stringent control over relocatees, at least in some parts of the zone, some of the time.[38]

Similarly, the favorable features of the East, another long-standing communist base area, were attributable to better food conditions and delayed implementation of the more restrictive policies. In Chhloy, refugee-survivors recalled that rice was available until the end of 1976, and that monks were still present and New Year celebrations still permissible through April 1976. In most parts of the zone, communal eating was not enforced until 1976, which meant that families could rely on their resourcefulness in managing their food situation. The able-bodied could provide and care for the sick and the elderly, who otherwise would have suffered from compulsory reduction in their food ration. Relatively favorable food conditions made the exacting work quotas tolerable. In some parts of the East, urban relocatees were also given an initial period of adjustment before being assigned to more demanding work in the fields.[39]

As elsewhere, the favorable conditions in parts of the Southwest and the East were not generalizable throughout the zones, or over time. In places such as Chantrea and Memut, starvation set in as early as 1975, with conditions worsening after the introduction of communal eating. In Kompong Trabek, food rations consisted of watery rice gruel and banana stalks, a mixture previously used as pig feed. Control was also stringent especially after the introduction of communal eating, with life-sustaining activities such as foraging and family gardening prohibited, even when not conducted during working hours. Pech, a relocatee to Prey Veng, remembered that period of hunger: "My cousin would put whatever she could find in her underpants. She no longer cared about modesty or anything. I would wear pants to work in the fields, and then roll the crabs and insects that I could catch in my pant legs to bring home to my son." In some areas, "people died while sitting."

Along with food conditions, the number of arrests, disappearances, and executions determined the tolerability of an area. In the Northern and former Central zones, execution rather than starvation was the principal cause of death. In the Southwest, touted as the "model zone," over seventy-eight execution sites and 6,032 mass graves have been uncovered,[40] with the number of deaths estimated at over 153,000.[41] At Tram Kak, Takeo, where the remains of 10,045 people had been disinterred, survivors still remember the music from the loudspeakers used to mask the brutalization perpetrated inside the detention centers: "When you hear the loudspeaker, you know."[42] In the East, survivors recalled mass executions, especially of former officers, in Svay Rieng and Koh Satin.[43] In the Northwest, retribution against soldiers and pilots was carried out almost immediately upon the capture of the cities; possibly as many as 10,000 people were executed at Tuol Po Chrey in Pursat.[44] Nil, a former soldier, recalled that in Battambang

the troops were told to assemble at the Lycée Battambang. The officers were confined at Sala Sao Hoeur . . . for about a week. Our family
brought us food. We could have escaped but we were afraid. Later, the
high-ranking officers were told to go and meet Sihanouk. The noncom-
missioned soldiers were separated into two groups, one taken to Phnom
Sampeuv and the other to Mongkol Borei. But after one night in Mongkol
Borei, they brought us back to Phnom Sampeuv. Later on, I heard from a
Khmer Rouge relative that they had intended to kill us all and that some
of those who were sent to Mongkol Borei ahead of us were already executed; but something changed and they had to stop and send us back to
Phnom Sampeuv.[45]

Much of the extremism of the Northwest arguably was rooted in the
socioeconomic and political characteristics of the region.[46] Because of
its strategic importance, the region was among the most heavily contested during the war. It was also marked by deeply entrenched stratifi-
cations between hereditary landed elites and land-poor peasants, with
debt bondage, often borne across generations, persisting into the late
1960s. Ethnic differences further accentuated social divisions, as control
over the rice industry in this primarily agricultural region—from the
trucking business to the rice mills—was in the hands of ethnic Chinese,
while the lucrative gem mines and critical water rights in Pailin were
monopolized by the Kala, ethnic Burmese minorities who had settled in
the region.[47] Significantly, the most serious instance of rural unrest in
post-independence Cambodia, the 1967 Samlaut peasant uprising, took
place in the Northwest.

These experiences served as a backdrop to the reprisals against "class
enemies" that went unbridled in many parts of the zone after 1975. As
long-festering animus was vented in the headiness of victory, violence
in the Northwest was deployed, in many instances, with a degree of
senselessness and brutality that found few parallels. At Boeung Reng,
all seventeen members of a general's family, including a one-year-old
child, were brutally executed.[48] At Ampil Pram Daem, a survivor recalled coming across a site where a customs officer and his entire family
were executed. The only survivor was a baby, who was still alive despite
multiple stab wounds:

> Both the baby's legs had been broken and she was crawling—more like a seal flopping—toward her dead mother. She was attempting to nurse from her bloodied breast. We picked her up, but we were afraid that we would be killed by association, so we found an old base peasant and asked him to lie and say that the baby was his grandchild.

The attrition was particularly acute among the male population, as manifested in the gender imbalance in post–Khmer Rouge Cambodia. By 1977 in one region of the Northwest, "there were no more males in the village except for the base peasants."

The Human Factor in Necropolitics

In the centrality given to organization and ideologies, studies of revolution often overlook the importance of the human factor, which, in a system as fluid as that which prevailed in Democratic Kampuchea, played an even more pivotal role. Objective conditions notwithstanding, what determined whether life was tolerable in any given area depended, in large part, not on policies but on individuals, the *mé kang* and the *mé phum*,[49] who interpreted and implemented those policies, who possessed tremendous discretionary power to regulate work hours, determine food rations, grant small privileges, and punish or overlook their charges' transgressions. Survivors' reference to them as *sdach krangn* (feudal lords) evokes Achille Mbembe's concept of the sovereign whose power extends beyond control over life domain to the dictate "over who may live and who must die."[50] "They would stand there in crisp, new silk sarong. We never even dared look at their faces. Our body would shake uncontrollably at the sight of them even from a distance." The fear was visceral: "I looked up and saw him standing over me, dressed in black like *yum probal* from hell. I could not stop trembling."[51]

Many refugees thus attributed their survival to the willingness of those in charge to inject compassion into the implementation of policies. As famine spread throughout the country, starvation was minimized in some parts of the Northern and Northwestern Zones by the decision of the leadership to send less rice to the state granary.[52] In some locales, regional leaders reportedly urged sympathetic treatment of "new people" and imprisoned military personnel, noting that they were "our own flesh and blood."[53] Near Phnom Sampeuv, a cooperative leader interceded to prevent the relocation of a group of urbanites into the jungle, where there was no water, a humanitarian act that, in the end, cost him his life.

More commonly, altruism registered in small acts. As food conditions deteriorated, the freedom to forage and to barter became critical lifelines, privileges that were within the discretionary power of local authorities to grant, but that many refused. Nem, a relocatee to an area near Chonghor Thmar, described the place as tolerable because "they didn't check or confiscate much if they saw that we had worked hard." The same leniency was exercised at Phnom Sampeuv: "When things got really bad around the middle of 1976, some people were allowed to go to other *damban* to barter for our group." Likewise, conditions in the malaria-infested Northeast were tempered not only by the availability of forest resources but also by the lax policy regarding foraging. Mann, whose family was relocated to Phum Srong Prak, recalled that food in that very remote village was not plentiful but relocatees could forage for wild roots such as *kdouch*, which is poisonous but could be made edible if left to soak in a flowing stream. Like many evacuees, Sarn relied on his own ingenuity: "We were so hungry that we picked some bitter fruits and rolled them in ashes to take some of the bitterness away. Then we put them out to dry or we boiled them." Many urbanites, however, did not possess the knowledge, skills, or resourcefulness necessary for survival, and could do little to deter starvation; equally many died from consuming the wrong things out of desperation.

In settlements composed strictly of urban relocatees, "new people" were sometimes placed in positions of authority, often with little supervision from the Khmer Rouge. Some, like Yoeun, a middle-aged woman who was assigned to lead an orange harvesting detail, used these privileges to ensure the well-being of their charges: "Whenever we were alone, I would tell my group to eat the oranges and use every opportunity and means to stay alive." Another refugee who was relocated to Phum Chrey attributed his survival to a compassionate work team leader: "There were only three of us in our group and the man in charge told us secretly that we could eat as much as we wanted from the storage as long as we don't get caught." Such solidarity and consideration (*yok-yul khnear*), however, could not be taken for granted. Under a regime that measured loyalty by one's ability to sever all emotional ties (*kat chet*), denunciations of friends and relatives were all too common.

Conversely, malevolent leadership was one of the contributing factors to mass death. Famine at Beng Veal in the Northwest, for instance, was aggravated by the authorities' callous disregard of the conditions: "There was so much death . . . but still we were not allowed to mix with the base people. It was not until 1976 that we were finally permitted to interact with local villagers; by then many had already died." Similarly at Beng Kosal, the prohibition against barter left the village without provisions: "Without salt and sugar, many people swelled up and could no longer walk. Those too sick to forage would pick up the discarded snail shells that people had already eaten, just to suck on them." In Koh Kong, one survivor recalled, "we begged for the little stubs that were left in the ground after the potato had been dug up, but they wouldn't let us have them." That many of these policies were not only draconian but also punitive and senseless was apparent at Preah Andong, where "there was so much fish and grain, but we could not touch them. If you had so much as caught one small fish for yourself, you would be killed immediately." Prak, a middle-aged farmer, remembered that in the Northwest "there were many paddy fields in the lowland that were left fallow but they wouldn't allow us to work them." Instead, many like Chanthou were sent to the top of the mountains to grow rice, evoking the imagery, as she puts it, of what the elders had foretold "about the shrimps climbing to the mountains."

Hunger and violence worked in sinister tandem. Brutality increased in direct proportion to the level of desperation as starvation drove people toward fatalistic choices. As one child survivor puts it, "If you didn't steal, you would certainly die; if you steal, there was a slim chance that you might not get caught and would live another day." Stripped to "bare life," as Agamben puts it, existence was reduced to one basal need— food: "Our life was worth the moment of savoring a snail or a morsel of potato. As long as we could satisfy hunger for the moment, we could die without regrets." In this death world, it was not uncommon for extremist measures, including summary executions, to be meted out for trivial transgressions. At Svay Doan Keo, eight Khmer Krom (ethnic Khmer from Vietnam) were clubbed to death for having stolen some cucumbers. Near Phnom Sampeuv, a *yothea* savagely beat an old woman simply for trying to gather some *sa-ngè* grains that grew in the swampy wild. At Preah Andong, one man was executed for squirreling away some insects, and another for foraging for food for his wife, who had just delivered a baby. She, too, was killed. Nhet, a refugee-survivor, recalled the violence in Kompong Speu: "Ta Choeun's son was caught stealing some pig feed. They gouged both his eyes and left him for almost two weeks without water before he died. Another person caught stealing food was split open, and those trying to escape would get their limbs cut off." The evidence in scattered fields amplified the terror. Oun recounted how "in Kompong Chhnang, when I went to dig for potatoes, I pulled up so many bones along with them." Under these depraved circumstances, power revealed its sadistic features. Srey observed that the Khmer Rouge would often resettle a family under suspicion near an orchard in order to tempt them into sealing their own death. The saying "Plant a banana tree near your house and you have planted your children's graves" became part of the encoded reality of Democratic Kampuchea.

The Year of the "Four-Legged": Temporality and Internal Conditions

Conditions in Democratic Kampuchea also reflected the political vicissitudes. As the Party Center proceeded to consolidate its power, campaigns to investigate and "smash" enemies who had penetrated the revolutionary ranks[54] set off widening purges of the leadership and cadres, and persecution of base peasants in different zones, which began in early 1976. In Siemreap, the Chikreng revolt was brutally suppressed. The greatest convulsion, however, was in the East, where mass arrests resulted in the dramatic increase in the number of prisoners from the zone detained and killed at Tuol Sleng, reaching the highest in 1978. These political shifts reverberated to the local level as changes in the leadership were accompanied by policy changes. In some areas, previously intolerable conditions improved. In others, relatively favorable conditions deteriorated, especially following the introduction of communal eating, which in some parts of the country occurred as early as 1976. Elsewhere still, difficult conditions worsened. In Patheat, when even the ration of "only about one tablespoon of rice grain in watery porridge" was no longer available, relocatees were given some salt and instructed to fend for themselves: "We traded with the base people for the taro branches that they threw away." In the West, conditions had become so extreme by 1977 that one can[55] of rice grain had to sustain fifty people; Nhet's daughter, who was only sixteen, "looked like an eighty-year-old woman."

Though deprivation was endemic, some of the most horrendous accounts were of the Northwest, where, despite a good harvest, starvation was widespread because of excessive requisition by the Center following the purge of the zone leadership in 1976.[56] At Sala Ta On, children would swim under the stilt houses of base peasants, waiting for the potato skins that they threw out with the garbage. One survivor recalled, "I was so hungry that sometimes I would suck on tree bark. Little children fought over a single grasshopper." Neang spoke of how hunger deprived her cousin Pom even of her dignity before death: "Before she died, she was stricken with such a high fever . . . she was always naked, and her head was shaved. There was just no shame left anymore." Others, like Neang's father, clung to their dignity despite the deprivation:

> He died after having nothing to eat for one month. . . . Once, he said that he saw a pile of potato skins that the base villagers had thrown away. . . . He was so hungry, but he was embarrassed to pick them up. We were able to trade with other evacuees for seven potatoes, but he got sicker after eating them. Then he ate some wild fruits without knowing they were poisonous.

As in many parts of the country, hard labor and starvation left many so debilitated with edema that they could no longer walk; survivors still refer to this period as the time "when your kneecap is bigger than your head" (*kbal chongkong thom cheang kbal*). Kieu, another survivor, was so weak that he had to crawl over the paddy embankment: "It was only about one and a half feet high but I could not step over it." The year 1977 was indeed, as he put it, "the year of the four-legged."

By late 1976, death was rampant. Bopha, who was part of the young women's *chalat* (mobile work detail), recalled that "flies followed us everywhere; we were like walking corpses." In many areas, illness, death, and disappearance left virtually no one to bring in the harvest from the fields. Sambath, who was assigned to transport straw from Moung, re-membered, "Each bundle was no bigger than my ankle, but no one could lift it. There was so much rice in the fields but there was no one left to harvest it." The death toll from starvation was high especially among children and the elderly. Pros, who was assigned to a transport unit, once came upon some toddlers at an area near Leach whose diminished state, and his inability to save them, left an indelible imprint upon him. Orphaned by the deaths that devastated the entire village,

> they were so swollen and stricken with starvation that they could no lon-ger move or talk. They sat in the huts and barely had enough strength to wave to me as I drove by in my oxcart. I couldn't do anything for them so I boiled them some potatoes that I had hidden for myself, but they couldn't even eat them. They just sat there blinking their eyes at the po-tatoes with flies swarming all over them. They begged me to take them along, but I couldn't. Nobody could help anybody. Each knew that further ahead, he would be like that too, so we could not take anybody with us. I just left the potatoes there and prayed that they would live long enough until another cart passed by.

In some places, death consumed whole villages. Sim remembered that in Phum Kampeang Poy "you could smell death everywhere." Another survivor recalled, "While cow herding I would sit on top of this hillock and look down at this village. It used to bustle with people, but later it was completely deserted. There was no sign of life. Only the tips of the bamboo poles from the huts still stood." The prophetic words of Puth thus reverberated: *There would be houses but no one to live in them.*

The political turmoil also engendered other punitive repercussions. In the West, mass relocation, including of base peasants, took place fol-lowing the leadership purge in 1976, fostering even greater animosity toward the "new people," who were blamed for their plight: "We heard the *mulathan* say that because of us, they were relocated . . . and that if Angkar would let them, they would kill all of us." Similarly, most of the Eastern Zone population was also forcibly relocated, many to the North-west, where most perished in mass graves. Leung, who stumbled upon one of the killing sites, recalled, "People relocated from the East, . . . they usually wear blue checkered *krama*. The pit was full of blue *krama*."[57] Of the violent developments in the East, Kiernan concluded that, though "in no way can the actions [of the leadership] be described as enlightened or benign,"[58] the subsequent years of political turmoil created such death and dislocation that they made previously imposed hardship seem like "benevolence."

As campaigns to expose "enemies" intensified, the terror net was cast even more widely. "We were told to write our biographies," one survivor remembered, "and they would cross-check them with those of the rest of our family members. At night, they would come and take some people away."[59] One of my interviewees recalled,

> The ten- to twelve-year-old *yotheas* were the worst. They called themselves *mit bang* [elder comrade] and would count our heads with a club. If one person were missing from the group, the leader of the group would be pulled out, made to kneel down and be executed immediately in front of everyone.

In a cultural context where age commands respect, and the head considered the most sacred realm, the boy cadres' self-designation as *mit bang* and the touching of an older person's head marked a reversal of power and the inversed social order that Democratic Kampuchea came to represent. While the regime infantilized adults by destroying all aspects of their self-determination, children once at the nadir of the social hierarchy were entrusted with absolute power over life and death. As it happened, the most brutal guards at the Tuol Angsaom prison were children who gleefully tortured other children for stealing an ear of corn. These were children upon whose childish whims countless lives were made to hang. Kassie Neou, a survivor and activist, for one, attributed his survival to his ability to entertain the child cadre in charge of the detention center with Aesop's fables.[60]

In the East, beginning in late 1976, wives and children of those already arrested were taken away. The number of executions grew from fewer than 10,000 in 1975–1976 to over 100,000 between 1977 and 1978.[61] Chanthou, then only sixteen, recounted the tragedy that struck her own family:

About two months after the old village leaders were taken away in the middle of 1978, the new *yotheas* started to gather all the males from the work sites . . . they were arrested and clubbed to death. Later, they came and took the rest of the evacuee families. . . . My whole family was killed, including my five-year-old nephew and my six-year-old sister. . . . The carts that transported them later returned with their belongings and clothing.

When I got permission to visit my family, I was so happy that I started to run toward my family's hut. But the village was so quiet. It seemed that even the base peasants were in shock. Some children asked me why I came back, since my family had been taken away. One of them was playing with my mother's pouch. I walked back to my hut and saw that everything was still there, in place, as if the people had just left. My sarong was neatly folded by the door. The kettle was still on the stove.

This young woman was told that her family had been relocated to Chamcar Krabas. Other than the sight of her mother's pouch, and the sad warning from the people not to inquire about her family, she was never able to confirm their fate.

Spying and denunciations amplified the terror. A picture of a loved one, a foreign-language book, or old school uniforms could be the cause of someone's unexplained disappearance. The moral anguish was still palpable decades after when Malis spoke of how she reached the painful decision to destroy the last link she had left to her past: a picture of her grandfather in court regalia, yellowed with age, the very last thing that her mother had given her before she died. In a culture that places an inordinate importance on genealogy, this decision amounted to an act of self-erasure.

It was more than just a photograph. It was my life history, my ancestors [*chi doan, chi ta*]. I had lost everything and everyone. At times, I almost forgot who I was before. To destroy it would have meant letting go of the very last link I have to my past. All these things—once gone, I can never get back. My children may never know their roots [*pouch ambo*]. One day I may not even remember what my grandfather looked like. But to keep it would mean death. So I said a prayer and buried it in the forest.[62]

Prisons, Death Camps, and the Moral Abyss

Under a regime where the "state of exception"[63] applied not just to a camp or a prison but the entire country, hence where the "state of exception" was not an exception but the rule, prisons and death camps, the ultimate Khmer Rouge terror institutions, stood at the very abyss, not just outside accountability but beyond the pale of humanity. Though the regime proclaimed that prisons did not exist in Democratic Kampuchea,[64] the Khmer Rouge internal security apparatus crisscrossed the country. While S-21 has acquired notoriety as the "artifact of Khmer Rouge brutality,"[65] it was only one of 196 formally organized prisons that have so far been uncovered, and was reportedly not even the site of the most killings.[66] Many more detention centers and unmarked prisons were scattered throughout Democratic Kampuchea, at least 250 of which were located in the Southwest alone.[67] Many were hidden in vacated monasteries—traditional sanctuaries of nonviolence—and in innocuous-looking villages, often shrouded from external scrutiny by verdant banana groves. There, hundreds of thousands of former soldiers, intellectuals, professionals, and individuals who for reasons unknown even to them, were imprisoned, tortured, and killed. Ton, who was sent to an area near a killing ground, recalled, "When you cut the banana trunks, they oozed of bloody sap."

Such a system worked through secrecy and compartmentalization. Until the collapse of the regime, this vast and complex security network, ranging from makeshift village prisons to the highly structured "bureaucracy of death"[68] of S-21 in Phnom Penh, was largely invisible to the outside world. One of the few accounts of prisoners detained in Phnom Penh in 1975 was that of Prum, a former student cum soldier,[69] who was held along with professors, students, pilots, and military personnel in the early months at a prison that he claimed was part of what later became the Tuol Sleng extermination center. As he recounted, "Regularly, four times a day, I was beaten with a bamboo stick. After the morning beating, they took me outside to work on the grounds with the wooden block still attached to my leg." Because of the practice of imprisoning people away from their village or cooperative, many refugee-survivors recalled having "simply seen prisoners being led away into the jungle," but not knowing who they were, where they came from, where or why they were taken, and what ultimately happened to them. The fate of those arrested was uncertain. Individuals "sent to Angkar Loeu" could be summarily killed in nearby forests or end up in a prison or labor camp, where death, escape, or release awaited them. Those who survived often changed their names to eliminate any ties to their past. Bunna was among the lucky few who were released following an arrest:

> There were two "prisons"—converted granaries actually—one for women, one for men, and one chicken coop for the special group of people who couldn't speak Khmer very well. In my holding area, thirty-five prisoners were kept there at a time. Each night they would take ten or twenty away and replace them with new ones. At night you could hear the *phoas, phoas,* noise of people being clubbed to death.
>
> Luckily they released all thirty-five of us. . . . They said that this was the first time anybody had been released and that so far, five thousand had been brought in. They told us not to go back to our *phum* because we might be accused again . . . that we must never tell anybody where we had been or anything about our past. Then they opened up the coop and we trotted out like chickens.

More pervasive than the detention centers and prisons were the re-education camps *(konlèng lot dam)* where individuals with tainted political biographies, including many students and professionals who had voluntarily returned from abroad,[70] were sent, purportedly to be reformed. In the already extreme world of Democratic Kampuchea, these "topographies of cruelty"[71] represented graduated extremism, with the most punitive being death camps in remote desolate areas. Reminiscent of the Soviet gulags, they were the ultimate manifestation of Agamben's *conditio inhumana*, here characterized not just by social abandonment and depravity, but by the complete obviation of humanism; there the condemned were not simply killed but "discarded" like refuse, as the term *vay chaol* (which was never part of the pre–Khmer Rouge vocabulary) implies. Mot, a former soldier, recalled being unceremoniously dumped with other military personnel from Battambang at the jungle fringes of O Paung Muan without adequate provisions or implements to ensure survival:

We were directed to clear the forestland for farming. But we were given no tools. Those without implements had to dig with their hands. . . . They brought in some seeds for planting, but no plough. So I took a branch with some thorns and dragged it along so that the loose soil could cover the seeds somewhat. There was also no water. We only had one well, but fortunately, it was the beginning of the rainy season.

Despite the rhetoric of rehabilitation, most reeducation camps were nothing more than holding areas for condemned individuals where human existence was instrumentalized[72] and maximum labor and productivity extracted from them before they perished. There, rather than positivist reform, the intended outcome was social death, the destruction of worth and vitality that extended beyond that of the body, and that lives in and through even those who survived. It was not just life that was erased in bestial treatment and mass disposal; it was humanity itself, such that even the life that was spared was imprinted with death. At Phum Chamrous, political prisoners were assigned to break rocks for road-building projects, a death sentence given their starvation ration.[73] Phoeun described his encounter with some of these condemned souls while working near the prison camp: "As they were led to the work site, some prisoners would pick some corn leaves to eat. Another approached our *krom* to beg for *katuok*. A *yothea* saw him and shot him."[74] At a prison camp in the East, 80 out of 120 prisoners died of starvation and hard work.[75]

It was in these death camps, "prisons without walls" (*kouk ot chanchaing*), that people came face-to-face with their dehumanized selves. Lok Ta Som, a traditional healer, recounted his imprisonment at Tuol Angsaom:

There were about two hundred prisoners and whenever the guards were displeased, they would beat us with a thorny club. It was like the pictures you see on the pagoda walls about the condemned who were sent to hell [*norouk*].

The leader was afraid to beat me because he had seen me cure people, so he would tell the six- to seven-year-old kids to kick me. Sometimes they would push our heads[76] into the puddle and hold them down with a forked branch. Some of the prisoners were women who had stolen food for their children. They would hang those children upside down by their ankles.

> We were no longer humans, . . . our clothes were so tattered that we could barely hold on to our decency. We were like *pret* [people from hell] who fought over an eaten corncob that they had thrown away.

Under these conditions, depravity surfaced. Executions often involved not only the physical destruction of the body but its mutilation. Sopheap, who was relocated to the Northwest, recounted how her neighbor's husband was killed, split from behind and had his liver and gallbladder ripped out. Rorn, another relocatee to the Northwest, still shivered at the memory of being instructed to cook human livers for the Khmer Rouge leaders: "They popped in the pan not like other types of liver." Pin, a refugee-survivor, recalled seeing pouches of human gallbladder stashed between the bamboo slates of the Khmer Rouge leader's house and being haunted by nightmares about "ghosts coming back to look for their missing gallbladders." Though there has been recent scholarly attention to these macabre acts,[77] it is important to note that these practices were rooted in Khmer fringe subculture and beliefs founded on the notion of power transference,[78] and were also known to have occurred during the time of the Issarak.[79] That both movements drew membership from certain segments of the peasantry meant that these forms of violence continued to be perpetrated in places where traditionalist authority remained entrenched.

In the deprived and depraved world of Democratic Kampuchea, the moral yardstick invariably shifted. Survival itself was purchased through daily acts of moral compromise. Rany lamented her own degradation in the face of hunger and desperation: "I had never ever stolen in my life, but they turned me into a thief. Every chance we had, we stole, because the hunger never stopped." In her autobiography, Loung Ung painfully recalled her theft of a handful of rice from a dying old woman, and her feeling of being morally implicated in the woman's imminent death:

> The fist-sized rice ball rests weightily in my pocket as the face of the old woman comes back to me. Her gray oily hair clings to her skull and her chest contracts and expands in shallow breaths beneath her black clothes. Her helpers will return to find the rice missing and they will have nothing

more to give her. . . . By taking her food I have helped kill her. But I can-not return the rice. I lift it to my lips. . . . The hard rice scrapes down in a dry lump, thus I put a marker on the old woman's grave.[80]

Dehumanization and self-implication reached the ultimate moral abyss with stories of cannibalism among the desperate. Pen, who was assigned to a work detail in Moung, an area devastated by starvation, was warned not to stand too far away from the railroad tracks, as people had been known to be ambushed and cannibalized in desolate areas. Phoeun recounted the execution of a man caught in the act of cannibalism:

> My neighbor's wife had died, and then his three-year-old child started to get sick. For days we didn't see him at the dining hall. Finally, the Khmer Rouge went to search his hut. In his kettle, they discovered boiling chunks of meat. They went and dug behind his hut and saw the skeletal remains. They dragged him away immediately. In this case, they didn't hide the execution because they said, "We don't need that kind of people—they are not human, they are *yeak*" [ogres].

It was through these daily compromises that the system worked to implicate everyone, abusers and victims alike. By leaving the victims in a state of moral ambiguity, plagued by self-questioning, the system in effect dulled their ability to condemn. Individuals forced to confront the diminishing of their own selves may feel compelled to recognize the same debasement in their victimizers: "*Yoeung anchoeung, prohel ke ko anchoeung der*" (We were in that situation, so perhaps they too were in that situation). Such a system thus thrives in the gray zone where nor-malcy and deviancy, morality and compromise blur together in a sinister synthesis.

It is virtually impossible to determine with certainty why, subjected to the same conditions, one individual survived and another perished. Chance and hope were the two themes that emerged in survivors' ac-counts. The Khmer Rouge practice of lying about the death of families was not merely for sadistic pleasure, but to keep survivors accountable to their loved ones, thereby thwarting any acts that despair may provoke. In so doing, the regime succeeded in divesting individuals of their final act of self-determination. Some, like Thida Mam, abandoned the idea of suicide out of fear of recriminations against their families: "I wanted to commit suicide but I couldn't. If I did, I would be labeled 'the enemy' because I dared to show my unhappiness with their regime. My death would be followed by my family's death because they were the family of the enemy."[81] For many, the *force de vivre* transformed into resilience and ingenuity. It was especially remarkable among child survivors. Though the revolution may have left its bloody imprint upon them, it was unable to destroy the spirit and the will that shone through their determination to survive and to hope.

2

The Children of Angkar

I tried to escape from the children's group . . . but the soldiers intercepted me. I told them that I was on my way to my village. They said they would take me there. Instead, they took me to Phum Sdok Krasang. I spent twenty-eight days in that prison. There were approximately two hundred prisoners, in separate halls, one for male prisoners and the other for the women. Many were there for stealing; others were former soldiers. In my hall, there were about eighty people. Every day, ten or twelve died, and new ones were brought in.

I made a friend in prison. We never talked about anything except food—what we would like to eat if we could have our wish. These day-dreams made us even hungrier, but each day we looked forward to those few minutes before hunger and exhaustion overtook us. These talks kept us going. They made us remember that we were still alive, even the hunger pangs; and I would remember that I had found a friend. One night, I was talking to him as usual—then silence. He had died; but I didn't realize that until morning. I had huddled next to him as I had always done; his saliva was drooling on my head. But my friend was dead.

Prisoner: Sith

Age: 13

Crime: Attempted escape from starvation

Like many of his peers, Sith came across like an average California teenager, with his LA Gear high tops and college sweatshirt. With West-ernized names that reflect attempts to bridge the cultural gaps, the Cambodian American youths whom I interviewed[1] seemed no different from the thousands of students who file through the corridors of Ameri-can public schools. Their animated conversations about sports and the prospect of owning their first cars, their inner-city slang, all presented an unsettling contrast to the other reality that they embodied—of Khmer Rouge labor camps, starvation, loneliness, fear, and violence. The scars, however, remain just below that veneer of ordinariness—scars of having seen too much, too young, scars of war and genocide.

Under the extremism of Democratic Kampuchea and the unerring conformity that the system demanded of its populace, it is difficult to conceive that any element of individualism could survive. The sepulchral forms with twiggy limbs and disproportionately large heads that staggered out of Khmer Rouge child-labor camps were nothing resembling humanity. Yet somewhere behind those aged, soulless eyes lay a pulsating will to live. Story after story of the uncanny ability to survive against all odds, of ingenious designs to stay alive, of wisdom beyond their age, sometimes makes us forget that they were only children. It is always the little things, the childish thoughts and expressions, their pained unspoken longing for a mother's touch, that remind us of their youth, their innocence, their humanity. These were, after all, children in old people's skin, living old people's fears, starving with old people's hunger, but dreaming the dreams all children dream. They are survivors. They were the children of Angkar.

He dreamt of being king, a *neak mean bon*,[2] powerful and mystical, coming to save his country and his people. He would restore his kingdom to a land of plenty, where everyone could eat their fill and wear colorful clothing, where children could savor all the delicious rice cakes and palm sugar and play in the streets, and where real justice would reign. But he was only a cow herder, and his domain the six cows for which he was responsible with his life. His sole possessions consisted of a torn shirt riddled with holes with sleeves long severed, and a pair of muddied shorts—cut-offs from his old elementary school uniform. The dark blue had been blackened with a foul-smelling mixture of mud and *makloeur* that his mother had conscientiously brewed under Angkar's order to dye all the colorful "city" clothes they had brought out with them from Phnom Penh. That was the last thing she had given him when he was inducted into the *kommar angkapheap* (children's unit). Rithy was seven years old when he was taken away from his parents.

The selection usually began after the relocatees had been permanently resettled in a *phum* (village). In many parts of Cambodia, the process of separating children from their families started in early 1976 and applied especially to older children, but there were accounts of children as young as five years old having been taken away from their parents. Arn, who was forcibly relocated with his family to the Eastern Zone, recalled the fear and anguish with which the announcement was received in his hamlet in Kompong Cham. The directive came on the heels of the first evidence that the regime was killing its own people.

> They were constructing this new *phum*. Everyone wanted to go there. My father really wanted to go but they wouldn't let him. Nobody knew; they lied. When they took all those people away, about a month and a half or two months later, they sent the clothing back to be redistributed to the villagers. So we all knew that those people were sent to their death.
>
> It wasn't long after that that they began selecting the children for the *ang kommar* [children's unit]. My parents were scared. . . . There were two of us in that age group in my family, and they needed to take one. My sister and I fought, each saying the other should go. Finally, my sister said, "Little brother, I am older than you and I have lived many more years than you. . . . Let me go in your stead." I still remember the words she uttered; I felt so bad. And then she went, but she wasn't killed. She was put in *chalat* and at first she was given a scarf and she had enough food to eat. We, at the *phum*, had nothing. I was so envious.
>
> After a few months, I was sent to join the *kommar angkapheap* . . . I was the tallest and they chose the tall ones to be in the *kommar kang pises* [special children's unit]. . . . Special, but we ate the same amount!

The conscription was not always received with anxiety and fear. Some children went out of their naive belief in Angkar's promise to nurture and provide. Given the unspeakable privations, children like six-year-old Vithou grasped for the most rudimentary signs of a better life:

> The leaders of the *krom kommar* had these shirts with thirty-two buttons. But we were so poor; some of us had no buttons at all. I had lost my last one while working in the fields and my mother beat me because she could no longer trade for them. The buttons, they showed how rich they were and they gleamed against their dark shirt—*really* dark shirts, not like ours that had been unevenly darkened with the extract from boiled tree bark and mud. Who wouldn't want to join them?

He added, "After four years with them, all I got were two *krama*, a roll of white fabric just enough for a pair of short pants, and a shirt. But I was so grateful and happy. Other children never even had that much wealth." For some children, seduced by the power that contrasted so markedly with their own insignificance, there was perhaps even admiration for such a seemingly invincible force:

> We looked at the *yotheas* and we envied them. They ate so well. They were so strong while we were nothing but skin and bones with kneecaps that were bigger than our limbs. They carried guns. They had shoes; and people feared them. Theirs was a life of luxury. As a child, you didn't think about the killing. They were just so virile and people shook at the sight of them. When they showed up at the *phum*, you knew something important was going to happen.

Prior to the enforcement of communal eating, in most areas children assigned to work in the vicinity of the village were allowed to join their parents for the evening meals. Subsequently, unauthorized contact with families was prohibited, and the children were sequestered when in the vicinity of a village, permitted to venture into hamlets only when they needed to secure farming implements or when they were granted leave. Even those housed within sight of their parents' hut were denied unauthorized interactions with them or with other villagers. Despite her father's status as the zone herbalist, seven-year-old Kanya was not spared: "We were sent to do orcharding in the jungle. Every time we returned to the village to get implements or attend the general meeting, we were not allowed to talk to our parents. Anyone seen talking to their families would be punished when they returned to camp." Socheat recalled the painful agony of having to suppress her maternal instincts in order to protect her child:

> They walked the children back from the worksite at the end of each day to line up at the dining hall, but before they approached the hamlet, they made them cover their heads with the *krama*. I recognized my little girl and she looked so thin and pale. I felt so sad and I went up to her, but she just turned away. I kept on repeating, "Phal, this is your mother. Why won't you talk to me?" She just looked at me coldly and said, "I'm not

your daughter. I'm the child of Angkar." That little girl standing in front of me was not my little girl but a stranger. Later, she secretly whispered to me, "Please don't call out to me anymore. They will beat me if they see me talking to you." My heart almost exploded at the thought that I cannot even talk to my daughter but the thought of her being beaten and chastised because of me was even more unbearable. I had to let her go.

A lucky few were permitted short and infrequent home visits. Many, however, were able to see their families only by escaping from their camps. Given the system of shared accountability, the risks were not only to themselves but also to their families: "My sister and I used to run to our mother's camp, which was about thirty miles from the orphans' home. Sometimes we were caught and punished. They warned my mother that if we did this again they would kill the whole family. We stayed at the orphans' home for about two years without seeing our family."[3] Many children were never to see their parents again.

During short-term assignments, the children would be sheltered in houses requisitioned from the base peasants. Mala described one of the structures: "The house only had a roof with brick shingles and wooden floor, like a typical Khmer house. . . . We had three houses, one for the head of the group, . . . one for the boys and the other for the girls. There were about fifty of us." At other times, they were housed in simple halls, built raised from the ground, often with no walls or partitions. Separated by gender, they slept on wooden floors, packed against each other, sometimes in groups of thirty, fifty, or even a hundred, depending upon the size of the project to which they had been assigned. Where accommodations were scarce, all the children would be sheltered together, often with one group sleeping inside, and the other under the house on stilts where cows were customarily kept. Rattana remembered,

> We were always so tired from working all day and sometimes half the night. We were also too afraid of the dark to go down to relieve ourselves. So the floor of the sleeping quarter was always wet. It smelled so badly that many times I went and slept in the oxcart instead.
>
> My brother's group had to sleep on the ground beneath us; the inside was for female workers. Always starving and with disease spreading everywhere, many of us became ill and we no longer had any control of

our bowel movements. I really felt bad for the boys who had to sleep below us. My brother would always have to wash off the filth, and was always late for work. He was punished all the time.

The difficulty and intensity of the assignments varied, depending upon the age group. Children too little to perform strenuous tasks were sent to sprinkle water on the dirt road "so that it would not get too dusty when people traveled by. This was especially important when we had dignitaries touring the countryside."[4] Others were assigned to collect manure and human fertilizer or work in the fields. As one recounted,

> They made us take planks out of houses and dismantle the walls. They drilled holes into the planks and then had us lay the planks down on the ground and place these special rice shoots from China exactly inside the holes. It did look really nice and symmetrical. People said the plants sprouted very quickly but did not bear any grain.

The older children were given more exacting tasks such as cutting wood to fuel the trains in Pursat. For evacuee children from the cities, what made the situation intolerable was not necessarily the hard work, as many assignments involved tasks that, in time, they were able to master. As Pin noted,

> It was as Darwin said. Those who survived were the fittest, those who were able to adapt to any situation. I had never come close to a cow before in my life, but I learned by watching other children. At first, one of the cows knocked me down when I tried to tie him from the front, and gored me. After that I saw others tie the cows from the side. I learned.

Rather, it was the abject conditions, the constant exposure to harsh elements, chronic starvation, violence, and fear that brutalized them. As life was rendered bare and barren, "color vanished, like laughter, song and dance."[5] The same tasks that previously were carried out by peasant children with levity and fun were now performed under the threat of beatings and disappearances, and always in hunger, made even worse by the oppressive conditions under which they lived and toiled. During the dry season, it was the heat that tormented them, especially at remote work sites such as Prey Nob, in Koh Kong, where water was scarce: "There was no water at all near that work site. Each person only got a small glass of water each day. After the canal was finished we got to bathe once a week. After laboring under the heat, carrying dirt and rocks, water was the sweetest-tasting thing in the world." The monsoons brought little reprieve, as their ragged clothes and dilapidated shelters provided little comfort from the rain and cold. At times, they slept huddled on the ground in rain puddles:

> We had no hammock, no pillows, no blanket. Nothing. It was the beginning of the cold season. My mother had given me one *krama*; that was all I had; and when it got so cold, I went to sleep in the hay. It was so itchy because the haystack was near the cows . . . and we didn't have much clothing on our backs; our clothes were all tattered by then. Sometimes we would crawl into a stack of rice husks just to keep warm. It didn't matter to us if there might be snakes or something in that pile. We just wanted the cold to go away.

Working conditions also deteriorated.

> During the flooding season, we had to wade through the water to the work site, about ten kilometers away, and we worked in the water all day. Where it was dry enough to walk, the grounds were so slippery that we would slip and fall. If that happened, they would beat us.
>
> Most of us only had two changes of clothes, if we were lucky. Usually, both would be soaking wet. If we were fortunate, the moist clothing that we wore to sleep would get somewhat dry by the next morning, but it would just get wet again. For this reason, the clothes we had did not last long. We ended up with only tattered clothes on our backs.

Over the loudspeakers, the same indoctrinating leitmotif spurned the lived reality: "Angkar will nurture and provide."

The backbreaking toil and abject conditions were exacerbated by the starvation ration. In some areas, priority was given to adults, and children, with less productivity, were given only watery gruel. In other places, as in parts of the East, children, considered by the regime to be the nation's future, received better rations. Regardless, by 1976, rice was generally no longer available in most children's camps. Bo recalled that

> during the worst period, it was watery porridge . . . [and] one bowl of soup for every six of us. As soon as the soup bowl hit the table we jumped on it, six spoons diving into the bowl searching for invisible pieces of fish or meat. We fought like dogs over a piece of bone. . . . Like animals, just like animals.
>
> Sometimes, we would be lucky and be given a grain of salt with our meals, but that was very rare. In my area, salt and sugar were very scarce. Every three months or so, we might get ten grams of sugar. If we didn't have sugar, we would swell up. "They" [the base peasant children] ate separately.

During some of the worst times,

> after starting work at 5 or 6 a.m., we wouldn't get any food until three o'clock in the afternoon, and the evening meal wouldn't come till midnight. The paddy fields were all flooded so we would perch on the dikes in the rain like monkeys waiting for them to row their boats alongside the dikes and distribute our food—a ladleful of watery watercress porridge, supplemented with watercress soup [and] the rain pouring into our plate. . . . In Sisophon, sometimes they used the water from the puddles made by buffalo tracks to cook for us and we would find leeches in our soup.

Isolated, alone, starved, and scarred by emotional distress, many children found themselves unable to do more than obey:

> After a month or so at that place, working in the water from dawn to midnight with no food, we started to feel disoriented. Our brains just stopped functioning. We just did what we were told. There was no sensation anymore. . . . One day we were working next to an adult group and I saw this woman. She looked so familiar but I couldn't recall where I had seen her before. Then the woman started to call out to me. I heard the voice but it sounded so far away, just a thin voice. I thought my mind was

playing tricks and the voice was not even real. But I kept hearing it. So I kept looking around at the voice that was calling me. Finally, the woman touched my shoulder and scooped half of her porridge onto my plate. From some deep recesses of my mind, I heard myself thinking out loud, "This must be my mother because she shared her food with me." Then the food hit my stomach and . . . I was back in this world.

With plaguing hunger, food became a disciplinary apparatus.

> The hunger is not like anything you've ever experienced. It was the kind of hunger that is raw. The thought that it would never end made it more intense. Today you starve; tomorrow you will still be starving.
>
> After a while, we couldn't walk erect anymore. . . . Some of the children were so debilitated by fatigue and starvation that if they slipped and fell into the paddy fields, they couldn't pick themselves up. So they drowned.

This was the ultimate irony of Pol Pot's Cambodia—to die of starvation in a rice field.

Work was key to survival: "If you don't work, you don't eat." Mom, whose family was relocated to the Eastern Zone, was injured and temporarily crippled, during which time she was constantly castigated for being lazy:

> It was just a small scratch but it started to spread and got deeper. Every time I moved my toe, the blood would shoot up. But they said that I was lazy and was just trying to get out of work by pretending to be crippled. I had to crawl to the eating hall to get my ration, otherwise I wouldn't get any food. But before they handed the food to me, they would chastise me every time.

In what I refer to as the necroworld of Democratic Kampuchea, the reality, as seven-year-old Rithy saw it, was that "even if you worked, you would probably still die—just a little later."

Separated from their families, they could rely only on their own resourcefulness and wit to survive. Kosal, then a sheltered ten-year-old, attributed his survival to his sharpened instincts: "When I walked, my eyes were never fixed straight ahead. They were always darting everywhere—looking for a fruit here, an insect there, a convenient route to escape or hide—anything, but always looking for options. I ate everything I could find—grasshoppers, field mice, insects—anything that moved." For seven-year-old Veasna, a fortuitous assignment guarding the orchards near Phnom Sampeuv was a lifesaving reprieve:

> It wasn't too bad because we could eat the corn that had been pecked by wild parrots. Sometimes we would spot the tendrils of the *damlong chreuv,* and we would cut off the vines so no one would know there were potatoes in the ground. We would put a stick to mark the spot. After work, we would sneak back and dig them up. Sometimes when no one was really watching, we pretended to warm ourselves by the bonfire that they kept burning to keep the cows warm and we would grill whatever insects or bits of potatoes we had hidden away. Sometimes, we would catch and eat the insects that were attracted to the light and had crawled toward the fire.

Hunger pushed individuals to the moral precipice:

> I once saw a wild duck and knew there would be eggs where the duck was. . . . I found one! It was lying in the middle of a human skull. I picked it up and took the egg out and searched and found three more eggs. One egg was stuck close to a set of teeth. I thought that the dead person wanted to eat this egg [so] I put it back.[6]

With pervasive starvation, food became one of the most effective implements of governmentality used to purchase loyalty and undermine solidarity: "When a child is hungry, you can get him to do anything for food. Children followed whoever gave them food. They renounced and denounced their parents and each other."[7] Laurence Picq, the French wife of a high-ranking Khmer Rouge official, saw the metamorphosis of her own children, enticed by a sliver of grapefruit: "Naren and Sokha, seated with other children, were savoring their first fruit in a long time. Staring into the center of the circle, they acted as if they didn't see me. I turned away sadly, thinking that *Angkar* had found a powerful tool—food—to keep my children from me."[8] Pech similarly recalled the effects of hunger on her young son: "We were all so hungry that once, when I made a little porridge, I couldn't resist dipping my little finger into it to taste it. My son was so mad and shouted at me, 'It'll be all gone, wait your turn like everyone else.' Hunger had changed him."

Where life hung on a spoonful of porridge or a sliver of potato, seemingly small decisions involved life-and-death consequences and left deep, enduring effects. Shame and guilt hovered like a shadow over many survivors. Now in their adulthood, child survivors still speak with lingering shame at what they had to do to stay alive, admitting in some instances to having kept food away even from their parents. A retired psychologist in Long Beach, Dr. Sam Keo remained plagued by his mother's chastisement at his unwillingness to share his meager ration with his dying sibling: "She said, 'If you gave your brother just half of your rice, he would still be alive.' . . . I know one spoonful of rice could not save him. But I still carry the guilt."[9] Often, that guilt is wedged in silence, in the downcast eyes and abbreviated two words "they died" that narrate a lifelong struggle to reconcile.

While starvation and inhumane toil wrecked the body, terror, constant and pervasive, gnawed at the very being of the children. As it was for adults, the past hung over many evacuee children, a reminder of the imminence of death. Scrutinized for the smallest transgressions, they were marginalized, tormented, and made to atone for the political sins of their families. Theavy was eight years old when her family was relocated to their native province in Kompong Cham. Her grandmother had been a wealthy landowner, and little Theavy was made to bear the cross for her family's privilege that even their current state of dispossession could not redress:

> Every time they [base peasants] saw me walk by they would shout from their huts, "Hey, *mi kachen* [pejorative term for a Chinese girl], did you come back to claim your grandmother's fields?" They used the word *ngeng* [pejorative third-person pronoun] and my heart burned because I've never been called that before in my life. At work, they assigned me to do the hardest tasks. If everyone else was tending the orchard groves, I would be the one who had to carry the water. They looked for every excuse to beat us. My sister would just cry at the abuse but I would fight back. Then, at night, they molested me and laughed about it in the morning.

As the regime's obsession with exposing "enemies" and "traitors" intensified, children were also swept up in the purges that consumed the country. In Pursat, a campaign to weed out "Vietnamese" (a term that came to be applied generically to those who were fair-skinned) struck the children's camp in 1977. Peou was taken out of his work group with six other children to be "reconstructed":

> I was arrested because I was light-skinned. They tied my hands behind my back and asked me who my mother was. They wouldn't believe that she was my real mother. They kept saying that she had adopted a Vietnamese baby. I had to weed and clear an area of a hundred square meters each day. Otherwise, I would be given no food ration.

For Vibol, the family's torment did not end with his father's execution:

> After my father [who was a soldier] was killed, they started calling us the children of traitors—enemies of the people. They treated us differently. We were always the ones woken up at night to go fetch errant cows after having just lain down to sleep for a few hours before having to go back to work.

Not unlike the notion of "collective responsibility"[10] that Thompson wrote about in the early 1900s, Khmer Rouge deracinating violence was totalistic, aimed at the destruction of the *pouch*, the very "seed" of the threat. It was violence grafted onto the biopolitics of culpability. The many faces of children on the walls of Tuol Sleng and the remains in mass graves are contemporaneous evidence of this totalistic mindset.

With all things belonging to Angkar, unauthorized foraging and hoarding were considered theft, a subversive crime against the state, as was escape, an evidence of individualistic agency. Many children, like Rith, were imprisoned and tortured simply for wanting to survive. An untold number did not survive the punishment:

> You could not last more than one month in there. We had to walk to the work site that was about a half to a kilometer away from the prison . . . and work from five in the morning to five in the evening on just one saucerful of watery porridge. At work, we would get whipped if we were

slow. One day we were transplanting rice shoots. There was a boy in the group who always stopped. They beat him but he couldn't go any faster. They dunked him into the water and lifted his face back up. But after the second or third time, he did not lift his face. He had died sometime in the process. The *yothea*—they just laughed. They always laughed when they punished us.

Fear is transformed into terror by the sense of utter helplessness. In this state of exception, violence as a disciplinary technology was both public and suggestive.

> We could not escape. . . . Sometimes they would pull a boy out of his hut at night and we wouldn't see him again. Sometimes they would take a boy into the jungle and we would hear him scream. Sometimes they would throw the body parts of a boy they had cut apart into the rice paddies as we worked. "Fertilizer," they would say.[11]

If the body, broken and discarded, was the political text[12] that proclaimed the sovereign power to dispense disproportionate judgment with impunity, terror in the unseen affirmed Angkar's omniscience: "You may not see the killings, but you hear things. And the rumors, things that happened without explanation—they were perhaps more terrifying than knowing for certain." An unlifting sense of doom, the haunting of social death, shadowed their existence: "When night came I always worried. . . . I was afraid that maybe next time it would be me. I would die before I saw the sun rise. . . . I always prayed, 'God, please don't let the sun go down.'"[13]

The New Citizen-Soldier: Education and Social Engineering

Through the destruction of the self and systematic unraveling of social bonds, the Khmer Rouge aimed to create the perfect citizen for revolutionary Cambodia—pliant, unthinking, and unfeeling save for unquestioning loyalty to Angkar and zealous dedication to the revolution. Like hunger and fear, education was a tool for social engineering. The regime not only had a profound distrust of the educated (*neak rean soat*) and the knowledgeable (*neak ches doeung*), but also a disdain for conventional education, which it perceived to be irrelevant to the needs of the new Cambodian society. Genuine education, according to the leadership, must be "close to the realities of an agricultural country" and must be conducted "in factories and cooperatives."[14] As a result, except for rare instances mostly in the early months of the regime, formal education ceased to exist for evacuee children. Instead, youths were subjected to political socialization carried out through the almost daily meetings, though little teaching or discussion of Marxism or any other political thought actually took place. Ratha, then thirteen years old, recalled having seen a picture of "Marx-Lenin" being held up "from very far away" only once during a meeting at the children's camp. More in-depth instructions, vocational training, and political education were reserved essentially for children of the party faithful; it was not until late 1978, when efforts were made to widen the political base, that children of the "new people," mostly orphans, were included in the special study sessions. Loung Ung recalled that at a special training center for child soldiers to which she was sent, the "elder comrades" spoke gloriously of Pol Pot and attributed all success to him.[15] Given that most Cambodians had never heard Pol Pot's name during the Khmer Rouge years, this revelation underscored the special status of these young recruits.

Rather than imparting political education, the meetings were aimed at fanning revolutionary fervor and blind optimism in the nation's future. More importantly, they were designed to inculcate in the youths a belief in the benevolence, infallibility, and omnipotence of Angkar.

They just told us to work hard, to go from one ton to six tons per year. They said that soon we wouldn't even have to feed ourselves; we would have machines to do it for us, that we would have three meals a day and dessert with every meal. They built model houses on stilts, with two bedrooms and . . . said that in five years every house would have electricity. Everything sounded so wonderful. I believed them because I could never imagine how something like this could go on forever. They said that if we were starving, it was because there were traitors among us. So I didn't blame them when I was starving. There was no other information going in or out of that place so after a while, if you say things often enough, people would believe it. I found myself believing them.

In the formation of the new citizen, violence was used to instruct and harden. After she was made to participate in a public execution, the memory of the brutality was graphically and indelibly imprinted on Bopha's mind:

> At Prey Kloth, one *yothea* violated a child. A meeting was called of five hundred children. The *yotheas* shredded his skin little by little and each group of children was given vinegar, or salt or chili to go and put it on the prisoner. I saw them turn his penis inside out and put chili in his eyeballs. . . . I was afraid . . . but I was also afraid that if I didn't do anything I might be accused of collusion. So I just picked up some dirt clods and threw them at him.

Before the "new people" could be instilled with new social and political identities, however, the regime had to first destroy all forces and institutions that competed for their loyalty. Given its centrality in Khmer life, Buddhism came under systematic attack. Rom recounted the systematic undermining of faith in the divine and its transference to Angkar:

> They would say, "Here is a candy. Now pray to Buddha and see if you would get the candy. You can pray all you want but you won't get it from Buddha. But if you ask me, I can give it to you." To a child, four or five years old, that was a very convincing argument. You see that in the children who joined them completely. Many of the Khmer Rouge *yotheas* were not much more than children themselves. They didn't flinch at any command.

Similarly, the regime, itself described as "a family dictatorship,"[16] worked to systematically dismantle the family institution, perhaps the most important of Khmer society.

> We were always told that there is no more *bang-phaaon* [relatives]. We are all *mit*, and Angkar is our *mè-ov* [parents]. They told us that we didn't owe anything to our parents because the only thing that they did was deliver us into this world and even then, they were only amusing themselves.

Eager to demonstrate their unassailable revolutionary stance or to ensure their own survival, families had been known to reject and denounce each other. At a children's camp at Pravel, survivors recalled how Ta Ngen, the camp leader, would tie up his own son and leave him to be eaten by red ants. Holding his actions as a model of revolutionary conduct, he would state emphatically, "Here nobody can help you. Families mean nothing." To many children, like Pros, it was their parents' inability to protect them that underscored Angkar's power:

> They had killed my father. As a small child, I thought he was the strongest man, the one to help me if I ever got into trouble. But they had enough power to kill him, and I feared them. When they beat you, they would say, "See, your parents can't stop that. Only Angkar can stop the beating."

A regime like Democratic Kampuchea, however, demanded not just severance of familial ties but the total negation of human connections, as captured in the Khmer Rouge aphorism "sok muy, kbal muy" (one hair, one head). The regime tested revolutionary loyalty and self-sacrifice not only by forcing relatives to watch or even participate in the execution of their own kin, but by prohibiting the expression of grief: "Sometimes, if they had already taken the man, they would ask the wife or mother whether she missed him. If she said 'yes,' she would be taken too." Forced to watch his mother's execution, Sophea Mouth recalled, "I was determined not to cry—not that I didn't feel horror; but my heart was frozen."[17] Fear and distrust sealed individuals into themselves, isolating them even from the person whose back pressed against theirs in work and sleep:

> I was lonely and alone all the time. I didn't have any friends at all. Nobody did. The children never talked to each other or anything. If one of the children was sick or just disappeared, we never knew what happened to him. We never asked. Our work leader also changed often. They didn't want us to get to know each other.

The loneliness and longing for community often remained with these young survivors. For Sat, orphaned by genocide, his only wish was to grow up and "live with other people."[18]

The systematic and unrelenting assault on parents, faith, and humanity left its mark. Perhaps even more devastating than fear was the feeling
of abandonment that many children like Seath carried with them into
adulthood: "I believed the Khmer Rouge soldiers when they told us that
our families did not love us . . . when I cried [and] they didn't come to
me."[19] The helplessness, guilt, and resentment were to torment many
survivors long after.

What the system sought to do was to destroy not just the physical
being but what Agamben refers to as "vitality," or as Khmer would put
it, to crush one's inner fortitude (*bam bak sbat*) and leave an individual
cowering in terror.

> It was fear that motivated most of our actions. We obeyed and followed
> because we feared. You eventually came to feel that nobody could help
> you. . . . They seemed so omnipotent. You couldn't escape the feeling
> that there was nothing that you could do without them knowing about
> it. You were even afraid to think. They seemed to know even your silent
> thoughts.

Bereft of protection, children, like those conscripted by Duch into
his institution of terror, were transformed into a blank page, onto which
violence as a singular reality could be imprinted: "It was a society of hatred, and with nothing else to challenge it, that's what the children grew
up appreciating—hatred. We sang their songs, we listened to their songs
when we worked, when we ate. It was the most effective tool of indoctri-
nation. You started to believe in them." Values and beliefs changed, and
past norms no longer held any validity. Instead, a child's survival, and
perhaps that of his family, hinged on the ability to lie, steal, cheat, and
even denounce a fellow human being. Forged by violence and hatred
that stripped them of whatever little humanity they may have harbored,
the true "children of Angkar" emerged. The transformation that could
be seen in their peers and in themselves was slow, at times imperceptible, but to some extent inevitable. Vithou reflected on life in Democratic
Kampuchea:

> The key to survival was to play dumb and obey. . . . One did not think.
> If you think, you die. But if one does not think, one does not know what

is right or wrong. I remember a public execution that we were all made to attend. Two people were brought in, accused of "wrongful moral conduct" [khos selathor]. The village leader started to shout, "Crush them." Soon, everyone was saying, "Crush them, crush them," myself included. The thought never even entered my mind whether the punishment was right or wrong. I just obeyed.

I found myself changing. I found my friends changing. The boy who was the leader of our team was fine, normal, until he was selected to be a leader and started being around them. Then he started bragging about being capable of killing his parents if they were to do anything that Angkar considered wrong. Everyone was affected. Maybe not to the point of actually doing the killing, but you changed. To a certain extent—a little or a lot—you changed.

Not all children, however, shared the ideological convictions or were seduced by absolute power, and not all complied either out of fear or loyalty. Despite their attempts, the Khmer Rouge failed to destroy social vitality. Small gestures of friendship, altruism, leniency, and humanism miraculously surfaced even from the abyss of the most depraved of human conditions. As it was with the adults, "acts of ordinary virtue," as Todorov puts it, are heroic simply because they were never intended to be heroic acts. They are simply human acts in the most inhumane conditions, a "refusal to accept what seems an implacable necessity."[20]

Once in our group, two brothers were arrested for stealing some palm sugar. . . . As soon as we found out about the imminent arrest, we snatched the youngest brother, who was about thirteen years old, from their hut. When the yotheas [who were new to the area] came to get them, the rest of the group told them that those three were not brothers, that the little boy was not sleeping with them and therefore could not have been sharing the stolen food with the other two. He was saved.

The other two were brought out with their arms tied above their elbows. The yotheas pushed the prisoners down and stomped their feet on their backs. Oh, Buddha, it was just like watching the arrest scene from the play Mak Thoeung![21] The head of the village, the mé phum, said, "You have been crushed by the wheel of the revolution!" Then, the yotheas fired. "Pong, pong," right in front of us, in front of the little brother.

For Pom, the realization that someone else's life depended upon her was the source of unimaginable courage and ingenuity:

> I was ten years old. My mother was near death from starvation. . . . I stole some potato vines that they had thrown out, and planted them. Meanwhile, I would steal away at night to the river where there was a lot of *sa-ngè* (wild grains) growing. I shook the grains into the boat and brought them back. Each night I was able to get about three or four cans of grains. I dug the ground and laid down some banana leaves. I wrapped the *sa-ngè* in a piece of cloth and put it into the ground, covering it with some banana leaves. Then I covered the hole with dirt and built a fire on top of it. Anyone passing by would think that we were just building a fire to warm ourselves. The *sa-ngè* sustained us for a while. After my potato plants sprouted, I took the buds that were still young and boiled them for my mother. She sucked on them. She lived.

In the depraved world of Democratic Kampuchea, these clandestine acts of selflessness were the "hidden transcripts," as James Scott puts it, that attested to the defiant nobility of the human spirit. They were also fleeting, as human relations all too often strained and broke under these extraordinary conditions.

From the world of death and deprivation, children sought refuge in tattered fragments of their forgotten childhood. They dreamt—some of kings and saviors, others of simple things like the taste of preserves, candies, and ice that hadn't touched their lips in close to four years. They dreamt of playing soccer in the schoolyard, of laughter. Above all, they hoped. They hoped that things would change someday, and they hoped to live long enough to see that eventuality.

> I thought that the starvation couldn't go on forever. They said we starved because we needed rice to pay back the debts to China. In five years we would have everything. All I had left was hope—hope that things would change. If you give up, you might as well die. I guess deep down inside I *really* wanted to live. I wanted to see my father again. I just had to believe that this couldn't last forever. And every time we got some food, we felt so revived and felt that we could go on another day. We just lived from day to day.

At times, hope appeared so ephemeral that they denied its existence even to themselves, for fear that that too would be robbed from them. The balance between needing and fearing to hope was precarious, but one that had to be maintained if one was to survive another day. In the peril-filled world of Democratic Kampuchea, where treachery could be read into virtually every gesture and expression, hope could be a damning evidence of seditious thoughts, punishable by death, hence as fatal as despair. Thus, when the guns thundered over the Northwest in that bright morning in early 1979, breaking through the hermetic silence of Democratic Kampuchea, twelve-year-old Sim knew nothing of the conflict that had convulsed the country. All he knew was that the sounds were a harbinger of change, and any change from the conditions he had had to endure could only have been for the better:

> The sun was just rising over the mountains and we were bending over harvesting when we heard *poc thong, poc thong*. We looked around, then we looked at each other. Then smiles were on our faces. But we didn't dare laugh out loud because people who had shown the wrong emotion had been killed. So we just looked around at each other, but our hearts were filled with joy. I can still remember the feelings of that day. I thought, "freedom!" Now everything would be normal again.
>
> What struck me the most was that here we were, children, feeling so much happiness at this sound. The only thing that went through my mind was "home!" I just wanted to be home, that's all.

Stain

Khmers used to say that children are the soul of the nation. Now it is said, "The children of the Pol Pot times are like cotton, tarnished with blood and soil."[22] The personalities of the average five- and ten-year-olds were stripped away and new ones superimposed. For many child survivors, the transition was never complete, leaving them in a state of flux. Arn, with his baseball cap, Washington State sweatshirt, and six-foot stature, revealed in his soft-spoken Khmer way something that was utterly "un-Khmer." He told me he was *lob-lob*, a term that loosely translates as confused or muddled, but that in the Khmer cultural context, clearly signifies something less than whole. For Arn, the years of unquestioning obedience, of living daily with the knowledge that his life had absolutely no value, had sapped his spirit and sense of confidence:

> Ever since Cambodia, I forget a lot, and I still fear . . . all those people threatening me all the time. I feel like I have no confidence left in whatever I do because during that time, whatever I wanted to do I could not do. I could not give opinions or anything. Everything was *prochea pdach kar*, an absolute command. People just told me to do this and that. Now whenever I see people using force, I am afraid because in Cambodia they made us *bak sbat* [broke our will]. They did what they wanted. I felt like I had no worth, that I was not a human being. Even today, I sometimes feel that my life has no value.

One of the casualties of terror and auto-genocide is trust—trust in people, trust in the predictability of things, and above all trust that there is a rational, or at least a comprehensible, order. Now in high school, Roth sadly remarked, "Sometimes when I think back to those days, I just don't want to do anything. . . . The world doesn't make sense." Robbed prematurely of their innocence, they are burdened by the shadow of a nightmarish past that they did not understand and of which they still have little understanding, a past that sets theirs vastly apart from ordinary childhood: "They treated me like I was an animal. They beat me, kicked me, starved me. . . . Other people have families and relatives. I am all alone in this world; it is hard to talk to someone who hasn't lived through that—hard to put into words."

That invisible demarcation between past and present, between extraordinary and mundane, is permeable and unstable: "Sometimes, it doesn't feel real. Sometimes, it is hard to say what is not real—the present or the past. . . . If I think of the past and the present, it gets all mixed up and things don't make sense." Against the surreal, the normalcy of laughter, marriage, intact families, work, and everyday life can be disquieting. Like a loyal but unwanted companion, the feeling of aloneness, of an estrangement from the world, that filled their childhood remains with many of the child survivors into their adult years. It is a constant that, when momentarily absent, sets the spirit in panic.

The scars may always be with them, but the resilience that had ensured their survival remains their source of strength. Some, like Boun,

attributed their determination, adaptability, and ability to endure and triumph over all adversities to their experiences under the Khmer Rouge:
"I survived the Khmer Rouge. I have been starved, beaten, thrown in
jail. What else can anyone do to me that would be worse? From here on,
whatever life hands to me, it won't kill me." That inner strength, however, also enables them to suppress all that is too painful to recollect.
When I first began my interviews of the child survivors, I was struck by
how well many appeared to have adapted to their new environment, of
American public schools and middle-class lives. As the questions became more penetrating, they perceptibly retreated ever further into that
"other-world," a world into which few have entered and returned. The
innocent smiles, wide-eyed curiosity, and general openness can still be
discerned in these young adults. The scars lie at a deeper level. The distrust of the human race that had brutalized them and that had remained
oblivious to their brutalization is often unconcealed. The instincts for
self-preservation that had been honed under the Khmer Rouge remain
sharp, detectable in the perfected manner of evading questions and in
speaking in generality and ambiguity. Above all, it is the eyes that betray
the loss of innocence. They have seen too many horrors, lived too many
horrors. For many of these child survivors, the war is still with them.
Perhaps it always will be.

PART II

Historicizing Diaspora

3

Prelude to Terror

Peace, War, and Revolution

Our country that we called Kampuchea, in reality it is "Kam-pum-chea," the bad karma that is never lifted. Our present suffering has a very long and entangled history.
—Cambodian refugee in California

There can be no precise count of how many perished under the Khmer Rouge. Estimates of the death toll in Democratic Kampuchea vary from 740,000 to 3.3 million,[1] of which 31–50 percent[2] were attributed to executions. From the records that survived at S-21, we know that at least 12,772[3] individuals, including approximately 2,000 children,[4] were tortured and killed at that one extermination center alone, many on the eve of the regime's collapse. Throughout the country, hundreds of thousands more simply "disappeared." Through nationwide areal mapping, some 20,492 mass graves have been found scattered throughout the country, from which over one million remains have been disinterred. With yet-to-be-uncovered sites, it is projected that the number of those executed alone could be as high as 1.5 million.[5]

The relative paucity and unreliability of Khmer Rouge documentation mean that many estimates of the death toll in Democratic Kampuchea are extrapolated from prewar data. This approach presents its own methodological problems as the latest prewar census and arguably the only real nationwide census conducted in Cambodia was in 1962, followed by one completed in 1998. This means that there is no accurate accounting during at least three major periods of the country's political history that included a full-scale war, genocide, and foreign occupation. Population statistics for 1970–1975, one of the benchmarks for determining losses during the Khmer Rouge regime, are largely based on natural growth projections and do not account for the demographic

shifts engendered by war and ethnic expulsion. In light of these methodological limitations, any estimate of deaths in Democratic Kampuchea,
as Heuveline stresses, "is subject to high uncertainty."[6] This caution notwithstanding, even the most conservative estimates far exceed Khieu
Samphan's incredible statement that only "11,000 Khmer Rouge" were
killed for "being Vietnamese agents," of which 3,000 "died from our
mistakes."[7]

By any measure, the magnitude of loss is staggering. Of Democratic
Kampuchea, Ponchaud wrote, "It is a perfect example of the application
of an ideology pushed to the furthest limit of its internal logic. But the
furthest limit is too far, and 'too far' is akin to madness."[8] But was it, in
fact, madness? And if so, what kind of environment needed to be present to allow such a feverish condition to afflict so many so pervasively?
If not, what forces and conditions produced such extremism? Accounts
of revolutionary developments often give way to a monopoly of concern
for the drama of revolutions. The sanguinary outcomes are often taken
to be an episodic explosion of societal psychosis, so extraordinary as
to be inexplicable by any rational measure. Some observers looking at
developments in Democratic Kampuchea are tempted to delve into the
psyche of the Khmer Rouge leadership or to Khmer cultural traits for
explanations of the violence.[9] Essentializing ideologies uttered by the
French archeologist Groslier that in Cambodia "beneath that carefree
surface, there slumber savage forces and disconcerting cruelties which
may blaze up in outbreak of passionate brutality"[10] resonate in contemporary references to the Khmer "warrior" or "warring" personality, with
the implied cultural predisposition to militancy and violence.[11] Others
evoke the cultural predisposition to disproportionate revenge;[12] arguably, Shawcross's contention that Khmer Rouge violence was the result
of their brutalization by American carpet bombing could be taken as
an extension of this argument. Others, like Philip Short, attributed it
to the lack of "rational thinking" and other frailties in Khmer culture,
contending that "such behavior comes more naturally to Cambodians
than to other nations because their culture regards forgiveness as a form
of weakness."[13] Others still see Khmer Rouge violence as a response to
structural and cultural oppression, a revolt of long-oppressed peasantry
against landed elites or a "revolution from the forest"[14] that marks the
resistance of indigeneity against foreignness.

As subsequent discussion will underscore, structural arguments fore-grounding economic inequalities and immiseration often advanced in works on revolutions are challenged by the socioeconomic reality of prewar Cambodia. Similarly, while culture informs the way survivors make meaning of their experiences, cultural explanations, beyond re-inforcing the essentializing of political violence, are limited in their ex-planatory power. Many falter on their internal contradictions, for just as there may be a culturally framed justification of violence, there is also a culturally framed prohibition against the exercise of violence, especially given the Buddhist emphasis on nonviolence and avoidance of karmic entanglement. This normative tension is often unaddressed. The theory of disproportionate revenge, for instance, cannot account for the relative absence of retributive violence against former Khmer Rouge, many of whom are known to, and living in proximity of, their victims. Cultural values such as loyalty, submission to authority, and the importance of "face" that are seen as contributing to violence have long existed without genocidal eruption, and are also not uniquely Khmer. It thus leaves unexplained how and why societal restraints that heretofore have impeded the wanton exercise of violence have been undermined, or how such occurrences could have taken place unsanctioned given the draconian discipline of the Khmer Rouge.[15] Rather than culturally framed, Democratic Kampuchea's rhetoric of killing was political and ideological, and rather than loyalty or honor, it was often fear of being implicated and killed that former Khmer Rouge proffer as an explana-tion for their violent actions. Moreover, many aspects of the Khmer Rouge genocide, such as the dehumanized "other," the besieged mindset, and the perceived corruption of the body politics by infectious enemies, are also present in other genocidal instances outside specific cultural frames. This is an argument not for universalism but for a move away from exceptionalism. As Todorov reminds us, "great criminals are as human as we are" and "great crimes of the Khmer Rouge were not the work of sadists or the mentally ill. They resulted from reactions familiar to everyone."[16]

Though spontaneous, retributive violence was an undeniable feature of Democratic Kampuchea, it would be too simplistic and erroneous to regard the dynamics of the Khmer Rouge revolution simply as an eruption of the irrational, the psychotic, and the criminal. Granted, all those elements *were* present to some degree, in one form or another. The sadism manifested in some of the killings could not have been anything but psychotic and criminal, just as some of the brutalizing acts could not have been anything but gratuitous and wanton. Like many other revolutionary movements, the Khmer Rouge did not only attract the Hofferian "true believers."[17] There were present within Democratic Kampuchea's "pyramid of murder," as David Hawk terms it, the more pedestrian operatives of terror whose unchecked destructive potential gave way to indiscriminate killing that promoted the appearance of the irrational. Although their presence may explain some aspects of violence, it cannot, however, by itself sufficiently account for the Khmer Rouge regime of terror. Individual savagery alone did not cause the death of over a million people. The scale, protracted nature, and patterns of violence in Democratic Kampuchea point to factors and dynamics that extend beyond spontaneous killing. Radical and large-scale undertakings such as the systematic evacuation of urban centers were consciously formulated, preemptively planned, and centrally directed initiatives,[18] not ad hoc responses to exigencies, as the Khmer Rouge leadership has contended. Some of these measures were undertaken in anticipation of the victory in 1975, while others were pushed through regardless of the challenges. The strategic decision and methodic way violence was carried out *before* and *after* victory undercut the argument of a brutalized army on a retributive rampage.

Though tragically flawed, many of the policy decisions were not without an internal logic, albeit a "logic fundamentally rooted in illogic,"[19] as Ronald Aronson puts it. As Gurr contends, "men's resort to political violence is in part unreasoning, but does not occur without reason."[20] What, then, were the circumstances and conditions that produced such a genocidal outcome, that made it viable for mass support to be abandoned and state terrorism substituted as a viable policy alternative? If the Khmer Rouge regime is not to be taken as a spontaneous eruption of violence but as a historicized phenomenon with a much longer genealogy, what can we cull from Cambodia's colonial and postcolonial experiences that stoked the political awakening of men like Nuon Chea, Democratic Kampuchea's "Brother Number 2,"[21] to illuminate this tragic chapter? What were those ruinous sites that fostered "alternative senses of history,"[22] as Ann Stoler puts it, that accounted not only for the desire for apocalyptic change, but for the form and tenor that it acquired, so fervent and righteous that it justified a genocidal recourse?

In his study of the Soviet Union, Conquest pointed out that the seeds of Stalin's reign of terror were deeply rooted in the Soviet past, traceable to the development of the party and the consolidation of the dictatorship. Khmer Rouge extremism was similarly rooted in Cambodia's long and tumultuous history, incubated in the shadow of a glorious past and a precarious present, of colonization and postcolonial disenchantment, in the contradictions between imported ideologies and local realities, and in the synergistic interplay between internal and external developments. Understanding Democratic Kampuchea thus requires a critical examination of the social, economic, and political topography of colonial and postcolonial Cambodia as located within the larger global context that produced both the possibilities and the limits of revolutionary mobilization. The forces and conditions that stymied Khmer communism from the 1950s to 1970, in fact, are just as analytically significant as those that made their eventual victory possible. The unmatched pace of social mobilization and institution building, systemic intransigence, and failure at genuine reforms in post-independence Cambodia ultimately convinced some in the burgeoning Left of the futility of political accommodation. For others, there was never any alternative to total revolution. While the exportation of the Vietnam War across the border did not create the Khmer Rouge, it did shift the political fulcrum inside the country, catalyzing forces that heretofore had been insipid, and creating conditions that enabled the movement to grow exponentially and for ideological extremism to prevail and intensify.

Myths Revisited

Girling once argued that perceptions and discussions of Cambodia were shaped by "myths" that enveloped the country and its leader.[23] Veiled in the "personification myth," prewar Cambodia was seen as an extension of its reigning monarch, Prince Sihanouk, and the image finely crafted and projected to the world was one of a national "family," with a patriarchal Samdech Euv (Father Prince) overseeing and ensuring the welfare of his *kaun-chao*, his progenies.[24] His ability to juggle, manipulate, and neutralize domestic opposition gave the appearance of stability and internal consensus. With deftness, political acumen, and personal charisma, he effectively cultivated the notion that he alone could ensure that Cambodia would remain an island of peace (*kos santapheap*) in the midst of a war-ravaged Indochina. Nothing better attests to the power of this myth than the incredulous manner with which the news of his ouster in 1970 was received at home and abroad. For many observers, it was inconceivable that domestic forces could have engineered his overthrow.[25] In contrast, the "internationalist myth" places singular importance on regional and global forces. Cambodian politics were understood largely in terms of the Cold War and its regional manifestation in the widening war in Vietnam.[26] This focus on the external context and on Sihanouk's efforts to balance the polarizing forces in the East-West conflict overlooks both the domestic ramifications of these developments and Sihanouk's simultaneous maneuvering to balance domestic forces. His adroitness notwithstanding, it was unlikely, given the rising stakes, that even Sihanouk could have prevented Cambodia's embroilment in war and, by extension, the shifting political tide at home.

While both "myths" illuminate our understanding of prewar Cambodia, they are limited in their reductionism. Despite the intrusive, constraining, and at times determinant power of external factors, Cambodia's leadership was not devoid of agency. From Sihanouk's neutralism to the Khmer Rouge determination to forge their own revolutionary path, local dynamics were not simply reflective of external dictates. Looking at politics in Cambodia purely through an internationalist lens, as such, obscures the plural histories that inform not only the formation and growth of the communist movement but also the fears and aspirations of Democratic Kampuchea, and thus not only how they came to power but what transpired after they came to power. The political turbulence that convulsed the nation in the 1970s made it relatively easy to forget that Democratic Kampuchea emerged a mere two decades after almost a hundred years of colonial rule. In its cultivation and co-optation of traditional elites—namely, the monarchy, the aristocracy, and, to some extent, the *sangha* (Buddhist clergy)—French colonial rule helped define the terrain for conflict and accommodation after independence. In the same vein, its racialized policies, and the tension and resentment that they fostered, were to cast long shadows over ethnic relations, reinforcing and radicalizing Khmer nationalism into

Democratic Kampuchea's national chauvinism. Despite its desire for an apocalyptic break from the past, Democratic Kampuchea was defined no less by these histories. It was within this intellectual milieu in the intersection of colonial and postcolonial encounters that the ideological virulence of the Khmer Rouge emerged and intensified.

Colonialism and the Shaping of Cambodian Politics

France has received from Providence a higher mission . . . of bringing into the light and into liberty the races and peoples still enslaved by ignorance and despotism.[27]
—Francis Garnier

While France looked toward Vietnam with commercial aspirations and the fervor of its *mission civilisatrice*, Cambodia was almost an after-thought, provoked more by the need to deny Siamese and British access to Indochina than by the country's intrinsic appeal.[28] Thus, while Vietnam became the focus of the *métropole*, Cambodia was regarded as little more than a "private hunting preserve of the French resident superior."[29] Expediency and racism justified subjugation and neglect. To the French, the Khmer was a "non-perfectible race,"[30] "doomed to disappear" before Vietnamese immigration,[31] thus warranting little investment in their development. Le Myre de Vilers, the former governor of Cochinchina, contended, "We will lose our time in trying to galvanize this race that a fatal flaw seems to have condemned to disappear. In intervening in its administration, we would create innumerable difficulties without obtaining any result, for we would have to resolve most grave social issues."[32]

Given France's limited interest, indirect rule through traditional authority was optimal for France, allowing for maximum gain with minimal investment. Over four decades after the establishment of the protectorate, the entire colonial administration in Cambodia consisted of only 254 *fonctionnaires*.[33] The progressive tightening of colonial control notwithstanding, Cambodia's social and political systems were left relatively undisrupted, except when and where they threatened French interests. Given the centrality of the monarchy in Khmer political and cultural life, French interest was deemed better served by maintaining

on the throne a king who, ideally, would be responsive to French demands or, at the very least, would not thwart colonial interests.[34] Thus,
whatever French colonialism may have disrupted in Cambodia, it preserved Khmer traditional authority and even strengthened the legitimacy, though not necessarily the power, of the monarchy as a pivotal
force in the country's politics. This was to have profound implications
for Cambodian politics in the decades after independence.

French racist ideologies engendered a self-fulfilling logic that was
acutely felt in the educational arena. According to Marie A. Martin,
"The accepted view held by the French administrators that Khmers . . .
possessed defects 'inherent to their race' such as laziness, contributed
to the colonial power's lack of interest in educating them."[35] The bud-
get earmarked for education in Cambodia was the smallest in French
Indochina.[36] By the early 1900s, almost four decades after the establishment of French control, and despite the importance of French language and education for socioeconomic mobility in the protectorate,
only four French-language primary schools existed in Cambodia—the
School of the Protectorate in Phnom Penh, and three in the provinces
of Kampot, Takeo, and Prey Veng.[37] Of the fifty-seven educators in the
modern schools, the majority were non-Cambodian, and non-Khmer
speakers. Rather than increasing, the number of French educators actually declined from forty in 1912 to twenty-eight in 1939,[38] with virtually
no effort to build local capacity. Of French neglect, Tully wrote, "Their
performance in Cambodia pales in comparison not just with what they
did in Vietnam, but also with the achievements of some other colonial
powers in Asia."[39]

Even more disconcerting than the lack of educational development
was the gross underrepresentation of ethnic Khmers in the few modernized schools that did exist. With the exception of a negligible handful of
elite and mostly male children, most of the students who attended colonial schools were French, Chinese, Vietnamese, and *métis* of French and
Vietnamese parentage. Alain Forest noted that of the over one hundred
students in the School of the Protectorate, only eight were Cambodians.[40]
By 1939, out of an estimated population of three million, only four Cambodian students had graduated from the local high school.[41] Ninety-one
years after the establishment of the protectorate, only 144 Cambodians
had completed the baccalaureate;[42] by 1944, after over eighty years of

French rule, there was only one engineer in the entire country.[43] Impeded access to French education, particularly French-language competency, essentially meant limited chances for advancement.[44] Nguyen-Vo argues that educational disparity provided Vietnamese graduates with an advantage in the French civil service examinations in Indochina and accounted for the disproportionate number of Vietnamese clerks in Cambodia's colonial bureaucracy.[45] The Cambodian absence was now embedded in the colonial structure of inequity.[46]

In a move that they deemed more cost-efficient than the attempt to develop the "indolent and untrainable Khmers," the French instead facilitated the immigration of Vietnamese and Chinese, whom they considered more industrious,[47] to fill critical functions in the protectorate, namely, administration and commerce. Of Le Myre de Vilers's expedient calculation, Osborne wrote, "He believed that within fifty years the Vietnamese would constitute the most important element of Cambodia's population. When that situation had been achieved, Cambodia, and Cambodians, would no longer present a problem."[48] The disproportionate representation of non-Cambodians in the country's bureaucracy and economic sectors attested to the ruthless efficiency of colonial expediency.[49] These technologies of imperial rule, as Ann Stoler puts it, were to engender ramifications that reverberated long after independence, a manifestation of which was the virulent nationalism of the Khmer Rouge and their disdain for all things considered tainted by colonial association.

While French schools were inaccessible to, and unaccessed by, the majority of Cambodians, education especially in the periphery continued to be delivered by the *sangha*, the Buddhist monks, as it always had been. In the 1910s, the majority of the eighty thousand students in the country were enrolled in modernized monastery schools. The Buddhist community thus became an important incubator of Cambodia's stirring intellectual and political life, and the Buddhist Institute a critical space for the fledging anticolonial intelligentsia.[50] Aided by the introduction of the printing press, men like Pach Choeun and Son Ngoc Thanh and writers with pseudonyms such as Khemarak Bottra (Khmer Son) slowly stoked Khmer nationalist awakening with their critiques of the racialized structure of privilege and entitlement.[51] What Daniel Hemery termed "reactive nationalism"[52] began to manifest itself in the agitation against the prevailing system of inequity in which "the most miserable white man," as Virginia Thompson observed, "is above the best native."[53] The expansion of indigenous education, as Tully points out, thus "contained the seeds of colonialism's own destruction."[54] Of the unforeseen effects of colonial policy, simultaneously conservative because of its promotion of entrenchment and the status quo and revolutionizing because of its unintended, destabilizing effects, Kautsky wrote, "It was just like a man who with one hand keeps adding wood to a fire under a kettle of water and with his other hand holds down the lid of the kettle. When the man leaves . . . the fire keeps burning, but the lid (the aristocracy) is blown off."[55]

Cambodia after Independence

The political scenario the French left in Cambodia in 1953 was one in which, unlike in Vietnam, where French colonialism had produced an early and sustained revolutionary condition, conservative forces and institutions remained strong and viable in Cambodia's post-independence politics. The centrality of the monarchy, though preserved, was not uncontested by newly mobilized individuals and groups with divergent political agendas and visions of the society that they sought to bring about. The politico-intellectual difference between those who opted to work within the system and those who sought its destruction, barely concealed beneath the thin veneer of unity during the anticolonial struggle, was to become increasingly evident and irreconcilable in the ensuing decades.

Thus, when independence was granted, the monarchy, tainted by colonial patronage, was faced with the immediate task of consolidating its authority; Sihanouk, after all, rose to the throne not on a wave of support, but because the French opted for a presumably more docile heir. The peaceful way independence was acquired was nonetheless an ingenious coup, one that he effectively used to wrest the nationalist mantle from his political opponents and position himself at the epicenter of the country's politics. This early indication of his unwillingness to be a mere figurehead was to foreshadow the conflict between the monarchy and the politicians in the years to come.

Given this constellation of forces, political collision, arguably, could at best have been only forestalled. Nevertheless, the years immediately following independence were relatively calm, something that, as Vickery noted, "the country had not known within living memory."[56] Many Issarak leaders such as Dap Chhuon had rallied to the royalist government in exchange for positions in the national armed forces or the bureaucracy. Others, like Lek, who wanted nothing more than secure routes for his teak logging enterprise,[57] simply sought economic stability. Others still had difficulty adjusting to life in an ordered society and continued to engage in social banditry, less out of political conviction than accustomed lifestyle. A few treaded prudently on frayed edges of respectability, relying on highly placed patronage and connections to ease their transition into a life of normalcy.[58] Most refrained from overt anti-regime activities, and a notable few resurfaced on the Cambodian political scene, on both sides of the ideological spectrum, following Sihanouk's deposition in 1970.

The communists were similarly defanged after independence. The Khmer Vietminh who had fought alongside the Vietnamese communists were divested of international recognition and a territorial base by the Geneva Accords. In 1954 their only options were to leave surreptitiously for Hanoi, go underground and embark upon clandestine activities, or disband. Many did in fact leave with the Vietnamese troops.[59] Some who stayed shed their militancy for legal membership in the Pracheachuon, the Khmer People's Party,[60] while others, like Sao Phim, Ke Vin (who later became the notorious Ke Pauk of the Pol Pot era), and many rank-and-file cadres, resumed their agrarian lives.[61] With most of the leadership neutralized by self-exile, demoralization, and defection, many in the anticolonial movement came to view "the end of colonialism as the end of the struggle."[62] Even the Buddhist *sangha*, once an important force in the anticolonial movement, joined the national appeal for an end to the struggle. The revolutionary fervor of the anticolonial era had been snuffed. A new direction had to be found if left-wing opposition was to have any political viability in post-independence Cambodia.

Though neutralized, challenges to Sihanouk's regime, particularly from Republican elements, were not absent in the years immediately after independence.[63] An assassination attempt against the royal family,[64] followed by a plot in 1959 to secede Siemreap, all underscored the ever-looming right-wing threat. Despite its failure, the "Dap Chhuon affair,"[65] which implicated South Vietnamese and Thai elements, exposed the internal fissures beneath that deceptively harmonious and unified facade that the kingdom strove to project, and the country's vulnerability to external subversion.

The challenge from the Left, in contrast, though not moribund, was insipid. With death and defections of party leaders,[66] including the party secretary Tou Samouth, and nearly half of the already minuscule membership killed or apprehended between 1955 and 1959,[67] the networks, especially in rural communities, were atrophying. What remained was an embryonic movement with a weak organizational and ideological foundation. Other than the party's pronouncement in 1951 that King Sihanouk, "already gone fat, should not rule,"[68] it had neither a blueprint, a coherent structure, nor an impetus for revolutionary change. That the communists did not constitute a serious threat was underscored by their ability to use the capital as their political base. Non Suon, a veteran of the Indochinese Communist Party (ICP)[69] who was later arrested, tortured, and killed at Tuol Sleng, recalled that "there are places [in the capital] to do secret work. The enemy has not yet become very concerned. There are houses where we can live and easy communication routes."[70]

Efforts were made to rebuild the network, and not wholly without success. In the 1960s, leftist influence effectively permeated some critical sectors. With the teacher's college under the leadership of Son Sen, who later became Democratic Kampuchea's defense minister, the country's lycées and technical high schools became a haven for the country's leftists and the loci of left-wing recruitment.[71] Pol Pot, then known as Saloth Sar, worked at Chamroeun Vichea until his flight in 1963. Similarly, left-wing infiltration of the Department of Public Works facilitated the mobilization of rail workers with their history of activism dating back to the 1940s. A woman whose brother was a railroad technician remembered Khieu Samphan as "a wiry man, pedaling a bicycle, wearing a simple short-sleeve dress shirt, coming to talk to the workers and showing a film." To her brother, he symbolized the humbleness and moral purity (saat sa-om) that contrasted starkly with Phnom Penh's status-conscious, materialistic, and widely corrupt urban bourgeoisie. That the convening of the 1960 Party Congress was held at Phnom Penh's railway station under the gaze of Sihanouk's police attested to the absolute confidence in their constituents. Pol Pot later wrote, "Had the enemy discovered the site of the Congress, the entire leadership of the Party would have been destroyed."[72] The Left was also active among factory workers such as at the Phnom Anlong cotton factory near Kompong Speu and the maize and cotton cooperatives near Toeuk Pous.[73] A former worker noted that when the Khmer Rouge finally came to rally the workers in 1971, "their people were already inside there. Right away, they just switched into black clothes." Similarly, at Koh Kalor, "as soon as the Khmer Rouge came in, three of the workers immediately put on black clothes. We never knew that they had their own people among us."

These political inroads notwithstanding, communist mobilization was gravely undermined by the fact that Cambodia was an agrarian society with only a nascent industrial base and a fledging proletarian class. Under these conditions, the destruction of the rural networks was a critical setback, while the decision to shift to an urban-centric strategy further distanced the organization from the peasantry; it was only in 1963 that the party, pressed by mounting challenges, made the belated decision to shift its political base back to the countryside.[74] Left-wing success was also undermined by Sihanouk's political maneuverings. His accommodation of China and North Vietnam divested the Khmer communists ideologically of the anti-imperialist platform, while his strategy of selective co-optation and repression weakened them politically. Through the Sangkum Reastr Niyum party, with its theater-politics and highly orchestrated congresses, Sihanouk effectively mobilized populist support for his policies, controlled the electoral process, and, through a system of co-optation and marginalization, neutralized domestic opposition "by immediately allying with or appeasing the more powerful enemy . . . followed by a quick reversal of policy as soon as the balance of power begins to shift."[75] While some prominent leftists were given scholarships and positions in the government, those regarded as politically threatening were harassed, periodically arrested, and jailed, and left-wing newspapers were repeatedly banned. More violent measures were also adopted. The editor of the left-wing magazine *Pracheachon*, Nop Bophann, was fatally shot in front of a military barracks. In another incident, Khieu Samphan, who later became Democratic Kampuchea's head of state, was beaten and stripped in the streets of Phnom

Penh. The repressive measures were effective. As Pol Pot later recounted, "The movement was active in each factory, but it could not withstand enemy repression. Every time the movement rose up, it was soon destroyed. . . . Take the railroads, for instance. The movement there was the most powerful movement of the working class in our country, but it was crushed."[76]

Internal factionalism further undermined the Left. The late 1950s and early 1960s saw the return from Hanoi of the Khmer Vietminh, also known as "Khmer-Hanoi," the "Hanoi 1000," or *khmer muok duong* (Khmers with conical Vietnamese hats), endowed with tremendous political currency in terms of their political training, guerrilla experience, and Vietnamese patronage.[77] Simultaneously, new leadership was emerging from the burgeoning, mostly French-educated intelligentsia. Individuals such as Son Sen, Pol Pot, Ieng Sary, Hou Yuon, and Khieu Samphan were gaining prominence in the party. Divergence within the party registered essentially on two fronts, externally with regard to the relationship with the Vietnamese communist party[78] and internally with the Sihanoukist regime. Some, like Hou Yuon, who felt that "class conflict should be resolved by a method that will not damage the unity of the nation,"[79] saw the viability of an accommodationist stance and ideological alignment with Sihanouk's "anti-imperialist" platform. Others, like Pol Pot, saw the political struggle as uncompromisingly and simultaneously two-pronged, for "there were two enemies who had to be fought, the first was imperialism. The second was the feudal class, the landlords."[80] Given their distrust of Vietnam, they viewed Sihanouk's accommodation of Hanoi not necessarily in terms of anti-imperialist solidarity, but as injurious to Cambodia's long-term interests. To the hardliners, the twin objectives could not be attained within the politico-legal framework, only through revolution. By 1960, this new and more radical faction had risen to the third, fifth, and sixth positions within the party, with Pol Pot in the position of party secretary by 1963.[81] These internal fissures and "separatist tendencies," which Pol Pot considered "the most difficult thing we have to deal with,"[82] however, remained largely invisible to the outside. They were to magnify over time, culminating in convulsive purges after 1975.

Combined with Sihanouk's political machinations, these dynamics worked temporarily to neutralize domestic opposition, but they could

not eliminate it. Both on the Left and on the Right, dissenters were bid-
ing their time. Within a decade, Republican forces had gathered sufficient momentum to launch a coup that abolished the age-old monarchy.
Five brutal years of war thereafter, the communists marched into Phnom
Penh.

Myths Disenchanted

*Should we ever learn that elsewhere man has succeeded in
improving the weather, we would soon demand that similar
improvements be made for us.*[83]
—*John Kautsky*

In his study of revolutions, Crane Brinton once wrote, "These revolu-
tionists are not worms turning, not children of despair. These revolutions
are born of hope, and their philosophies are formally optimistic."[84] Not
unlike France on the eve of the revolution, post-independence Cambodia under Sihanouk was marked by modernization and progress and
an unprecedented level of social mobilization. Growth was especially
evident in the educational arena. Public education expanded, and the
adult literacy campaign registered marked success. In Kompong Cham,
Milada Kalab noted that "except for the very old ladies everybody can
now read and some of them actually do read."[85] School enrollment, overall, increased exponentially, reaching one million at the primary level[86]
and 117,000[87] at the secondary level by 1968, with a concomitant expansion of the teaching corps from 3,500 in 1955 to over 13,000 in 1968.[88]
Following the establishment of nine universities where none existed less
than a decade prior, enrollment in higher education also grew to 17,000
by 1970.[89] An increasing number of Cambodians also went overseas for
advanced training, many on government scholarships.[90] The return in
the 1950s–1960s of some of the country's budding intelligentsia who
had been educated overseas added to the intellectual vibrancy of post-
independence Cambodia.

These positive developments were not without challenges. The rapid
expansion of higher education was constrained by an acute shortage
of qualified professors, resulting in the decline of academic standards.
The relative ease with which degrees could be obtained produced not

only an enlarged pool of matriculated students with few employment prospects, but also a devaluation of higher education, resulting in an unprecedented number of not only graduates, but also dropouts. The mobilization of new social forces, furthermore, severely tested the system's absorptive capacity. In a country where most educated young men and women aspired to a civil service career, the bureaucracy, already bloated, could accommodate only a nominal few, with access further constricted by nepotism and corruption. Of the many disenfranchised graduates, Roger Smith observed, "They had learned too much ever to contemplate returning to the soil, and they had learned too little to attain positions in the civil service—the only career possible—for which they mistakenly believed themselves qualified."[91]

Opportunities for inclusion were also undercut by the lack of political will to absorb new and innovative ideas, particularly those that threatened the status quo. Steeped in the political headiness of student life in Paris, young leftists such as Khieu Samphan, Ieng Sary, Saloth Sar, and their wives returned with a vision of a more egalitarian and progressive Cambodia, not realizable under royal absolutism. Despite the fact that individuals like Hou Yuon and Khieu Samphan were among a small handful of Cambodians to receive doctorate degrees and the Khieu sisters among the first Cambodian women to obtain advanced degrees, they were marginalized by their politics. With opportunities in the private sector equally limited in the fledging economy dominated by Europeans, Chinese, and Vietnamese, many of the nation's youths came to see their future as stymied under Sihanoukism. Reflecting on a conversation with a gem miner in Pailin, Osborne drew the following conclusion:

> The heretical opinions that the young man offered me were the reflection of a feeling, far more widely held than I realized at the time, that Sihanouk's Cambodia provided no answer to the hope and aspirations of the young men and women who had struggled, sometimes at the cost of real financial sacrifice, to work for a high school diploma or a University degree.[92]

The regime's responses to these mounting challenges were largely symbolic. Efforts to promote inclusion of the nation's youth produced little more than the creation of the Royal Socialist Youth.[93] For the politically astute, it was not difficult to see through the orchestrated myth-making of wide-based populist support for Prince Sihanouk, and recognize that the system yielded little opportunity for any real involvement in the nation's political affairs. Many began to question Sihanouk's paternalism and absolutist control, seeing in his treatment of the populace as his "children" not nurturance but purposive infantilization, emblematic of the regime's inability to provide for genuine participation. Many saw in the prince's newfound diversion in filmmaking, mostly featuring Phnom Penh's decadent elites, a disconnect between the world of Chamcar Mon palace, with its intrigues and self-indulgence, and a country mired in underdevelopment. The opening of a casino in 1968 epitomized the country's moral bankruptcy.[94] With the demand for genuine reform yielding not only cosmetic concession but, simultaneously, repression, the gap widened between the modernizing monarch and the society that he attempted tentatively to modernize.

These sociopolitical conditions were exacerbated by the economic challenges facing newly independent Cambodia. The country's agricultural sector was underdeveloped and long plagued by rural indebtedness, while the industrial sector was fledging at best. The adverse impact of the rejection of American aid in 1963 was especially felt by the urban elites and the military, the latter growing increasingly anxious about the escalated war in Vietnam and its cross-border spillover. Because of its neutrality, Cambodia had become an important sanctuary and transit point for weapons and rice destined for the Vietnamese communists.[95] According to one high-ranking officer, the sanctuaries had also become increasingly fortified and seemingly "permanent."[96] Given Sihanouk's interest in currying favor with the Chinese and Vietnamese communists,[97] there was at best no political will to curtail these transactions,[98] and at worse, complicity.[99] By 1966, illegal sales accounted for 50 percent of Cambodia's rice "exports" and a loss of state revenue of some $20 million annually.[100]

Prompted by economic deterioration, and with leading leftists Khieu Samphan, Hu Nim, and Hou Yuon finally given prominent positions, the government introduced a series of reforms as part of a "Khmer Socialist" development strategy. Banks were nationalized, trade regulated, and state control over the country's financial and commercial sectors expanded to increase fiscal soundness and promote Cambodia's industrial and agricultural potential. State-owned enterprises such as SONEXIM[101] were established to enable the government to directly engage in wholesale import and retail of foreign goods. To facilitate government control over the rice trade and alleviate rural indebtedness, the Office du Crédit Populaire and the Office Royale de Coopération (OROC) were established to enhance state competitiveness in the purchase of rice and other agricultural products, and to provide the rural poor with a viable alternative to usury.[102]

Because of persisting structural problems, insufficient planning, weak administrative capacity, improper pricing policies, inefficiency, and corruption,[103] many of the initiatives failed to meet their objectives. Sihanouk had to concede that the rural scheme "hardly profits anybody, except well-off peasants."[104] Attempted reform of the industrial sector was similarly challenged. Many enterprises operated at a deficit[105] and could survive only with government subsidies.[106] Despite the policy of austerity,[107] luxury foreign imports continued to flow into the country while state industries and enterprises became, in the words of one observer, "appanages for Sihanouk's mandarins, who grew wealthy while the accounts were in the red."[108] Rather than progress, some of the reform measures produced unintended effects that exacerbated the economic conditions. Nationalization shook investor confidence and spurred capital flight as Phnom Penh's wealthy entrepreneurs sought safer investment havens in places like Hong Kong and France. The biggest scandal, involving the flight of Songsakd, a Thai-Cambodian banker, with an estimated $10 million, implicated many of Phnom Penh's prominent personalities.[109]

The Gathering Storm

The subterranean rumblings grew as many came to feel that the Sangkum reforms, as it was with prerevolutionary France, "had aggravated, not alleviated, their condition."[110] Unrest began to register in the cities and the countryside. Labor strikes took place in various state enterprises in 1963, while student protests erupted in Siemreap and Kompong Cham.[111] Though they never acquired a nationwide momentum, these instabilities were dark clouds over Sihanouk's "oasis of peace." With profound insight, Osborne commented, "To realize the existence of continuing disruptive pressure beneath the surface calm of Cambodian politics is to make Siha-nouk's ultimate fall from power much easier to understand."[112]

To the government, the growing unrest especially among labor and the nation's youths was seen as instigated by the communists,[113] whom Sihanouk labeled the Khmer Rouge (Red Khmer), and their external sponsors. In an effort to undercut leftist influence, the teacher corps was reshuffled, privately owned newspapers suspended,[114] and prominent leftists such as Phouk Chhay, head of the pro-Peking Khmer Student Association, and Chau Seng, editor of *La Nouvelle Dépêche* and minister of national economy, were removed from their positions. To contain external sources of influence, the government dissolved the Khmer-Chinese Friendship Association, restricted study abroad opportunities, and revoked scholarships held by some leading members of the anti-Sihanouk Union des Etudiants Khmers de France.[115] As repression intensified in the cities, many leading leftists fled to the *maquis*. Among them were Son Sen, Ieng Sary, and Pol Pot, who sought refuge with the Vietnamese communists in their border "Office 100" in 1963.[116]

The elections of 1966, which marked the ascendancy of the Right, were an important point of departure for the Khmer communists.[117] As Ieng Sary later recounted, "An actual war was begun against us. We had to answer their guns with our guns."[118] While a handful of known leftists continued to work within the legal political framework, the changing political tide underscored for the more radicalized faction the futility of seeking peaceful change, and the necessity of taking the struggle to a different arena—more rural, more clandestine, and more militant. Pol Pot later spoke of the necessity to relocate the revolutionary base to the countryside:

> The city was small. . . . The networks of the enemy's repressive apparatus were concentrated there, and the social composition of the cities was very complex. By contrast, the countryside was vast. The enemy was spread thin there. In some communes, there were only one or two soldiers or police. . . . The peasants there were numerous. The class composition was good.[119]

With the deployment of 90 percent of the Central Committee members to the countryside,[120] defunct cells of the anticolonial period were reactivated. Unrest percolated in areas where local conditions were ripe for exploitation.

As it worked to rebuild and fortify itself, the movement became enshrouded in secrecy.[121] The party leadership was so effectively veiled that, before the collapse of Democratic Kampuchea, few, including his own brother, even knew that Saloth Sar and Pol Pot were the same individual, or the extent of the role that he played in the Khmer communist organization. Pol Pot later claimed, "They knew me but they did not know exactly who [what?] I was."[122] Whether deliberate or incidental, the combined strategy of accommodation and militancy adopted by the Khmer Rouge allowed the attention and repressive arm of Sihanouk's internal security forces to target the more renowned but moderate leftists, while the power fulcrum within the party shifted imperceptibly in favor of the hard-line, Pol Potist faction.

The Khmer Peasantry in Prewar Cambodia

Despite growing signs of instability, left-wing mobilization in the 1950s and 1960s was gravely thwarted by the objective conditions that prevailed in prewar Cambodia. While rural Cambodia was not the bucolic "democracy of small owner-tillers [that] knows no agrarian problems"[123] that Jean Delvert had described, the relative abundance of land and natural resources mitigated rural discontent. Unlike many other Asian countries, including neighboring Vietnam, Cambodia was not burdened by population pressure. Further endowed with fertile plains and rivers, Cambodia enjoyed relatively favorable economic conditions had earned it the compliment of a Chinese metaphor "wealthy as Cambodia."[124] In 1937 Virginia Thompson observed that "living requires little exertion as the natural resources of the country are great and the population small,"[125] and that "whole villages decamp when the soil around them had become exhausted."[126] Close to twenty-five years later, the average national density was thirty-two persons per square kilometer and grew only incrementally to forty per square kilometer by 1971.[127] Even with increased population pressure, land was still abundant in the late 1950s, with only an estimated one-quarter of the country's cultivable land and one-tenth the total area having been put under cultivation. In the early 1970s, almost two-thirds of the country was nowhere near saturation.[128]

While soil conditions are rather poor in many parts of the country, the abundant rainfall and rich alluvial deposits and resources of the Mekong and its tributaries contributed to the relative ease of agrarian life in Cambodia despite the relatively low standards of living, as captured in the old Khmer saying "If it grows, why plant it?"[129] Ta Phouk, a native of the Tonle Sap region, described how local fishermen had devised a method of catching fish by simply digging holes into the riverbanks and waiting for the tide to recede and leave them teeming with fish.[130] Though such natural endowment could not be said to have existed throughout the country, in areas where conditions were more challenging, peasant families could usually supplement their earnings with the cultivation and sale of produce from the family's orchards or other part-time activities such as making and selling palm sugar.[131] Neang, a woman from Baray, Kompong Thom, noted that in her village, "people rarely had to borrow money on any big scale because they could combine farming with laboring on other people's farms—not a necessity to live but to supplement." Many from Kompong Cham could also find employment on the rubber plantations.[132]

Thus, for the majority of the Khmer peasantry, economic marginality rarely, if ever, translated into starvation; in fact, they were among the most well nourished populations in Southeast Asia.[133] As one elderly refugee pointed out, "In our myths and folktales . . . from the story of *Pous Keng Kaang* to *Neang Pi Damdab Neak* ["The Twelve Sisters"], the sweet potato from the earth had always cushioned us in times of privation. When nothing else avails, we can always forage for potatoes." Pich, a poor subsistence farmer from Takeo, reflected, "[We] didn't have much left after filling the stomach, but life was easy. We never imagined that this [Pol Pot] would happen." Given perceptions of Cambodia's relative abundance, poverty was often attributed to the moral defects of the poor rather than to structural impediments. Chanthou, a wealthy landowner from Prey Veng, commented, "They are poor because they are lazy and stupid. They don't create work for themselves. During the winter months, they just sit there hugging the bonfire." Despite their revolutionary stance, the Khmer Rouge leadership subscribed to the same mindset. The prewar Khmer aphorism "All you need is a sickle and you will survive" found a gruelingly literal application during the Khmer Rouge rustication campaign, as thousands of evacuees were sent to previously uninhabited forestland with only the crudest implements and the barest provisions.

Additionally, many features of structural oppression found elsewhere in Asia were also absent in Cambodia. Landlordism did not plague the Khmer peasantry in the way that it did those in prerevolutionary China and neighboring Vietnam. In his analysis of prewar Cambodia, Kiernan noted that there was never a rigid class structure in the countryside, and that "landlordism never really became an explosive national issue in Kampuchea although Pol Pot later stressed that it was crucial."[134] Because of the relatively favorable conditions and a tradition-sanctioned system of bestowing rights to the person who cultivated a previously fallow plot, tenant farming and sharecropping were not pervasive in Cambodia. Though plot sizes may have been small and progressively shrinking for many, averaging between 0.9 hectares and 4 hectares depending on the region, the majority of peasants owned their own land and draft animals.[135] In her study of a Khmer village in one of the more densely populated provinces, five years prior to the onslaught of war, Kalab noted that 83 percent of the land was privately owned[136] and that "fragmentation of holdings has not so far caused serious difficulties in a country with large areas of virgin land."[137] Interviews with Cambodian refugees in the United States,[138] the majority of whom were from modest farming families, corroborate this portrait of prewar, rural Cambodia as comprising small, self-sufficient farmers (*neak srè*) or garden cultivators (*neak chamcar*). Of the landowning refugees, the majority reported owning at least one hectare of riceland. One woman from Ampil, Kompong Cham, recalled that in her village "four out of ten were 'poor' people" but "most people owned their own plots, however small they may have been," adding that life was hard but it was "never as bad as under Pol Pot." This was a poignant indictment of the view of Democratic Kampuchea as rural Cambodia writ large posited by some scholars.[139]

Prior to the onslaught of war, these objective conditions accounted for the relative stability of rural communities.[140] Despite increased mobility, it was not uncommon for areas adjacent to more densely populated communities to remain relatively uncongested. Internal migration was often seasonal and not large-scale. Mass flight, when it occurred in contemporary history, was compelled essentially by political upheavals. This reflects both the strong attachment of the Khmer peasant to the land and the continued tolerability of the rural conditions despite the challenges.

In his study of popular revolt, Gurr argued for the importance of understanding not just the economic and social structures that produce grievances but equally how people perceive and interpret these conditions.[141] In Cambodia, cultural norms further buffered against social discontent. In her ethnographic study, May Ebihara observed that in the farming community in which she lived, structural inequalities were mitigated by a

> general ethic of fundamental egalitarianism manifested not only in the villagers' regarding themselves as "poor people of the rice fields," . . . but also in the fact that material wealth in and of itself was not the basis for high status among fellow villagers [but] rather on the basis of qualities such as age, religiosity, and especially "good character" (chet l'oo).[142]

Along with these norms, Khmer belief systems further militate against social tension. In the Buddhist *Weltanschauung*, the concept of *bon-barb*, karmic merits and demerits accumulated through one's actions, informs how most Khmers assess, understand, and rationalize their social positions. While it can also justify change, the notion of *kam* (bad karma) can dull revolutionary impulse, as those who find themselves at the lower stratum essentially believe themselves fated to be there. As Pol Pot contends, "The belief that bad and good deeds from another life resulted in present conditions served to deceive the peasants and prevent them from seeing the contradictions."[143]

Though without many of the oppressive features of other agrarian societies, Khmer peasant life could be marginal and precarious. Vulnerability to the vagaries of nature, reliance on family labor,[144] and limited capital constrained productivity. While many farming families owned their own rice fields, the plots were often small, in part because of the non-primogenitary inheritance system that generally produces a progressive dwindling of parcel size. These factors combined accounted for the persistently low production in certain areas and may have underscored for the Khmer Rouge leadership the importance of collectivizing land and labor, and of achieving "mastery over water" in order to maximize agricultural yields.

While landlessness was not a principal affliction, indebtedness plagued many rural families. The yields from small, individually cultivated plots may have been sufficient for basic subsistence, but often left little in the form of working capital needed for medicine, farm implements, and other necessities such as weddings, funerals, ordinations, and the multitude of ceremonies that are important to Khmer Buddhists. For these, the peasants had to turn to local moneylenders. The usurious interest rates, in some areas at 60 to 100 percent per year,[145] created a virtually unbreakable cycle of indebtedness. Already in the 1930s, the country was described as "eaten by usury."[146] The high presence of ethnic Chinese and, to a lesser extent, Kala (ethnic Burmese community, largely of the gem-mining towns of Pailin) in the moneylending business made the issue of rural indebtedness even more volatile. Among the grievances raised in the Khmer-language newspaper during the protectorate was the Chinese moneylenders' practice of charging a repayment of "ten times the loan."[147]

Little changed in the decades that followed. Where a landless peasant had to lease the land as well as secure a cash advance, repayment for the loan was deducted from his projected share of the harvest, which in Preng Veng, for instance, was as high as 50 percent of the yield.[148] Thus, even before the crop was sown, it was already spent on debt payment, with unpaid balance carried over to the next year at double the interest. From this state of dependency, a peasant "rarely returns to a state of solvency, like an 'insect trapped in a spider's web.'"[149] It was not uncommon for a debt to be shouldered over generations or for a peasant to be eventually dispossessed, first of his draft animals, then of his small plot, and eventually of his wife and children, who had to be sold into servitude. Though "debt slavery" was supposedly abrogated in 1947, such debt spirals could transform temporary servitude into permanent bondage. For many, flight was the only escape. Refugees from Sangkè recalled that those who fled to the *maquis* in the 1960s and 1970s were often those "with debts spun around them" (*champek roum kloun*). Others from around Thnal Bot and Prey Chas, areas of widespread poverty, recalled that those who willingly followed the Vietnamese communists when they came to recruit in 1971 were "the very poor and the orphaned— those without anybody in the world." Though a small minority in 1970, these "agricultural proletariats," as Hou Yuon referred to them,[150] and other *déclassés* became the backbone of the Khmer Rouge.

Reinforcing the structural challenges were the social barriers. Though without the rigidity of the caste system, Cambodia was and remains a stratified society, with notions of class (*vannak*) and social hierarchy embedded in the Khmer language and in the Khmer social consciousness. Social divisions, however, are defined along two intersecting cleavages, namely, class and geography—more specifically between town (*krong*) and country (*srè*). In Buddhist Southeast Asia, power is understood as emanating outward in concentric spirals from the capital city. It is thus that Khmer coronation ceremonies involve the ritualistic circumambulation around the capital in the symbolic act of claiming the seat of power. The social and cultural space of cities, as such, signifies more than a place of residence. Cities represent a world that connotes classism (*vannak niyum*) and modernity (*tomneub, samay,* or *civilay,* a transliteration of "civilized"), separated from and juxtaposed to the countryside, with all the negative and positive features that it implies. In this rural-urban divide, social distinctions in pre-1975 Cambodia were measured in terms of distance from the rice fields.[151] Townspeople (*neak krong)* thus commanded greater social capital than those on the periphery, where the *neak chamcar* (orchard cultivators) commanded higher social standing than the *neak srè* (rice cultivators). This town-country divide was to inform Democratic Kampuchea's sociopolitical classification system, more rooted in Khmer social reality than in classical Marxian concepts of class.

All told, famine and starvation were not common calamities in prewar Cambodia. Though poverty was widespread and on the rise, abject immiseration remained confined to geographically isolated pockets, sparsely dotting an economic landscape of rural self-sufficiency. It was thus that Kuon Lumphuon, who spent nine months in the *maquis,* concluded that the weakness of the Communist Party of Kampuchea stemmed from the fact that "Cambodian society does not have a farmland problem."[152] This relatively calm rural landscape, however, was slowly changing, with disconcerting signs emerging by the mid-1960s. The system of land registration, marred by corruption and nepotism, disadvantaged the poor and illiterate peasants who could not easily navigate the bureaucracy, and contributed to increased dispossession and immiseration especially for those who relied on customary laws and on access to communal land, a situation that was exacerbated by inadequate compensation made to dispossessed farmers.[153]

The land issue intensified with population growth and rising land speculation stimulated by rural development. According to Ben Kiernan, landlessness climbed from 4 percent in the 1950s to 20 percent in 1970.[154] In the area around Samlaut, a northwestern region known for its agricultural bountifulness, construction of new roads and plans for the expansion of fruit, jute, and cotton plantations spurred speculation, concessions, and land grabbing.[155] Sok, a farmer who lived near Samlaut, recalled that "the big people were coming in to buy land around there." The construction of a sugar refinery further dislodged peasant families from their land.[156]

In the highland, state plans for regional development, including the establishment of commercial plantations, threatened land heretofore protected by customary laws and the well-being of communities subsisting on forest resources. Where relations between the Cambodian state and upland minorities, generically referred to as the Khmer Loeu, had been buffered by social and geographical distance, the progressive extension of government and lowlanders' presence into the highland encroached upon economic and cultural lifeways of communities that had existed in virtual autonomy. Along with private land speculation, state-sponsored development projects such as the expansion of the Labansiek rubber plantation were carried out through government requisition of communal land. Likewise, the creation in 1963 of two new northeastern provinces, Rattanakiri and Mondolkiri, and the introduction of a new policy of appointing the provincial governor from Phnom Penh eroded local authority and undercut the communities' sense of self-determination.

As the war in Vietnam escalated, the arrival and resettlement of cross-border refugees, many of whom were ethnic Khmer Krom families, aggravated the situation especially in land-poor border provinces such as Kampot and Kompong Chhnang.[157] In some areas such as Beng Khtum, government concessions to new settlers, especially of communal land, became the source of intracommunal tension.[158] In the highland, the establishment of these new settlements fanned the already

volatile situation. Social tensions increased with rising rural immiseration. Peasant unrest, sparked by land contestation, became more registered.[159] The most explosive instance took place in Samlaut, when
villagers rioted against the brutality of a military party assigned to collect the paddy tax.[160]

Though short-lived, the Samlaut uprising was significant in a number of ways. At one level, it exposed the social discontent that prevailed.
While one can debate the degree of societal disequilibrium, there is no
discounting "the immense gap . . . between the rich and the poor" in
prewar Cambodia that Khieu Samphan noted in his memoir.[161] Equally
significant, the uprising underscored the *limits* of revolutionary impetus in prewar Cambodia. While it is tempting to look at the revolt as a
"prelude, in a microcosm, of the conflict that would sweep across the
country three years later," as some have argued,[162] Samlaut, though a
milestone development, was an isolated example of peasant mobilization
in the two decades following independence. The province was atypical
in the heightened disparity that existed between large landowners and
landless cultivators. As Pol Pot described it, "This was a region of vast
rice plantations. Some 90 percent of the rice paddies were in the hands
of the landowners. Of the tens of thousands of people in Thmor Koul,
only four to ten persons were landowners. Tens of thousands of peasants
shared the remaining ten percent of the rice paddies."[163] Revolutionary
impetus was still in its emberred state in prewar Cambodia.

Though revolution was premature, these conditions were ripe for exploitation by the communists—first Vietnamese and Laotian (the Pathet
Lao), then Khmer—who appeared in these communities. While the full
extent to which the Khmer communists were involved in rural unrest
remains to be conclusively determined, they appeared to have at least
exploited peasant discontent that began to register in different parts of
the country.[164] Given the incipience of the proletarian class and general
lack of receptivity of the Khmer peasantry, the communists concentrated
their mobilization in these economically marginalized, geographically
isolated, and socially alienated pockets of Cambodia's rural communities. One refugee described this encounter:

When I was young, I used to travel to the remote parts of Battambang,
near Phnom Vay Chap. We were sent there to clear some forestland.

These people have never seen a tractor in their lives. They used to come up to us and say, "Uncle, what is that beast that makes so much noise?" So we tricked them and told them, "That's what we called *neak* [mythical dragon]. It only eats at night, so why don't you bring it something so it won't roar so loudly." That night they brought us a basket of fresh *ombok*[165] and we ate it all and said the beast ate it. Those people were quite naive.

Another survivor recalled being asked by a female cadre who saw a train "what kind of animal that was that made such a noise."[166]

It was in this small but growing community of the rural disenfranchised that the Khmer Rouge initially found their most trusted followers. When asked about the Khmer Rouge with whom they had come into contact, surviving refugees, most of whom were themselves of rural background, frequently described them as *pouk prey* (forest people), "black with frizzy hair," or *neak srok loeu* (people from the upland),[167] less in reference to ethnicity than to geographic and social distance. Heretofore peripheral, these groups could find in the membership in a revolutionary movement the sense of belonging and social import that were denied to them in the old order. While they did not produce rural revolution in Cambodia, once mobilized, they contributed significantly to the Khmer Rouge's virulently anti-urban stance.

In addition to disenfranchised peasants, ethnic minorities—namely, Vietnamese, Chinese, and the Khmer Loeu (upland Khmer)—were also targets of communist recruitment. Prodded by the Chinese embassy working through the Kampuchea-China Friendship Association and the Chinese-language schools, segments of the Sino-Cambodian community responded to the call of the Cultural Revolution.[168] Maoist buttons, Mao's Little Red Book, and "pamphlets denouncing Sihanouk and his administration and calling for the overthrow of the Cambodian 'capitalist' state" circulated in Phnom Penh.[169] The communists were also active among ethnic Vietnamese, particularly in the eastern border provinces and among fishermen and plantation workers where the Indochina Communist Party had previously made inroads.[170] A teacher from Peareang recalled that those who came to recruit in the area were Vietnamese plantation workers from Chup and Memot.[171] Another refugee noted that in Baray, many factory workers and their families left for the *maquis* after being "turned around" (*pravel*) by the communists and that mobilization efforts intensified in 1970 "after Sihanouk left for Paris." In the northeast, the Khmer Loeu, who had long been in contact with the Vietnamese communists because of the Ho Chi Minh Trail, which cut through the area, also became increasingly politicized by the growing presence of Vietnamese and Khmer communists in the border sanctuaries.[172] With people now equipped with an ideology and an organization for redressing grievances, passive resistance soon catalyzed into organized revolts. Violent confrontations erupted between government forces and the upland Jarai community in 1968. At Labansiek, an uprising broke out in the face of government repression of the local Brao tribe, which had protested against state appropriation of its land for agriculture.[173] The northeast, once a sanctuary for anti-French rebellion in 1876, became an early Khmer Rouge base region.[174]

Though Sihanouk's Cambodia may have fallen short of the myth of the "serene oasis," communist influence, overall, was not extensive. While much of Southeast Asia in the 1950s and 1960s was destabilized by left-wing insurgency, communist proselytizing in Cambodia fell on infertile grounds. As Willmott concluded in his study of prewar Cambodia, "There was little social basis for rural discontent (except in pockets) where the KCP began to organize the peasantry in Kampuchean revolution."[175] As it was in China before 1937, where the communist bid for power, based on an appeal to peasant economic interest, was "a conspicuous failure,"[176] the Cambodian peasantry largely was still a passive element in politics in the decades prior to the outbreak of war. The country's prewar socioeconomic condition was not "ripe" for a revolutionary outbreak, and the Khmer communist movement incipient, unstructured, and geographically disparate. Organizationally challenged and ideologically weak, they were unable to exploit the seeds of instability or to translate the few instances of rural unrest into sustained peasant mobilization. Pol Pot later acknowledged that the Samlaut uprising was "set off by the people, through their own movement," for "the Party Central Committee had not yet decided on general armed insurrection throughout the country."[177] In the face of government reprisals, the two remaining leading leftists, Khieu Samphan and Hou Yuon, took to the *maquis*. Their flight effectively severed the last physical links to the accommodationist line. As the movement became radicalized, it also became more clandestine. Justified by the new political environment, the party veiled itself in secrecy; the progressive consolidation of power in the hands of a small radical group was imperceptible both from within and from the outside.[178]

"When the Elephants Fight"

As is true with many small states, internal developments in Cambodia cannot be viewed in isolation, for they were integrally and dialectically linked to external developments, particularly to dynamics engendered by the Cold War. While they were not the sole determinant, externalities did impact domestic developments, creating both opportunities and impediments to the revolutionary dynamics. With the introduction of American ground troops in 1965 and escalation of conflict in Vietnam, access to cross-border sanctuaries in neutral Cambodia became even more important for the Vietnamese communists. The decision of the Khmer Rouge to resort to armed struggle was inopportune and threatened the quid pro quo that Vietnam and China had reached with the Sihanouk government, whereby in exchange for the prince's tacit cooperation, they agreed to restrain the local communists.[179] For the Khmer Rouge leadership, Hanoi's ambivalence reinforced the distrust between the two communist parties and reaffirmed for the hard-liners the necessity of a political break with Vietnam. These experiences with uneasy alliances, subjugation, and betrayal reinforced their worldview.[180] According to Stephen Heder, "It was in this period that the CPK finally decided that it had little choice but to learn how to make a virtue of the necessity of isolation and independence from all other Communist Parties, especially the VWP [Vietnamese Workers' Party], and that such policy could work."[181] Following victory, distrust and the feeling of besiegement saw to the dogmatic insistence on self-reliance that amounted to a virtual autarky, and to the militant posturing toward the outside world and self-consuming purges at home.

At least for a while, Sihanouk was able through careful balancing of external forces to neutralize threats both at home and abroad. As Osborne noted, however, "Sihanouk had been astute in choosing a foreign policy that was in tune with the times, but he could not ensure that those times would last."[182] By 1970, the confluence of internal and external developments was to set Cambodia on an unalterable course. The rising stakes in Vietnam were to thrust America, the Vietnamese communists, and the war westward, launching Cambodia into a historic tailspin.

Storm over the Oasis

As the above discussion indicates, the predicaments facing Cambodia in the fifteen years leading up to the outbreak of war in 1970 were largely those of a newly independent state struggling with the colossal tasks of postcolonial development while facing challenges both at home and in the international arena. The issue was not the absence of change, but rather the inability or unwillingness of the regime to effectively respond to and manage change. While Sihanouk, like other modernizing monarchs, may have regarded reforms as necessary and perhaps even desirable, the institution of the monarchy itself is inherently traditional. As such, it ultimately views genuine expansion of political participation as a threat to its interests. The resulting tentative reforms succeeded only in alienating the middle class and the military, and in frustrating the hopes of the disenfranchised.

Of Sihanouk's dilemma, Chandler wrote, "Ironically, Sihanouk's triumphs . . . led to his downfall, because those he educated and those he pulled together, came to doubt (as Sihanouk never did) that he was the only conceivable leader for Cambodia."[183] As the regime proved itself increasingly less capable of responding to internal problems and managing the seeping effects of the deteriorating international situation, resentment and dissension emanated from both ends of the political spectrum. They became differentiated only by the degree of radicalism, some advocating democratic reforms, others seeking nothing short of revolution.

While seeds of discontent did exist in prewar Cambodia, as they do in all developing countries, social dislocations and tension that elsewhere had translated into systemic disequilibrium were relatively insipid and effectively contained through Sihanouk's combined strategy of rewards and suppression. The inability of the communists to translate peasant unrest into sustained mass mobilization speaks to the political and economic landscape of prewar Cambodia, in which the legitimacy of the monarchial regime, though increasingly contested by urban elites, remained largely unquestioned by the majority of Khmer peasants. Ideo-logically unrooted and politically insipid, the Khmer Rouge as such did not constitute a significant threat in the years preceding the onslaught of war in 1970. Estimates vary, but after close to a decade in the *maquis*, presumably in constant contact with potentially recruitable members of the exploited mass, the Khmer Rouge according to Pol Pot's own fig-ure could boast an armed force of no more than four thousand men. Most estimates placed the number at three thousand,[184] others as low as eight hundred armed men at the time of the coup in March 1970.[185] The greater challenge throughout Sihanouk's governance thus emanated not from the Khmer communists but from the Right, culminating in the Republican coup in 1970.

Domestic instability by itself did not bring about regime change in Cambodia. Rather, it was the convergence of internal *and* external stim-uli that proved to be most destabilizing. By the mid-1960s, the com-pounding pressure of domestic and international exigencies increasingly undermined the delicate equilibrium that Sihanouk sought to maintain both at home and in the international arena. As the war in Vietnam escalated, Cambodia's options, including that of staying "neutral," and Sihanouk's political maneuverability narrowed and eventually became nullified. His inability to sustain the political balance eroded his author-ity, further reinforcing the disequilibrium.

The precarious peace that Cambodia was able to enjoy heretofore and upon which much of the legitimacy of the Sihanoukist regime had rested was dealt a final blow by the coup of March 18, 1970. It was the ultimate vote of no confidence delivered by the country's urban elites and the mil-itary. For the first time in the nation's history, Cambodia was without a ruling monarch as the centuries-old kingship was abolished and Prince Sihanouk forced into exile in North Korea. The auguries and prophe-cies that had reverberated in the preceding months acquired an uncanny realism as the country was irreversibly drawn into the vortex of war. *The princely white heron did fly north* into exile; and it was not long before *the country was bathed in blood as high as the belly of the elephant.*[186]

The regime change in Phnom Penh and widening conflict altered the power balance on the ground. The establishment of the Khmer Repub-lic, with its pro-American stance, signaled an official end to Cambodia's neutrality, albeit one that had long been compromised by Vietnamese communist sanctuaries and American secret bombings. The westward expansion of the war and the catalytic role of external forces were to have profound implications for revolutionary dynamics in Cambodia. In her study of the "grand revolutions," Theda Skocpol argues that competition for acquisition and control over imperial domains has contributed significantly to revolutionary crises.[187] Cambodia provides an important argument for looking at the *effects* of major power contests on smaller nation-states. Despite the overreach in her description of political developments, Laura Summers's point regarding the revolutionizing impact of war is important: "It was not by any means historically necessary that Cambodia should experience widespread revolt or revolution. Although there were conflicts in the pre-coup period, no national uprising on the scale observed since 1971 was foreseen. The Cambodian liberation forces seem to have been created by the military logic of foreign intervention."[188] Like the Chinese communists, the Khmer Rouge were catapulted to power after decades of political marginality not by rural immiseration but by war. The conditions necessary for national mobilization that the communists could not engender in almost two decades of struggle came to bear after 1970 with the widening conflict on mainland Southeast Asia. The unlikely contexts that brought about an unexpected Khmer Rouge victory, in turn, accounted in large part for the challenges of post-victory governance that they came to encounter, and for some of the extremist policies that they adopted in response.

What, in fact, were the forces and conditions that made it possible for a movement, organizationally weak and ideologically unpopular, to emerge victorious? What were the consequences of such unlikely beginnings? For many older-generation Khmers, war and destruction were part of the historical memory that replayed itself. When asked about the Khmer Rouge, Ta Chin, an elderly refugee in Stockton, recalled how as a young boy growing up in colonial Cambodia's eastern province of Prey Veng, he had asked his father, "Where did the Issarak come from?" to which his father answered, "The Issarak was born of the ashes,"[189] in other words, of the destruction brought on by conflict and the anger it provoked. This, he pointed out, was also the story of the war in 1970.

4

From Peasants to Revolutionaries

I don't know who started what and why. But in my lifetime, I have witnessed power changing many hands, since the time of the Issarak. All I know is that when the big people clap their hands, the little people get smashed.
—A Cambodian elder in Stockton

The right-wing coup of March 18, 1970, that overthrew the monarchy shattered the illusion of serenity that had enveloped Sihanouk's "island of peace." If the end of the monarchy caught many by surprise, the fact that it was brought about by the prince's trusted ministers was even more disconcerting. The calamities unleashed were far greater than what even the coup leaders may have imagined. Almost in somnambulance, the country found itself swept up in a whirlwind of unforeseen events. The American military support that some may have anticipated did not materialize; instead, the U.S.–South Vietnamese incursion into Cambodia on April 30, 1970, was brief and limited in both scope and objective. As Nixon made clear, the goal was not to protect Cambodia but "to protect our men . . . in Vietnam and to guarantee the continued success of our withdrawal . . . and end[ing] the war in Vietnam."[1] As for Cambodia, the administration was emphatic: "We have no U.S. formal commitment."[2] Aimed at shifting the conflict to a new theater, thereby securing that much-needed margin of time for South Vietnamese forces to be strengthened so as to allow for an "honorable" withdrawal, the invasion of Cambodia was the "Nixon Doctrine in its purest form,"[3] the "sideshow," as Shawcross aptly described it, critical to the administration's Vietnamization campaign. That the operations were planned and carried out without the involvement of the Phnom Penh government[4] revealed the extent to which Cambodia's fate had spiraled away from its leaders' grasp. As American tanks rolled across the Cambodian border, Lon Nol, head of the new Khmer Republic, was informed that American troops would be withdrawn within one month. He reportedly wept.[5] This was the man who, in the days of the Jeunesse Internationale in Vietnam, had impressed his childhood friends with his inner strength.[6] Even in moments of uncompromising idealism, he knew that Cambodia's fate was sealed.

When war broke out in 1970, the major threat facing the Khmer Republic was not the Khmer Rouge, but the forty thousand Vietcong/North Vietnamese (VC/NVA) forces inside Cambodia.[7] Alerted by Soviet and Chinese sources to a potential coup against Sihanouk, the VC/NVA pushed deeper into Cambodia[8] to secure militarily what they could no longer achieve politically through their courtship of Prince Sihanouk. Hastily mobilized and ill-equipped, the 35,000-men-strong Republican forces proved no match for their battle-seasoned opponents. Within a few months of the coup, approximately 50 percent of the country and 20 percent of the population were firmly under Vietnamese communist control.[9] By 1971, U.S. intelligence estimates placed two-thirds of the countryside under the communists.[10] The Khmer Republic was never to regain its footing. It was a feat that the Khmer Rouge had not been able to achieve in two decades of struggle.

Of the political *élan* provided by their Vietnamese allies, Burchett reflected, "Rarely did a national liberation movement have such an excellent take off condition."[11] At least in the first two years of the war, Vietnamese communist forces, shielding themselves behind the Sihanouk-led united front, the Front Uni National du Kampuchéa (FUNK),[12] shouldered the brunt of the fighting in Cambodia,[13] while local Khmer recruits were largely confined to menial roles. One interviewee, Saath, recounted her first encounter with the Vietnamese communists in Kandal in 1971: "They would come sometimes [in a group of] four to ten . . . with a Khmer Rouge. But they never crossed the village, . . . they just walked along the edge of the hamlet. Father saw them when he was tying up the cows. Claimed they were Khmer Rumdos [Khmer liberation forces]." To maintain the façade of an independent, nationalist movement, the VC/NVA was also careful not to expose its involvement when implementing campaigns to promote "hatred-killing of cruel tyrants," meting out punishment, or manipulating local elections.[14] In Takeo, a former Khmer Rouge cadre recalled that "they appointed a Khmer commune chief, but in practice he answered to a Vietcong official. It was like the colonial system."[15] The strategy was effective. Both Father Ponchaud and François Bizot, who were detained by Vietnamese communist forces, were unable to convince their colleagues of their presence in Cambodia.

Vietnamese communist military strength, in effect, delivered for the Khmer Rouge the secured base areas needed to build their infrastructure. Within one year, Khmer communist forces grew to an estimated ten thousand full-time soldiers and fifty thousand operatives,[16] becoming progressively visible both in the fighting and in the administration of base areas.[17] By early 1971, the administrative apparatus in more than half of Cambodia's provinces now under communist control reportedly was staffed mostly by Khmers.[18] The war became increasingly Khmerized. Refugee interviewees confirmed that by 1972–1973, "you don't see the Youn (Vietnamese) anymore, only Khmer." This "almost complete transformation of the face of the war"[19] from one of foreign aggression to one of civil war undercut the political platform of the Phnom Penh government, which had depicted the conflict as a nationalist struggle against Vietnamese communists. A former soldier recalled, "By 1972, it became just between Khmers and Khmers. It was not like the Issarak days with the French when we could speak about foreign imperialism."

Born of the Ashes: War and Revolutionary Mobilization

Theorizing about populist revolutions often centers on oppressive class relations and economic conditions as a catalyst for revolutionary mobilization.[20] The leadership of Democratic Kampuchea themselves explained their revolution in terms of peasant exploitation and class struggle. However, as Trotsky contended, the mere existence of privations "is not enough to cause an insurrection: if it were, the masses would be always in revolt." Peasant discontent is often not the immediate instigator of revolutionary outbreak, nor is it the principal determinant of revolutionary success. While misery and frustration are important catalysts of popular mobilization, they do not automatically produce either the coherent ideology or the necessary organization needed for the making of a revolution. In *States and Social Revolutions*, Skocpol notes, "What is at issue is not so much the objective potential for revolts. . . . It is rather the degree to which grievances that are always at least implicitly present can be collectively perceived and acted upon."[21]

In many revolutionary instances, it is war, with its indiscriminate destruction, made even more impersonal and massive by technological advances, that lends cohesion to discontent and makes collective action possible. Of rural mobilization in China, Chalmers Johnson argues that the peasantry was finally moved to active rebellion by the Japanese invasion, which drastically destabilized their quotidian lives and transformed local grievances into nationwide mobilization.[22] In Cambodia, after decades of political inconsequence, the Khmer Rouge owed their organizational expansion largely to war-engendered, particularly rural, dislocations rather than to the intrinsic appeal of the communist ideology. Communism was not only insignificant to Khmer Rouge mobilization success but was seen as an impediment, which accounted for the fact that the communist party was kept hidden not only throughout the war but for two years after their victory. Countervailing Kissinger's position that "the Khmer Rouge had always been killers," Shawcross argued that regardless of their predisposition toward brutality, it was the war of 1970–1975 that catapulted them to power and essentially put them in "the position of being able to kill so many, so indiscriminately." In fact, he wrote, "the five-year war . . . created the conditions, the *only* conditions, in which they could grow. Just as the Bolsheviks could come to power in Russia only after the destruction wrought by World War I, so the Khmer Rouge were brought to control in Cambodia only by the 1970–1975 war."[23] During his trial, Duch asserted that "the Khmer Rouge would already have been demolished" by 1970, had it not been for Kissinger and Nixon's policies.[24]

While one can debate Shawcross's thesis that American bombing radicalized the Khmer Rouge, accounting for their post-victory extremism, it is undeniable that the westward exportation of the war, largely waged by the United States through air campaigns,[25] dislocated lives and communities and fundamentally altered the political dynamics on the ground. The scale of the destruction was not only in the quantity of bombs, which was three times that dropped on Japan during World War II,[26] but in the concentration on less than 25 percent of the country.[27] Contrary to Kissinger's claim that the bombings were confined to unpopulated areas, the direct orders from Nixon and Kissinger were "to hit everything,"[28] "anything that moves."[29] That pilots often had to work with outdated maps and ever-shifting battlefronts contributed to the indiscriminate nature of the destruction. Describing an area near Kompong Chhnang, Jon Swain reported, "The war damage here, as everywhere else we saw, was total. . . . The entire countryside had been churned up by B-52 bomb craters, whole towns and villages razed."[30] As Ponchaud recalled, at night "it was like the skyline was burning."[31]

The war devastated the rural economy. Rice production plummeted from 3.8 million tons in 1970 to 762,000 tons by 1973–1974. With domestic supplies further siphoned off through illegal sales to the communists, Cambodia, once a rice exporter, became dependent on food imports, a situation made increasingly acute as the country's urban centers became swollen with refugees. Phnom Penh's population grew from approximately half a million to almost two million by 1974. While the Khmer Rouge population shuffles are well documented, comparatively little is known of the extent of dislocation that preceded it. Of the refugees interviewed, most indicated having moved at least twice during the five years of war. Families were fractured, as it was not uncommon for children, especially daughters, to be sent to live with relatives in more secure areas or, in the case of young boys, to avoid conscription. In the first year of the war alone, over 30 percent of the population was internally displaced.[32] They came in waves. The first brought in families of government functionaries and merchants from communist-held areas. Fortunes were amassed from others' misfortune, as smuggling of marked individuals (that is, "class enemies") to government-controlled areas became a lucrative business. Then came the general victims of war: peasant families forced to abandon their farmland, propelled toward urban centers by the desperate search for security, a human flotsam cast off by the forces of circumstance, losing pieces of their humanity at each makeshift settlement.

The Reluctant Revolutionaries

In the anarchy of war, the average peasant is often confronted with constrained choices, namely, to remain neutral or to choose sides, and in the latter case, decide which side to join. The question, as Johnson posits, "is how the peasantry came to have any side at all."[33] In their focus on ideology and political agency, studies of revolution often underempha-size the power of exigencies in compelling revolutionary participation. As refugee-survivors have pointed out, whether on the side of the gov-ernment or of the *Khmer krahom* (red Khmer), it was more often that individuals *found* themselves there rather than that they *chose* to be there. With both armies vying for control over population and territory, it was largely chance—or fate, as the Khmer would have it—that deter-mined whether someone ended up on the side of the government or the Khmer Rouge: "The bullets were flying over our heads. . . . We crouched behind the dikes of the paddy fields, not daring to lift our heads. Then someone from behind shouted, 'Go forward, go forward.' And we strug-gled to our feet and just went; didn't know where we were going. We just forged ahead without thinking of anything." In its 1976 annotated history, the Khmer Communist Party acknowledged that "although they did not want to join us, when the storm came they had to come and take shelter in our refuge." Refugees also spoke of entire hamlets being corralled by Khmer Rouge forces in the midst of battle or villagers kid-napped while working in the rice fields and forcibly taken to the jungle. Those individuals who ended up with the Khmer Rouge, like those who flocked to government-controlled areas, never "joined" in any willful sense. This was to shape the Khmer Rouge relationship with the masses in the post-victory period.

By no means is this to argue that ideology or political choice was not important. Like most revolutionary movements, the Khmer Rouge did build their organizational core from a small minority of "true believ-ers."[34] Most Cambodians, however, simply "asked to stay alive" (*som tè rous*). As it was with the Chinese revolution, agency was demonstrated not in establishing a political stance but in making pragmatic calcula-tions. For the peasantry, the only thing greater than the desire for bet-terment was the need to minimize risks, which could be achieved by aligning with the preponderant force. In Cambodia, the power balance on the ground was tilted first by the military prowess of the Vietnam-ese communists and subsequently by the incipience of the Republican Forces Armées Nationales Khmères (FANK). Mobilized under fire, FANK consisted largely of young conscripts who, with little training, were simply trucked off to battle. Of the raw recruits from the Koh Kong fish cannery, U Sam Oeur wrote, "They had received only rudimentary training. . . . Some of them didn't even know where the trigger was on a rifle or where to load the cartridges. They just threw down their guns and ran. The majority of them were mowed down in one day."[35] The inexperience of the rank and file was compounded by the lack of training and ineptitude of many of the commanding officers. A former air force officer recounted bitterly,

> That was what killed many of the men—all those guys in command who knew nothing about military affairs but who either bribed people to temporarily enlist or who were in cahoots with people who lied about the headcount. There was the incident of that well-known actor who ordered his men to chase a Vietcong who appeared to have been crippled and actually sent all those men into a deadly ambush. It was his stupidity that killed them.

With casualties reaching a thousand per week at one point,[36] increasingly less-experienced officers were promoted, creating a spiral of incompetence. Corruption, fueled by the massive influx of foreign aid, further strained the system. With high attrition and a system that made anyone who could amass a battalion-size force its commanding officer, opportunistic officers padded the payroll with "ghost soldiers." Troop under-strength accounted for many battlefield defeats. A pilot who flew air support for ground operations recalled that where there was supposed to be "a broad, fan-like operational sweep, only a thin, tattered and highly exposed column moved out."

A vicious cycle emerged in which fear and inexperience drove government troops to use force to shield themselves against an elusive enemy, while indiscriminate deployment of force further galvanized the populace to the side of the opposition. Ill prepared to engage the enemy, "unseen" and ever more omnipresent, government troops confined themselves largely to provincial centers and to the vicinity of the national roads. Beyond these enclaves, the countryside belonged to the warriors of the night. By 1973, all areas, except for the capital, some key provinces, and the riverbank outlets, had either been evacuated or designated enemy territory.[37] As Jon Swain reported, "The front was close to Phnom Penh, . . . a thirty minute drive in almost any direction provided a grandstand view of the war."[38]

The inability of the Republican government to reassert control over the countryside essentially left these areas uncontested and the Cambodian populace with no option but to support the communists—first Vietnamese, then Cambodian. A peasant from Snaang stated with poignant simplicity, "They were already there. What could we have done? We lived under them so we worked under them." Another pointed out that the communists "may come and go but they left behind their *mé khum* [subdistrict chief] and their *mé phum* [village chief], who could always summon the troops if we didn't cooperate. At night, they would come and summon us [those who disobeyed]. The government soldiers only stayed in their barracks." Moreover, many who were caught in communist-held areas were often regarded as "compromised" (*mean khlun*). Held hostage by this cloud of suspicion, they had little choice but to submit to communist authority.

Elsewhere, "multiple sovereignty"[39] prevailed, and even those who lived in government territories and essentially supported the Phnom Penh regime were compelled to "balance the pole on our shoulders" (*rek oy smaer*). Like other villagers in his area, Tun, a farmer from Battambang, was forced to deliver to the Khmer Rouge a monthly requisition of two to three burlap sacks of rice grain and salted fish. Nim, a woman who lived in the remote part of Pailin, told of the practice in her hamlet of "packing some rice in banana leaves and leaving it under the eaves of the thatched roof for the *pouk rumdos* [liberation forces] when they passed through the area."

Once the Republican forces were neutralized and no longer posed a threat to communist control over the "liberated areas," the façade of the united front crumbled: "After 1972, Sihanouk was no longer mentioned. A film was shown in the village showing the royal family and the KR pointed out the extravagant lifestyle of the leaders stating that they had stolen from the people, that 'they were no better than the Lon Nol traitors.'"[40] In his court testimony, Ponchaud recalled hearing pejorative references to the prince and his wife as "*a-knouk* and *mi-kneak.*"[41] Campaigns against Khmer-Hanoi who had returned to participate in the war, including clandestine assassinations, also intensified, forcing many to flee back to Vietnam.[42] One surviving veteran recalled, "We were transferred from our jobs; some of us were sent to grow pepper, or supervise cattle. Even a doctor was sent to raise pigs, to be 'forged.'"[43]

In the Southwest, ninety of the one hundred returnees were killed in 1974.[44] Force was also progressively directed at the general populace as the initial campaign to cultivate popular "hearts and minds" gave way to a hardened stance. By 1972–1973, mobilization became increasingly coerced. A woman told of her four sons who were inducted into the Khmer Rouge army in 1974: "They were forced to go. If they did not go with them, they would be killed."[45]

With uncontested control over expansive base areas that had been "effectively cut off and isolated from the rest of the country,"[46] the Khmer Rouge proceeded to build their administrative and political infrastructure. Tapping into the traditional legitimacy of monks, teachers, and village headmen, they formed village committees, set up their own taxation system, and conscripted. In the process, force was wielded strategically to compel submission. Pich recounted how her brother-in-law, a village headman in Kompong Cham, was killed because of his refusal to cooperate. Where the Khmer Rouge had consolidated their control, radical reforms were also introduced. In some base areas, commerce was disallowed[47] and land redistribution undertaken. In some locales, private holdings were limited in size, while elsewhere they were abolished, with land and other means of production collectivized as early as 1971[48] and "superior level" cooperatives, as Khieu Samphan termed it, established by 1973.[49] Pol Pot spoke in retrospect of the economic imperative for communalization: "The landowners and merchants gathered all the rice to sell it out to the Lon Nol clique and to the Vietnamese. . . . As for the Revolutionary Army of Kampuchea, . . . they were running out of rice and fed with rice soup at every meal. . . . If this continued, we would have been defeated."[50]

Granted, these reforms were not wholly without popular support. Impoverished peasants, especially in land-poor regions such as parts of Kampot, Kandal, and Takeo, had much to gain from land redistribution, and many actively supported the movement. The average peasant, including those who stood to benefit from the reforms, however, found Khmer Rouge extremist measures difficult to reconcile. Where they were established, cooperatives paved the way for tightened control over movement and the ban on religious and cultural practices, which found little support among the peasantry; the prohibition against the wearing of traditional clothing, for instance, triggered a Cham revolt in 1973. Once a common feature of village cooperation, the mutual aid system (*provas dai*) as enforced by the Khmer Rouge, took the form of mandatory communalization of labor, imposed without the volunteerism and altruism associated with traditional practice. Khieu Samphan later wrote that the hasty introduction of high-level cooperatives "had to be imposed on the population because peasants in any country would never agree to give up all the fruits of their labour to any organization."[51] A peasant protest at Chamcar Andaung in which even the village poor participated was only one such documented instance of resistance.[52] Given the Khmer peasant's attachment to the land, this radical policy was particularly alienating. Within six months of the introduction of collectivization, some sixty thousand people fled communist zones. They exercised their final act of defiance, as Russian peasants had done during Stalin's collectivization campaigns, by slaughtering their livestock rather than relinquishing them to Angkar.[53]

Even more alienating than the socioeconomic dislocations engendered by the reforms was the draconian way the Khmer Rouge enforced their will. To compel absolute and unquestioning compliance from an increasingly recalcitrant populace, they frequently meted out capital punishment for minor infractions. A former Khmer Rouge recalled having to intervene to stop the killing of innocent civilians at Baray.[54] Beginning in 1973, forced population relocation became more frequent and with rising brutality that presaged later developments. In Kratie, the city's residents, irrespective of their class background, were forcibly relocated from the provincial capital to remote, malaria-infested areas in Cambodia's northeast.[55] In Kompong Cham, fifteen thousand residents were taken away from their homes by the Khmer Rouge. The city of Oudong was also evacuated in 1974. In numerous instances, mass evacuation was accompanied by executions and deliberate destruction of towns, Buddhist monasteries, and religious icons.[56] Massacres of high school students and nuns in Oudong in 1972 and 1974, and of villagers of Sasar Sdam in Siemreap in 1974, were among the early evidence of Khmer Rouge brutality against the populace.[57] Whereas prior to 1973, those seeking refuge in government-held areas often cited the U.S. bombing as the primary reason for flight,[58] thereafter, many stated that they were fleeing the brutality of the Khmer Rouge. These early developments foreshadowed the extremism that came to characterize Democratic Kampuchea.

Terror used against the populace did more than create a power vacuum. It exposed the government's fundamental weakness—its inability to protect its people. To the formerly apolitical Khmer peasantry "swaying with the wind" (*bok taam kchol*) in constant search for security, the inability of the government to meet the most fundamental need of its people—namely, physical security—eroded its legitimacy. As Che Guevara had observed in Bolivia, "Peasants are always with forces of power and strength."[59] For many of the situational revolutionaries, their support of the Khmer Rouge was born not of conviction but of necessity.

Nationalism and Political Mobilization

While war is perhaps the greatest catalyst for the anomie and social disorganization that Hannah Arendt linked to totalitarianism, the Cambodian and Chinese experiences suggest that peasant mobilization was not only on the basis of war-engendered structural dislocations but also the *source* of the dislocations. When brutalization is given a foreign face, it transforms feelings of helplessness and alienation into nativistic indignation. Tempting as it may be to focus on the internationalist aspects of communist revolutions, it is often local histories and sentiments that give texture to popular discontent, and resonance to revolutionary ideologies. What transpired in Cambodia was not just a war between communism and republicanism. It was essentially a contest for the mantle of Khmer nationalism in which the Republican government presented itself as a defender of Cambodian sovereignty against Vietnamese communist aggression, while the Sihanouk-led united front presented itself as fighting imperialist America and its South Vietnamese and Cambodian allies to restore the monarchy that alone could ensure Cambodia's security and prosperity.

In this contest for legitimacy, the Khmer Republic, already drowning in ineptitude and corruption, was further weighed down by its Faustian alliance. While American troops withdrew soon after the incursion, South Vietnamese forces were left behind to militarily assist the nascent government in Phnom Penh, evidence of the U.S. disregard of local realities. Unlike the VC/NVA, which understood the political imperative of hiding behind the united front, South Vietnamese forces, deployed at the heel of the killing and expulsion of ethnic Vietnamese by the Lon

Nol regime, unleashed retributive violence.[60] A U.S. intelligence report concluded, "Cambodia was open house for the South Vietnamese Air Force. They and the army were free, for the first time in decades, to give expression to their historical contempt for the Khmers. They behaved as if they were conquering a hostile nation, rather than helping a new ally; every Cambodian was a VC and a target."[61] Abuses, in many cases sanctioned by the officers, were widespread.[62] Along with organized banditry, systematic brutalization of innocent civilians such as that which took place in Prey Veng became all too common: "The soldiers surrounded the temple. . . . They accused us of being Vietcong, and wanted to know who was killing the Vietnamese people. They brutally beat some of our men, and sexually abused all the women, forcing them to undress and raping them with wooden sticks."[63] In Kompong Soeung, "young girls were forced to strip for the pleasure of the soldiers."[64] An ethnic Khmer officer in a South Vietnamese unit who served as a field monitor recalled numerous occasions in which Khmer Krom (ethnic Khmer in Vietnam) soldiers had to threaten their own Vietnamese comrades with the use of force to prevent the brutalization of Cambodian peasants.[65] At times, South Vietnamese troops appeared more intent upon settling scores than on conducting their operations against the communists. Nuon Siphy observed that no fighting erupted even though South Vietnamese and VC/NVA forces could clearly see each other across the river.[66] Near Kompong Trabek, villagers also noted that the South Vietnamese army deliberately refrained from attacking a concrete bunker complex that had been occupied by Vietnamese communist forces for over a year, and instead concentrated on terrorizing Khmer villagers in the area.

In the face of widespread lawlessness and violence, the inability of the Cambodian government to stop the abuses underscored its moral bankruptcy. CIA field reports warned that South Vietnamese excesses had caused "grave physical and moral suffering" and that "it will be difficult to hold down the rising tide of hatred and rancor,"[67] something that Lon Nol had feared when he warned Alexander Haig against maintaining heavy South Vietnamese troop presence in Cambodia and the "affront to my people which can be exploited by the enemy."[68] In Kompong Speu, popular anger at the powerlessness of the government catalyzed into active support of the opposition: "When the [South] Vietnamese troops

came, they stole chickens, pigs and furniture and they killed some people. When we took our complaints to the government, the government
was helpless to do anything. We were told that if we joined the liberation
forces, we could protect our people and our country."[69] It was reported
that that village alone generated at least a hundred new recruits.[70]

Echoes of History

South Vietnamese brutality became a battle cry for the Khmer Rouge.
More than the devastation that it engendered, it pricked the historical memory of loss and subjugation and breathed life into the nation's
deeply held anxieties about national survival. The brutality associated
with Vietnamese westward expansion and annexation is inscribed in
national chronicles and encoded in historical memory.[71] Of this history, Chandler wrote, "For the twenty years or so in the first half of the
nineteenth century, before the coming of the French, the Vietnamese
took over most of Cambodia. . . . The brutality of their rule has passed
into Cambodian folklore."[72] Khmer children grew up with the *kapub
tè ong* story, in which Khmer forced laborers, buried alive with their
heads used as pit stones to prop a teapot, and in their death throes, were
admonished not to "spill the master's tea!" (*kapub tè ong*).[73] This saying
became a signifier for the trauma of subjugation and lost sovereignty,
and like the lost provinces of Kampuchea Krom that are now part of
South Vietnam, a leitmotif in the mobilizing ideology of successive post-
independence regimes in Phnom Penh.

French colonialism added new layers to this vexed history. The
growth of Vietnamese and Chinese settler communities during the
protectorate exacerbated Khmer anxieties and interethnic tension.
Of the French attitude regarding Vietnamese immigration, Osborne
wrote, "If the French no longer spoke of 'Vietnamizing' Cambodia, as
Champeaux had in 1889, they nevertheless did not look with disfavor
on the seepage of Vietnamese into Cambodia."[74] In 1908, Vietnamese
numbered over sixty thousand in a population of less than one million.[75] By the 1930s, they accounted for about 10 percent of the population, totaling some 250,000,[76] concentrating in the urban centers. With
ethnic Khmers accounting for only about one-third to one-half of the
population,[77] the capital was demarcated into three informal but dis-

tinct residential zones—the Vietnamese and the Chams to the north, especially along the riverbanks, the Chinese and the French in the commercial center and around Wat Phnom, and the Cambodians to the south and west of the royal palace.[78] The spatial demarcation reinforced the social distance, which was inflected with essentialist "othering," resentment, and distrust. Noting that Vietnamese and Khmers are "perhaps the most sharply contrasted neighbors in Southeast Asia,"[79] Chandler wrote,

> The Vietnamese, who keep themselves apart [from the Khmers], have different customs, and often make no secret of their contempt for Cambodian culture. The Vietnamese way of life, derived from that of the Chinese, . . . stresses their identity as a superior race of people, and the fact that the Khmer, like all outsiders, are "barbarians."[80]

Nayan Chanda also observed that "in many conversations with official and non-official Vietnamese, their feelings of superiority over the Khmers—in political education, organization, and leadership ability—can be clearly sensed. When charitable, the Vietnamese tend to view the Khmers as children."[81] Many Khmers, in turn, claim moral superiority in their Buddhist piety (*klach bon, klach barb*), which they contrast with Vietnamese caprice and "lack of compassion,"[82] as captured in the familiar saying *Khmer men chaul kboun, youn men chaul puth* (Khmers never abandon the tenets, the Vietnamese never abandon their caprice).[83] As Chatterjee notes in the case of British India, where the material domain has been usurped, colonized, and monopolized, the spiritual domain becomes a nationalist countervail to domination, a domain where the subjugated could still claim superiority.[84] With differences often described in terms of "essence" (*khos thheat khnear*), hence unalterable, exit was a common response. Land scarcity that compelled their westward migration brought Vietnamese settlers into direct conflict with Cambodian peasants, often resulting in the displacement of the latter. Virginia Thompson's observation in the 1930s that "the Khmers prefer to move away, even in their own country, rather than to share a village with immigrant Annamites,"[85] remained salient decades later. A native of Svay Rieng recalled that "when the Vietnamese settlers move into the area, the Khmers would simply relocate." It was a process that some perceived as the progressive annexation once termed by a Vietnamese general as "slowly eating the silk worm."[86]

Numbers and concentration alone did not fully account for the anxiety posed by immigration. The colonial structure of privilege rested on racial and ethnic hierarchies in which foreign settlers, both European and Asian, were extended certain protection, rights, and entitlement not available to natives, including extraterritoriality and exemption from the dreaded *corvée*.[87] A French policy enacted in 1881 made it possible for Vietnamese in Cambodia to register for an identity card that listed them as French subjects and entitled to French protection, hence immune to local laws.[88] A farmer from Peam Chor recalled that during the protectorate, "many Vietnamese sneaked in to live and farm the land because they had the support of the French. At that time there were more Vietnamese than Cambodians in the region, so the Cambodians moved out and settled near Neak Loeung."[89] Moreover, given the symbiotic relationship between church and empire, the protection and patronage extended by French missionaries to Vietnamese immigrants, many of whom were Catholic, further shored up the system of privilege inaccessible to the Khmers, who were largely Buddhist.

Within this racialized hierarchy, ethnic Khmers became marginalized in their own country. Except for a small coterie of nobles who were part of the royal administration, they were impeded in their social and economic advancement by structural barriers and institutional racism. With a small handful of French at the pinnacle of the power structure and Vietnamese and Chinese settlers dominating the middle and lower tiers of the bureaucracy and key economic sectors such as the rice, pepper, and fishing industries, the oppressive features of the colonial system that an average Khmer would encounter—the bureaucracy, the courts, the shopkeepers, mill owners, and moneylenders—came to acquire foreign features.[90] This was to inform the Khmer Rouge vision of revolutionary change after independence.

The French exit from Cambodia in 1953 paved the way for the introduction of new bases for determining legal status and rights through the legislating of nationality and citizenship laws. Many Vietnamese settlers without proof of legal residence resorted to the illegal purchase of Lang Tay identification cards, while some had to move off the land they had illegally occupied with colonial protection. Nuon recalled instances of violent altercations that occurred in his village:

> Some Vietnamese who were illegal residents did not want to give back the farms to the Cambodians. Some who did agree to give back the farms did not want the new owners to keep the farm products they grew. . . . Occasionally, conflicts escalated into death because the Cambodian people had to use force to get their land back. My father . . . paid a great deal of money to own his land and was not able to grow any crops on it, since there were five Vietnamese houses located there. When my father did try to grow things, sugar cane, corn, bananas, vegetables, etc., the Vietnamese residents tried to destroy all the production.[91]

In the months following independence, the threat of communal violence was such that the Cambodian government had to deploy troops into conflict areas to guarantee the safety of displaced Khmer villagers seeking to return to their native provinces. These episodic sparks forecasted the tension that was to resurface in the decades to follow. They provided the historical backdrop for understanding not only the role that nationalism played in the mobilization of the 1970s but also the virulent antipathy of the Khmer Rouge toward Vietnam, and everything and everyone associated with it.

In Search of the God-King: Traditional Authority, Political Culture, and Revolutionary Mobilization

Like many conflicts, the war of 1970–1975 was as much a political contest as it was a military one, which underscores the importance of situating revolutionary mobilization not only in the context of structural instabilities, but also in the context of the political culture and belief system that shape and inform the ways individuals perceive, interpret, and respond to their objective conditions. For the masses to be moved toward active political participation, they need to be not only alienated *from* a system but also drawn *toward* the alternative. Amidst war-engendered dislocations and anomie, some looked for an escape in a "fantasy of salvation,"[92] as Cohn puts it. In Cambodia the communists, both Vietnamese and

Cambodian, not only worked actively to undermine the Republican regime but to strengthen their own legitimacy by tapping into traditional sources of authority, namely, the monarchy and Buddhism. It is one of the many ironies of Cambodia's political history that the movement that was to later reveal itself to be the most radical in its rejection of traditionalism owed so much of its mobilization success to those paramount symbols of conservatism.

Of revolutionary dynamics in Cambodia, Serge Thion noted that it is precisely this interplay between traditionalist and communist forces that marked its particularity.[93] The decision of exiled Prince Sihanouk to form a united front with the communists anointed them with much-needed legitimacy. While many in Phnom Penh may have welcomed the demise of the monarchy, in the countryside, where the institution remained a powerful force, news of Sihanouk's overthrow was received with stunned disbelief, anxiety, and outright anger. In the weeks following the coup, violent demonstrations broke out in Kompong Cham, Takeo, and Kampot, where some officials, including one of Lon Nol's brothers, were brutally murdered, reportedly by pro-Sihanouk demonstrators. Though these instances were few, and many of the participants motivated as much by anger at government use of force as by loyalty to the prince, the moral outrage felt by many Cambodians attested to the persisting centrality of the monarchy in Cambodian society. To most Khmer peasants, kingship and nation were inseparable entities. As it was in ancient times, it is believed that "if the kingdom was to survive, the rains to fall, and the crops to yield in full measure, a king must reign and through his powers ensure that the realm was at one with the cosmic forces";[94] conversely, an unrighteous ruler could engender adverse consequences through his misconduct.[95] The quasi-divinity attributed to kingship is attested by the popular belief in the mystical power of the "Sangkum cloth," coarse cotton pieces dispensed by Prince Sihanouk during his *tournée* that soldiers were known to wear as amulets. A monarch's quasi-divine power is also believed to be incontestable by common people, or at least those with less meritorious power, less *bon*; those who seek to do so would only invite tragic consequences.[96] Many elderly Khmer refugees like Ta Pen regard the tragedies that befell the nation over the last forty years since the 1970 coup as *chanh vineas*, the fatal consequences of having challenged someone more powerful.[97]

Given the interconnectedness between earthly and spiritual realms, the political pulse of the nation-state is believed to reverberate in cosmological manifestations. As anxieties grew over the escalated conflict across the border in Vietnam, elders looked to the sky at the comet, the *pkay dos katuy*,[98] and pronounced that war was not afar. On the eve of the coup, Phnom Penh, the country's capital and politico-cosmological center, was enveloped in auguries. Sightings in the Tonle Sap of the mystical white crocodile (the country's mythic guardian), a medium delivering admonitions from the pillars of Preah Ang Dangkar in front of the royal palace, and the moon in red halo all forecasted turbulent days ahead. Upon news of the prince's overthrow, Phnom Penh was gripped by whispers seeping through the palace walls that the royal scabbard, a symbol of the nation's security and well-being, was found blackened with rust.[99] Sihanouk himself recounted several inauspicious incidents that he later read as ominous forebodings of his political demise.[100]

With the monarchy representing order and protection, Cambodians historically have sought refuge in royal paternalism during times of duress. The calamities of land disputes, taxation, and conscription that afflicted their lives could always be redressed through royal intervention. In one of the rare instances of mass uprising, thousands of Khmer peasants, strangled by colonial taxes and *corvée*, made their way to the capital to present their grievances to the king, and peacefully returned to their villages after receiving a royal audience.[101] This dyadic relationship between the king and his people—that is, between state and society—remained important in Khmer political culture. It was, in essence, the basis of the Sangkum "populist" ideology and of Sihanouk's popularity.

The abolition of the centuries-old monarchy in 1970 thus left many Cambodians feeling rudderless, and others with the customary trepidation muted by fatalistic resignation. Phoch, who described her personal sense of disorientation as that of "a child bereft of a father," explained, "Our people were like driftwood. First, we had Samdech. Then we ran to Lon Nol because of all the problems with the Prince. Then we discovered that we had even more trouble, and we were at a loss. We didn't know where to go." Khom, a village woman, noted, "For a small country like Cambodia to be without a king is like a house without a big, central pillar; the four corner stilts will bend and cave toward each other." It was a sentiment shared by Chuon Thy, a Khmer Rouge commander who joined the revolution "[mainly] to demand that Samdech Sihanouk come back and [retake] power" because "a country without a king would be in chaos."[102] The sense of reverence and longing is captured poignantly in the words of an elderly woman who, decades after the coup, continued to bemoan the absence of "Father Prince," saying, "Every time I look at the moon, I see Samdech's face." It was thus that during the war, many clung to the hope that the prince would return to prevent a bloodbath and restore peace. It was this enduring faith that accounted for the quick surrender in 1975 and that compelled many during the dark Khmer Rouge years to openly court death just to touch Sihanouk's hand on the rare occasions when he was allowed to tour the countryside. In one instance when the prince was rushed away by his Khmer Rouge guards, the people were seen kneeling down to touch the ground where he had stood.[103] However elusive hope may have been in the terror-filled abyss of Democratic Kampuchea, the vision of this quasi-divine presence was, for the doomed, the long-awaited sign of impending salvation.

Speaking of the "ideology of dissonance," Eric Hoffer saw the "hunger for faith" as an important instrument of revolutionary mobilization.[104] In Cambodia, the royal call to arms had historically been a major catalyst of internal uprising. Of those who joined the 1885 revolt, Osborne wrote, "They fought because the King ordered them to do so; they believed and obeyed."[105] This scenario was to replay itself in the war of 1970–1975. Villagers in Kompong Cham and Prey Veng recalled the communists playing Sihanouk's taped appeal from Beijing, in which he pleaded for the people not to forget "Euv" (Father) and urged that "if my beloved children wish to see Father, go to the jungle." As Nhem remembered, "Samdech had said that if you love your nation, and if you love your Father, you must rise up and join the maquis. So they [the villagers] went."[106] Yeay To, an elderly peasant woman from O Ngo, recalled how she and other villagers followed the communists into the forest in hope of *literally* finding Sihanouk, the "god-king": "The *youn thminh khmao* [Vietnamese with black teeth][107] came. There were also Khmers with them. They said they were *khmer rumdos* [Khmer liberators] and that they would take us to see Sihanouk. But when we went, we didn't see Sihanouk." In the political imagining of the average Khmer peasant, national politics, already abstract and distant, resonated of familiar themes from the Ramayana, of exiled princes forced to seek refuge in the forest and await the auspicious moment when they could battle their adversaries to recapture their rightful kingdoms.[108]

Especially in the early phase of the war, the monarchy was critical to the mobilization success of the united front, indispensable to the Vietnamese communists whose presence in Cambodia was politically volatile. To maintain the royalist facade, the communists adhered to the practice of wearing badges displaying Sihanouk's picture and representing themselves as the king's soldiers.[109] Sonn, a native of Peareang, also recalled the Vietnamese communists bringing in a large statue of the prince and forcing local teachers to sign a statement renouncing their loyalty to the Phnom Penh government.[110] In Doan Tri "at least four out of ten villagers, . . . those who loved Samdech," actively supported the front with food and medicine. Within two months of the coup, an estimated twelve thousand "Sihanoukists" had joined the movement.[111] Dudman, who was captured by the communists in 1970, noted that in almost all of the houses in which he was lodged, Sihanouk's picture adorned the altar alongside the statue of Buddha.[112] Tragically, it was also in the very name of "Samdech" that the Khmer Rouge induced the surrender of Republican forces. In Svay Sisophon, the communists held up a large portrait of Sihanouk when they entered the city in 1975, prompting the soldiers in the area who initially were determined to fight to the bitter end to lay down their arms, thinking that victory was to the king's men and not to the communists. It was also in the name of the prince that they summoned thousands of high-ranking officers and civil servants to their death. One refugee remembered, "They [the Khmer Rouge] told all the *neak thom* [high-ranking people] to dress up in their official uniforms, with all the insignias and ranks, because they were to go pay homage to Samdech. There was no way for them to hide their background. They were all taken and killed." At the killing grounds, individuals were told they had to be tied up for security reasons as they would be taken to meet the prince.[113] In Siemreap, survivors recalled seeing high-ranking officials in their court attire, being taken away in a *raa-mork*,[114] purportedly to receive Prince Sihanouk. They were never seen again.

The Power of the Robe:
Buddhism and Revolutionary Mobilization

Just as the Khmer Communist Party "had to cut its fingers to exploit Sih-anouk's political credit,"[115] they also capitalized upon another source of traditional authority—the Buddhist *sangha*. In a land where there were at least three thousand monasteries housing over a hundred thousand bonzes for less than three million people in the late 1940s, Buddhism, as Osborne pointed out, "no less than the King's symbolic position, was an essential aspect of the continuing sense of Cambodian national iden-tity that persisted throughout the colonial period."[116] With the myriad of religious activities cementing communal bonds, the Buddhist *wat*, customarily located at the center of the village, is, as Jean Delvert puts it, "the heart of rural life."[117] From birth to death, the existence of the majority of Khmers is interwoven with Buddhism, with each life passage marked by rituals and ceremonies. Irrespective of wealth or status, *bon* (merit) is the singular insurance of good rebirth. Ordination is the high-est form of merit-making, the noblest fulfillment of filial duties. The *bon* acquired is especially important for mothers, for women have no other venue for attaining this level of actualization.[118] Prince Sihanouk himself was ordained, and Pol Pot, under whose leadership thousands of bonzes perished, once served as a novice at the Wat Bottum Vaddey, patronized by Phnom Penh's aristocracy.

Because of the enduring importance of Buddhism, a monk occupies a special place in Khmer society, serving as a moral beacon, a living cultural depository and transmitter of knowledge. It is to monks that the people turn, not only for religious counsel, but also for personal ad-vice, conflict mediation, and the performance of rituals that fill a Bud-dhist life. Their moral authority stems not only from their religious training but also from their ascetic lives. It is thus that boys of humble background are often placed in the service of monks so that they could acquire not just food and shelter, but also academic and moral educa-tion, discipline and piety, essential qualities without which an individual would be considered *monus komraul buoun chrung*, "a person with four raw edges . . . rough and crude."[119] From this early monastic experience, a young Khmer boy is introduced into a network of social relations that bind him for the rest of his life. The loyalty of the pupil (*koan soeus* lok), which is how a temple boy is identified,[120] to his teacher (kru), is based on the fact that "even after leaving the monastery [the kru] will remain his guide and his friend, his counselor and sometimes even his confidant."[121] For this nurturance, he is bound to his mentor by a moral debt (kun) that can never be fully repaid. The loyalty that it extracts is an important element in Southeast Asian political culture, where, in most instances, affective ties between leaders and followers, rather than ideologies, influence political behavior.[122]

From the early dynastic struggles to the anticolonial uprisings, religious figures thus have been a mobilizing force in Cambodian history, at times in defense of traditionalism, at other times in pursuit of revolutionary change, and at other times still in the simultaneous quest for both.[123] With an embryonic intelligentsia and a restrained monarchy, anticolonial resistance was incubated within the protected sphere of the sangha, who regarded French initiatives, such as the romanization of the Khmer script, as undermining traditional institutions and authority.[124] With the Buddhist Institute acting as a galvanizing force and a political hub, popular mobilization was carried out through traditional networks. A former governor recalled how the nationalists solicited the cooperation of local achar (laymen with religious training) and monks, who were often called to preach to Khmer soldiers in the French army, to help secure their support in the event of an anticolonial uprising: "We appealed to their Khmer-ness. The monks would pass on the message and try to convince them. They [the soldiers] told us not to worry and that they would take care of the tanks if anything were to happen."[125] Immediately following independence, monks were instrumental in urging the surrender of insurgent forces to the royal government. Later, during the Samlaut uprising, the sangha was a force both in anti-regime mobilization and in the restoration of order, leading villagers into the forests during the conflict[126] as well as helping mediate the end to the peasant revolt.[127]

The importance of Buddhism and of the sangha was no less important during the war in 1970–1975.[128] Both sides sought to harness their moral authority: the Lon Nol regime portrayed the conflict as a holy war (chambang sasna) waged against the godless communist thmils, while the opposition, with its royalist façade, presented itself as defenders of Khmer culture and tradition. That the surrender on April 17, 1975, to the

Khmer Rouge was prefaced by an address to the nation from the Supreme Patriarch calling for peace, unity, and reconciliation attests to the enduring legitimacy and sanctity of the Buddhist institution. Tragically, the intercession of the *sangha* served only to reinforce popular belief and illusion in the possibility of a brokered peace and of a nonviolent transfer of power.

The moral authority of the religious teachers extended to secular educators. That Khmers consider ingratitude toward a teacher (*ot doeung kun kru*) one of the greatest sins (*barb*) speaks to the moral authority of educators and to the importance of loyalty to one's mentor. The traditional legitimacy bestowed on teachers, combined with the oratorical skills that many possess, makes them one of the most influential forces in Khmer society.[129] As noted earlier, the Left was also successful in penetrating the educational sector. Many senior Khmer Rouge, including Pol Pot and Son Sen, were former teachers. It was thus not surprising that many students who fled to the *maquis* were inspired to do so by their teachers. A young man from Baray, Kompong Thom, who joined in the protest described how following the overthrow of Sihanouk "many people were incited by monks and teachers from Phnom Penh." In Kompong Chhnang, unrest among students and teachers reached a level where the town had to be declared a state of insurgency.

It was from this reservoir of the committed and the compelled, of *ralliers* and captives, that the Khmer Rouge were able to expand their organization. The ability of the communists to tap into traditional sources of authority allowed them to effectively widen their base of support. Kuon Lumphuon, who spent nine months in the *maquis*, noted that only one out of the thirteen members of the Front's Bureau of Information was a farmer by occupation. As in other revolutionary instances, many who joined the movement were, like Pareto's intrinsic elites, underemployed professionals and urban intellectuals "of modest origins, sons of farmers or of small employees";[130] if educators, they were mostly mid-level teachers in private schools[131] or provincial *lycées*. Class and ideological differences were temporarily set aside, and more radical agendas not revealed until the Khmer Rouge had consolidated their control over the base areas. The strategy was effective. According to one FUNK defector, the Khmer Rouge was able to deceive the masses, of whom "nine out of ten, though living in Communist zones do not know that there's a

Communist Party of Cambodia [and] usually do not see the Party even when they are looking right at it."[132] Once control was firmly established and they no longer needed to hide behind the united front, however, the Khmer Rouge became bolder and more draconian in implementing their revolutionary programs. As they proceeded with revolutionizing the areas under their control, all that were considered "old dandruff" had to be ruthlessly shed. Royalist elements in the movement were progressively neutralized, and traditional and religious practices prohibited in some areas. These policies were to foreshadow the extremism that followed their victory in 1975, when the royal family was essentially placed under house arrest and monasteries were not only desecrated but, in many instances, transformed into human abattoirs.

A Portrait of the Enemy

In building their political base, the Khmer Rouge did more than tap into the cultural reservoirs or the basic human need for security. They also instilled hope. While exposing the Republic in its dependency, ineptitude, and corruption, they inculcated in the popular imagination a vision of change that appealed to the desire of the people for the return to a peaceful and ordered life and for a new, "clean" (*saat sa-om*) society. Though careful to avoid any mention of communism, they touted social justice and egalitarian principles, promises that were revolutionary in Cambodia's class-conscious society. While the Republic was mired in decadence, life in the *maquis* was austere. Provisions for the cadres consisted of rice "filled in tubes of cloth draped over his shoulders, and packets of salt sewn into the hem of his pants," and provisions for the leadership were "neither more plentiful nor of better quality than that of the people,"[133] their accommodations consisting of "some chairs and a hammock."[134] Manual labor (*polakam*) was compulsory for everyone regardless of rank. To the masses, accustomed to rigid hierarchy and gaping class disparity, the vision of this alternative social order, freed from an ossified social system in which the *neak ches doeung* (the wise and the knowledgeable) lived in a different, exclusive, untouchable, and alienating world from the common peasant, must have been unimaginably liberating. It promised the intoxicating possibility of change. In this regard, parallels can be drawn with the experience of Bengali peasants during the rebellion of 1937–1947, when the purposive disregard of ritual pollution by the communist movement's higher-caste organizers effectively created a social leveling that became the basis of their mobilization success. In Cambodia, Ith Sarin concluded that more than any theory about socialist revolution, the "sentiments of openness and friendliness" that Angkar was able to manifest toward the people was most effective in securing peasant support.[135]

At least during the mobilization phase, when winning popular hearts and minds was critical, conscious efforts were made to avoid alienating the populace. Ta Meas, an elderly man from Prey Chas in Battambang, described the Khmer Rouge who came to that impoverished fishing community as "very helpful," assisting the sick and the vulnerable, and not eating food "except when given," adding mournfully that "the Lon Nol soldiers ate my duck." Of the communist success, one Republican officer reflected, "There was nothing invincible about the Khmer Rouge. The only difference between us and them was discipline. Our troops shot at their own generals. On their side, theirs was the discipline of death." By presenting themselves as self-denying, pure, and incorruptible, the Khmer Rouge painted themselves as true nationalists (*neak sralanh cheat men*) who sacrificed their personal comfort and material well-being for the service of the nation. Though post-victory developments in Democratic Kampuchea were to later expose the fragility of these tenets, these imageries and representations constituted a powerful ideological weapon in the political war that was being waged.

The contrast with the Republic, drowning in incompetence, intransigence, and unchecked corruption, was stark. As the Khmer Rouge tightened their control over transport routes, prices for basic staples skyrocketed. The official pay, irregular for most soldiers, did not keep up with the spiraling inflation.[136] A bag of rice would have divested an average clerk of almost an entire paycheck, and depleted the average soldier of a month's salary.[137] With the practice of allowing families to accompany them to the front, soldiers were often more concerned with daily survival than with fighting.

The state of wartime economy fostered an environment in which the gray market thrived. Basic provisions such as sugar, garlic, and oil destined for neighborhood cooperatives often ended up on the black market. Weapons, equipment, and supplies destined for the troops as well as loot from overrun villages made their way to Phnom Penh markets. Bribery came to govern all aspects of life, as common a protocol as the *bonjour* (the handshake) by which it was known. Trash would not get picked up without added incentives; a house going up in flames would be left to burn while its hysterical owners negotiated the price with the firemen. During a riot in Kompong Chhnang, shopkeepers deterred vandalism by bribing the military to move their tanks in front of their shops.[138] In Kratie, Chinese businessmen were threatened with conscription until they agreed to pay a bribe. If corruption is that which "oils the system," the war in Cambodia had indeed created an oil spill.

More than the economic crises, it was the relative sense of deprivation engendered by war-generated extreme misfortune and opportunism that fueled popular alienation. Bolstered by foreign aid, the Khmer Republic was marked by a high degree of social mobility and flux, with new wealth and widened class disparity. Alongside mushrooming squatter camps, Phnom Penh brimmed with restaurants and luxury cars. By 1972, the capital was awash with unconcealed criticism of "how the generals ran the war from their Mercedes cars and restaurants, while the young people, civilians and soldiers, [were] dying each day."[139] General Sak Sutsakhan noted, "The progressive decline in morale among our soldiers . . . as contrasted with the enthusiasm they showed during the five years of fighting, was frightening."[140] A villager from Kompong Chhnang recounted the defection in his area:

> What was the use of staying in the army? What do you get from it? Nothing except the corpse! The thing that got people mad . . . was that when the wife went to collect the death compensation, she didn't get the money. Instead, she got violated. . . . That burned in their hearts.

Yet many fought on, not out of patriotism or loyalty to the government but out of a simple compulsion—fear for themselves, for their families, and for each other. In many instances, it was only the strength of these sentiments that sustained the ragtag bands of fledging adolescents and wide-eyed country boys rushing to their deaths, often with only cheap rubber flip-flops (*sbek choeung Chip Tong*). It was not the system that sustained them. The system was what had robbed them of the shoes right from their feet, sending them to frontline combat with only cal-lused soles. It was the system that had seen to it that the wounded could not be transported to the hospitals because fuel had been siphoned off the military trucks and sold on the black market, and it was the system that had promoted that cowering officer to their command. The system was indeed, as one former soldier puts it, absent of *manos sathor*, flayed of its humanity. Ultimately, it was that very system that turned those bleeding soles into callous souls.

As the war progressed, Phnom Penh increasingly became "an isolated city under military siege,"[141] submerged in lawlessness. Desperation bred deviancy. In restaurants and food stalls, government soldiers were known to order meals and then put a grenade on the table as "payment," at times appealing to the humanitarianism of the shopkeeper: "Uncle, just let us eat this one meal. Tomorrow we are going to our death." Amidst the deteriorating economy and eroding social order, alienation thickened over Phnom Penh, once the base of support for the Lon Nol regime.[142] With fraying loyalty of intellectuals and the youths who had been among the Republic's most ardent supporters, Phnom Penh's elite became increasingly fractured. By 1973, "the country's seams were vis-ibly tearing."[143] The power struggle among the elites on one hand, and the disillusionment, malaise, and overt anti-regime agitation among other segments of the population on the other plunged the Republic into "political and military asphyxiation."[144] As frustration and misery deepened, people began to reminisce about the Sihanouk days, when "at least there was peace." The Phnom Penh once inebriated with its new-found freedom from monarchical absolutism was nostalgic for its lost innocence. Nothing better attested to the popular desire for change than the way victorious Khmer Rouge soldiers were received upon their entry into the cities.

In his study of millenarian movements, Cohn argues that societal crisis engenders a collective need for solace and escape that a salva-tionist organization provides.[145] In Cambodia, the political turbulence that convulsed the country from 1970 to 1975 brought about more than physical destruction. It undermined many of the "signposts" by which a Khmer related to the social world. The abolishment of the monarchy, the politicization and polarization of the Buddhist community, and the fracturing of the nation by a conflict that rapidly degenerated into a fratricidal civil war engendered an anomic disruption to the Khmer social world, while war-compelled displacement produced social unraveling and the destabilization of critical norms and institutions. The uprooting of individuals and families from their villages eroded communal bonds, destabilized critical institutions, and weakened social accountability.

Where social institutions collapse, organizations emerge in the vacuum to provide the needed structure and order. In war-ravaged Cambodia, a movement such as the Khmer Rouge can and did offer, especially to the marginalized and the youths among whom they drew their most fanatical recruits, a new frame of reference and opportunities denied them under the entrenched classism, ageism, and nepotism of the ancien régime. Moreover, where faith and values have been undermined, force may be the singular language comprehensible to all—those who wield it and those who fear it. Hannah Arendt thus may be right in suggesting that the basis of loyalty is not so much the belief in the infallibility of the leaders but in the conviction that anybody who commands the instruments of violence with the superior methods of organization can be infallible. While insufficient to explain radicalization, these factors combined can account for gravitation toward a radical organization. When force becomes the governing logic, however, it produces a certain dynamic that, in the absence of internal restraints, leads the system to consume itself.

Just as there was nothing predetermined about the outbreak of revolution in Cambodia, so was there nothing predestined about the outcome. The victory achieved by the Khmer Rouge was as much a product of their strengths as of the weakness of the incumbent, for the war was as much political and psychological as it was military. Nationalism and communism, traditional norms and revolutionary ideals, all reinforced one another in powerful synergy. Ultimately, success and failure hinged in no small part upon political will and morale, for few things could not compensate for administrative paralysis, absence of genuine leadership, and loss of political will. Of the French Revolution, Simon Schama once noted that the parent of the revolution was incompetence rather than tyranny, but its offspring were dictatorship and extremism, and the results, blood and terror.[146] In Cambodia, the war was not launched by the Khmer Rouge, and it was not won by the Khmer Rouge. It was launched by the Vietnamese communists, and it was lost by an insipid Republic that capitulated under the weight of its own self-destructiveness. As the U.S. embassy had concluded, "FANK was out-thought, outmaneuvered, outfought, and out desired—in a word, outclassed—every step of the way."[147] The Republic was analogous to a diseased body that succumbed to death less from the virulence of the virus than from the weakening of the body politic. There was no need for Khmer Rouge conquest; Phnom Penh was like a ripened fruit, waiting to fall.

5

Instrumentality of Terror

Totalitarian communism can dispense neither with enemies
nor with utopia.
—Erich Goldhagen

From the storming of the Bastille to the Long March of the Chinese revolution, the power of conviction and invincibility of mass will are sacrosanct tenets of revolution. It was evident, however, that even prior to their victory the Khmer Rouge challenged many revolutionary principles, particularly in their disregard of popular support and substitution of fear for conviction. Democratic Kampuchea thus provokes an interrogation of the role of violence in societal transformation, and of the conditions that gave paramountcy to violence as a technology of governance. Writing about revolutions, Chalmers Johnson argued that rather than an "insensate rage of destruction,"[1] revolutionary violence is *purposive*, deployed strategically to effect societal change.[2] This intentionality, which Tucker argues distinguishes mobilization regimes from past autocracies,[3] sanctifies revolutionary violence with the moral righteousness that feeds its virulence. For revolutionary movements, the aim is not merely to redress inequities but to bring about a systemic overhaul from which a new society can emerge, hence to engender apocalyptic change rather than to simply modify the status quo. What is sought, then, is not just reform or accelerated development but the propelling of society toward a course that it would not naturally take. In the "frontal attack on traditionalism,"[4] violence is employed as a strategic technology of control and transformation.

Whereas most studies of mass atrocities focus on either the quest for utopias or the quest for purity as a catalyst for violence, what the Khmer Rouge sought was purity *and* utopia. In Democratic Kampuchea, extermination was not an end but the means to a greater end, which was the organic purity necessary for the realization of the utopian goals. As Angkar impressed upon the populace, the success of the revolution required only "one million of the *ang-kor daem*—the finest grains." Of those without political merits, "to keep [them] is no gain; to take [them] out is no loss" (*took ka men chaneng, yok chench kor men khhart*). As Rithy Panh reflects, "the revolution is pure; it wants nothing of people."[5] Given the totalistic change that is sought, the scope of destruction necessarily extends beyond specific forces and institutions to *all* threats to the regime, actual or potential. Consecrated by the "murderous arrogance . . . of a messianic zeal that parades itself as divine consciousness for the redress of history,"[6] as Wole Soyinka puts it, violence becomes the response to all obstacles, real or perceived, encountered in the chiliastic pursuits.

While state-sanctioned violence may be a feature of revolutionary regimes, not all revolutionary regimes are genocidal; few manifest the extremism of Democratic Kampuchea. As Leo Kuper states, "Revolution and war, though necessary conditions, . . . are only potentially genocidal, depending on many variables that influence the final result."[7] What were the conditions and confluence of forces that gave rise to the primacy of violence in Cambodia and that allowed it to acquire the genocidal dimension that it did? What intellectual rationale sanctified violence with the moral righteousness that not only justified its commission but, moreover, transformed it into an instrument for societal purification? Of the "sanctifying power of ideology," Ferrero wrote, "They did not spill all the blood because they believed in popular sovereignty as a religious truth; they tried to believe in popular sovereignty as a religious truth because their fears made them spill so much blood."[8] Democratic Kampuchea underscores the importance of looking not just at regime insecurity *or* at ideology as the singular catalyst of violence but rather at the interplay between structural *and* ideological factors in engendering the genocidal outcome. In essence, Khmer Rouge extremism emanated from the uncompromising determination of an organizationally challenged and ideologically unrooted regime, ushered to power by an unexpectedly speedy victory,[9] to impose its revolutionary vision upon a largely unreceptive populace. Already colossal, the challenges of postwar governance were magnified by the regime's unerring determination to bring about a revolution that was not only total but historically unprecedented in pace and scope.

It was thus the interplay and tensions between ideological imperatives and structural constraints, between "power and impotence,"[10] that made the process of revolutionizing Cambodian society even more costly in human lives. Framed against the Sorelian ethic of crisis, with "all the stress on purity and all the fear of contamination,"[11] both the Herculean drive and the setbacks spurred the spiral of violence: "What the Khmer Rouge sought was purity; what they obtained was emptiness."[12]

Of the Russian Revolution, Lenin once wrote, "Nowhere in the world is it easier to capture power and so hard to keep it."[13] In the way state power was seized, and in the strategies that were adopted to sustain it, the Khmer Rouge revolution draws parallels with the Bolshevik experience. In essence, what was attempted in Democratic Kampuchea from 1975 to 1979 was the making of a radical communist revolution without the necessary organizational and ideological base. At the time of their victory, Khmer Rouge forces reportedly numbered some seventy thousand, a ratio of approximately one Khmer Rouge cadre for every hundred civilians, the vast majority of whom were raw recruits of children barely in their teens, hastily inducted into the army in the face of high attrition.[14] A large number were subsequently deployed to deal with mounting problems at the border, leaving the zones and villages with "insufficient strength to grasp hold of all the cooperatives."[15] The resulting challenges in controlling (*chap kandab*) urban evacuees led to the proposal made at the 1976 Zone Assembly that the majority of the forces be retained at the cooperatives.[16]

If the regime was without sufficient security forces, it was also without a broad political base; one estimate placed political membership at the time of victory at fourteen thousand.[17] The Khmer Rouge not only had a limited foothold in rural Cambodia in the prewar years but also a deep distrust of the peasantry they purportedly championed, as reflected in the party's directive to "be like the people but don't let them lead you by the nose."[18] The challenges were especially acute for the small extremist faction led by Pol Pot, Ieng Sary, Nuon Chea, Son Sen, and Khieu Samphan, which came to dominate the Party Center and security apparatus. Despite their involvement with international communist parties,[19] most of the members could not be said to have had a deep understanding of Marxism or other socialist thought. Ta Mok once asserted, "When we talk about economic life, I have no theoretical ideology. . . . When we talk about life we talk about land and water. For the people, having these is having freedom and democracy."[20] However, unlike Ta Mok and those who came from the leadership of the Issarak movement, who were largely of rural background and remained in those communities, many in this small faction were part of the urban privileged.[21] Their grasp of Cambodia's socioeconomic conditions was limited and essentially flawed. Stephen Heder argues that Pol Pot and Nuon Chea were blinded to local realities in their insistence on applying a formulaic revolutionary template to Cambodia.[22] In a society where 80 percent of the population lived in rural communities, this intellectual disconnect and the inability of the organization to root itself politically and structurally amidst the peasantry was to have profound implications for Democratic Kampuchea's utopian vision and postwar governance.

Thus, though the political requisites may have been achieved with the seizure of state power in 1975, what Lenin termed "sufficient civilization" needed for immediate passage into socialism[23] was not present in Democratic Kampuchea. While the party relied almost solely upon political consciousness to bring about its communist utopia, it was clear that such consciousness was gravely lacking. The party would later acknowledge that "our system is already Socialist but its philosophy and consciousness are not yet clear,"[24] noting one year after victory that in the cooperatives "socialist revolution has not yet penetrated deeply" and "socialist consciousness and the collective relationship [are] . . . still inadequate."[25] Though it recognized the problem and the importance of rectifying it, the party provided no more concrete recommendation on how to effectively expand its political base than to propose the selection of potential candidates on the basis of their life histories, who "would then be summoned to study" and "would all produce new life histories," projecting that "from every hundred people, at least ten will be swift."[26] The party later acknowledged that these efforts were outright failures.[27] Similarly, while the need to raise political consciousness was emphasized, the issue of political education was addressed only in a cursory reference made to unspecified "short texts which can be studied."[28] In fact, as Chandler pointed out, the *Report of Activities of the Party Center* gave more attention to the collection of urine for fertilizer than to education.[29] In the limited form that did exist in Democratic Kampuchea, political education appeared to have been provided only to a select few. Even then, the study sessions conducted at the special camps for returning "intellectuals," some of which were led by Pol Pot and Ieng Sary, were more dedicated to self-criticism and the history of the Khmer communist struggle than to serious engagement with theories of socialism.[30] Rather than rehabilitated and integrated into the revolutionary fold, hundreds of returnees were subsequently killed. It was thus unlikely that the party's projection of 100 percent expansion of membership within two years, with "Party branches in [all] the collectives,"[31] could be realized.

Mao once contended that the peasantry may be capable of fueling *social* revolution, but not of making a *socialist* revolution. To assume otherwise and proceed accordingly, as Lenin also pointed out, would be tantamount to "building on sand."[32] It was this expedient need to co-opt other critical forces in society, especially in the initial stages of reform, that prompted the Chinese and Soviet leadership to make concessions to the interests of other social groups in the early phases of their revolutions. The Khmer Rouge, on the other hand, dispensed with the need for broad-based support, and looked instead to a small committed core (*snol*) of "at least six to eight firm people" in all zones[33] as the sole force needed for the success of their revolution. This stance fundamentally altered state-society relations in Democratic Kampuchea. Within this "diffuse hierarchical structure, . . . in which the top provided only vague and general guidelines,"[34] as Heder contends, power came to rest in the hands of "the chosen few" who wielded it with a great deal of subjectivity and impunity in the name of Angkar. Dogmatism enabled local cadres and leaders, many of whom were newly catapulted into positions of power and responsibility by their revolutionary credentials, to hide their intellectual or administrative shortcomings by claiming unquestioning adherence to the party line. Since Angkar's will could not always be comprehended and decisions made by the "higher-ups" (*neak khaang loeu*) never unreasoned, even seemingly irrational directives must be obeyed. Revolutionary discipline became a justification both for the subjective interpretation of policies by those with the latitude to decide, and for their mindless execution by those who followed, an effective insulator against accountability. Self-servingly, Pol Pot later attributed the "mistakes . . . both large and small . . . from top to bottom" committed under his regime to the fact that "base people, assuming state power for the first time . . . had little experience" and that "three years was too short a time [for them] to gain experience."[35]

The victory achieved in 1975, unexpected even by the movement's own leadership, in effect delivered state power into the hands of a small and vulnerable group. If the political base of the movement was narrow, that of the Pol Pot group was even more incipient. Though they had succeeded through political acumen, manipulation, the harnessed strengths of politically and militarily powerful allies, and sheer fortuitousness in dominating the Party Center, the Pol Potists had not consolidated their power base at the time of the power seizure in 1975. As Barnett observed, it was "in a minority, despite the fact that it controlled the leadership positions. The objective it set for itself was to try to secure the power it had won in such precarious circumstances."[36] As late as 1969, less than a year prior to the outbreak of war, the Khmer communist movement was so fragmented and dispersed that according to Pol Pot, "no zone could come directly to the aid of another. . . . Each area had to rely on itself."[37] This internal division remained at the time of victory, with differences and even tense confrontations evident among the Khmer Rouge groups even during the seizure of Phnom Penh.[38] According to Marie Martin, "At least until the end of 1975 the city remained divided into as many pieces as there were zones that the Khmer Rouge had created in the country. . . . For several months, each regional authority administered a part of Phnom Penh that it received in the country's division."[39] Molyda Szymusiak recounted an instance when a Khmer Rouge soldier from Prey Veng was fired upon when he tried to reenter the city.[40] Rochoeum Ton, a Khmer Rouge bodyguard, noted that in 1975 in Phnom Penh, senior Khmer Rouge all had their own "forces and people," and spoke of security concerns because of the "power struggles within zones after the liberation."[41] Because of distrust, zone secretaries were required to leave behind their weapons and bodyguards before entering the Central Committee area, S-71.[42] Whatever understanding may have been reached in the ensuing months was insufficient to consolidate power in the Party Center. Ta Mok, who controlled the Southwest, reportedly said that the only "'head' to whom he answers was his own."[43] Most of the local power bases were not neutralized until late 1976–1977, when the zone leadership and the networks were arrested and liquidated at Tuol Sleng. Despite efforts to eliminate them, the Khmer-Hanoi continued to retain key positions particularly in the Eastern Zone, which did not capitulate until 1978.

From this unconsolidated perch, the new leadership of Democratic Kampuchea had to not only confront the colossal challenges of postwar governance but to do so amidst threats, real and perceived, in multiple arenas that fanned the all-consuming preoccupation with regime survival. Despite the violent blow dealt to Republican forces, isolated units such as those of Prince Chantaraingsey continued to hold out in Cambodia's forests, while other resistance groups sprouted along the Thai-Cambodia border.[44] Within months of the Khmer Rouge seizure of power, a Cham rebellion erupted in Kompong Cham and was brought to an end only by the destruction of the insurgent villages. Following the uprising, Kos Phal (the island of abundance) came to be referred to by the Khmer Rouge as *kos phes* (the island of ashes), a harsh reminder of the regime's exacting retribution for dissent. As death and starvation escalated, reports of popular resistance, both small- and large-scale, also grew, developments that are largely unacknowledged in dominant narratives of Democratic Kampuchea.[45] In November 1975, base peasants and new evacuees in Prek Pdao village rose up in collective protest of their abject conditions and seized a weapons depot at Kohe in anticipation of a coordinated uprising in the Eastern Zone and in Kang Meas district that never materialized. They were brutally suppressed.[46] Protests erupted even in the "model" Southwest.[47] In his August 1976 report to the General Staff, Son Sen cited "enemy unrest" at Ang Prouch and other parts of the Southwest in which protestors "raised a white banner with the slogans 'Long Live Buddhism,' 'Long Live the White Khmer Front of Liberation From the Rice by the Can.'"[48] The expressed desire for rice and faith exposed individual and collective agency that constituted a threat to the regime. From these protests, some 160 people were arrested.

Perhaps even more disconcerting to the leadership was the threat that emanated from the party's inner sanctum. Though they were never successfully challenged in their policy decisions or dislodged from the helm, the Pol Potist leadership was not unopposed. Dissension over the nature, pace, and scope of reform was reportedly voiced within the party as early as 1971.[49] While he disagreed with the dichotomous categorization of the Khmer communists as being "pro-" and "anti-" Vietnam,

Heder posited that there were contending views on *how* to deal with Vietnam and how to proceed with the implementation of the revolutionary agenda.[50] Reservations about certain party decisions could also be culled from the Tuol Sleng confessions.[51] Saom Chea, a Southwest regional secretary, stated that "there were powerful contradictions within the ranks," and that "most of the leading cadres . . . were not in unity with the Party over its contents, because the new road of making socialist revolution that was being traveled was repressive, dogmatic and constricted the rights and freedoms of every human being."[52] Some, like Hou Yuon, who was liquidated in 1975, were said to have opposed extremist policies such as rapid collectivization and de-urbanization.[53] Others found the methods of executing those plans too draconian. Sao Phim, secretary of the Eastern Zone, appeared to have been especially concerned about mass starvation and purges of cadres while war with Vietnam was imminent,[54] and also objected to the regime's dogmatic stance, purportedly saying, "One little false move and it was [viewed as] an ideological, political or . . . moral error."[55] Another leading official of the Eastern Zone, Phuong, admitted to harboring similar concerns about the populace "losing all popular democratic rights and freedoms, [and that] all the cadre and state power are under the examination and surveillance of the Communist Party of Kampuchea at all times."[56] Among the rank and file, dissatisfaction was less ideological. Some were arrested for remarking that "making socialist revolution means eating rice gruel with bindweed, and when we reach communism, we'll be eating plain bindweed."[57] While dissenting opinions are not to be dismissed, it is also important to note that most of the opponents appeared to have broken rank only *after* they were at risk of being purged.[58] What these confessions do indicate, nonetheless, is that at least at the time of their arrest, these leaders *knew* of the situations on the ground and may even have been concerned about them.

In a few instances, intra-party dissent took the form of active opposition. Though not all instances can be substantiated, reports of attempted assassinations and coups against the leadership predated the victory in 1975 and persisted thereafter.[59] Relocatees to the North recalled heavy fighting erupting "soon after the fall of the country" and of seeing "a small plane circling above the village."[60] Of the protests and uprisings that seemed to mark all major anniversaries,[61] perhaps the most disconcerting to the Party Center was the attack led by Chan Chakrey that struck at the regime's seat of power.[62]

To a regime that saw dissent as externally instigated and foreign infiltration in "almost half" of the Standing Committee,[63] the threat presented by these domestic instabilities was accentuated by external uncertainties. With a stridently anticommunist government in Bangkok and Cambodian resistance units along the border to the west, a hostile Vietnam to the east with firm control over Laos, and uncertainty in China following Mao's death to the north, developments, both internal and external, could only have reinforced the sense of beleaguerment felt by the DK leadership. The state of siege thus legitimated the "state of exception"[64] that sanctified a new modality of killing in which no distinction was made between the external and the internal enemy.[65] The wave of arrests and executions, mostly under the charge of treason, that first convulsed the Northeast in late 1976 spread not only to other zones[66] but also to segments of the population heretofore spared in earlier purges.

Terror and the Disciplining of the Nation

It is against this political montage that the atmospherics of terror in Democratic Kampuchea must be understood. The regime of terror, in essence, emerged from the conflagration of organizational challenges, internecine struggle, regime paranoia, and, as will be discussed subsequently, ideological dogmatism. Driven by the dual imperatives of consolidating power and making total revolution that were deemed essential for the survival of the party and the utopian order that they strove to establish, but confronted with grave organizational and ideological shortcomings, the regime relied on force as an instrument of governmentality. If the populace could not be moved by conviction to pursue utopian goals, they would be compelled to do so by violence and terror.

News footage of masses of humanity being herded out of Phnom Penh presented the first and most graphic visual of the regime's extremist features. The official and long-adhered-to explanations focused on urban evacuation as a "temporary" measure to protect people from either American bombing or food shortage. Ieng Sary, DK foreign minister, contended,

We had estimated the population of Phnom-Penh at two million, but we found almost three million when we entered it. The Americans had been bringing thirty to forty thousand tons of food into Phnom-Penh daily. We had no means of transporting such quantities of supplies to the capital. So the population had to go where the food was.[67]

While the food condition in the capital was a serious concern, the scale, scope, and above all the nature of the rustication process belied the soundness of the regime's explanations. For one, food insecurity could not account for the displacement of people in rural communities or in provinces such as Battambang, where the food condition was not serious. Moreover, in some base areas, villagers were moved, almost pro forma, a mere short distance from their homes, only to be put to work in the same fields that they had always cultivated.[68] Finally, the regime's professed concern for the welfare of the people was inconsistent with the inhumane manner with which the evacuation was carried out, during which, according to one estimate, twenty thousand lives were lost.[69] In some sections of Phnom Penh, this process was deliberately brutal; elsewhere, it was characterized by a malevolent disregard for human lives that could only have stemmed from the presumption of their dispensability. The abruptness, brutality, and deception with which the order was largely carried out denied the possibility for preparation that could have saved lives. The Khmer Rouge not only emphasized the temporariness of the evacuation but also insisted that urban residents leave everything behind, since "Angkar would provide" for them. This virtually guaranteed the high levels of immiseration and death that ensued. Many of the starvation-related deaths in the new settlements, in fact, occurred between the time of relocation and the first harvest. Like the relocation, the process of resettling evacuees into new communities was also incongruent with the rationale proffered by the regime. If productive labor was in fact needed in the countryside, as the leadership had maintained, necessary measures should have been taken to ensure the welfare of these valuable human resources. Instead, insufficient planning and coordination left many evacuees without the means for basic survival and in conditions that virtually ensured a high death rate.

Contrary to the rationale proffered by the regime, the systematic nature and nationwide scope of the population transfer point to more overriding strategic and ideological imperatives, driven largely by the security concerns of a leadership acutely aware of the precariousness of their situation. Given their fear of counterrevolutionary activities[70] and resistance, emptying the country's urban centers was a preemptive move to neutralize what the regime perceived to be "entrenched, organized, and well armed" vestigial opposition, tantamount to digging "the trunks out by the roots."[71] The same security logic extended to the elimination of markets. As Nuon Chea reportedly contended, "If the market existed, internal enemies would exist. Only the evacuation of people from the markets to the base could help [us] find the internal enemies."[72] As such, rather than an ad hoc decision prompted by unforeseen exigencies, the emptying of cities was a deliberate, pre-planned strategy to secure control,[73] a decision that the Khmer Rouge later acknowledged was made prior to victory and spurred in large part by the "success" of earlier evacuations, because "we knew our strength was not strong enough to defend the revolutionary regime initiative in our hands."[74] Bizot contends that the plan was laid out as early as 1970 in a Khmer Rouge document that "foreshadowed the horror: already there was mention of the evacuation of the towns and the establishment of a state-controlled collectivism based on a reduced population. But these warnings, duly relayed to Paris, had fallen on deaf ears."[75] It was clear from party statements that the regime never intended for the residents to return to the cities.[76] The population shuffles, which the party considered to be "one of the important factors (for our success),"[77] did in fact have a neutralizing effect. Surviving Republican soldiers confirmed that even with access to buried weapons, population dispersal made coordinated uprisings virtually impossible.[78] Moreover, the manner in which the evacuation was carried out delivered a shock that disoriented the populace and effectively undermined the prospect of organized resistance. Compounding the effects of mass relocation, the process of resettlement further contributed to the violence as local authorities had to manage, with little forewarning, preparation, and experience, the influx of new and presumably hostile relocatees (e.g., as many as 1.5 million in the Northwest[79]) into their administrative areas. Faced with this colossal undertaking, the leadership could rely neither on available forces nor on broad-based legitimacy to ensure compliance and order. Terror presented itself as the most efficacious technology in the neutralization of all that the leadership regarded as a threat, actual or potential.

As challenges and setbacks increased, they breathed life into the figure of the "enemy"—ubiquitous, masked, burrowing into the body politic—fueling what Jacques Sémelin terms an *imaginaire* of fear that set in motion the terror campaign. With echoes of Lenin, Nuon Chea noted, "We worry most of all about the enemy inside."[80] As the regime strove to achieve the organizational purity that it perceived to be the basis of its strength by "distilling out" (*samret samrang*) ideological impurities, the definition of the "enemy" became progressively elastic in the party's "hyperinflated imaginings"[81] to include not only those accused of transgression but also those implicated by association. Whereas previously, violence was propagated in the name of "class struggle," widening purges came to ensnare not only supposed class enemies, but also infectious class "carriers," not just the bourgeoisie but "bourgeois tendencies."[82] Ultimately, nonconformity itself was treason, as any expression of critical thought was regarded as subversive. In the same vein, distrust of Vietnam translated into distrust of Cambodian communists who were, or were perceived to be, associated with Vietnam. The term *kbal youn, kluoun khmer* (Vietnamese head, Khmer body) connotes not only the corruption of the physical body but its infectious effect on the body politic.

The institutionalization of "permanent revolution"[83] and concomitant march of terror followed in tandem, implicating first the upper stratum of the party apparatus, then the rank-and-file cadres and base peasants. In 1976 alone, some 2,250 of the movement's adherents were detained and killed at Tuol Sleng. As with the Stalinist terror campaign, the concentric circles of purge grew simultaneously wider in scope and narrower in targets, tightening onto the inner sanctum of the movement. By 1978, five of the thirteen members of Pol Pot's cabinet had been eliminated,[84] and all the zone leaders (except Ta Mok) and virtually all Central Committee members had been killed, arrested, or put under suspicion.[85] By the collapse of the regime in 1979, Tuol Sleng prisoner lists reflected arrests from virtually every zone, every ministry, and every unit in the country. The fire of revolutionary retribution knew no bounds, ultimately becoming self-consuming. As Chhouk Rin, a Khmer Rouge commander, reflected, "My leader was like a hungry tiger. If there was no food, that tiger might eat his subordinates."[86]

In the effort to combat unseen enemies, national defense was made to rest on "high revolutionary vigilance and [the] maintenance of secrecy in every field."[87] As in many totalitarian states, a well-honed and extensive network of informants (*chlop*) buttressed the system of control in Democratic Kampuchea. Comprising mostly children and young adults simultaneously invested with tremendous power and shielded from accountability by the omnipotence and anonymity of Angkar, the *chlop* became the executor of its quasi-divine will. The very existence of this clandestine force that was at once embedded and ubiquitous, panoptic and unseen, added yet another facet to the architecture of terror, enabling the regime to extend its punitive reach and compensate for its organizational limitations. The regime's motto, "Angkar has eyes like pineapples," allowed the regime to veil itself with the illusion of omnipresence. As a surviving refugee explained, "You may see only one or two of them in the village but you don't really know how many more could be hiding nearby. We could not see them, but they appeared when they needed to take people away." Another recalled,

> Sometimes, you couldn't see them but when you go into the bushes at night, you could almost step on them. It happened to me once. I almost ran into them. I was terrified. I said to myself, "That's the *kser tream* [patrol network]!" and I started to shiver all over. You don't see them but you can see the small light at the tip of their charoots. You know they are there.[88]

Violence and clandestinity were mutually reinforcing, contributing to and relying upon the erosion of accountability. Angkar's gaze was not only all-watchful but, like the legend of Akineth,[89] fierily destructive. Comparing state deployment of terror in Germany and the Soviet Union, Maier contends that whereas "the principle of German terror . . . was to enforce an iron law of predictable consequences, . . . the principle of Soviet terror was to enforce the arbitrary discipline of nonpredictability."[90] In Democratic Kampuchea, the saying *Angkar samlab men del prab* (Angkar kills without explanations) captured the sense of the impunity and arbitrariness of Khmer Rouge violence that amplified its disciplinary power. In fundamental ways, terror reaches its optimal effectiveness when its stochastic appearance belies the fact that it is actually highly discriminate.[91] In that sense, even that which Primo Levi termed "futile violence" has a "delirious rationality," as Jacques Sémelin[92] puts it, if the ultimate objective was to paralyze and discipline.

Terror, with its power to disorient and atomize, became a highly reliable technology of societal control. The fear, disorientation, and hopelessness that it engendered made it possible for the regime, despite its organizational challenges, to exercise an absolute hold over the populace. With disappearances and an informant system that subverted even the family, the unraveling of sociality reinforced the structural dislocations. In the "battle against counter revolutionary thoughts," solidarity was the first casualty, as "each person is a potential enemy, a traitor to crush."[93] As Duch put it, "Everyone, fearing for their lives, surveyed everyone else."[94] Fear and distrust assured "the automatic function of power," for "surveillance is permanent in its effects, even if it is discontinuous in its action."[95] Under its panoptic gaze, and subjected to what Foucault describes as "a state of conscious and permanent visibility,"[96] the individual came to feel that Angkar in its seeming omnipresence and omniscience knew not only their every physical movement, but their very thoughts. Ultimately, people were afraid not only to resist but to even *think* of resistance. In that sense, life in the death world of Democratic Kampuchea was even more "bare" in the Agambenian sense than in the gulag, which Solzhenitsyn described as one place "where one could think as one wished."[97] The effective disciplining of the individual, and of the nation, is achieved when the individual is transformed into "at once the persecuted and the persecutor, each censoring himself."[98] This, in essence, was the "perfection of power [that renders] its actual exercise unnecessary."[99] While it may be effective in coercing unquestioning compliance, terroristic violence exacts a grievous toll on the state and the society. Ultimately, echoing Arendt, "To substitute violence for power can bring victory, but the price is very high; for it is not only paid by the vanquished, it is also paid by the victor."[100]

Terror and Secular Salvation

It all starts with purity and ends with hate.
—Rithy Panh

Though structural factors accounted in large part for regime reliance on force, revolutionary violence in Democratic Kampuchea was not simply an expedient response to organizational challenge. It was also integral to the revolutionary quest for apocalyptic change. The Khmer Rouge revolution was not only about seizing power but also about ushering in a new era of independence and sovereignty, "unprecedented in 2000-year history of [the] country."[101] As with the French Revolution, "violence *was* the revolution."[102] Rather than merely a shroud over power interests, as Arendt contends, ideology identifies the inherent contradictions of the old order and proffers both a vision of an alternative and a blueprint for its realization. In so doing, it delineates not only the possibility of change but also the parameters of acceptable societal costs in the pursuit of noble ends. By channeling the mobilized passion of the masses to a "higher" purpose, ideology moves revolutions beyond the banality of power, providing an intellectual rationale and moral justification for sacrifices that otherwise would be unacceptable to the humanist conscience.

It is thus not sufficient in the study of regimes such as Democratic Kampuchea to focus solely on the features and narratives of atrocities, the functionality of violence as a technology of control, or the effects that violence has on the social system. It is important to also look at the ideas for which all sacrifices, including the dispensing of humanity, are worth making, *and* at the intellectual and objective environment that gave resonance to those ideas. In that sense, one must consider not only "the teleology of functions but also of purpose."[103] Whether the ultimate goal is development or a quantum leap toward a utopian society, once a set of ideas has been crystallized, it becomes a self-sustaining reality. Of the power of ideology, Henri Bergson wrote, "The strength of faith manifests itself not in moving mountains but in not seeing mountains to move."[104] Whether the faith is in the intrinsic goodness of man, the invincibility of popular will, or the infallibility of historical determinism, it is above all the ability of a movement to "kindle and fan an extravagant hope"[105] that makes for its mobilization success. Of the Khmer Rouge revolutionary vision, Bizot wrote, "The hope this utopia engenders has justified the bloodiest exterminations in history."[106] What vision of apocalyptic change stirred this utopian hope for "nationalist-revivalism," as Kiernan terms it, that was to be Pol Pot's Democratic Kampuchea? What life force did it draw from antiquarian inspiration and thwarted ideals? If Khmer Rouge desire to erase history and rebuild from "Year Zero"[107] is to be read as a response to long-frustrated aspirations, what were the historical experiences that could illuminate our understanding?

Nationalism and Khmer Political Imagining

Mao once wrote that "Marxism-Leninism has no beauty nor has it any mystical value. It is only extremely useful."[108] For Cambodia, as it was for many postcolonial states, the achievements and optimism of the post-independence period were tempered by frustrated development. To many postcolonial leaders, socialism, with its ability not only to stir the "malady of the soul"[109] but also to provide the instrument of insurrection, possesses a potency that is unmatched by other intellectual traditions. For a people colonized and subjugated, it was the notion that things that appear to lie beyond the realm of possibility can be manufactured right here on earth that is most intoxicating. As Foucault asserts, utopias afford consolation.

Equally important as the utopian hope that it engendered, socialism provided the developing world, especially nonaligned countries like Cambodia, the opportunity to turn their gaze away from the West as an intellectual referent. As Sihanouk later said, "We felt in a more or less confused fashion that it was an instrument for national development and a weapon against imperialism."[110] While they may desire modernization, many postcolonial regimes do not necessarily wish to uncritically replicate but to forge their own paths to development. As Pol Pot contended, "In order to be masters of our own destiny,"[111] Cambodians had to "maintain our national character, that is, without copying from abroad."[112] What they sought, in essence, was not only progress but also self-determination. Thus, from Sihanouk's "Buddhist Socialism" to Pol Pot's virulent communism, Cambodia's post-independence ideologies, not unlike those of many newly independent states of the 1960s, reflected the "Khmerization" of imported ideals.

While they may have sprung forth from a shared political wellspring, it was the extreme literalism with which the Khmer Rouge translated some of those ideals, and the totality of their prescription for change, that splintered them from the nationalists. It has been said that no single intellectual tradition spawned the ideological anomaly of the Khmer Rouge and that what prevailed in Democratic Kampuchea was a "unique alloy" minted from the extreme and literal application of "untried, romantic revolutionary schemes."[113] Even Pol Pot admitted that his political beliefs were shaped not by "any single influence, [but] maybe it's a little from here, a little from there,"[114] claiming that "I started as a nationalist and then patriot and then I read progressive books. Before that time, I never read *L'Humanité* [the French communist party newspaper]. It scared me."[115]

While inferences have been made about their Paris days and the intellectual debts to the French Communist Party (FCP), then the last bastion of Stalinism,[116] it is important not to overstate these early leanings.[117] As one prominent Cambodian progressive recalled, "Initially we were very Stalinist. . . . We turned towards China in the late 1950s because the Russians were playing the Sihanouk card and neglecting us. . . . When everyone began to criticize Stalin, we became Maoist."[118] In the same vein, Pol Pot's participation in a youth brigade in Yugoslavia, by his own admission, "wasn't influenced by any ideology, . . . [just] pleasure,"[119] and simply affordable. To delve into the early intellectual formation and writings of the Khmer Rouge leaders would reveal little of the radicalism of Democratic Kampuchea. For the most part, the political activities of the Khmer communists in France in the 1950s and 1960s, many of whom relied on government scholarships, were not exceedingly radical, amounting to little more than participation in Marxist discussion circles and production of anti-regime student bulletins.[120] That they did not present a serious threat was underscored by the fact that at least three of the leading intellectuals, Hou Yuon, Hu Nim, and Khieu Samphan, later rose to political prominence in Sihanouk's Sangkum government. According to Pol Pot, the source of his real political awakening was not the Parisian intellectual milieu, but rather "the actual situation in Cambodia" that he encountered upon his return from France.

Like their student activities, the ideals the Khmer Rouge leaders espoused then were not unique or radical. In the 1950s and 1960s, the neo-
Marxist concerns with the contradictions and inequities of the capitalist
world that threaded through Khieu Samphan and Hou Yuon's writings
resonated with many postcolonial leaders equally preoccupied with
chronic underdevelopment. To many of Cambodia's French-educated
progressives, the country's dependence upon foreign capital, goods,
markets, and expertise was the principal impediment to development.
The influx of foreign imports stymied the country's nascent industries,
while the outflow of capital and profit from essentially extractive and
exploitative foreign ventures left little in the form of local investment.
Echoing theorists such as Samir Amin, whom he cited in his doctoral
thesis, Khieu Samphan concluded, "Without the oppression and aggression of the imperialists, and old and new colonialists, Cambodia
would not have remained an underdeveloped agricultural country but
would have changed through a natural historical trend."[121] As such, for
national development to occur, without which genuine political self-
determination cannot be realized, economic self-sufficiency was imperative. For the extremists who came to dominate the leadership of
the Khmer Rouge, this could be realized only through total revolution.

Nationalism, Myth, and Ambivalence

Of the leadership of Democratic Kampuchea, Nayan Chanda stated,
"They may have read a lot of Marx, Lenin, and Mao, but the ideology
of the present Khmer leadership is virulent Khmer nationalism."[122] In
essence, what the Khmer Rouge did was to wed nationalist agendas with
a Leninist organizational structure, discipline, and militancy; hope was
tethered to historical determinism. Beneath the veneer of internationalist creeds, the reality was undeniably local. Both the aspirations and
the anxieties that they harbored had long genealogies. That is not to
say, however, that there was no aberration. To emphasize threads of
continuity is by no means to assert that the Khmer Rouge was simply
mirroring the past. In its militancy and extremism, Democratic Kampuchea bore no resemblance to any previous regimes in Phnom Penh;
what the Khmer Rouge sought to do was indeed radically revolutionary.
It is merely to argue for the importance of reading that chapter of Khmer

history, extraordinary and tragic as it was, as an interconnected albeit anomalous part of Cambodia's historical continuum, and as a postcolonial footnote of much wider implications for developing countries.

In the inspiration that they drew from the nation's glorious past and their emphasis on Khmer exceptionalism, the Khmer Rouge leadership amplified many of the nationalist underpinnings of preceding regimes. If the essence of nationhood lies in a rich heritage of memory, as Renan contends, then for the Khmer, Angkor memorializes and mythologizes Cambodia's imperial past. An eloquent testimony to the indigenous prowess that once took the nation to the zenith of civilization, it is held up as evidence of Khmer exceptionalism, an inspirational referent for the future. Rather than reflecting a loss of self-confidence, as has been posited, the ancient Khmers' attribution of this architectural feat to the works of *tevada* (celestial entities) can be read as a perception of themselves as a people "chosen" to be bestowed with this divine gift. Standing in disconcerting contrast to the diminished state to which modern-day Cambodia had been reduced, Angkor is Khmer sovereignty and greatness edified, its glory a leitmotif in Cambodian politico-cultural imagining. In quotidian discourse, self-identification as Khmer Angkor (Angkorian Khmer) is, for many Cambodians, a way of claiming indigeneity, racial and cultural purity, and a genealogy of greatness. Pol Pot himself sought claim to this political and cultural pedigree by adopting the pen name Khmer Daem (Original Khmer) during his Paris student days.

This "return" to the originary source and "authenticity," in essence, indexes the postcolonial struggle to reaffirm the self and the nation's identity against the corruptive grain of colonization and Westernization. Rather than a distant memory, Cambodia's memorialized past inspires nationalist imagining of what could still be if only the nation's latent potential could be unleashed. In so doing, it kindles revivalist nationalism.[123] It was thus that for Democratic Kampuchea, as for other preceding regimes, the inspiration for future salvation was made to rest in the nation's past. Despite the radical break from the past that it sought, the standard over Pol Pot's Democratic Kampuchea, as with all preceding and successive Cambodian regimes, flaunted not the apocalyptic severance of the past, but rather its exaltation.[124]

Like most salvationist regimes, there was an inherent paradox to the Khmer Rouge. In their forward-oriented vision, they were fundamentally inspired by antiquities. Pol Pot spoke of "this great power sleeping for centuries . . . [that's] now awakening and thriving,"[125] and echoed the sentiment of other Khmer leaders before him in his proclamation that "if our people were capable of building Angkor, they can do anything."[126] National development became imbued with a chiliastic sense of mission. In fundamental aspects, Democratic Kampuchea's work camps evoked the powerful imagery of mass mobilization upon which the whole structure and greatness of Angkor was founded. That the Khmer Rouge was inspired by the very oppressive features that it disparaged and demanded of its populace the same costly human toil that made such a feat possible was among many historical ironies.

Paradoxically, this backward gaze is compelled equally by pride in the nation's glorious past and by anxieties over its diminished present. At the core of Khmer sentimental nationalism is the frustration of a nation denied, constantly living with the memory of the distant past and the unrequited aspiration to reclaimed grandeur. Progressively dispossessed of its territories by Siam and Vietnam, Cambodia by the late 1800s was able to purchase a modicum of security only at extreme injury to its national pride, namely, by submitting to French rule. The price was paid with not only compromised sovereignty but also territorial dismemberment. To the Khmers, the loss of Kampuchea Krom, Cambodian provinces that are now part of Vietnam, stands as a reminder of the country's geopolitical vulnerability and the external powers' disregard of Cambodia's interests. The memory of humiliation and loss bore heavily on Cambodia's postcolonial regimes. That older-generation Cambodians continue to refer to Saigon by its Khmer name, Prey Nokor, is a linguistic resistance to the forced territorial divestiture, and an unyielding claim over the lost provinces. Unresolved border disputes with both Vietnam and Thailand that intermittently erupted in the post-independence period did much to keep historical anxieties alive. Sihanouk's sentiments that Cambodia's neighbors only "wish to see our glorious Khmer nation disappear forever"[127] resonated with many Cambodian leaders, including the leadership of Democratic Kampuchea.

The inability to reconcile a glorious past with a diminished present accounts in large part for the deep-seated ambivalence about the nation, and for the national egoism and complex that constitute the Janus face of Cambodian political culture. The interplay of excessive pride and insecurity is most pronounced in foreign policy; in the 1950s and 1960s, diplomatic relations were often strained by offenses that Prince Sihanouk perceived as having been directed at his person, hence at Cambodia, which he described as "very small and very weak, but . . . an organized state well ahead of the greater part of the countries of Europe, let alone the young United States of America."[128] The nation's "moral and social superiority"[129] thus was made to compensate for its territorial and political insignificance. Cambodia's nonalignment, for instance, was presented not as a constrained choice but as a Lilliputian defiance of the Manichean logic of the Cold War, delivered "with the courage and energy disproportionate to our size,"[130] to be held up as an example to other nations.[131]

Though they took them to illogical and suicidal extremes, the Khmer Rouge leadership inherited both the nation's hopes and fears. The leitmotif of excessive pride and insecurity, especially the deep-seated anxieties about Vietnam's intentions harbored by previous regimes in Phnom Penh, reverberated in Democratic Kampuchea. The distrust was amplified by the movement's own political experiences. As it was with Vietnam's relations with China, domination and resentment, condescension and distrust characterized the relationship between the Cambodian and Vietnamese communists in which self-interests often trumped internationalist solidarity.[132] The quid pro quo between Hanoi and the Sihanoukist government, maintained throughout the 1960s at the expense of the Khmer Rouge, and the pressure put on the latter to subordinate their struggles to the war in Vietnam were some of the thorny issues that reinforced the acrimony between the two communist movements. Even when the Khmer Rouge was still in their nascent state and their dependency on Vietnamese patronage acute, the party declared that Vietnam should be treated "as a friend, but a friend in conflict."[133] These textured local realities, nuances, and contradictions are often lost beneath the more overriding preoccupation with the East-West conflict, or within the monolithic categories of ideology and race. It took the eruption of the Third Indochina War between China and Vietnam to expose the fissures and the fragility of the "red brotherhood" in Southeast Asia.[134]

National Salvation and Totalistic Reform

Though these vexed histories provide a significant context for understanding Democratic Kampuchea, it is important to recognize that national humiliation, loss, and ethno-racial divisions, which factored centrally in early theorizing about political violence,[135] are insufficient to explain genocidal developments in Cambodia. Without discounting the fact that many ethnic minorities, particularly Vietnamese and Cham,[136] did suffer colossal, even disproportionate, losses, a race-based reductionist analysis cannot account for Democratic Kampuchea's close relations with China and corresponding treatment of Sino-Cambodians that, though by no means tempered, was generally not as virulent as that of ethnic Vietnamese. Similarly, while many Cham were brutally persecuted, some occupied key positions in Democratic Kampuchea and were also implicated in the regime's repressive campaigns.[137] Above all, to focus centrally on race as the primary factor for the genocidal policies of the Khmer Rouge[138] would be to ignore the fact that the majority of the victims were ethnic Khmer.

Though not a catalyst, these historicized experiences, social distancing, and "othering" of differences can serve as an important frame for understanding the appeal and resonance of a virulent, chauvinistic, and restorative ideology. They also illuminate the emergence of the state of siege and the figure of the "enemy"—masked, chimeric, subversively usurping the body politic—that fueled the regime of terror in the name of progress and self-determination. Given the history of colonization, subordination, and loss, the Khmer Rouge saw national revivalism as possible only with genuine self-determination. This, in turn, rested on achieving self-sufficiency that could only come from accelerated and total reforms. Rather than being anti-industrial and anti-modern, as is often assumed, the Khmer Rouge saw industrialization as dependent on the fruits of agriculture,[139] noting, "If we have rice, we can have everything."[140] The necessary doubling, and even tripling, of rice production, in turn, rested on the ability to acquire "mastery over water at all times."[141] Like Angkor, Pol Pot's Kampuchea was to become an advanced society, sustained by a hydraulic complex. A former child soldier recalled how Khmer Rouge cadres would entice villagers with visions of a bucolic and prosperous country, crisscrossed by canals, particularly seductive to that segment of the population that had never known the world beyond their natal villages: "They used to tell us that these hardships won't last forever, that in the future, Cambodians, old and young, can enjoy ourselves, traveling by motorized boats anywhere and everywhere. When you think about it, it sounded so nice. . . . [People will be] so happy."

For Democratic Kampuchea to achieve these lofty goals, Cambodian society had to be reordered and forces of production reorganized for optimal efficiency. According to Khieu Samphan, Pol Pot saw the continuation of wartime economy, particularly the establishment of high-level cooperatives, as key to ensuring postwar food security.[142] This was especially critical given the loss of the massive international aid that had previously shored up the Khmer Republic, and the resurgent conflict with Vietnam. To address these exigencies, the whole country was transformed into a vast labor camp, with the entire population mobilized to toil on collectivized fields.

Wholesale rustication was not just strategic but also integral to the utopian ideology. For the Khmer communists, the schisms and inequalities in prewar Cambodia existed not only between classes but also between town and country. Cambodia's socioeconomic development had been urban-centric and uneven, with the outlying areas largely neglected despite their economic importance. The power asymmetry and underlying resentment echo in the Khmer saying "The fruit is grown in the country but is eaten in the city." During the colonial period, this schism was accentuated by preponderant settler presence in the capital, where Vietnamese accounted for 62 percent of the total urban population in 1921,[143] and by the transplanted aesthetics of the *métropole* inscribed onto Cambodia's urbanscape, with colonial ordinances legislating against the intrusion of the periphery.[144]

Post-independence Cambodia continued to manifest the imprints of its colonized history. With tree-lined boulevards, open-air cafés, and French-style villas, Phnom Penh was coloniality edified, its residents embodying Francophilic socialization reinforced through the French system of education and emulated lifestyles. To the colonial remains, the war of 1970–1975 introduced new forms of cultural taint and decadence. As American goods flowed into the local markets and American popular music beamed through military airwaves, Phnom Penh's wartime bourgeoisie, especially the city's youth, rushed to embrace the new creed. Reminiscent of Fanon, the Khmer Rouge leadership wrote, "We lost all sense of national soul and identity. We were completely enslaved by . . . the cultural and social ways and lifestyle and by the clothing and other behavioral patterns of imperialism, colonialism and the oppressor classes."[145]

It is thus that, to the Khmer Rouge, cities came to represent both class, racial, and cultural oppression. With a settler presence, foreign-dominated commerce, and market economy, they signified ethno-racial and capitalist exploitation and greed, cultural corruption, and coloniality. While Cambodia's cities became progressively divested of native traits, the denizens embodying the cultural and normative distancing of colonized subjects, the countryside remained steeped in tradition-honored agrarian lifeways. In their desire for reclaimed "authenticity," the Khmer Rouge saw the village as the locus of an idealized past, which accounted for the peasantist ideology that they embraced. The checkered scarves and blackened uniforms, the village vernacular, valorization of agrarianism, and privileging of poor peasants within the power structure all marked the return to the perceived seat of Khmer-ness. What emerged was a gaping disconnect between town and country, foreign and indigenous, privileged and disenfranchised that the Khmer Rouge sought to erase with punitive violence. The "us against them" attitude turned inward as the ideological disdain for the parasitic city transformed into animus, a fusion of hatred and envy, toward urbanites and all that they personified. Ping, a factory worker, recalled the vindictiveness of the base villagers when told of her deportation to the countryside: "They said they were going to send us to dig the soil . . . where the red ants would bite us, where our hands would blister and our knees would swell bigger than our heads because as *neak psar* we never had to do anything like that."[146]

If, as Zevedei Barbu contends, "communism is not simply an industrial revolution, but rather the total negation of Western civilization,"[147] then de-urbanization for the Khmer Rouge was not simply to disperse and neutralize potential threats but to erase vestiges of coloniality, and ultimately the very idea of cosmopolitanism. As a tainted colonial relic, the city was not just a security threat but a cultural and moral threat that was regarded as a security threat. The stoicism of some notwithstanding, to many peasant boy soldiers long deprived of material comfort, cities, that tantalizing world that only inhabited their imagination, were undoubtedly places of temptation. Ieng Sary spoke of the threat to revolutionary discipline and ideological purity posed by the social ills associated with urbanity,[148] citing an alleged conspiracy to subvert the revolution by corrupting the troops and "weaken[ing] their fighting spirit with girls, alcohol, and money."[149] That urban centers were not only evacuated but kept empty of the general population throughout the Khmer Rouge regime suggested that cities were regarded not only as corrupt but irredeemable: "People can be reformed, but not cities." De-urbanization, as an act of cultural purification, necessarily entailed not only depopulation but also a physical alteration of Cambodia's urban landscape. Upon their capture of Phnom Penh, the Khmer Rouge dynamited the national bank and the Catholic church, symbols of the subversive influence of capital, foreignness, and religion, and transformed Phnom Penh's once manicured parks and tree-lined sidewalks into lush vegetable gardens and banana groves. In the ultimate societal reordering in which, to borrow from Richard Rubenstein, "the fringe became the center,"[150] the reversal of the social order acquired a geopolitical and cosmological dimension as the center acquired features once associated with the "uncivilized periphery"—desolate, controlled by unseen forces mysterious and powerful, inaccessible, and feared.[151]

If cities were regarded as colonial constructs, urban residents by extension were embodied coloniality; the elimination of the former mandated the erasure of the latter. In Democratic Kampuchea, the definition of political undesirability thus came to be less about socioeconomic status than about geographic association. The regime's suspicion of the urban poor was encoded in the directive not to employ "people from the lower layers who have recently emerged from the cities."[152] This urban-rural binary, however, overlooked the fact that many of the city's residents were recent, war-displaced refugees from the countryside. For the Khmer Rouge, however, these exigencies mattered little, as flight was viewed as opportunism and treachery.

While urbanites in general were regarded as marred, the educated class in particular was deemed morally and politically suspect because of their French-style education, an ironic stance given that many high-ranking Khmer Rouge officials were themselves products of French education. With training "alien to the concrete conditions of the country," they were also considered irrelevant in the new society, where the emphasis was not on certification but on observable "truths."[153] With the customary Khmer wordplay, cadres often stressed that unlike "foreign countries [that] needed twenty years to train an engineer," what mattered in the new Kampuchea was not credentials—*sagnabat* (a homonym of "the lost sign")—but *sagna-khhoeugn* (visible sign), tangible practical knowledge acquired through labor and honed through political convictions.[154] This new knowledge form and approach to education were held up as "the model for the entire world."[155]

From the romanticization of rural life, exaltation of indigenous ways, renunciation of intellectualism, reliance upon militarized mass will, and self-reliance, the Khmer Rouge espoused many ideals and rhetoric that were also touted by other revolutionaries. In its fervor and militancy, Khmer Rouge language of mobilization harked back to China's Great Leap Forward and the Cultural Revolution: "Our male and female combatants . . . all are waging the offensive and thereby achieving the very spectacular victory . . . of the great leap forward."[156] Even the reference to the "great leap forward" (*moha lot ploah*) reflected Maoist lexicon. Chinese intellectual influence is hardly surprising, given its extensive support of the Khmer communists and the fact that many Khmer Rouge leaders had spent time in China during their revolutionary career. If nothing else, the importance of militancy and permanent struggle must have been impressed upon Pol Pot during his visit to China at the dawn of the Cultural Revolution.[157]

For the leadership of Democratic Kampuchea, as it was for Mao, the concept of "struggle" was wedded to the principle of change: "In growing rice, there are two battles. First, a battle with nature. Second, the battle with destructive enemies. . . . Raising crops is a technical struggle, [and] a class struggle, a struggle between revolution and no revolution."[158] To the Khmer Rouge, the victory in 1975 was not a political but a *military* feat, fought for and won through sheer determination. Given this wartime success, the same strategy and militant program of action were to be applied to postwar development. With the political arm of the party stunted, the military was the most organized institution and, with a monopoly over force, virtually the sole institution to step into the political vacuum created by the arrest, imprisonment, and liquidation of Republican elements. The military became a critical force in the building of the new communist utopia: "Our revolutionary army, whose clothes still smell of gunpowder, is launching a construction offensive with ardor and revolutionary optimism."[159] A wartime martial spirit, untempered in its zealous fervor, was applied to all tasks; all revolutionary objectives had to be met with assaults and offensives, and all impediments "crushed under the wheels of the revolution." Militancy marked not only the rhythm of work and life, but also death in Democratic Kampuchea, as combative revolutionary songs were beamed not only over the worksites but also the killing fields to mask the sound of executions.

In the pairing of Maoist ideals, Leninist discipline, and Stalinist methods, force and militancy became not only the organizing principles but the governing norms over a society that was no longer conceived of in terms of a peaceful, family-centered social system, but as one engaged in a constant state of war.[160] As Sigmund Neumann puts it, "The nation is seen as an army. Its life is a constant battle."[161] Calling for resoluteness and tenacity, the party warned that "the approaching class combat is sharp and lean, uncompromising, bitter, thorough, and life-and-death in form . . . and long into the distant future."[162] In effect, the regime was working at cross-purposes by attempting to whip up revolutionary fervor and institutionalize wartime mobilization while simultaneously and systematically depoliticizing and atomizing its populace. With striking similarity to the Soviet experience of the Great Terror, where the party insisted that "we must impose our will to victory on our exhausted and dispirited followers,"[163] the Khmer Rouge also failed to recognize that the Cambodian people, broken by war and paralyzed by terror, were empty vessels from which no additional sacrifice could be extracted. After five years of brutal, fratricidal war, it was peace, not permanent mobilization, that they desired.

While the articulated goals and principles of Democratic Kampuchea were not unique, the extremism, literalism, and unconscionable disregard for societal costs with which they were interpreted and implemented by the Pol Potists found little precedence. Whereas all newly independent states aspire to self-determination, Democratic Kampuchea's self-reliance amounted to virtual autarky, with the ultimate aim being to ensure not only economic independence but also impermeability to all corruptive external influence. Where other communist systems eliminated capitalism, Democratic Kampuchea abolished currency, markets, and all forms of privatization through communalization of life and property. Even though new bills had been printed,[164] currency was banned, a measure the regime proudly proclaimed as "unique in the world,"[165] because "money is a tool of dictatorship of the capitalist class,"[166] and, as Nuon Chea puts it, "the most important and powerful weapon of the enemy."[167] While the notion of cities as "the source and manifestation of most glaring inequality"[168] was espoused in revolutionary thoughts from Babeuf, to early Russian thinkers, to Mao, to Fanon, as was rustication held up as a prescription for reform, Khmer Rouge radical anti-urbanism was unprecedented. Where Mao extolled the countryside, it was to support the cities. The Khmer Rouge, on the other hand, essentially did away with urbanization, with cities kept vacated of all except for select personnel and a handful of foreign dignitaries. Whereas intellectuals were "sent down" to learn from the peasants in China, the Khmer Rouge worked systematically to eliminate the educated class, formal education, and, for the most part, much of learning except through labor. Nor was the definition of intellectuals in Maoist China so broadly interpreted that it became virtually synonymous with the literate. In Democratic Kampuchea, those sent to hard labor camps or summarily executed included not only students and teachers, but also individuals who were *assumed* to be educated. The Robespierrean "contempt for the genius" was so all-consuming that the wearing of spectacles could mean a death sentence.

The extremism of Democratic Kampuchea was manifested not only in the nature and scope but also in the pace of reform, as the Khmer Rouge was determined not only to achieve total revolution but to do so at a historically unprecedented speed. It was to be an apocalyptic achievement in the context of both Khmer and world history. As Ieng Sary proudly proclaimed, "The Khmer revolution has no precedence. What we are trying to do has never been done before in history."[169] Emboldened by an early victory, the regime sought to catapult the country from its incipient capitalist state to a classless communist society virtually overnight. Whereas in China, land reform took almost a decade to be fully implemented and collectivization not undertaken until close to two decades after power had been consolidated,[170] Democratic Kampuchea boldly proclaimed the goals of achieving full collectivization and food sufficiency within three years and a complete transition to modernized agriculture within ten to fifteen years. Less than two years after assuming power, and despite indications of serious misprojections and mass starvation, Phnom Penh proudly announced the export of "tens of thousands of tons of rice."[171] Compared to socialist Vietnam, where economic reforms were introduced incrementally, the Khmer Rouge reduced the nation's economic life to premodern bartering within months of their victory, proudly proclaiming that "there are no markets." Privatization was also dealt an immediate blow by mass relocation and collectivization of life and property. Just one year after coming to power, the party declared that "nothing at all is private in the entire society."[172] As Roeuth, a child survivor, recalled, his entire possessions during the Pol Pot years consisted of "a metal spoon tied around my neck, so that no one can steal it when I am asleep, a *krama* [traditional peasant scarf], and a change of tattered, blackened outfit." Ultimately, as Ong Thong pointed out, even parental love had to be renounced as proof of one's ability to relinquish one's "proprietary" hold over one's children.[173]

In part, this breakneck pace of reform was driven by strategic imperatives. For a regime that felt besieged by threats "both inside the country and coming from outside the country, especially in our revolutionary ranks and even in our Party,"[174] rapid and total reform was deemed essential to the survival of the nation: "Outside enemies are just waiting to crush us. Enemies of all kinds want to have small countries as their servants. So in order to prevent them from crushing us . . . we must strive to move fast."[175] In part, it reflected regime arrogance. Dismissing Zhou Enlai's admonition against reckless haste,[176] the party flaunted its ambitious "stage-leaping" and ability to produce "a socialist society straight away" as unique to Cambodia,[177] noting that China and Korea "didn't carry out a genuine Socialist revolution until 1958. They needed fourteen years to make the transition. . . . As for us, we have a different character from them. We are faster than they are."[178] "We are four to ten years ahead of them."[179] "There is a great difference between us and other countries."[180] The Khmer Rouge regarded the relative restraint of other communist regimes such as Vietnam, which they considered to be "neither a revolutionary nor a socialist" country,[181] as ideological frailty rather than prudence. Democratic Kampuchea was thus to serve as a model for other developing nations: "The world is looking at us. . . .

Our revolutionary movement is a new experience, and an important one in the whole world, because we don't perform like others."[182] For the first time in modern history, Cambodia could claim historical primacy: "The name of our country will be written in gold letters in world history as the first country that succeeded in communization without useless steps."[183] This prospect must have been intoxicating to the leadership.

Already recklessly ambitious, Democratic Kampuchea strove not only to achieve these utopian goals but moreover, to do so with uncompromising self-reliance. For Pol Pot, dependency was a moral affront and a source of vulnerability: "We must not permit other powerful states to decide the destiny of our nation, our people, our revolution. . . . Aid from abroad, even if healthy and unconditional . . . can never play a decisive role. . . . [We must] rely on our own forces and endure difficulties and suffering."[184] Citing the importance "of being masters of our destiny and to rely on our own strengths, and on our own resources,"[185] Democratic Kampuchea held up its wartime experience as an inspiration for post-victory sacrifice. Political memory was edited to eliminate debts to external patrons—namely, China and Vietnam—while the regime mythologized the supposed bare-handedness with which the movement battled its way to power: "We made a revolution . . . with empty hands";[186] "When we won the victory over the U.S. imperialists . . . this army had no planes, tanks or artillery pieces and was short of ammunition; however, our fight was crowned with success."[187]

For the Khmer Rouge, self-reliance was made to rest on national strengths drawn from the moral capital of being Khmer *and* communist. Of the country's ports, the leadership noted, "The political and ideological stand of our fraternal dockworkers . . . more than compensate for any lack of technical skills."[188] Faith in the nation's exceptionalism also shored up the "illusion of numbers" and sense of invincibility that emboldened Democratic Kampuchea to take on battle-hardened Vietnam, with the second-largest army in Asia. With the belief that "one Khmer equals thirty Vietnamese," the regime boasted that it would take "only 2 million troops to crush 50 million Vietnamese and we would still have 6 million people left."[189]

Stretched to its illogical extreme, Democratic Kampuchea's prideful insistence on self-reliance produced a virtual autarky. Foreign presence in Cambodia was limited to advisers and technical teams from a handful of socialist countries, namely, China, North Korea, and Romania.[190] Besides unregulated border bartering between Thai and Khmer Rouge forces, trade with the outside world was essentially confined to China, North Korea, and a few European countries.[191] The regime's isolationist stance was most extreme in its rejection of much-needed foreign assistance.[192] As thousands perished from endemic famine, Phnom Penh rejected a Canadian offer of wheat and, instead, announced its plans for rice exports. While an untold number died from lack of basic medical care, a planeload of French medical supplies on standby in Bangkok was denied permission to fly into the capital.[193] As malaria ravaged the population, especially urban relocatees, the government finally conceded to the purchase of DDT (some of which was used in mass graves) over a year and a half after population relocation had begun and many had already perished.[194] Finally, though in dire economic shambles, Democratic Kampuchea steadfastly refused to demand reparation from America,[195] contending that "we Cambodians believed that the blood freely shed by our people is priceless and should not be 'reimbursed' in dollars or other material indemnities. . . . We prefer to dress our wounds ourselves however serious they may be."[196] It was the same defiance and national pride that also spurred Sihanouk's rejection of American aid in 1963.

Self-deluding faith notwithstanding, the process of transforming Cambodia into a communist utopia was at best unrealistic and at worst suicidal. In addition to the reckless pace and unrealistic scope of reform, what contributed to the derailment of the Khmer Rouge revolution was the disconnect between political vision and objective conditions, and the primacy given to ideological and political concerns over pragmatic considerations. Ideology governed the way the Khmer Rouge construed reality; the blueprint that was worked out in theoretical abstraction reflected little of Cambodia's socioeconomic conditions. Key policies such as radical land reform essentially were based on erroneous premises. Though the party identified class struggle between peasants and landlords as the one "overwhelming, dominant" contradiction in Cambodian society[197] that the peasantry decided "to resolve through revolutionary violence,"[198] class antagonism in prewar rural Cambodia was not sufficiently intense as to produce the totalistic revolution that the regime sought to bring about. As noted earlier, the gravest rural affliction was usury rather than the "feudal landlord class" denounced by the Khmer Rouge.[199] To fuel revolutionary fervor, the regime worked to "arouse the peasants so that they . . . burned with class hatred."[200] What resulted was a virulent class struggle that did *not* emerge naturally from societal contradictions but instead was systematically and violently induced by the Party Center to "reveal those contradictions."[201]

Dogma also subverted the rational formulation and execution of policies and blinded the leadership to practical concerns. Contrary to assertions made by some Western scholars,[202] Democratic Kampuchea had no sound analysis and virtually no concrete plans for realizing its utopian vision. Many policy initiatives were recklessly pursued in virtual absence of real data, objective analysis, or blueprint, and with few if any discernible contingencies to address potentially adverse outcomes.[203] With "delusional rationality," as Sémelin terms it, plans for the construction of an oil refinery, for instance, were made without any indication of how the project was to be financed except for oblique references to the "work of the people" and "national savings from the absence of salary."[204] Similarly, increased revenue from rice and other export commodities was projected and, as Chandler noted, in some instances meticulously documented, without any supporting data of its feasibility or actual crop production. The absence of systemic planning was evident in this report about jute production: "We have calculated the profits from this crop. Scattered, unclear reports allege that we have enough seed, but it's clear that in fact we're short of seed."[205] Similarly, decisions on crop substitution were often made with little, if any, assessment of the suitability of the area and with equal disregard for the wider impact of the change in production patterns.

On numerous initiatives, there was an apparent disconnect between ends and means, and among multiple and conflicting objectives. While the regime pushed mercilessly for increased crop production, cultivators were relocated from their native villages, made to abandon their fertile fields, and put to labor in unfamiliar and often hostile environments, with devastating results. In Moung, local rice farmers were instructed to shift to jute cultivation while new, mostly urban evacuees unaccustomed to farming were made to grow rice in their stead. In one instance, relocatees unfamiliar with riverbank cultivation planted water-intolerant seeds, which were devastated by the rising water.[206]

If they were proffered at all, solutions were often simplistic: "The land is fertile and there is plenty of water. But now the land is left unused. There are only potatoes left over from last year. We must plant a lot so that each plot will become a garden."[207] Nor was there any effective attempt by the party to correct problems in the few instances when they were reported. From references in the Standing Committee meeting notes to "the problems of many sick people in the worksite, a loss of 40 percent of the labor force,"[208] it was evident that the regime was aware of the conditions as early as 1976. Khieu Samphan also indicated that "certain abuses" were "noted and severely criticized," with directives given "to correct them."[209] Given that those adverse conditions persisted, whatever corrective measures were put in place were ineffectual.

As with many salvationist movements, the leadership of Democratic Kampuchea saw the "higher purpose" as transcending pragmatic considerations, believing mass will, purity of "socialist consciousness," and infallibility of the party to be the sole ingredients needed for revolutionary success. Of the blinding power of ideologies, Arendt wrote, "Once their claim to validity is taken literally, they become the nuclei of logical systems in which . . . everything follows comprehensibly and even compulsorily once the first premise is accepted."[210] As educators were "disappeared" and formal education virtually eliminated, the regime announced that the country had succeeded in eliminating 90 percent of adult illiteracy through "mass line and the great mass movement."[211] As hundreds of thousands perished from disease, hard labor, and starvation, the leadership of Democratic Kampuchea described the conditions inside Cambodia as "excellent,"[212] with the populace "basically assured of all needs in all fields."[213] While starvation raged, Pol Pot proclaimed that 80 percent of the rice production target was reached within one year, and praised the regime's ability to provide "an average of 312 kilograms per capita" and to "begin exporting tens of thousands of tons of rice in 1977."[214] Nowhere was this "rupture with reality"[215] more evident than when the regime proclaimed the goal of raising the population "to 15 to 20 million in the course of the next 10 years or more"[216] while the state continued to exterminate its own people.

Of ideological fanaticism, Hoffer observes that "though ours is a godless age, it is the very opposite of irreligious."[217] The transformation promised by communism was apocalyptic, perhaps even more compelling than religious sects, for it was not of paradise in the world beyond but an earthly paradise in the here and now.[218] The fervor of conviction with which this was pursued in Democratic Kampuchea was for the party faithful no less than that of a divine "calling." As with other salvationist movements, what organizational membership provides is not simply a chance to improve one's lot but to be part of a chiliastic mission of stupendous importance. For the average peasant boys- and girls-turned-cadre, accustomed to feeling powerless in a class- and age-conscious society, there must have been a tremendous sense of empowerment that came with knowing that he or she "is working for a great task which occurs but once in 2000 years."[219] The moral righteousness that these convictions impart is quasi-religious. Once bestowed with a monopoly over "truth," the small and hardened core of true believers is elevated to the role of the "chosen few," the embodiment of the secular sacredness of revolutionary conviction. Winnowed and set apart for their ideological purity, these *ang-kor daem* (first rice grains), in Khmer Rouge parlance, must be protected from the corruptive forces of the mundane. The self-distancing of Khmer Rouge cadres was evident when they marched into the conquered capital, unmoved by the masses that greeted them, prohibited from touching evacuees with their hands, only their rifles,[220] lest their humanity remind them of theirs. Subsequently, all aspects of life and work in Democratic Kampuchea were structured to reinforce this stratified order, with base peasants segregated by power and privilege, and even spatially, from the "new people." In the villages, survivors noted that Khmer Rouge cadres often sequestered themselves apart from the populace, confining their presence to areas barred to the common people. What this primacy ultimately imparted was a sense of the indispensability of the chosen few, and conversely the disposability of all others.

The Dialectics of Fear and Violence

A leadership that believed itself infallible could never accept the idea of failures or rejection. Hence, setbacks and failures were never the result of erroneous policies, but of revolutionary lassitude, insufficient trust in the infinite wisdom of the party, or subversion. Confronted with the report that three-quarters of the country was without food reserves, the party responded by blaming the people for having "grasped the line with insufficient firmness."[221] In drawing these conclusions, the leadership could deny responsibility for failures, while justifying mass violence in the name of defending the revolution. If revolutionary lassitude and treason were the cause of all setbacks, the only policy responses needed were more exacting demands of the populace and elimination of counterrevolutionary elements.

Be it in the form of frenzied killing or criminal disregard of human life in the attempt to extract the impossible, violence was motivated not simply by hatred of the old order, ideological conviction, or loyalty to the party, but also by fear. More than the cowering fear of the victims, it was the fear of those who possessed power and wielded it with deliberate ferocity that shored up the totalitarian state. Under a regime that considered revolutionary lassitude a capital transgression, the only means of purchasing immunity was to make one's dedication to Angkar unquestionable through excessive fervor. As state terrorism escalated and imploded, consuming even the movement's own adherents, personal insecurity grew in dialectical proportion, spurring revolutionary fanaticism and zealous absolutism (*pdach kar niyum*) that contributed to the brutalization of the populace.

Fear of moderation was matched by fear of disclosure. The inability of the regime to regard failures and setbacks as anything but treason encouraged falsification of information. Of the effects of such a system, Sao Phim was said to have quoted an old Khmer proverb: "When the teacher is mean, the student connives" (*Kru kach, soeus khoch*).[222] While mass famine was decimating the population, local authorities were unwilling to report the gravity of the conditions or to resist grain requisitions by the Center for fear of being accused of treason.[223] According to one survivor, "We grew a lot of rice. The fields were green; but when the time came, they just came and took it all away. All we had was watery porridge." Instead, many capitalized on unreported deaths by using the extra allocation to illegally barter with the "new people."

As the regime embarked on Promethean reforms and encountered mounting challenges, paranoia intensified. Turning inward the fiery gaze, the party admonished that "there is a sickness inside the Party; ... we cannot locate it precisely,"[224] noting that "sometimes there is no active opposition; there is only silence. Sometimes opposition emerges as confusion, breaking down our Solidarity."[225] Enemies became ubiquitous and veiled: "From every direction, traitors continue their activities. . . . They are waiting. They operate under every kind of appearance: not . . . open, secret, tender, vicious, and so on."[226] Speaking of persisting "life-and-death contradictions"[227] that must be rectified through violence, Pol Pot noted that "1 or 2 percent of the population"[228] (totaling at least 60,000–120,000 individuals) and an estimated 40–50 percent of those living in the cooperatives were reactionary elements and to be considered "enemies."[229] Pervasive reference to *merok* (disease-carrying microbe), burrowing itself into state and society, evoked both the language of political biology and the imagery of the body politic, debilitated by autocidal "antigens": "If we wait any longer, the microbes can do real damage."[230] Lest they infect others, such "rottenness" had to be cut out. In the totalitarian mindset of Democratic Kampuchea, killing thus became a form of societal cure.

The "permanent revolution" needed to purify the party and the society saw to the unrelenting drive to unearth and destroy real and potentially corruptive elements, paving the way for the institutionalization of state-sanctioned terror. Reminiscent of the Stalinist purges of so-called industrial saboteurs, a high official was made to confess to the counterrevolutionary act of "having believed that a fire that destroyed a boat carrying petroleum products was the result of a battery explosion rather than politically-inspired 'wrecking,'"[231] while maintenance workers were killed when power failed.[232] Seeing external machination in all setbacks, the regime branded those caught drinking beer as "CIA drinkers."[233] Ultimately, treason came to be indiscriminately applied to virtually any transgression, from breaking rice stalks during transplanting, to "allowing" an ox to eat the paddy, to allowing a suspect to escape by not being "sufficiently clandestine."

As with the Stalinist purge, the "proof" of seditious acts was in the tortured confessions extracted from high-level Khmer Rouge who had been arrested and killed at Tuol Sleng.[234] As Chandler profoundly noted, those arrested and purged were "guilty because they had been arrested rather than arrested because they were guilty."[235] In effect, places like S-21, as Duch noted, were "the end of the line. People who got sent there were already corpses. Human or animal? That's another subject."[236] Once proclaimed as such, however, "traitors" could be crushed with impunity, for treachery was cause for disavowal by the state and the nation. Pol Pot instructed, "These counterrevolutionary elements which betray and try to sabotage the revolution are not to be regarded as being our people. They are regarded as enemies of Democratic Kampuchea, of the Cambodian revolution and of the Cambodian people. We must deal with them the same way we would with any enemy."[237] The totalistic manner with which the regime eliminated not only political opponents but also their family members, even their newborns,[238] was a demonic reflection of the party's distorted notion of associative guilt. Though it insisted on the erasure of kinship, the regime regarded political impurity as an inheritable trait. According to the party, an offspring inherits 50 percent of his parents' class taintedness.[239] Rather than a social construct, class was imbued with biological, hereditary traits. Like the ancient despots, Angkar demanded the "killing of the entire seed" (*samlab muy pouch*) in retribution for an individual's transgression.[240] As the Khmer Rouge put it, "When you weed the field, you must pull out the roots."

Of totalitarian regimes, Hoffer wrote, "The ardor which yesterday found an outlet in a life-and-death struggle with external enemies now vents itself in violent . . . clash of factions. Hatred and violence have become a habit. With no more outside enemies to destroy, the fanatics make enemies of one another."[241] Pierre Vergniaud's prophetic admonitions about the French Revolution reverberated in Democratic Kampuchea: "The Revolution, like Saturn, successively devouring its children, will engender, finally, only despotism with the calamities that accompany it."[242] Given the belief that the nation's fate depends on the success of the revolution, which only the party can ensure, regime survival became synonymous with national survival, hence paramount. The imperative of protecting the *kbal massin* (head of the machinery), as Nuon Chea put it, came to justify the most punitive sanction. What may have begun as a necessary but temporary deviation from the original goals eventually became the *only* goal. In the final analysis, all that was left of the initial revolutionary vision was nothing more than a grotesque caricature of distorted ideals. What emerged in Democratic Kampuchea was not simply the despotic rule over man, but a system in which man was superfluous.[243] In their determination to achieve something unprecedented in the history of revolutions, the Khmer Rouge dispensed with all regard for human and societal consequences. In one of the many paradoxes of Democratic Kampuchea, humanity was ultimately sacrificed in the name of humanist principles.

The Permissibility of Violence

While violence may have resulted from organizational constraints and ideological fanaticism, what in effect made its rampant, indiscriminate, and ultimately self-consuming expression possible? In particular, what accounted for the seeming absence of institutional restraints that allowed political extremism to reach such a magnitude in Democratic Kampuchea? While seeds of radicalism existed in many other revolutionary experiences, violence in many instances was bridled by moderating forces that were essentially absent in Democratic Kampuchea. Unlike in China, where key apparati and forces prevailed to eventually countervail the "reckless advances,"[244] the sweeping purges in Democratic Kampuchea essentially eliminated all viable intra-party opposition, while profound disorientation and atomization of the individual produced by starvation, hard labor, and institutionalized terror stifled the possibility of organized resistance. Ultimately, the reign of terror was brought to an end not by domestic forces but by a foreign army.

The ability of the system to effectively compartmentalize and immunize against individual culpability further neutralized opposition. A survivor recalled that many of the *yothea* had no real understanding of the reasons for the killings; they simply surmised that those they were leading to the killing fields "must have done *something* wrong."[245] That which has been referred to as "the numbing of the Auschwitz self"[246] also worked during the Khmer Rouge regime to accentuate the moral distancing that was, in turn, reinforced by euphemisms deployed to veil brutal acts with the illusion of normalcy. Rather than arrests and executions, terms such as *prochoun toeuv rean* (sent to be educated) proffered hope for the victims and their families and freedom from accountability for the arresting cadres. Simultaneously, the system worked to encourage the feeling that there was "no exit."[247] Everyone caught in the system, both regime supporters and victims, was made to feel compromised. Its ultimate efficacy was underscored by the attenuation of blame by some refugee-survivors, some of whom projected their own helplessness onto the Khmer Rouge cadres: "We wouldn't know who to blame. Maybe they had to do what they were told just as we had to do what we were told." This moral buffering may account in part for the fact that although revenge killings did take place in the days immediately following the regime's capitulation, they were relatively contained both in scope and in duration. In the refugee camps and in diaspora where survivors have identified their persecutors, retributive acts of violence were relatively rare. One refugee woman in Oakland laughingly recalled how she felt compelled to give money to her abuser so that the latter "could buy some sweets for her little girl because I felt sorry for her child." Though many survivors attribute their unwillingness to exact retribution to Buddhist sensibility, the reticence conveyed speaks, in no small part, to the ability of the system to dispossess even the very people it victimized of the power to condemn. It is a resounding indictment of the complex effects of auto-genocide on the entire nation—perpetrators and victims alike.

The Heretics

Just as the earlier messianic movements had claimed that reason cannot comprehend the will of God, so it is with modern-day chiliastic regimes that the "higher purpose" was seen as transcending human comprehension, hence moral sanction. As the Khmer Rouge often pointed out, "Angkar moves by leaps and bounds, and one cannot hope to understand its will"; in its infallibility, the totalitarian state demands unswerving conformity. The myth of omniscience was shored up by the facelessness of the Organization. The few references to the party leadership that appeared in Khmer Rouge documents were only to their *noms de guerre*. While this emphasis on anonymity contrasted with the personalistic features of Khmer political culture, it reflected elements of traditional autocracy. Like the semi-divinity of the *devaraja* (god-king), Democratic Kampuchea's sovereign—Angkar—was distant, all-seeing, and omnipotent, commanding absolutist control over the populace without any need for accountability.

This belief in the infallibility and righteousness of the ideals and, above all, in the inevitability of the historical outcome justified the wholesale negation of all forms of restraint. The will of Angkar and the actions of the cadres who unquestioningly executed it were deployed with sanctimonious self-vindication and moral impunity. As the Khmer

Rouge cadres often admonished, "The wheel of the Revolution is un-relenting. Those without resoluteness or firmness of stance (*chamhor*) would be crushed in its path."[248] Prisoners at Tuol Sleng often "con-fessed" to lassitude in carrying out their orders as their "crime" against the party. In *The Anatomy of Revolution*, Crane Brinton argues that "as the crisis of the revolution approached, only the man with a touch—or more—of fanatic idealism in him, or at least with the ability to act the part of such a lunatic, could attain to leadership."[249] Arguably, many of those who were swept away by the waves of purges that convulsed Dem-ocratic Kampuchea were those who lacked the ideological fervor needed in a militantly revolutionary society, or who had simply grown weary of struggle. With militancy and violence sanctified by a salvationist ideol-ogy, Khmer Rouge terror was, in essence, revolutionary morality in ac-tion. Armed with a sense of historical determinism, the regime regarded those perceived to be thwarting the mission not just as mistaken men or political enemies; they were "heretics," hence corrupted beyond redemp-tion. Even in the face of advancing Vietnamese troops, brutal campaigns continued, especially against base peasants and cadres accused of having betrayed the party.[250] A couple from Battambang recounted how their daughter was caught escaping from her work group to search for her family when the Vietnamese invaded, and brutally executed. Accused of being a "traitor," she was tied on the ground, nine months pregnant, while a female *yothea* repeatedly jumped from the verandah onto her swollen stomach until the fetus was squashed out of her.

Of chiliastic movements and their intrinsic seed of self-destruction, Hoffer wrote, "Even if [the] division into schism and heresies may not threaten its existence, fanatics can still wreck the movement by driv-ing it to attempting the impossible."[251] Utopian ambition ruthlessly dis-pensed with humanism and conventional logic, for when successes and failures are measured in millenarian terms, the notion of "limits" takes on a different dimension and the sacrifices that were demanded, nec-essarily defiant of rationality. The Khmer Rouge revolution, however, must be understood not simply in terms of the historical conditions that spurred the desire for change or in terms of the ideological vision, but as they were framed against the backdrop of blind zeal, endemic fear, distrust, a totalistic mindset, and systematic devaluation of humanity that can transform otherwise rational convictions into absurdity. What emerged was a world in which an individual's fate was made to hang precariously on a sliver of stolen yam or the errant judgment of a child informant. With tragic irony, policies aimed at achieving uncompromising self-determination, in the end brought about not enhanced security, self-sufficiency, and progress for the Cambodian nation, but the loss of sovereignty. Less than twenty-five years after independence, the fear that had long dominated Cambodia's foreign policy thinking was made concrete by Vietnam's invasion and decade-long occupation, the one historical specter that had haunted all postcolonial regimes in Phnom Penh.

In his analysis of revolutions, Gordon Wood emphasized the dialectical importance of intended and unintended dynamics:

> The purposes of men, especially in a revolution are so numerous, so varied, and so contradictory that their complex interaction produces results that no one intended or could ever foresee. . . . Historical explanation which does not account for these "forces," which, in other words relies simply on understanding the conscious intentions of the actors, will thus be limited.[252]

In the pursuit of its utopian goals, the Khmer Rouge regime deluded itself with the belief in the determinant power of mass will, in the infallibility and invincibility of organization, and in the efficacy of force. In so doing, they lost sight of the human dimension and failed, with grave consequences, to recognize that force incurred its own costs. In the end, ideological fanaticism, blinding dogmatism, national egoism, regime paranoia, and criminal disregard for the human cost combined flung the nation into a self-destructive, genocidal spiral. It was to be another chapter in the annals of history where the blood of a people was spilled in the name of saving it. To the Cambodian nation, crushed with wanton disregard under the wheel of historical progress, the "human face of Socialism" was transformed into the grimace of death.

Annihilation

Exhausted by torture and degradation, the past had been his anchor. There was no real "explanation," only the warm solace of faith that, in all of Angkar's omniscience, there must be a reason for his arrest. The party's will is infallible and often incomprehensible to lay minds. All the party faithful who had been led away by Angkar's far-reaching grip had reaffirmed with their last desperate breath their unyielding faith in the party. It was, after all, the movement that had nurtured them and imbued them with the life force of conviction. Without the belief in the absolute correctness of the Path, the life led would have been of lies and senseless violence. If not faith in the party, then what?

As the shovel struck him from behind, he slumped into peaceful release. The prisoner never lived to find out that the place where he had been incarcerated was Tuol Sleng, otherwise known as S-21, and that at least twelve thousand political prisoners—"traitors", heretics—would have walked through its door, never to exit, before the revolutionary flame was snuffed out by advancing Vietnamese tanks.

PART III

Cambodian/Americans and the Legacies of Genocide

6

Fragments

Life is difficult. . . . Even the tears have left me.
—*Cambodian survivor*

That Khmer culture and the Khmer people will never be the same after "*a-Pot*" is a leitmotif in post-genocide Cambodian discourse. With almost a generational death, virtually no Cambodian is left untouched by this national tragedy. The "radioactive"[1] effects of this collective trauma transcend spatial, temporal, and generational boundaries. Even those born after the Khmer Rouge period live under the unlifting shadow of this history. As Samphy Iep puts it, "We all have a part of us that has been torn away, something special, precious that is gone."[2] The totalism of the Khmer Rouge reign of terror meant that chance was the principal, if not the singular, element separating life and death. In the words of one Cambodian Canadian woman, "Those who survived were leftovers from the dead."[3] The proximity with death and loss, as such, is measured only in terms of immediacy and relativity. For these reasons, all Cambodians of the genocide generation are survivors in the Lyotardian sense of "an entity that is dead or ought to be [but] is still alive,"[4] for this collective trauma has branded us all.

In Cambodia, what is engendered by the death of almost one quarter of the population is a material and metaphysical rupture, involving not only structural but also tangible cultural loss. Over 63 percent of the country's Buddhist monks perished or were forcibly disrobed, and 90 percent of the Buddhist texts lost or destroyed.[5] Of the nation's master artists, only a small and aged handful survived in 1979. Where much of the cultural traditions are orally based, there is an underlying anxiety that the physical deaths would also mean the cultural death of the nation, that the erasure of time would leave behind nothing more than a suggestion of a richly textured culture. As Dr. Sam Ang Sam, a Cambodian American ethnomusicologist, points out, "In the oral tradition, when the musicians die they take along with them the knowledge and memory before it can be passed on, so it's gone."[6] Through five pendular regime changes since independence, linguistic integrity has frayed; royal vocabulary, for instance, was vacated from the Khmer language for over two decades, first by the Republic, and subsequently by the Khmer Rouge and socialist regimes that followed. Cambodian elders have commented that, in this generation of "children of the bombs,"[7] the Khmer language has lost its richness and complexity. If language informs consciousness, what implications might this have on the continued fracturing of Khmer cultural identity?

More than structural and institutional destabilization, this historical trauma injures social connectivity, ethos, meaning, and collective memory that make for social coherence. For many Cambodians, the cultural world they inhabit in which behaviors are prescribed, roles and relations clearly defined, and norms and expectations readily understood may be constraining and even oppressive in fundamental aspects but it also yields a sense of security in its ordered-ness. Even the Khmer language, with its rigid and stifling hierarchical forms, allows an individual to determine his or her sense of place and positionality vis-à-vis the larger collective. Similarly for Cambodian Buddhists, who constitute the majority of the population, solace is found in the karmic doctrine of actions and consequences that provides not only an explanation for even the seemingly inexplicable but also hope in karmic redress. It was this need for a spiritual anchor that compelled many, like the poet U Sam Oeur, to risk their lives during the Khmer Rouge period just to light an incense and utter a prayer;[8] even the Khmer Rouge, Nuon Chea later acknowledged, prayed in secret.

It was this sociality and existential frame that the Khmer Rouge strove to shatter. With the fracturing and corruption of the familiar, what survivors experience in the aftermath is a loss of coherence, a "wound in the order of things"[9] that punctuates their life continuum, leaving the past with little relevance to the present. With this loss of continuity, Hannah Arendt wrote, "what you then are left with is still the past, but a fragmented past, which has lost its certainty of evaluation."[10] Extreme violence, as Robben and Suárez-Orozco point out, "un-makes" the culturally constituted norms, conventions, social webs of relations and trust, worldviews, and the "safety of the familiar everyday world." What results is the "negation of what binds human beings together," which engenders overwhelming feelings of terror and anxiety.[11] The Khmer aphorism *kalab phen dey* (world turned upside down) speaks to the inversion of order that renders void all sociocultural and metaphysical "signposts." The unraveling of familial bonds is particularly disorienting. For Bunna, a teen survivor, the relational tear inflicted by one of his own, a signifier of auto-genocide, was irreparable: "If it were strangers, perhaps I can understand. But this was my own uncle, my own blood, who turned against us. Because he wanted to live."[12] What results is the loss of ontological security[13] that leaves in its void a post-genocide reality constituted of "an unending desolation, . . . ineradicable images, gestures no longer possible, silences that pursue."[14]

In the face of this dramatic loss of identity and meaning that Eyerman defines as cultural trauma,[15] survivors come to question their basic assumptions about community, life, and faith, about the orderliness of the universe, and the explicability of things. The growth of the Cambodian Christian community is, in large part, a reflection of the inability of Buddhism to effectively reconcile the genocidal realities. Survival thus involves the process of recovery and restoration, not just of life and meaning but also of self, and the reaffirmation above all of one's own humanity. Bereft of all that had made them whole, survivors found themselves, in the aftermath, struggling to piece together fragments of their identity as individuals, as a nation, as human beings. Thida Mam recalled,

> In April 1979, the Buddhist New Year, exactly four years after the Khmer Rouge came to power, I joined a group of corpselike bodies dancing freely to the sound of clapping and . . . folk music that defined who we were. . . . At that moment, I felt that my spirit and my soul had returned to my weak body. Once again, I was human.[16]

For Daran Kravanh, music similarly provided a lifeline out of the genocidal abyss: "I came to understand that playing music recreated everything that I had lost: my mother, my peace, the closeness of brothers."[17] Phanny, a young woman survivor, also spoke of her rediscovery of beauty and faith amidst the squalor of the refugee camps and under the pall of Khmer Rouge depravities:

I had arrived in the refugee camp. Dirty, poor, clothes tattered, alone. I was almost at a point where I could no longer see any reason to go on living. I was sitting under a tree and thinking about my life, my bad karma, when I heard this sound. I have never heard anything so beautiful. They were voices, singing. It was so beautiful that tears flowed uncontrollably down my cheeks. I stood up and started to follow the sound until I came upon this makeshift church. After that afternoon, I found myself drawn back there again and again. . . . That's how I found Christianity.

In an article about the Cambodian auto-genocide, I used the metaphor of a "broken chain"[18] to depict the sense of discontinuity, anomie, and rupture that survivors feel in their lives. In the broken chain of their historicized selves, the links are severed but there still remain the ghost imprints of past connections. For many Cambodians, the wounds are kept raw by the absence of any real opportunity for mourning. Most who survived have no way of knowing what happened to their loved ones, only that they "disappeared." Lives have withered in the liminal state of impaired mourning in wait for the return that in their heart of hearts they know will never be. Mrs. Ouch, now over sixty-five years old, spent "months and years" waiting for her family, or someone who may have known her family, to turn up: "I used to wait by that crossroad—just looking at all the passer-bys. Finally, my cousin who lived with my parents showed up and she told me that my parents had all been killed."[19] Even those who after three decades of hoping have come to conclude that their loved ones are dead, still clung to the thread of possibility of their survival, however improbable that may be. After thirty years, Mrs. Oeun, whose husband fled from their village one evening in 1976 never to be heard from again, still looks up at the sound of a car or a bicycle peddling by on the village road in hope of her husband's return.[20] Yet others search in the faces of young passersby for signs of recognition of a long-lost child who had been taken away or a possible surviving kin whom they knew only as a child. For the known dead, there can be no markers of remembrance, save perhaps on mass or makeshift graves. Upon my initial return to Cambodia, I found myself, as others must have done, looking at lone trees lining the roads leading out to the countryside, or past verdant rice fields, and wondering whether this could have been the place where my relatives had perished.

Memory works thus involve the biopolitics of remembering, the injury that is inflicted by the absence and unknowability of the missing body. Fisher speaks of disappearances as a "censorship of memory"[21] that denies an end to mourning, and possibly any hope of transcendence. Mourning is thus not just for the lost presence but also for the lost body that makes the lost presence forever present. In that sense, what may appear as fatalism or apathy in survivors is often relief from the unbearableness of not knowing, a register of the metaphysical sigh at being freed from the lifelong shackles of uncertainty. An elderly refugee listened quietly to the confirmation that all his siblings, nieces, nephews, and close cousins had died under the Khmer Rouge; in his twilight years, he found himself all alone in the world, and in a country that will never be his. With an impassivity that is culturally Khmer in which the most poignant expression is often communicated through silence, he said, "It is better to know that they are dead than to live with not knowing." In a social system of vastly extended kinship, for every Cambodian there is always uncertainty, somewhere, about someone.

For many survivors, the ability to move on is hindered by the remembering of things left unresolved. Many are plagued by the tormenting self-questioning about what they could have done to save their loved ones, the self-chastising at their own inability to withstand hunger and spare some food for a dying kin, or their inability to cry when forced to witness a relative's execution, thus letting someone go to his or her death feeling disavowed, essentially for choosing life over family. In his painting *The Last Look*, Ngeth Sim relived his father's final glance as he was led away to his execution and sought atonement for his helplessness: "At the moment when the Khmer Rouge led you away, . . . I did not have the force to protest in front of these torturers, to prevent them from taking you and killing you. . . . Father, I pray every night that your soul will pardon me."[22] Similar guilt threaded through the testimony of Mrs. Thouch Phandara, a civil party to the Khmer Rouge tribunal:

> The conditions in which they [my parents] died were not worthy of animals. . . . Thrown into the ditch, naked. I don't even know the place where he was discarded, and I retain a terrible feeling of guilt about this—not having been able to save my parents. If I was perhaps a little braver I

might have been able to feed them, bring them some rice, something. You never erase memories like that.[23]

By provoking this self-questioning, the genocidal regime had artfully and sadistically succeeded in implicating its victims. If mourning is what constitutes "the human for humans," as Nichanian asserts, its denial is a revoking of humanity. Rather than acknowledgment, witnessing in this context becomes a forced confrontation with the unraveling of social bonds and the dehumanized self. In effect, the regime perpetuates the devaluation of personhood, the denuding of life to its barest, by forcing survivors ultimately to question their own right to life: "Why did I live?"

In a culture where filial duty extends into the afterlife through the ritual honoring of the ancestors, mass graves and disappearances deny survivors the ability even after the genocide to conduct the appropriate funereal rites, necessary for the successful transmigration of the soul and, by extension, for the well-being of the living. The dead, especially in the context of a violent end, are otherwise caught in the hindered passage between life and death, and are denied a place not only among the living but also among the ancestors. Given the Buddhist practice of cremation, mass graves become a literal, metaphorical, and metaphysical "crypt"—to build on Derrida—in which the victims are simultaneously confined and scattered in anonymity. Loss as disappearance, as such, ruptures not only the social system but also the cosmological order, engendering trans-temporal disturbance in the world of the dead and of the living. For families of the disappeared, there is a psychic sense of "being stuck"; there is no "after" as the atrocity lives on in the ambiguity, a "mourning without end."[24] Reburial, as Antonius Robben notes, thus "reconciles the bereaved with their loss, restores the public honour of the victims, reincorporates them into society as deceased members."[25] Bou Meng, whose wife was "disappeared" at Tuol Sleng, wanted nothing more from Duch, the head of S-21, than an answer: "My question is just to tell me, just to tell me where she was killed or smashed. Then I would go . . . and get the soil from that location to pray for her soul."[26] Thouch Phandara's appeal to the court was to give the deceased "back their souls" because they are "lost between the living and the dead."[27] It was, in essence, an appeal for the dead, and for the living, to be made whole.

The wound is pricked to life by the memory haunting that registers when "an unquiet history returns to inhabit the present."[28] Often in the form of dreams, nocturnal visitations are not necessarily traumatic; they may in fact make up for the physical absence and rupture with a trans-temporal relationality affirmed through ceremonies and rituals from which the living may continue to draw solace. The disconcertment may be in the message they convey. Saneth, a young refugee woman, recounts her recurrent dream about a favorite aunt who had died under the Khmer Rouge: "I saw her in tattered clothes, hungry, insisting that she has nowhere to go. She told me before she died that she wanted to be with the rest of the family. I believe that she is still looking for them." For Youk Chhang, as it is for many Cambodians, Pchum Ben, the Khmer "Day of the Dead," evokes memory of the unresolved:

> It always reminds me of my older sister who died from starvation in the Khmer Rouge regime. It is believed that Pchum Ben is the time when the souls of the dead are set free from hell and the living relatives must make offerings . . . to their dead ancestors or the spirits. I always think that my sister's soul always comes and rests with my family during the days of the festival. And I still maintain the same feeling that she is still very hungry. And I want to give her rice to eat.[29]

In fundamental aspects, the world of survivors is peopled by the dead. The losses constitute an ever-present absence that punctuates the clutter of reconstructed lives. Ceremonies and ritual offerings, as such, are technologies of repair that make possible the "re-membering" of the dead through recall and reintegration; in that sense, mourning itself is a reparative act. Out of a sense of obligation made collective by the magnitude of loss, even the nonreligious find themselves compelled to partake in merit-making "not for us the living, but to send on to those whose debt of gratitude we were unable to repay when they were alive." Post-genocide ceremonies and rituals are thus imbued with uncanny poignancy, inculcating the past with a perpetuated contemporaneity.[30] During religious observances, altars are crowded with pictures of the deceased, marking simultaneously a "pseudo-presence and a token of absence."[31] Even more disconcerting are the lists of names of individuals of whom not even a picture is left as a reminder, an "absence even of shadows," as Cambodians would put it (*ta samowl ka menkhoeunh*), that nonetheless insists on being acknowledged. These ruinous debris, to borrow from Stoler—the unknown, the unmet, and the unresolved— essentially impede survivors' ability to move forward, for their backward gaze prevents them from focusing on the present and what they could envision for the future. For many refugee-survivors, above and beyond the political, the economic, and other, perhaps loftier motivations, it is the simple yet insistent need just "to light an incense for those to whom we owe a debt of gratitude," the *neak mean kun*, that beckons return. In that sense, *survivors do not come back. They never left.*[32]

History, Memory, and the Unreclaimability of Loss

*"When I close my eyes, I can still picture my friends, I can hear
the laughter, as if they were right there."*
*"At least when you close your eyes, you still hear the laughter.
When I close mine, I hear silence. Silence of the dead."*
—*Conversation between two Cambodian American friends*

Where home and history evoke the imageries not only of familial warmth and belonging but also of reeducation camps and killing fields, memory itself is fraught with contestation and contradictions. That which connotes the solace of home, belonging, and the security of same- ness also provokes the recollection of death and deprivation, signifying both an indelible connection and, simultaneously, a rupture. For many Cambodians, "Year Zero"[33] is not simply a marker of an apocalyptic shift in history: it is an *erasure* of history, an untraversable temporal divide that is encoded in the way national and personal histories are narrated. An elderly refugee spoke of living with "one body, two lives"— one before and one after Pol Pot—straddling the schism engendered by the "otherworldliness" and irreversibility of that historical trauma. Rithy Panh poignantly reflects, "When you survive genocide it is like you are dead already and have been reborn again. But you are reborn with death inside you."[34] Democratic Kampuchea lay beyond the experiential realm of the average Khmer, for there is nothing within the nation's prior col- lective experience or its historical consciousness that defines hunger in terms of the literal starvation of hundreds of thousands of individuals, or hardship in terms of the enslavement of the entire nation. Laughter, tears, and other basic human sentiments are rendered banal by the immeasurability of the experience. Numbed to pain and joy, many survivors have lost the ability to feel: "There are no more tears left to cry."

While survivors may find ways to manage and mask the historical traumas, many cannot free themselves from the hauntings. The dreams, differing in images but consistent in themes, are invariably filled with scenes of impending escape—the suitcases that will not close, the agony of having to choose and never knowing how to choose among life's artifacts, the panic of having to evaluate and compact all of one's life meanings into a final, desperate, and arbitrary choice. If there are people in these nocturnal intrusions, they are usually nameless and faceless, but unfailingly exuding omnipotence, and if victims, tortured helplessness. American friends often ask in what language refugees dream. For many Cambodians, the dreams are mostly of silent agony, such that both in the dream world and in the conscious world, they could not speak. In effect, these are dreams from which one awakens to remember nothing but choking terror and muted helplessness.

When Words Are Injured

The auto-genocidal encounter was such that it left survivors in a psychic flux, caught between the need to give form and expression to their extraordinary experiences and the inability to recall and articulate. The corruption of language deters articulation. With words vacated of their original meaning, language under the Khmer Rouge in effect became an unstable weapon, deployed by perpetrators as a tool to deceive, lure, threaten, and injure, and by the oppressed to protect each other with veiled admonitions such as "plant a *kapok* tree," ironically suggestive of life and renewal despite the foreboding.[35] The neutering of language began when euphemisms were employed to distance killers from their acts of violence, and potential victims from their impending fate. Khmer Rouge atrocities were carried out under linguistic ambiguity and amorphousness: people were not killed, they were "sent up"; they were taken away not to be liquidated but to be "reconstructed," hence not physically destroyed but "rebuilt," with the implied positivism of reform and transformation. Vocabularies were also appropriated and transformed into the lexicon of terror. The executed, unceremoniously discarded, were "still working in the field as fertilizer." When language denies, reality deceives.

Linguistic corruption culminates in the loss of words to describe that wounding encounter, which for many survivors is evacuated of comprehensible meaning, and which remains, as the writer Vaddey Ratner asserts, "unanswerable to this day."[36] Decades later, many Cambodians still punctuate their reflections about the Khmer Rouge era with the refrain "I just don't understand" (keeu men yul). What results is aphasia, that sense of disconnect that Stoler describes as "an inability to recognize things in the world and assign proper names to them."[37] There is nothing within the Khmer vernacular that could be used to fully capture that "unreal reality"[38] that resists description. Though it may approximate the idea of total loss or le catastrophe,[39] the word Mahantaray[40] has a very specific Buddhist connotation that refers to the end of the world, and not just the annihilation of one people nor the self-destruction of auto-genocide. The inability to capture through words the totality of the experience is in essence the inability to "translate the uncivilized into a civilized language."[41] Ordinary terms such as "rice," "farming," "marriage," when applied to the samay a-Pot, assume entirely different connotations. The hoe came to represent both the glorification and corruption of agrarian life, an implement of life-giving sustenance, but also of death and destruction. New vocabularies such as vay chaol, a combination of "beat" and "discard" that reflects the Khmer Rouge dismissive annihilism, have no significance outside the genocidal frame. Similarly, the Khmer term for "genocide" (samlab pouch sas or pralaay pouch sas) is a relatively recent coinage.[42] Despite its ubiquitous deployment in writings about post-1975 Cambodia, mostly done in the West and by Westerners, it is not a term that is colloquially used among Cambodians when speaking about samay a-Pot.

For survivors, recounting these experiences means "navigating between two sets of landmarks, trying to fathom two sets of code."[43] It is thus, as Wiesel suggests, that to put such experiences, which lie "somewhere beyond life and history,"[44] into words does not signify sharing but compromise.[45] For many survivors, the inability to reconcile the incompatibility of narrative and narration with what James Young refers to as "deep memories"[46] is rooted in the despair that if they themselves cannot make meaning of their experiences, they cannot hope that anyone else would fully understand them. The process of naming the experience thus becomes a struggle within language, which through the invalidation of past referents has fundamentally lost its power to communicate. It is thus not just voice but also language that must first be recovered. When words are injured, what other expressions are possible? As Takenishi Hiroko laments, "What words can we now use, and to what ends: Even: what *are* words?"[47] While many sought quiet transcendence for that which cannot be unburdened, for Socheata Poeuv's father, anger is the only tangible feeling: "I don't want to talk. I don't want to hear. I don't want to see. I hate."[48]

Of the land of shadows that was Democratic Kampuchea, where to survive one must render oneself mute and mindless like a *tiing maung* (scarecrow), the genocidal fracturing is also manifested in the physicality of silence. Daran Kravanh wrote, "The horrible reality of what our country has become began to be revealed to me, not so much by words, but by silence. No one talked, no one laughed, no one sang. . . . The people were as silent and half there as ghosts. In time, we too became silent."[49] In the aftermath, silence is the embodied "invisible violence of fear,"[50] a spirit crushed by the ravaging encounter, cowering in tortured recollection. Ronnie, orphaned and left for dead at a killing ground, still sees himself as one of the "walking emotionally wounded," tormented by nocturnal haunting.[51] Like him, Bunna, a Cambodian American professional and survivor, finds himself quivering upon hearing a taped recording of the Khmer Rouge revolutionary songs over a decade later. It is not uncommon for surviving refugees, in the safe confine of their homes in the United States, to instinctively lower their voices when speaking about the Khmer Rouge. One of the defining moments of my field research was when an interviewee, in the midst of a casual conversation over tea in his San Diego apartment, froze momentarily at the sight of my red pen, recovering with a tinge of apologetic embarrassment to explain that, under the Khmer Rouge, names of individuals slated for execution were marked in red ink.

Silence is reinforced by the culturally inscribed reluctance to "publicize" personal issues or private emotions, as both are regarded as character flaws. This cultural reserve and public performance of normalcy that may be mistaken for forgetting[52] challenge the Western regard of articulation and sharing as catharsis. Without dismissing trauma, this urges a different reading of silence, not as pathology but as fortitude and resistance, not mutedness and submission but a scream.[53] The "blank spots on a communicative landscape,"[54] as Leslie Dwyer puts it, are as such not vacuous ellipses, but laden with culturally audible conveyance of all that is left unuttered, hence equally as significant, if not even more significant, than speech.

Politics and Politicization of Memory

For survivors, silence is not only self-imposed but also externally compelled. Politics and polemics divide and fragment and, in the process, reinforce the silence. Like many aspects of their lived experiences, memory too has been politicized. In diaspora, the power of politics to invalidate was felt early on by refugees when their recounting was muffled by the ideological wars in the West, their pain unacknowledged under the weight of post-Vietnam cynicism and America's desire to forget the ignominy of Vietnam. When it was no longer possible to discount the atrocities, disbelief gave way to their dismissal as grievances of the once pampered urbanites now forced to live the life of the "average" Cambodian peasant.[55] The sufferings of those who escaped in 1975, in particular, were often rendered inconsequential by the presumed taint of privilege; even among social activists, the issue of granting refuge to this initial cohort was contentious.[56] Many refugees, like Mr. Ok, a former official, came to internalize this disavowal: "How can we talk about our sufferings? We made grave mistakes and as a result we lost our country." The silencing is perpetuated. Within these "incomplete frames of forgetting [and] schemes of strategic remembering" that Cathy Schlund-Vials terms the "Cambodia Syndrome,"[57] refugee presence was evoked largely to underscore America's altruism and moral leadership toward the stateless. Gratitude, rather than loss, was the sanctioned trope.

In Cambodia, memory was also co-opted by the post-genocide state. In the campaign to legitimate itself, the post–Khmer Rouge regime, tainted by its association with Vietnam and its decade-long occupation, has fundamentally appropriated the public space of remembering. Rather than serving as memorials, sites such as Tuol Sleng (S-21) have been transformed into a "politicized curatorial agenda,"[58] as Cathy

Schlund-Vials puts it, where archives of Khmer Rouge atrocities were strategically exhibited, complete at one point with a "map/ping" of genocide with human skulls. Designed for international consumption, it was not until 1980 that Cambodians were permitted access.[59] Despite the fact that public displays of disinterred remains such as at Choeung Ek violate Khmer Buddhist and cultural sensibilities, the resistance of the Phnom Penh government to proposed cremation, arguing their evidentiary importance, underscores the politicization of the genocide issue. A bag of bones, as Avery Gordon poignantly notes, "is not justice. A bag of bones is knowledge without acknowledgement."[60] The official rhetoric of reconciliation stands alongside the state proclamation of a national Day of Anger, with its promotion of collective hatred in the act of public remembrance.[61] Memory of the Khmer Rouge is also evoked to reduce the discussion of Cambodian politics into a moral and political binary that juxtaposes the threat of a return to the killing fields against all prevailing ills. In the reductive political frame of the immediate post–Khmer Rouge years, Cambodians who questioned the timing of a Khmer Rouge trial in the 1980s, or insisted that former Khmer Rouge remaining in power in Phnom Penh also be held accountable, or in any way challenged the legitimacy of the Vietnam-installed regime in Phnom Penh were branded as Khmer Rouge sympathizers.

As Hirsch contends, "These variable winds of politics influence the interpretation of history because the particular version that gains acceptance is used to justify present policy and future actions."[62] Be it through state-sponsored commemorations or the politicization of school curricula,[63] politics dictate what and how survivors can remember, and define what is to be considered legitimate, acceptable, and safe discourse about Cambodia's contemporary political history. Where, if anywhere, within these narrow confines of state-sponsored and otherwise dominant narratives, do other articulations and expressions fit?

Silence as Resistance

If trauma, fear, and power politics rob many of their ability to speak, mourn, memorialize, and move forward, silence is for others a defiant political stance. Reacting to the media flurry over the death of Pol Pot, an elderly refugee stated vehemently, "We should not be giving so much attention to *a-Pot*. Speaking about him, writing about him, is like honoring his existence, his evil. In so doing, we perpetuate the memory of him. Why would we want to memorialize such evil in our nation's consciousness?" This view has a certain resonance in Khmer culture, where moral transgressions are punished by the act of "disowning" (*kat kal chaol*). Historically, ostracism was often accompanied by a prohibition against public utterance of the individual's name, for the gravity of the malefaction is such that it should not be given actuality through speech. In a form of *damnatio memoriae*, the condemnation of memory, what is not articulated, therefore, does not exist. Conversely, to speak of evil is to give it life and to invite its presence. Just as villagers venturing into the forests would refrain from naming dangerous jungle animals, so are political evils denied actualization through their banishment from speech. Cambodian oral lore is replete with instances of royal decrees stipulating that the names of transgressors be banned from public utterance, hence from popular consciousness. Banishment, as such, is not simply a physical act but a nullification of memory. During the protectorate, a village implicated in the assassination of Resident Bardez was decreed by King Sisowath to be henceforth referred to only as Phum Derachhaan (the bestial village),[64] excommunicated from the realm of humanity, its previous history and identity erased from the nation's collective memory.

For others still, silence is a deliberate act to break the cycle of violence. As it is with Balinese women after the 1965 massacre, silence for Cambodian survivors like Theavy is "chosen,"[65] to avoid "burden[ing] and inflict[ing] pain" on themselves and on their children by reinhabiting the narratives of genocide: "I don't want my daughter to learn of these horrors, to feel my pain." In the refusal to perpetuate victimization by transmitting what Veena Das terms "poisonous knowledge,"[66] silence is a signifier not of victimhood but of agency.

The experiences of survivors, in effect, exile them to a world of their own, sealed off from the rest of humanity, apart and different. Silence becomes a refuge against banal empathy, incredulity, and the weariness of having to explain. Elie Wiesel's self-censure resonates with many survivors: "It's not because I don't speak that you won't understand me; it's because you won't understand me that I don't speak."[67] For many Cambodians, the "otherworldliness" of their experiences instilled in them the feeling that no one, other than people who have traveled the same road, or have "swum through the Pol Pot era" (*heil kat samay a-Pot*), could conceive of such existence, let alone comprehend it. Whereas in prerevolutionary Cambodia, social introductions were invariably accompanied by inquiries about kinship as a way of socially and relationally locating an individual, it has since become almost customary among Cambodian refugees to address each other with "Were you stuck during *a-Pot*?" Rather than kinship, genocide now defines the Cambodian identity. Though they seek the community of other survivors, it does not necessarily guarantee solace. The fact that every Cambodian life has been touched by this tragedy, paradoxically, can also impede the effective sharing of pain, as loss and suffering become a matter of degree; there is always someone who has suffered even greater tragedies that make one's own sufferings pale in comparison.

Whether in speech or in silence, survivors must live with the knowledge that they have lost something fundamental, something essential in their lives, and that nothing—no faith, no miracle—can ever bring it back. As Elie Wiesel puts it, "God Himself cannot change the past."[68] The reflection of an elderly Khmer refugee over the death and disappearance of his entire family speaks with eloquent poignancy to the totality of loss and the irreversibility of the genocidal realities: "They are all gone. There's just silence. Not a trace, not a sound, as if someone just took a broom and swept it all to the wind." Now in her late sixties, Mrs. Saath, who had lost everyone in her family, confronts the unalterable reality of loss: "Once in a while, I recall that history. My tears would just roll down on their own. I just sobbed by myself. I have lost everything and there is nothing that I can do to get it back. The dead, you cannot bring them back." The kind of violence that was done unto the Cambodian nation constitutes a tear in the metaphysical and social fabric that cannot be easily patched. Speaking to the irreparability of this historical injury, a Cambodian woman described herself as "damaged [like] a broken vase that has been mended [but] will never be whole . . . again."[69] It is this sense of finality that underscores the feeling of rupture, and for many survivors, the elusiveness of justice. Mrs. Sim, a middle-aged survivor, softly said, "I rarely ever speak about my experiences. People often ask me about those days, and now about the tribunal. There can never be justice. No courts in the world can bring back my mother, my father, my childhood." It is thus not surprising that only 3 percent of those surveyed in Cambodia listed justice, as ostensibly provided by the Khmer Rouge tribunal, as a personal priority.[70]

Betwixt History and Memory

If speech eludes, memory evokes and provokes. As one Cambodian refugee reflected,

> The memories of the escape and the terrible things that happened to all of us have permanently made scars on our souls for our entire lives. We are all wounded and there is little we can do to respond to the pain except get through our days the best we can. . . . I am silent and inside of me I cry. . . . But I say nothing.[71]

The survivors' relationship to memory is, thus, one of ambivalence. Memory, on one hand, is the thread that connects their multiple "lives." In the re-stitching of life and history, the past irreparably bleeds into the present, for the meaning that survivors attribute to the present is often framed by reference, consciously or subconsciously, to the past. These memory flickers that punctuate the receding temporality—sometimes a welcome illumination, other times jarringly glaring, bringing to the fore that which they wish to remain obscure—are not only central to the survivors' existence, they are also their constant source of pain because they are reminders of things lost, fragmented, shattered, things that can never be fully recovered. As a result, there is a void that will always stand between the world of survivors and that of ordered normalcy, and a sense of acute and permanent aloneness that permeates their lives: "The more I remembered, the more I felt excluded and alone."[72] It is thus that for many survivors, the trauma is not only in what they lived through but also in what they live with. In that sense, survival itself, as Caruth observes, "can be a crisis."[73]

Memory and recollection exacerbates this existential crisis by disturbing the fragile world that survivors inhabit, in which life instincts force the blurring and darkening of life traces, where History compels the rewriting of histories. Under the Khmer Rouge, memory was a place of both refuge and peril. As Rithy Panh reflected, "To survive you must hide within yourself. A picture can be stolen, a thought cannot."[74] To a regime bent on totalistic control over man and society, however, these hidden thoughts—memories—were the greatest threat, for they constituted the kernel of hope and resistance. "The mental enslavement of the subjects of a totalitarian regime," Paul Connerton notes, "begins when their memories are taken away."[75] With looming fear of denunciation, survival in many instances necessitated a deliberate severance from the past and fabrication of new identities. Life histories, reconstituted from ellipses and memory gaps, traumatic recollection and defensive response, acquired a permanency that belies the artificiality of their genesis. Even years after resettlement, it is not uncommon for refugees to retain the names that they had assumed during the various phases of their journey. In some cases, the new alias memorializes a certain moment in their lives, their meaning understood only by the individual. The renowned artist and playwright Pich Tum Kravel, for instance, took on a name that is a combined reference to his stage character and an earring, a "piercing" memory forever embedded as a reminder to never forget. Coming from a culture where a given name is believed to reflect a person's essence and influence the development of his or her character, survivors' decision to retain the names that they had assumed for themselves during the Khmer Rouge era reinforces the notion that so much of their identity is shaped by the proximity to death and the disconnect in life. Life "after *a-Pot*" is not just a new chapter in their lives. It is essentially an entirely new life, with the cleavage being not just between the present and the past, but between the present and a past that is at risk of never having existed.

Behaviors learned under the Khmer Rouge were subsequently reinforced in the border camps, where refugees found themselves once again placed in situations of having to hang their future on the credibility of their biography. This process of re-membering, of reattaching a fractured life, necessarily involved at times omissions, edits, and errors. Absences are often redacted from immigration papers, hence of their places in the reconstituted lives in exile; if they are ever reclaimed, as with the reappearance of the presumed dead, these past relationships are necessarily altered to fit the contours of new realities. This is especially true when one spouse had remarried or had registered himself or herself as unmarried when applying for asylum. It is one of the many paradoxes of post–Khmer Rouge reality that, in these instances, family reunification was possible only through denial or fabrication of new relationality.

Where one's welfare depends upon delivering consistent information, ambiguity and vagueness in disclosure become a safer and, eventually, an almost instinctual response. Among refugees, these ellipses are tacitly recognized and inconsistencies rarely contested, allowing ambiguities and secrets to live in the gray zone between recognition and acknowledgment. As a people whose lives have been torn and patched in many ways and in many places, refugees are reconciled to the tension and contradictions in their lives and in the lives of others. Living with the multiplicity of selves and layers of identity thus becomes a part of the liminality, ambivalence, and ambiguity that mark the post-genocide world of survivors. For many, the fear of revealing one's compromised past, even to one's spouse, means having to work through grief and trauma in even greater isolation. Women are further silenced by cultural prejudice. Chim Math, a former detainee of S-21, said, "I've tried to forget. I have never even told my husband or children. But I remember what they did, like it happened yesterday."[76] Though widowhood, abandonment, and rape, including state-coerced "red weddings," have become "normalized" by recent experiences, they remain disconcerting subjects in a community that continues to place import on the ideals of chastity and cohesive family. Trading silence for a chance at a redeemed future, Ms. Pen Sochan, a victim of a Khmer Rouge forced marriage, never again revealed her past, not even to her six children, after her betrothed's family rejected her for not being a virgin.[77]

These losses nonetheless hover in the background, palpable but unarticulated. They close survivors off from each other, and at times even from the intimacy of the family. With each member burdened by his or her own ghosts, no one can provide solace to anyone; there isn't any to go around. All too often, family members seek to shield each other from pain with their silence, afraid that speech and recollection would prick open the wounds that "may scab but rarely heal."[78] Hence, they remain walled-in by their own silence, visited only by private haunting. With each imprisoned by his or her past, family members often end up leading parallel lives, aspects of which will never, and can never, intersect.

"So That the Children Will Never Forget"

If, for some, silence is refuge and resistance, the need to bear witness is, for others, an unyielding insistence, compelling them to tell and retell the stories that the world should know but does not seem to care about. In the preface of his memoir, Pin Yathay wrote, "In just two years, I lost everyone I loved . . . and everything that was dear to me. I am left only with memories. In this book, I want those memories to live on."[79] As it is for many of history's battered subjects, the struggle to remember is also a struggle for relevance. It is a stance against the invisibilization of mass graves and the depersonalization and dehumanization of totalitarianism. It is this need to recover their humanity that distills the search for justice for survivors like Vann Nath, one of the few to have emerged alive from Tuol Sleng, into a quest for personal accountability, encapsulated in the simple question, "Why did you do this to me?" For Rithy Panh, it is through accountability that humanity will be restored for both the victims and the perpetrators: "I'm not looking for objective truth, . . . I just want words. Especially Duch's words. I want him to talk and explain himself. . . . I want him to answer me, and in so doing to take a step on the road to humanity."[80]

Of the destructiveness of totalitarianism, Connerton wrote, "What is horrifying in totalitarian regimes is not only the violation of human dignity but the fear that there might remain nobody who could ever again properly bear witness to the past."[81] Where the incumbent state is implicated, *le devoir de mémoire*, the duty to acknowledge and reckon, thus falls on the survivors. Among first-generation Cambodian survivors, there is a prevailing fear that in mass death, in the fading memory of the surviving generation, and in the generational disconnect, time will prove to be the ultimate tragedy. Witnessing thus is an ultimate defiance of the totalitarian attempt to render insignificant through arbitrary executions and daily transgressions on selves and being. After describing his experience as a human ox made to pull a plow in a Khmer Rouge labor camp, Phim spoke of his life's dream to paint a mural at the housing complex in East Oakland, so that "the children will never forget what we went through."

Though many recount "the Pol Pot stories" as testimonials, others do so as a way of making the unreal real, or simply as a reminder of being alive. These stories are often shared spontaneously and in ways that reaffirm the feeling of community, of people bound by experiences that cannot truly be shared by outsiders. Survivors would say that *roeung a-Pot doch ta knear* (the Pol Pot stories are all the same). In their world, in which contradictions and paradoxes coexist in familiar tension, "sameness" and "differentness" inhabit the same plane. In this process of "talking stories" (*niyey roeung*), or as Alessandro Portelli would have it, "history telling," each person would invariably chime in with his or her contributions to the mosaic of recounting, editing, supplementing, and reinforcing. One is often left with the impression that they are talking to everyone and to no one. It is for themselves that they speak. Even if the sharing is not in the narrative itself, it is in the narration. For a people whose feeling of community has been compromised by death, dislocation, and distrust, and whose experiences and narratives have been questioned by outsiders, by their own children, and even by their own inability to reconcile the surrealism of their experiences, such reaffirmation is important and necessary. Evoking Halbwachs's notion of the social frame of memory, Novick is right in underscoring the "circular relationship between collective identity and collective memory."[82] In the contradicting and the reaffirming of recounting, every refugee can participate in the shaping and memorializing of a collective history, and in so doing find comfort in the assurance of a shared identity. Given Khmer social stratification, genocidal losses, separation, and exile have been an essentially leveling experience. One survivor reflected,

> The one and only time that I felt that Khmers were really together was in 1978, when we first came out of Pol Pot. We all gathered in one huge clearing and one young woman stood up and started to sing "O, Phnom-Penh." It's an old song about the beauty of the city. But it was also about what and who we were. We all started to cry. Have you ever seen thousands of Cambodians sitting down and crying together?

Those who did not live through the experience, but whose lives had been undeniably marked by the tragedies, listened. They may even be compelled to ask for a recounting of the same stories, many times over, partly to concretize that which transcends the boundaries of their imagination, partly as a feeble attempt to connect with the experiences of their loved ones—the moments of suffering, the context of death and dying that they were not able to share. It is thus that these narratives exercise their reparative power on both the narrator and the audience, and above all on the social bond that needs to be restored between the individual and the collective.

Though in vastly different ways, both silence and compulsive recounting represent attempts at reconciling with that "something [that] one cannot understand," which constitutes "a painful void, a puncture, a permanent stimulus that insists on being satisfied."[83] As Rithy Panh stated with piercing eloquence, "What wounds me has no name."[84] In effect, those who speak appear to be no more reconciled with their experiences than those silenced by the memories. While survivors may manifest a certain readiness to recount their experiences, it is often delivered with the degree of generalization that is proportionate to the level of sensitivity and personalism of the subject at hand. What is often expressed is *bavardage*—shallow chatter.[85] As Wiesel reveals of his own experience, "The tales that I recount are never those that I would like to tell, or ought to tell."[86] As victims, as survivors, as exiles, they are torn between the need to reveal to others all the pain that they had experienced and the need to hide behind ambiguity. It is perhaps this same centrifugal pull between the compulsion to speak and the need to protect the self and the psyche against the vulnerability of disclosure that often makes survivors more willing to share personal narratives with relative strangers while remaining extremely guarded in more intimate conversations. The fact that "the essential will never be said or understood"[87] means that there will always be memories that survivors seek to remember as well as to forget. These memories—*snaam*—that connote both traces and stains, are simultaneously imprints that they want to preserve and stains that they cannot erase. As a result, there is a perpetual unrequited need, a gaping denial of something unfulfilled from which stems the yearning for community and communication in a context that is familiar, in ways that require no translation.

Writing History

If remembering involves a retracing of one's life paths, writing involves a journey across a different terrain. As with speech, the extremism of the experience impedes other forms of expression. Of the injury done to the Cambodian imagination, Soth Polin, a renowned prewar writer, reflected,

> There is something that we cannot get past. It just kills the imagination. It is the atrocity of the Khmer Rouge. Even if you are reaching in your imagination for a new destination, you cannot get past their cruelty. When you try to write something without mentioning the Khmer Rouge, you can't. The next generation will forgive that, they will forget, but for us, we cannot forgive it. . . .[88]
>
> Maybe this is why I cannot finish my writing: because of this story. Because of this, I lost my inspiration. Because the reality surpasses the imagination.[89]

The situation is the same, he notes, for the Cambodian nation as a whole: "What we have lost is not reconstructable. An epoch is finished. So when we have literature again, it will be a new literature."[90] It is this simultaneous mutilation of the mind, spirit, and body of those "who are no longer here" and, in fundamental ways, also of the survivors, that the artist Séra Ing seeks to capture with his limbless and headless sculptures for the genocide memorial.[91] The dismembered state not only invokes many ancient Khmer sculptures, hence continuity that threads through discontinuities, but also the embodied fractures of the genocidal experience, and that which Séra refers to as "the fragile remembrance of a tragedy."[92]

For many survivors, documenting their experiences involves moving beyond the realm of the personal, hence a "public" act even when devoid of the intention to publish. In that sense, it is an alienating form for dealing with issues that are intensely private and that call for private mourning. If remembering is to enter that which Blanchot has termed "the wounded space" and "to shine a merciless light on faces and events,"[93] as Wiesel notes, then to write a memoir is in essence "to draw up a balance sheet of your life,"[94] a process that can only be complicated by the moral abyss into which survivors were flung. That their own survival may have been purchased with others' untold sacrifices leaves long shadows over the present for many like Mardi Seng: "My father died so that my family might live."[95] The moral distance among the various realities that survivors have had to traverse in one lifetime are difficult to reconcile; articulation and documentation would mean confronting the unbearable and speaking of the unspeakable. The strain can be exacting. It took Sam Keo nearly twenty years to write his autobiography, a process so painful that, at times, he would break down after each paragraph. Of his own experience as a concentration camp survivor and writer, Jorge Sémprun wrote, "I had to choose between literature and life and I chose life."[96] Ultimately, it is perhaps the belief in the futility of the exercise that stifles the desire to document. In *The Boat*, Nam Le's father reflected about the futility of remembering: "Only you'll remember. I'll remember. They will read and clap their hands and forget. . . . Sometimes it's better to forget, no?"[97]

Though often without the vocabulary for articulation or the luxury of reflection, for many survivors forgetting is not an option. Of this history, a friend once stated so eloquently, "It has been almost forty years but it is so fresh. When will it ever be un-fresh?" Of the insistence of memory, Loung Ung noted, "I found out that memories are never silent, whether or not I speak or write about it, they are always there. And sooner or later, they'll come boiling back up. . . . The story . . . wouldn't go away."[98] Recall, recounting, and reckoning are therefore imperative, for things that are left unsaid, unresolved, and above all unrequited do not disappear. They return, as LaCapra puts it, "in a transformed, at times disfigured and disguised manner."[99] In his cultural reading of the sudden blindness that afflicted Cambodian women in the United States,[100] Trent Walker referenced the *Suvannasama Jataka*, in which Buddha's mother was blinded by snake venom.[101] It is thus that I argue that the concept of *peus* (venom) rather than *kum* (vengeance) carries greater analytic potency for understanding both the wounding encounter of autogenocide—the "poisoned truth," as Rithy Panh puts it—and the anger it provokes, that which Arn Chorn calls "the tiger in my heart."[102] Unlike *kum, peus* is externally inflicted but unconsciously internalized, and if left unattended, can become fatally destructive.

Against the backdrop of loss and fragmentation, documentation becomes an act of resistance against the threat of historical oblivion, hence a political undertaking that transcends the personal. In the diaspora, the last four decades saw the production of several published memoirs and many more unpublished writings. Cambodians, once uneasy with the seeming egoism of autobiographies, now find in the higher purpose a counterrationale to the cultural emphasis on self-effacement. Like the poet and playwright U Sam Oeur, who considers his work "a cry of anguish . . . of the world which cannot speak for itself,"[103] Sophal Leng evokes writing as an act of memorialization:

> Twenty years and what seems like a dozen lifetimes have passed . . . and although I can now look back, with less emotions, the memories of that time are as vivid as if they happened yesterday. I cannot completely explain my reasons for the need to write about these experiences except as a testimony to those whose lives were lost and can no longer speak for themselves.[104]

The need to document, publicize, and transmit thus can be read as an extension of the simple but insistent desire to proclaim that those swept into the oblivion of mass death were once here, that they were important, and, above all human, with personal dreams, hopes, and disappointments. These are identities that have been callously erased by "disappearances" and unmarked graves, and that must be recovered if wholeness and coherence are to be regained, both for the individual and for the nation. Writing is a way of giving form to the annihilation, the void, the absences. In essence, survivors sought to compensate in death what they were unable to do in life, by restoring dignity, humanism, form, and presence to those who had been denied them by the Khmer Rouge. The clay figures in Rithy Panh's documentary *The Missing Picture* are animated with soul, consecrated with the lives, identities, and memories of those who survived and those who did not. For survivors, as Marianne Hirsch posits, "memory is necessarily an act not only of recall but also of mourning, a mourning often inflected by anger, rage, and despair."[105] Art is thus transformed into an utmost commemorative act. This refusal to be denied constitutes "small acts of repair,"[106] and as Séra Ing reminds us, "Restitution is not restoration; perhaps small acts of repair is all we can do."[107]

As with rites of remembrance, through these articulations "the dead were given life" not just so that "they would eventually cease to distress the living,"[108] but ultimately so that the living could actually begin to have a life. It is perhaps only by giving significance to those rendered insignificant that survivors can reclaim *their own* significance, their own sentient self from the "numbness to life itself,"[109] to recover a bit of the "shrinking surface of the soul that [came] in contact with the bloody and menacing world out there."[110] As Alessandro Portelli puts it, to speak is "to preserve the teller from oblivion,"[111] and the same is true of writing. Before the convening of the Khmer Rouge tribunal, writing was one of the few ways that survivors could provide public testimonials, to insist on their relevance, and as Helen Leslie puts it, "to challenge entrenched power structures and to rebuild the moral and social order for themselves and for their communities."[112] For Loung Ung, writing was the road to self-recovery: "The KR tried to take my power, my voice and it took me years to find it again."[113] It is also redemption: "As I tell people about genocide, I get the opportunity to redeem myself. I've had the chance to do something that's worth me being alive. . . . The more I tell people, the less the nightmares haunt me." There is, as such, a dialectical relationship between memory, identity, and writing. Of creation as a critique and negation of power, Rithy Panh reflected, "It means that we are alive. It means that we can express our feelings. It means that the Khmer Rouge didn't destroy our imagination; they couldn't destroy it."[114] To memorialize one's life in writing, however, requires an investment in the future, which has become elusive for many who have been reduced to living as creatures of the day. Above all, the memorialization of one's life experiences requires the recovery of the self, for as Wallace Stevens so eloquently puts it, "In this mind of winter, the pathos of summer and autumn as much as the potential of spring are nearby but unobtainable."[115]

Given the plurality of loss, what individuals determine to be important to remember and how varies. The bucolic past that is not only lost through time but also altered by the memory of violence reveals itself in Vann Nath's painting *My Village of Birth*. For the visual artist Sopheap Pich, his installation of the morning glory, the staple food of the Khmer Rouge era, gestures toward not only the painful past but also the present that is threatened by neoliberal greed.[116] With the Boeung Kak lake landfilled for private development, the aquatic bed of the morning glory may soon disappear from the city's urban landscape, marking the erasure of yet one more memory trace. In the same vein, for Kalyanee Mam, a Cambodian American filmmaker and environmental activist, the Cambodian tragedy is not temporally bounded and left behind; it persists in the perpetuation of violence and precarity that bear daily upon vulnerable communities in post-genocide Cambodia;[117] the imperative, thus, is not to simply protect the memory of the Cambodia past, but the Cambodia of the present. Others, like Sophiline Shapiro, whose choreographies interrogate themes of violence, retribution, accountability, and self-recriminations, illuminate and provoke the confrontation of post-genocide ruination and debris through the veil of abstraction. Others still, like Emmanuelle Nhean, who sees her art as a "duty to Cambodia," choose to focus only on the beautiful: "I have overcome this painful period. As Matisse, I have chosen to show what is beautiful . . . above everyday life, something related to dreams."[118] Whereas the older generation often assert their presence through fluidity and blurred and untranslated lines, veiling disconcerting realities with ambiguity, younger-generation Cambodians, especially those in the diaspora and perhaps because they are of the diaspora, find and define their identities and place in this history through deliberate self-assertion. For Prach Ly, music and poetry provide the platform for acknowledgment and justice:

> Twenty-five years have gone by. When will justice be served? If we keep quiet about it, what they went through will be for nothing. . . . I don't believe in vengeance. I don't believe in fighting. But I do believe in justice.[119]

For many survivors, the wounds are kept raw by the elusiveness of accountability. Efforts to bring the Khmer Rouge to trial have spanned over three decades, making it the longest wait in the history of international tribunals. Most of the Khmer Rouge leaders, including Pol Pot, Ieng Sary, and Ta Mok, the infamous head of the Southwestern Zone, have since died, and others are in failing health or incapacitated; Ieng Thirith, Pol Pot's sister-in-law, was recused from testifying at her own trial because of dementia. Bou Meng was insistent in his conversation with me, "We need to finish this before they all died. Otherwise we will never know the truth." The search for accountability, however, has been repeatedly thwarted by political expediency. In the 1980s, with communist Vietnam's preponderance over Cambodia and Laos threatening regional stability, the hope for an effective resistance movement was hitched to the remnant Khmer Rouge forces. Democratic Kampuchea's bloody record was conveniently expunged and its expeditious reintegration into the political community brazenly proclaimed in the name of the coalition government in exile. The issues became distilled into a Manichean choice between genocide and foreign occupation. Pointing to the importance of transcending the past, Sichan Siv, who later became U.S. ambassador to the United Nations Economic and Social Council, argued that "continued occupation of Cambodia by the Vietnamese is a greater danger in the long-term than what has already happened to our country under Pol Pot."[120] Lamouth, another Cambodian refugee, underscored the moral quandary:

> Yes, the Khmer Rouge killed. But as long as there are Cambodians left somewhere in this world, and as long as the land is still there, we can always repopulate. With foreign occupation, however, it is the death of the nation. In the future, Cambodia may no longer be on the map. My children would not know where they came from, who they are.

In the ensuing decades, politics continue to impair the quest for accountability. Fearing that a comprehensive and independent investigation might implicate those in the current government who were former Khmer Rouge, the Hun Sen regime has argued that such an endeavor would only "prick open old wounds" and undermine the process of national reconciliation. When resistance to the idea of an international tribunal proved insufficient to stop the process, the Phnom Penh government insisted on a mixed court with a narrowly defined mandate, limited to trying only the most senior Khmer Rouge leaders. The Extraordinary Chambers in the Courts of Cambodia (ECCC), which was finally created in 2006, was in fact a hybrid court, composed of international and Cambodian judges, while those brought to trial were, for the foreseeable future, limited to the five then-living Khmer Rouge senior leaders, namely, Kaing Guek Eav (Duch), Nuon Chea, Ieng Thirith, Ieng Sary, and Khieu Samphan. What is evident is that while justice, reconciliation, and healing are often spoken of interchangeably, these notions not only are not synonymous, but may even be conflicting. While the government repeatedly insisted that the quest for justice would undermine national reconciliation, many survivors like Bou Meng view the absence of justice, in its plural register, as impairing personal and collective healing: "The ghosts they came to visit me and ask for me to help find justice for them. Why did she die and I live? The wounds inside still haven't healed. The hurt won't stop until there is justice."[121]

Buried under the hyperattentiveness to macro forces—namely, the international community, the UN, the donors, and the state—are questions that essentially go unaddressed: justice for whom and in what form? Though Cambodians, both inside and outside Cambodia, have played prominent roles in genocide prevention and peacebuilding initiatives,[122] there is little room for Cambodians of different generations to speak for themselves, to articulate their issues as they define them, assert their perspectives on this important chapter of their history, complex and diverse as they are, demand accountability in ways that are legible to them, and as a nation publicly mourn their losses in ways they deem necessary. While the focus has centered on juridical process, a population survey conducted by the University of California–Berkeley[123] found that most Cambodians know very little about the court, its mandate, and its procedures. Of the respondents who had lived under the Khmer Rouge, over one-third know nothing about the ECCC, and almost half said they only know a little about who are on trial; only 3 percent can correctly name those five individuals; and some 54 percent of the respondents simply did not know. These findings point to the disconnect between these developments and the Cambodian society. With over 30 percent of the population younger than fourteen, the Cambodian population is young. Despite the magnitude of the historical trauma, coverage of the Khmer Rouge period in the country's educational curriculum was problematic at best, highly polemical in the 1980s and, until the publication and dissemination of the first textbook dedicated to this chapter of Cambodian history in 2008, tenuous. Given the generational disconnect that registers both in Cambodia and in the diaspora, the risk of social amnesia is difficult to discount. The Berkeley study indicated that 81 percent of the respondents in Cambodia who were born after or did not live under the Khmer Rouge regime described their knowledge of that period as poor or very poor.

Along with lack of awareness, there is also a profound distrust of the legal system, particularly the courts, which many Cambodians see as undermined by corruption and partisanship.[124] In the Berkeley survey, only 36 percent of the respondents said they trusted the Cambodian court system, and only 37 percent said they trusted Cambodian judges. Almost 60 percent of the respondents do not believe that "justice is the same for everyone."[125] While popular confidence in the process has since risen as a result of public education about the ECCC, it has been undermined by the scandals and continuing politicization of the tribunal and by the prevailing conditions in Cambodia, where law, order, and accountability remain elusive. Close to two decades after the peace settlement and despite the infusion of international assistance, force, in the form of extrajudicial killings, intimidation, and persecution of the poor and the politically threatening, continues to be deployed with impunity. A high number of respondents in the Berkeley study reported being a witness to rape and torture, and forced to kill someone. In fact, rape and humiliation were two categories perceived to be on the *increase* when compared to the Khmer Rouge period. Despite pervasive and brutalizing abuse of power, the Bertelsmann 2008 report noted that not a single high-ranking official has been prosecuted to date for these transgressions.

These enactments of the pathology of power in the everyday reanimate the terror imprints. Where victims live in proximity to their tormentors, and force commands impunity, fear continues to prevail and to censor. It is thus that many survivors in Cambodia and in the diaspora find themselves reluctant to opine about the Khmer Rouge trials for fear of retribution. Only half of those who participated in the Berkeley survey indicate a willingness to testify about their and their family's experiences under the Khmer Rouge. In the diaspora, the issues of the tribunal and even the campaign to create a national day of remembrance in the US are controversial. Of discourse in post-massacre Bali, Leslie Dwyer notes that, while truth-finding processes rest on the presumed possibility of "straightforward narratives of 'what really happened,' . . . the psychic imprints of terror, its de-stabilisation of social and cultural forms, and the shadows of fear it casts over political landscapes render the languages used to articulate violence ambivalent, shifting and even treacherous."[126]

Faith in the ability of the legal process to deliver justice is also tested by the limited mandate of the ECCC. In his opening statement, Duch's defense attorney, Kar Savuth, questioned whether justice could be delivered given that only a small fraction of the Khmer Rouge, and even of the leadership, will be put on trial. Despite the differences in intent, it is a concern that resonates among Cambodian survivors, many of whom felt that for full accountability to be achieved, the process should not stop with the five leaders, but extend to others who are implicated in these crimes, including former Khmer Rouge who continue to hold positions of power in the current Cambodian government.[127] Many also felt that true justice can only be delivered by trials not only of those in power positions but also of the persons who actually persecuted them or their loved ones. As Vann Nath reflected, "If I had ever met Pol Pot or any of his top henchmen I wouldn't have had anything to say to them. They were either top—the chiefs of them all—and far away from me. I never had any direct contact with them or saw their activities with my own eyes. But it [would be] different [with] . . . the guards who worked at Tuol Sleng."[128] Hun Sen, however, proclaimed, "The trial of four or ten people will bring justice for [Cambodia's] 12 million people. That is enough."[129] For Theary Seng, a rights advocate and orphan of the Khmer Rouge, the scope of justice as delineated by the court is grossly unmatched by the cost: "There's no magic number as to how many should be prosecuted and should be indicted. But five indictees after $200 million spent with only one verdict is not acceptable. The current five are not sufficient for the crimes that took the lives of 1.7 million Cambodians."[130]

If politics silence and divide, the nature of auto-genocide itself complicates. Unlike other genocidal instances in history, the Cambodian experience is particularly disorienting because the perpetrators not only "look like you; they are you."[131] It is an encounter with evil that gazes back: "People say foreigners were behind the killings so that they can take our land, that it was because the big countries were fighting each other and it spilled into Cambodia. . . . That's what I *heard*. But what I *saw* were Cambodians killing our own people." This unsettling reality shatters language because it takes the "extraordinary" to yet another level: "When Cambodians kill Cambodians, it is very difficult to speak." It is *hous peykh*, extreme, beyond words. It provokes not only the questioning of one's fundamental assumptions about the external world, but ultimately a self-questioning. Under the Khmer Rouge, fundamental values were made to change, beliefs altered, morality compromised by the instinct for self-preservation. From this stems a certain moral implication: "Coming out of the darkness, one suffered because of the reacquired consciousness of having been diminished. . . . Our moral yardstick had changed. . . . You find no obvious transgression; . . . nevertheless, you cannot exclude it."[132] By extension, if you yourself can be diminished by situational morality, it is possible that acts of brutality were committed not by inherently bestial characters but by individuals under similar duress.

> It would have been easy for me to think of them as faceless monsters devoid of human attributes. But the Khmer Rouge . . . were my fellow Cambodians who had grown up as I had on the rice and the fruit of our country. . . . I tried to understand why they had lost their Cambodian characteristics of kindness and generosity . . . maybe it was just the path of survival they had chosen. Maybe they were as helpless as I, as caught up in the whirlpool of social change.[133]

While this by no means implies an inability of survivors to locate accountability, it does explain those moments of reluctance to condemn, lest moral condemnation become inwardly directed. In the state of exception that was Democratic Kampuchea, where actions have gravity immeasurable by ordinary standards, what degree of complicity makes one a "perpetrator"? Tribunals often work with a clear binary between victims and perpetrators, but what about perpetrators who have become victims, or victims who were made into perpetrators? This is an unresolved tension that percolates over the proposal to create a Tuol Sleng memorial where names of executed former Khmer Rouge will also be etched in commemoration, thus making permanent the forced co-inhabitation of victims and perpetrators.

Reconciliation and Healing

While political rhetoric and interference, expediency, and survival imperatives may override and mask, they cannot eliminate the pain that continues to afflict survivors and their posterity. It is merely relegated to another place. The fact that many survivors have had to live in close proximity with perpetrators without retribution does not imply reconciliation, only the absence of enacted violence; Ms. Kem Vaing, a civil party to the tribunal, shared a taxi with Mr. Huon Kin, who had killed her husband, without exchanging a word. In the follow-up Berkeley study in 2010, 81 percent of those surveyed still harbored feelings of hatred toward the Khmer Rouge. In another study, over 70 percent of the respondents indicated that there had been no reconciliation between former Khmer Rouge and victims in their village.[134] In fundamental ways, it is not possible to talk about reconciliation and "closure" in the conventional sense. Many, like Rong, see in their present life the irreparable legacies of this history: "I lost my entire family, I have no parents, aunts or uncles, no grandparents. How can there be any happiness that way? Even today, my daughter is angry. She said no one is born so alone—just one head. Other people have aunts and uncles and relatives around them. All I have is one head." In the Khmer cultural context, where an individual's sense of identity is embedded within and informed by the social web of family and kin, the reference to "one head" speaks to the utter aloneness that many survivors feel. Asked how the trauma can be eased, Noun spoke emphatically: "I no longer think of release. How can there be any relief? I lost a husband, a son, seven brothers, and both parents. I am the only one left—like a lone reed."

Women, who constitute the overwhelming majority of the immediate post-genocide population, have found solace in both activism and disengagement. Of the civil parties who filed complaints with the tribunal, 69 percent are women. Others, like the *doan chi* who seek refuge in monasteries, have turned to spirituality for deliverance from worldly attachment, of which pain is a prominent feature. For some others still, solace could be found only in extreme disengagement. The blindness that afflicted Cambodian American women can in essence be regarded as a physical manifestation of this retreat from sight and sound (*leng chang khoeugn, chang leou*) and into themselves; they "had seen too much" for one lifetime. Withdrawn into a world where the eyes need no longer see and the mind no longer reasons, they exist "lost in a silence crowded with memories."[135]

Others revisit their own helplessness in search of reason, unreconciled between the need to give in to fatalistic acceptance that divests all guilt and responsibilities, and the inability to believe that forewarnings of such life-changing events could have bypassed them altogether. Friends and families would ask of each other whether they could have foreseen these fateful developments, each assuming the burden of thinking that if only he or she had known, so and so would still be alive, that they could have done this or that to alter the course of their fate and the fate of their loved ones. Vaddey Ratner spoke of the loss of her father as "still devastating every time I think about it, especially in my solitude and silence. A part of me still wonders if I hadn't revealed who he was, would he still be with us?"[136] That is the guilt that many survivors harbor within themselves, to some degree or another. The believers talked about signs and omens, looking for clues in premonitions, for the "out of the ordinary" in the ordinary, in order to make sense of their plight. Even decades later, my mother still spoke of an inexplicable experience she had the night before our flight to Thailand, in which the candlesticks on her altar appeared to have been wiped clean. To her, it marked the beginning of our exile, the candlesticks symbolizing the thoroughness of our dispossession and severance of all links to our past, the *tabula rasa* of our personal history. Like the candlesticks wiped clean by some unknown force, our past, our lives before *refugitude*, had been erased.

The search for healing continues, even if hope for true justice is tempered. As the judicial process battles politics, financial hardship, corruption, and scandal to deliver what many see as an imperfect but important form of justice, Cambodians continue to confront and work through their historical trauma in private mourning and communal commemoration. Over the last three decades, some eighty memorials and countless numbers of sacred sites have been erected and marked by survivors, overwhelmingly without state support or acknowledgment. Many Cambodians turn to spirituality and rituals to find comfort in the belief that that which cannot be delivered through the legal process will be delivered through karmic consequences: "I think often about fate. We are alive today because of our merits and we live today by our merits. . . . [By building good merits], we can be reborn into a good station." Buddhism, with its wheel of accountability, provides not only meaning for the seemingly incomprehensible but also a way out of the impasse; the key is to break the cycle of entanglement by not continuing to build bad karmic ties (*chorng kam, chorng pear*) through retribution: "I want [the young] to learn the Buddhist teachings so that they can free their minds of the violence."[137] Within this Buddhist frame, revenge, etymologically rooted in the idea of absolution (*vindicare*),[138] is not liberatory but implicatory. It is significant that while over 47 percent of survivors surveyed in 2009 did not wish to reconcile with former Khmer Rouge, and over 45 percent have not forgiven them, only 19 percent "totally desire" revenge.[139]

Of his victimizers, Im Chan, a Tuol Sleng survivor, reflected, "I would not like to meet them because I would really like to kill them. I would like to see them punished. . . . But truly I cannot do like that because I am a Buddhist—no revenge."[140] For all that has been implied about the Khmer predisposition toward "disproportionate revenge," the desire to break the karmic cycle expressed by many survivors is an important reminder of the pitfalls of cultural reductionism.

It is thus that for many like Chan Socheat, a civil party, the "apology requested is for the dead," for it is they who ultimately will have to render judgment on the perpetrators when they die.[141] In this reversal of the panoptic power in which "it is now the dead who do the surveillance, the dead who stare hauntingly back at the survivors and the killers,"[142] as Boreth Ly puts it, Chum Sirath redirected that brutalized gaze of the S-21 victims that accuse: "You saw the 32,000 eyes, the hopelessness, the despair, the incredulity. . . . How can you escape the 32,000 eyes, if Cain cannot even escape one pair of eyes?"[143] In the ultimate redress, the debased souls are now the only ones vested with the power to absolve.

For survivors like U Sam Oeur, healing can only be achieved by not simply confronting evil but by transcending it.

> In Cambodia, we have very bitter *sleng* seeds. They are poisonous. But when you use the seed as medicine, you halve or quarter it, and you chew it one piece at a time. The seed can heal malaria. . . . But if you eat the whole thing, it will kill you. . . . The positive and the negative—every strand is precious in the web of life.[144]

It is in remembering and retrieving that aspect of the nation's and one's own past, in reintegrating the "negative and the positive . . . in the web of life,"[145] that wholeness can be reconstructed, albeit not seamlessly. Ultimately, confronting and enfolding the loss is perhaps the way for the living to move through and beyond this history. For many survivors, reconciliation is not political or psychological resolution, but a quiet acknowledgment of the irreversible and a resigned coexistence with that reality, that may or may not ever lead to forgiveness, but possibly transcendence. It is a twofold process that involves learning to live alongside one's victimizers and learning to live with that unnameable something that lives inside and alongside oneself. What is implied is not a process of moving on but moving through, with the traces and stains present and submitted to the imprints of new encounters, and as a result may be altered, made more legible, or smudged over time. Taken in that sense, Youk Chhang was right to point out that Cambodians have been working on "reconciliation" for over three decades now.[146] The day before the court rendered its verdict on Duch, all the civil parties gathered at Tuol Sleng and conducted a *bang skaul*, a ceremony for the ancestors, an act, both collective and individual, that reaffirmed the accountability of the living to the dead and simultaneously declared both the importance and the insufficiency of juridical justice.

7

Homeland, Exile, and Return

Think back; happiness was in the country
Lake, stream, flowering tree,
Cicadas sounding their melodies
All this gone, past.
Want to return, but no
Can't, yet still want to go as
Slim hope grows slimmer still that the homeland
Will ever rest from war.

—Luoth Yin, survivor and poet

For genocide survivors, nothing accentuates the sense of rupture more than exile. Flight and dispersal further fractured the Khmer nation, creating yet another geo-temporal frame in which memory, memorializing, and healing must be located. For Cambodian survivors, *exiliance*, which Alexis Nuselovici defines as both the conditions and consciousness of exile, informs the prospects and constraints in post-genocide remembering and reconstitution.

The exodus began as a trickle, as the country's elites made what many thought was a temporary escape from the war, and grew in scale and level of desperation as conditions rapidly deteriorated inside Cambodia. A small handful, mostly staff of the American mission in Phnom Penh, left with the Americans in early April, the smallness of the group and the seemingly unremarkable exit a marked contrast to the much larger and chaos-filled American evacuation from Saigon. Many more civilians and military personnel made the eleventh-hour escape on their own in the face of the advancing Khmer Rouge. One high-ranking official who left without his family on one of the last helicopters out of Phnom Penh recalled,

> We made arrangements to be picked up but the transport never showed up. I could not turn back to get to my family. We drove out to the stadium

where we were told that the helicopters were waiting. There were three helicopters there but one of them could not take off because the batteries were not working. Prime Minister Long Boreth was aboard with us but then he saw his family waiting in the hangar and got off to join them. Our helicopter took off. We later heard that he never made it.[1]

Many air force pilots simply flew their planes across the border into Thailand and requested asylum. A shipload of marines took to the high seas after the naval base at Ream was overrun. After months at sea, they were eventually granted permission to land in the Philippines.

The collapse of the Republic in 1975 also left thousands stranded abroad, the majority of whom were diplomats, students, and civilian and military personnel who had been sent overseas for training, and who now found themselves essentially stateless. Those who could not stay and those who could not return converged in the Thai refugee camps. Kanika recalled,

We ended up in Bangkok but our papers were no longer valid because the government had fallen. My parents did not know what to do or where we would go. Then a friend of theirs told us to register with the Americans to go to Utapao [refugee camp], where we would at least be safe and we could decide what to do later.

I remember that bus ride. There were many important people on that bus—diplomats, generals, and high-ranking ministers. People were chatting because many had not seen each other for a while. Even though they were anxious and their hearts were heavy, there was, strangely, levity because everyone was together. Some were laughing incredulously at their situation. Then the bus slowed down and turned, and we could see a field of tents. The sun beating down was merciless and you could feel how desolate and oppressive that place was. The bus became dead silent. No one could speak.

In this makeshift refuge, families and individuals waited for news about Cambodia, which had become shrouded in silence. The sense of desperation grew palpable with each day of uncertainty and confinement. Resentment against former elites held responsible for the debacle began to percolate inside the camp, erupting in violent altercations. Unable to withstand the horrific news that trickled out of the country, a group of mostly soldiers who had left their families behind opted to return to Cambodia, to tragic ends.

If the 1975 debacle was a shock from which many who now found themselves disavowed and dispersed never fully recovered, the experiences of separation, loss, and dislocation were even more acute for those who fled after the collapse of the Khmer Rouge regime in 1979. After having endured and survived the infernal years of Democratic Kampuchea, refugees were subjected to another layer of trauma by the circumstances of flight—abrupt, secretive, and perilous—that further fractured family and community. Many who were separated from their families under the Khmer Rouge were unable to reunite with them before fleeing to the border. Others could never reconcile with the fact that family members had managed to survive the genocide only to die fleeing across battle-ravaged and heavily mined jungle areas. Organized banditry, rape, and murder were common occurrences in the no-man's land. Mrs. Noun, now middle-aged, recounted, "At the border, the Thais would line up, row after row. They had knives. They pointed them at us and poked us with them to make us turn over everything we had, groping and searching everyone, . . . the young girls [*shaking her head*] . . . no one was spared. Even the Thai children were doing this. The small children had small knives." In 1979, after having successfully crossed into Thailand, some forty thousand Cambodian refugees were forced back down the treacherous trails of the Dangrek Mountains by the Thai military. Mrs. Noun was among the repatriated:

> The cliffs went straight down, and there was no way for us to get down except to cling to the mountain vines. Then we heard *boom-boom*—the mines! Body parts were everywhere, . . . heads blown off with blood splattering like chili pepper seeds. People were pleading for help, and there were so many children crying because they lost their parents. But how could you help? No one could help anyone.

Thousands did not survive. Others found themselves back in Vietnam-occupied Cambodia.

For most of those who managed to stay in Thailand, what followed were years of living in liminality, danger, and fear, with essentially little or no rights or protection.[2] Many of the settlements were in conflict zones, straddling war and lawlessness: "The Vietnamese troops would fire into the camp. Sometimes, they came so close, I could hear them. At night, Cambodian bandits also attacked the camp." Lives that had been so devalued under the Khmer Rouge continued to be disparaged by the wantonness of violence that prevailed on the border. Particularly true of non–UN-recognized camps, refugees, officially classified as "displaced people," lived under the absolutist control of factional armies and the Thai military. Even some protective institutions such as the Thai Task-force 80 were implicated in violence against refugees, and with impunity:

> The greatest danger for us came from the Thai camp guards. They killed, raped, and beat people whenever they wanted. . . . I was there when they stopped a Cambodian woman from selling bananas in the market. She was not permitted to do that, so the guards took the boiling oil from her pan and poured it on her head. Her eyes blew up and she died instantly, right in front of her two small children.[3]

Confinement and loss of self-determination threatened the sense of self. As Yan lamented, "Soon we will grow tails."[4] Years of languishing in makeshift camps, marked as they were by uncertainty, artificiality, and social psychosis, further unraveled the social fabric. A whole generation of "camp children" were born and raised behind barbed wire. Of the Site Two camp population in the early 1980s, only 7 percent were older than forty-five, and approximately 50 percent were younger than fourteen. The generational and cultural disconnect was evident. The Cambodian nation that is rooted in agrarian tradition came to produce, in less than a decade of turmoil, a new generation who knew only that "rice came from the UN trucks."

In diaspora, refugee-survivors embodied the nation's traumatic history. Mai Lam, the Vietnamese commissar responsible for transforming S-21 into a genocide museum, once contended that "to understand the genocide, you must understand Cambodians," to which I argue that to understand Cambodians, one must understand the genocide. Of the Cambodian population in the United States in 1990, the majority of whom were genocide survivors, over 61 percent were under the age of twenty-five, and over 67 percent had no formal schooling,[5] a demographic index of Khmer Rouge anti-intellectualism. As in Cambodia, the disproportionate decimation of Cambodian males left a stark gender imbalance, with over 25 percent of the refugees in the United States registered as widows.[6] In San Diego, for instance, over half of the households surveyed during the peak of the Cambodian resettlement were single-parent households.[7] Fragmented and reconstituted families, including informal adoptees, became a feature of the surviving community. Both in Cambodia and in the diaspora, it is not uncommon to find households of unrelated individuals who came together for expedient reasons, some out of economic necessity, others simply because they have no one else to turn to. Lok Yeay Tem, a childless woman in her seventies whose husband had abandoned her for a younger woman, regularly deposits a small portion of her meager Social Security income with an acquaintance "just so that someone could give me a funeral when I die." As in Cambodia, where many women—widowed, abandoned, or without children to care for them—have formed small communities around temple grounds, seeking companionship and solace in a life of piety, a similar presence is emerging in monasteries in the United States.

Already acute, the genocidal injury is aggravated by the experience of exile. Resettlement, largely into blighted neighborhoods, may have brought reprieve but not an end to the challenges for refugees; a study of the Long Beach community revealed that 70 percent of the respondents have encountered violence after resettlement.[8] In America's racialized society, Cambodian refugees occupy a seemingly paradoxical place, simultaneously visible and marginal. With limited education and English-language proficiency, many refugees are unable to advance economically and socially in America. Though the rate of labor participation is not unfavorable, employment remains concentrated in highly vulnerable sectors. Over two decades after resettlement, only 4 percent of Cambodian Americans occupied managerial positions.[9] Statistics on labor participation also obscure pervasive underemployment, as many refugees hold multiple low-paying jobs without employment security or benefits. With a persistently high poverty index,[10] especially among single-female-headed households with small children, over 30 percent of whom live at or below poverty level, Cambodian Americans are part of that "implosion of the Third World into the First, the peripheralization at the core."[11] The refugee figure thus came to represent in the American public imaginary not the discarded human debris of America's failed imperial project but a social burden, not the consequence of corrupted ideals but the source of corruption of the imagined American ideals.

The challenges to integration into American society are not only structural but also sociocultural. For the majority of Cambodian refugee-survivors who came from a rural background, transitioning from an agrarian to a postindustrial way of life can be a highly daunting and disorienting process. Given the personalistic relationships and village communalism of the Khmer social system, the impersonalism of American society and bureaucracy is alienating. Language and cultural barriers further keep segments of the Cambodian refugee population in social isolation. Such are the paradoxes of the refugee condition—to be packed in an "overcrowded apartment but [still be] isolated and lonely."[12] This is particularly true of the elderly. Speaking of his daily existence, a Cambodian refugee, once a man of action and decision, pensively stated, "I stare at the wall and blink . . . until three o'clock, when the children come home from school. Then there is noise and activity . . . there is life."

Even more unsettling perhaps than the changes in the external environment are the changes that confront and confound them in their intimate spheres. The support system traditionally provided by the family continues to be eroded, first by U.S. dispersal policy in refugee resettlement, and later by the imperative of employment-related relocation. Once fixed and encoded in language and mores, the old paradigm for social interactions lost much of its relevance, as shifts in gender and generational roles impact family dynamics. They began during the war, when many women were left to fend for themselves and their families, and continued under the Khmer Rouge with the systematic destruction of the old social order and fragmentation of the family. In the refugee camps and later in resettlement, the practice of assistance agencies such as Aid to Families with Dependent Children (AFDC) of issuing allocations in the women's names reinforces these changing power dynamics.[13] Given the post-genocide demographics and the structure of opportunity that is marked by increased feminization of labor, women, including those in Cambodia, have also become principal wage earners. For Cambodian American women who are homebound, home industry such as piecemeal sewing provides the opportunity for generating supplemental income. With changing contexts, power relations alter as traditional bases of authority lose their relevance, calling into question critical assumptions about roles and relationality.

For Cambodian American women, this change can be a double-edged sword. The gains garnered from increased economic power are not without adverse trade-offs. The changes do not necessarily mean abandonment of old roles and expectations, but rather the layering of new roles and responsibilities that necessitates the juggling of multiple identities, norms, and expectations, forcing many to walk the "family tightrope."[14] These shifts are further complicated by the fact that women's enhanced economic upward mobility and independence, in many instances, contrast with the real or perceived downward mobility of Cambodian men, especially among first-generation refugees. Their inability to access jobs commensurate with their training or expectations, or to fulfill their traditional role as the breadwinner is a source of disempowerment and emasculation. As one Cambodian American man bemoaned, "We now have to live under the wings of our wives."

Changes also register in intergenerational relations. Revolution, protracted encampment, and migration have fundamentally altered the social position of Cambodian youths, who were once at the bottom of the social hierarchy. Because of the adaptation challenges of the older generation, youths in the diaspora have often had to assume the role of linguistic and cultural brokers, indispensable in the daily negotiations of a refugee family. A father explains his utter reliance upon his children: "We are blind and mute; the children are our bridge to the outside world." What has emerged in many refugee families, in essence, is filiarchy, with power residing in children. The responsibilities and power that came to rest on them, incommensurate with their age, became a psychological burden both for the youths and for the adults, and a source of intergenerational tension when juxtaposed with the latter's sense of disempowerment. In an America that equates Cambodia and everything Cambodian with nothing more than the "killing fields" and with politically and socioeconomically disenfranchised "refugees," many young Cambodian Americans have come to associate their parents—their "Cambodian-ness," their "refugee-ness"—with social stigma and regard them as possessing no inherent capital for success in America. For some, shame and disregard for elders translate into a loss of self-esteem as their own Cambodian-ness and refugee-ness become burdens they cannot unload. With the generational loss of the Khmer language and limited English proficiency of the older generation, linguistic barriers further impede intra-family communication, leaving tension and conflict often unaddressed and unresolved. Accustomed to culturally sanctioned corporal punishment but restrained by the fear of being reported for child abuse, in many instances by their own children, parents are at a loss as to how to resolve intergenerational conflicts: "When we discipline our children, the police come to take us to jail. When we don't do anything and our children err, we, as parents, are blamed. We no longer know what to do." With the rise in gang violence, Cambodian parents have come to fear that they had survived the Khmer Rouge only to lose their children to the streets of America. The neoliberal promise of refuge and betterment, for many, is transformed into "the shifting sands of hope mingled with the crippling sorrow of estrangement."[15]

For many refugee-survivors, genocidal traumas are thus layered with the "traumas of the everyday." Sitha, a Cal State Long Beach student, spoke of the compounded trauma in her family:

> I believe my parents were not able to soak in their experiences completely and move on. My father was so angry and depressed. . . . He lost many people in his life and he was the youngest, . . . the same for my mother. The war has traumatized them in different ways and leaves them mentally and emotionally wounded. My parents were forced to move to a new country, which they knew nothing about: new language, new people, and new land. Big changes occurring one after the other leaves no time for understanding and . . . to adapt.

The sobering realities and daily exigencies of life in resettlement impair reflection and healing. Exacerbated by acculturation stress, the prevalence of trauma-related disorder among Cambodian refugees remains high three decades after resettlement. A study of Cambodians in Long Beach revealed that 62 percent of adults over age thirty-two have posttraumatic stress disorder (PTSD), and 51 percent manifest symptoms of depression.[16] Other disorders, including those associated with the "concentration camp syndrome,"[17] are even more prevalent. A study of Cambodians in San Jose found that "sadness from obsessive thinking" about traumatic events they had experienced were root causes of common illnesses among the Cambodian elderly.[18] Dr. Sam Keo, a Cambodian American clinical psychologist, contends that as a result of social isolation and "lack of distractions," trauma-related disorder, reported to be at over 40 percent among Cambodians in Cambodia,[19] is perhaps more acute for Cambodians in the diaspora.[20] For many, long-suppressed memories did not dissipate over time but resurface with unabated virulence. After a long and successful career, an elderly Cambodian finds himself plagued by recurrent nightmares upon retirement: "Every night, I find myself running in my sleep, getting shot at. The bullets come right at me. It's as if I was still there. . . . It's exactly the way it happened . . . thirty five years ago." The 2011 murder-suicide of a Cambodian grandmother in Seattle is a shrill reminder of the ever-looming peril of latent trauma.

Combined, pre- and post-resettlement stressors contribute to social toxicity. Substance abuse, pathological gambling, and domestic violence are some persisting issues in the Cambodian American community.[21] In a study conducted in Massachusetts, home to one of the largest Cambodian American communities, 47 percent of Cambodians surveyed reported having been abused or injured by their partner, the highest of the Asian American groups in the study.[22] Of the respondents who have been abused, 22 percent felt that they should not reveal it to anyone.[23] Once frowned upon, divorce has become a common feature in the community. This is particularly true of marriages forced by the Khmer Rouge or by circumstances that took place during the Pol Pot regime or in the refugee camps.

The Cambodian social fabric thus continues to fray long after the genocidal encounter. If solace and support are not easily found within the fractured and reconstructed confines of the family, they are even more elusive on the outside. In the diaspora, the notion of community is challenged not only by geographic dispersal but also by the erosion of trust. Along with the physicality of trauma, genocidal violence leaves behind the imprints of social death. The most tragic legacy of the Khmer Rouge, as one survivor noted, "is that Khmers no longer trust. So many had trusted and died." In the immediate post-genocide Cambodia, Cecile de Sweemer of the World Health Organization noted that even in small communities, villagers choose to "isolate themselves to survive in silence and rather not cooperate with each other" long after the genocide, because of persisting distrust.[24] The challenge for survivors, as Robert Lifton observed, is thus not only to reestablish their lives, but also "to recover something else that they had lost—something on the order of trust or faith in human existence."[25] The proliferation of Buddhist temples, community centers, and heritage programs speaks to the refugee struggle to reweave the social fabric, one thread at a time.

Re-Membering across Generations

What Yolanda Gampel terms the "radioactive"[26] effects of the genocidal encounter bleed through multiple identities, geographies, and temporalities.[27] Many born after the Khmer Rouge period have few ways of making sense of this history and can neither relate to nor fully understand their parents' traumatic experiences. For most, it is the post-genocide present rather than the weighty past that is disconcerting. War and genocide, for them, are on the streets of America's inner cities and not the killing fields of Cambodia. This disconnect reflects not only the spatial and temporal distance from the trauma source but also the prevailing post-genocide conditions that impair and impede transmission of historical memory. The inability to traverse the metaphysical gap between those who had lived through the experiences and those who did not is compounded by linguistic erosion, if not outright loss. Sovanna, a young Cambodian American student, admits that "sometimes it's hard to communicate. My grandmother would speak in Khmer about what she lost in the war, but I could not understand her completely because of the language barrier. It builds a wall in between me and my parents." In some families, the wall was not language but silence. Em never spoke to his children about his experiences under Pol Pot: "Even if I were to tell them, they wouldn't believe me. They never went through it, so they don't believe." Where survivors are silenced by their inability to speak, *niyeay men chench* (when words cannot come out), trauma lives on in the unsayable, in the "crypt," as Derrida asserts, of buried language. As a result, family narratives are punctuated with blank spaces: "The only thing my mother tells me is that just about everybody from her side of the family has passed away. My father refuses to acknowledge anything about what happened during the war." It is not uncommon to hear young Cambodian Americans say that while they may learn of the Khmer Rouge atrocities from their college courses or the media, their parents have never spoken directly about the deaths and disappearances in their own families. Nita's experience is not uncommon: "I know something terrible had happened but my mother never talked about it. As a family we never talked about what happened, really. But I feel this terrible burden, because of the things that they had suffered." In *New Year Baby*, Socheata Poeuv, a Cambodian American documentary filmmaker born in a refugee camp after the genocide, spoke of discovering her mother's secret about a previous marriage one Christmas day: "My parents and even my sisters kept this secret from me for 25 years. I felt like I didn't know my own family. And I wondered what other secrets had they left behind in Cambodia?"[28] For Socheata, it was this desire to break this "culture of silence and denial around the Khmer Rouge history" that motivated her work.

In his work on memory and recall, Gobodo-Madikizela points out that "accounts given by victims and survivors are not simply facts. They are primarily about the impact of facts on their lives and the continuing trauma in their lives created by past violence."[29] Memory that lives in that context is capricious; just when you are ready to confront it, it retreats "like flowers curling back in on themselves."[30] Memory works, as such, are not just about remembering but also about forgetting, both of which involve a choice, however unwilled or unconscious. That which is deliberately edited out or muted by linguistic loss, thus, is as important as that which is transmitted; rather than vacuous and noncommunicative, silence is impregnated with significance. With recounting often bearing traces, gaps, and lacunae of trauma,[31] postmemory, that "secondary, belated memory mediated by stories, images and behaviors among which [they] grew up, . . . never added up to a complete or linear tale,"[32] and, as Hirsch argues, is therefore "as full and as empty, certainly as constructed as memory itself."[33] Pete Pin, a self-taught photographer born in the refugee camp, spoke to the transgenerational haunting:

> That tragedy casts a long shadow on the lives of Cambodians. It bleeds generationally, manifesting itself subtly within my own family in ways that I am only starting to fully comprehend as an adult. It is ingrained in the sorrow of my grandmother's eyes; it is sown in the furrows of

my parents' faces. This is my inheritance; this is what it means to be Cambodian.[34]

From this "compact void of the unspeakable,"[35] the immediate post-genocide generation is nonetheless made to bear witness "to lives and life stories forever scarred by the experience of violence."[36] Of this bequeathal, in which only the wounds of the past and not the meanings are transmitted, young Cambodians are left to patch together from the *mémoire trouée*, as Raczymow terms it,[37] "a history . . . they have never lived by using whatever props they can find, . . . photographs and stories and letters but also . . . silences, grief, rage, despair."[38]

In its transgenerational travel, genocidal memory leaves traces that are both legible and smudged. Though shadows of the past may grow long and progressively distorted with the passing of time, for many families, genocide remains a part of the architecture of everyday life. Though without vocabulary, trauma hovers like an unrequited haunting. The absences may be unspoken but not unacknowledged. They are in the pictures that look on silently from the ancestral altar, the list of names without faces written on a notebook page to be burnt at Pchum Ben, the casual lapses of reference to another life that refuses oblivion, the laden pauses that punctuate family discourse or the ghostly reappearance of a long-lost kin whose existence has been kept secret. Elsewhere, these "haunting legacies," as Schwab terms them, manifest themselves in "the emanations . . . that kept erupting . . . with frightening immediacy in that most private and potent family languages—the language of the body."[39] The bio-imprints of violence register in the tortured body wincing in pain in harsh winters, and other nefarious ways that the body remembers and narrates the trauma. For Mara's father, the guilt and terror that elude words manifest themselves in nocturnal haunting: "My dad would sleep-talk during his nightmares and scream at the soldiers in his dream. He also hated it when I watched violent movies." At times, the anger is unleashed against the living:

Sometimes I feel that my parents don't deal with their stress as successfully as they would like to. . . . Instead of talking about what they went through, I feel that my parents will take the anger out on each other. I feel like my dad had it worse since he lost his whole family in the Khmer

Rouge. As a result, my dad deals with his stress by taking out his anger on his wife and kids.

In other instances, memories struggle just to be acknowledged:

> Every now and then, my dad would walk up to me and just randomly tell me a story about an experience he had either during the war or when he was in school in Cambodia. Sometimes they're really sad and it seems like he is about to burst into tears and other times they are reminiscent of the good old days.

Trauma also conditions behavior, at times insidiously "normalized" in its quotidian form: "My mom keeps *everything* . . . . She has a habit of buying more than she needs and has a hard time getting rid of stuff. She always says that it's because we never know if we're going to need it." For many, like Thouch Phandara, trauma is embodied in the compulsion to hoard, consume food, and feed their children: "I can do without a great deal of things—comfort, money, whatever, even a roof over my head, but I need to have food."[40]

Trauma traces are also transmitted through the socialization of the next generation to a wounded view of the world that shapes the interpretation of the everyday. Of the trauma effects on her parents, Nita reflects, "It gives them a different outlook on life because they know that not everything is as good as it seems. It makes me more conscious about my surroundings and the people around me." For Bossiba, the ravages live in inherited behavior:

> At a young age, I felt my father's pain because of the way he treated us. His sufferings from the Khmer Rouge changed him, and he projected his sufferings onto his family. His depression and hostile nature made us feel detached and unloved. This affects the way we act and perceive ourselves. I thought he did not love me, or I thought I was a burden to him. My father especially taught me how to view the world and it was a dark one. He taught me to be afraid of others, and to be detached from others. He thought I shouldn't have many friends. . . . I became passive and submissive, . . . had low self-esteem [and it affected] the way I act towards others. I remember his negative thoughts clearly even though he has been gone

for years. We take on a lot of our behaviors and habits from our parents and I am still trying to change the way I think.

Transgenerational trauma, transmuted and internalized, can be deeply destructive: "I would feel really depressed at random moments after I see my father depressed." "My first semester in college, I was drunk all the time. I can't remember when I was ever sober. Looking back, I realize that my family is still living with the genocide—memories, divorce, pain and violence. It is still with us."

Elsewhere, loss, rather than vengefully corrosive, induces empathy and compassion, and strengthens the family bond:

> My family is quite different from other Cambodian American families. . . . They are very understanding, encouraging. . . . My parents seem to value spending a lot of time together. It may be because when my parents were in the war they lost a lot of family members and they were split apart from one another for an extensive period of time.

In his study of the former Yugoslavia, David de Levita noted that for war-traumatized children, it is often the grief and sufferings of their parents that they feel more greatly than their own pain.[41] Just as adult survivors seek to protect through silence, many youths like Phinath are compelled by loyalty and empathy to refrain from delving into their parents' pasts: "I wouldn't ask my parents about their experience or history because I know it will bring a lot of bad memories that I don't want to bring up." Similarly for Mara, "My family never really spoke about their experiences. Every story seemed to be a tragic story, so it was hardly brought up." They are thus made to live with this "something" that they can neither name nor understand but that inserts its presence "in abrupt, fragmented phrases; in repetitious, broken refrains"[42] or ellipses in family narratives. Of the silence that shrouds her family, Loung Ung wrote,

> It's not as though we sat down one day and decided not to talk about the war. . . . There are times that I still want him to tell me more about Pa and Ma [but] I do not ask because I cannot bear to watch his face light up at the memory of them, only to see it dim and darken when he remembers they are no longer with us.[43]

Though fear and distrust seep into the next generation, the empathy many feel for their family extends to the collective: "When I am out and about in the community, I often find myself wondering what this person or their family went through during the war. If a person is being a difficult person, I try to think that there is a valid excuse, they must have lost someone."

While memory of a traumatic past may be passed on, albeit in staccatos and discontinuity, and despite the obvious impact that it has on some second-generation Cambodians, it is not predetermined that trauma, defined as that which is injurious, is necessarily transmitted along with it. Though they may be shaped by this history, many like Phinath are not necessarily "damaged" by it but instead draw pride and inspiration from their parents' struggle:

> I admire them dearly for they are like trees; they were once tiny seedlings, all fragile and weak, but over time they have begun to grow to be big and strong. The stories of the pitch-dark escape through the jungle remind me of what courage and willpower the human spirit is capable of and how that same blood is flowing through my veins. To me, Cambodia represents the idea that one can overcome great odds and persevere.

Of postmemory, Hirsch argues that at its conceptual core is the "critical distance and profound interrelation" between the present and the past that constitutes an "uneasy oscillation between continuity and rupture."[44] For Sophea, the temporal and psychic distance means that what is received is mediated, filtered: "I can understand and learn from it, but I can never fully understand their hardships because I was never there." For LaCapra, it is this temporality that transforms witnessing to representation.

Despite the gaps and ellipses, young Cambodian Americans often recount those histories with an assumed poignancy, and inhabit family narratives with a vividness and an immediacy of those who had lived through them. In a fundamental way, they have. Theirs is a childhood nurtured in the shadow of this history, oppressive in its unshakable omnipresence. Though this history is often encoded in stuttered "brief statements followed by sobs" without details, shades, or textures, most feel its tangible weight and know that they are different from their

American peers because of it. Of the silence that compels her journey of discovery, Marina Kem, a Cambodian German filmmaker, muses, "How can something unsaid still shape a person?"[45] The pain, palpable in the family and community, is an insistent reminder of the collective trauma. As Vida puts it, "I can't specifically relate to my family's history. However, all the experiences my family has had is a part of me. My family's history has made me who I am today." Though born after the genocidal period, Prach Ly, whose music centers on the theme of loss and healing, refers to his work as an "autobiography." In his words, "(the story of the genocide) was inside of me."[46] Of this vicarious claiming, he posited,

> Some people ask me what gives me the right to rap about the war because I wasn't born during the time of the killing fields. I didn't go through that. But I have that in my blood. My mother, and father, my brothers and sisters went through that. I lost aunts and uncles. So how can they ask me that?[47]

By inserting themselves in the history *over there*, by claiming that which, for many, is at the core of the diasporic identity, American-born Cambodians attempt through borrowed identities[48] to carve out a sense of belonging here. It is a way to connect, signify, and claim ownership of that history, however mediated and distant, and in so doing, resist the ahistoricization and invisibilization of their own alterity. In that sense, the rupture is the re/connection. Through creation, they impart meaning and realism to forms, images, and presence that have shadowed their lives. Ironically, it is the very surrealism of these experiences that had rendered many first-generation survivors mute, with tongues parched and heavy with pain and rage and "trapped in the bitterness of those who cannot speak."[49] It is their generational perch, distanced temporally and geographically from the trauma source, however, that allows young Cambodian Americans to discern the optimism that eluded the older generation. Pete Pin opined, "It was a vision of hope and renewal, that we as Cambodians are endowed with an incredible resilience and strength in human spirit. I have seen this in the faces of Cambodians I have photographed and have been incredibly humbled. In the words of my mother, it is a miracle to simply exist."[50]

Exile and Diasporic Longing

Exile is a kind of death where loss is found
in every beautiful thing—a postcard, a sunset, a sonnet,
the way light kindles a wooden floor, jasmine

and rose water, moonlight on the tongue.

—Lois P. Jones

While *exiliance* may be a site of creation for some, for many, especially first-generation refugees, the gaping void left behind by the genocidal encounter is filled with an "essential sadness of the break [that] can never be surmounted"[51] that marks the forced and unexpected severance from the ancestral homeland. Having "swum across a-Pot" (*heil kat a-pot*), refugee-survivors find themselves essentially adrift, floating between two nations in their imagination, and between time and place in their consciousness. The place of their being is not necessarily, and certainly not singularly, the place of their longing. Refugees are here and there—simultaneously, and to borrow from Edward Said, contrapuntally.[52] The trauma lives on in, and is accentuated by that "discontinuous state of being."[53] The rupture of displacement and exile is, for many refugees, an inculcated wound that throbs, sometimes in conscious response and other times subconsciously to repressed memories, but always as a reminder of their liminality.

Distance and the seeming impossibility of return render even more acute the challenges of resettlement that many have to confront without much resources, support, or solace. While migration necessarily entails change, the context and process of flight for Cambodian refugees involve dislocations that are qualitatively different in nature and scope from many other migration experiences. Unlike E. H. Carr's self-exiled intellectuals, there is little of the romantic "redemptive motif"[54] in the exile of those carried in flight by the turbulence of history. To the politically displaced, as Barudy points out, exile "is never the fulfillment of a wish; it is a 'forced choice,' necessary to escape danger and survive, . . . always involv[ing] a break or a repetition of the break in the individual's personal and social history which began with the repression."[55] What it entails is "a removal in space as well as in spirit,"[56] a simultaneous physical uprooting and a psychic and spiritual disconnect from land, history, and identity that leaves behind an existence devoid of "the warmth of home and the history that gives meaning to every part."[57] Exile thus represents a "severing of one's roots, the source of sustenance, security, and ties to the familiar,"[58] a historicized traumata engendered by what Said describes as "the unhealable rift . . . between the self and its true home."[59] For the forcibly displaced, it is not just the physical state of being in a country that is denied but also "the community and togetherness, food and laughter, and the calm that comes from knowing one's rightful place and the right thing to do in all circumstances."[60] What they experience, in essence, is a loss of the entire social texture.[61]

It is thus, as Mario Benedetti contends, the "grayer, more opaque, nostalgias," the tranquility that comes with the "freedom from the surprises [that] made me tired,"[62] the ease of being that lead one to embark on the "route home" that frame exilic longing. What is sought, therefore, is not simply a re-territorialization, but a re-rooting of the individual. Re-emplacement alone does not make whole. Through forays into memory and recollection, what survivors seek to do is to reconnect and retrieve that which had been snatched away from them, in essence to "re-assemble . . . a broken history into a new whole."[63] This retrieval is necessary to reaffirm for many survivors the fact that they had existed, that they had a past, a history, and a community, that they had once lived in a world where reason did prevail. For young survivors, even the unrequited reach for a lost childhood is a necessary gesture, for reinserting memory into its rightful frame yields that release, however momentary, from the temporal prison of a life abbreviated by historical rupture: "I wanted to again relive the good memories before the Khmer Rouge walked into Siemreap. . . . I had to dig deep into my shattered memory bank to be able to go back in time for just a moment."[64]

In the interstices between the place of necessity and that of desire that mark the "perilous territory of not-belonging,"[65] Many Cambodian diasporas inhabit two simultaneous contexts of exile—exile *from* the ancestral home and the memory source, and exile *within* the new place of refuge. The ambivalence that is embedded in diasporic consciousness is toward both contexts and referents; Cambodia, at once distant and ever present, symbolizes history and grand tradition as well as turmoil and loss, while America—the now, the final—simultaneously represents sanctuary and marginality. For many refugees, "there is a sense that no one place is truly secure." Despite having achieved all the markers of the "American Dream" that accessorize his suburban life, an upwardly mobile Cambodian American professional questions the meaning of "security" in a society where the system of home mortgage could mean overnight dispossession of land and property, the two signifiers of "rootedness" for Cambodians, and where "no matter how well educated or rich, your skin will always be dark." The sense of non-belonging is evident in the rationalization that Cambodian refugees frequently provide for racist encounters in America: "What can we do? This is not our country" (*Men mene srok yoeung*) or "That's the way it is because we asked for refuge in their country" (*Som chrok nov srok ke*). The "nigh unpayable debt,"[66] as Mimi Nguyen characterized it, that refugees shoulder is amplified for many Cambodians, for the "gift," in the face of auto-genocide, is not just freedom but life. In this acknowledgment of gratitude, what, as Lisa Lowe provocatively asserts, is buried by the violence of forgetting?[67]

Above all, it is the sense of irredeemable loss that prevents exiles from focusing on what they do have rather than what has been taken from them, for "habits of life, expression, or activity in the new environment," as Said posited, "inevitably occur against the memory of these things in another environment."[68] Of this melancholia, David Rieff wrote, "For all its glittering appurtenances, its prosperity, and at times, its self-satisfaction, there was a level on which no leisure, no level of attainment, nor any material accumulation could make up for what had been taken away from these exiles";[69] such are the "wounds, unstanchable after three decades, of those who once felt themselves truly happy."[70]

Diaspora is thus a site inhabited simultaneously by continuities and discontinuities—ghosts, memory fragments, interruptions, and contradictions. Loss and joy, trauma and inspiration, despair and hope, death and renewal, all coexist in accustomed tension. Where rupture and entanglement, denial and remembrance inhabit the same metaphysical realm, the notion of time and space must be spoken of in terms of memory and imagination, that "endless temporal notion in which past, present, and future intertwine without any fixed centers."[71] It is in this context of fluidity and ambivalence that attachment to the "homeland" becomes most registered. Nostalgia constitutes an "assertion of belonging to a place, a people, a heritage,"[72] a route through which diasporas reclaim their history and identity. Though the word "nostalgia," a combination of the Greek word *nostos* (homecoming) and *algos* (pain), is often discussed as a negative, even pathological, manifestation, there is also a recuperative aspect that is often overlooked. While remembering is, for some of the forcibly displaced, a luxury that they can ill afford, for others, memories are their only solace against the unquiet realities of the present. The affixation of the diaspora's hopes on and preoccupation with the homeland is a way of coping with and rationalizing their present condition. More than the physical territory, it is all that the "homeland" represents that makes for the significance. Against the topography of poverty and marginalization, the homeland becomes a reference point, both as a reminder of all that is good and possible and a justification for all that is failed and unachievable. It is, as Homi Bhabha puts it, that "anxiety links us to the memory of the past while we struggle to choose a path through the ambiguous history of the present."[73]

Unlike other experiences of dislocation, mass violence—particularly the self-inflicted form that it took in Cambodia—complicates this process of "return." "Home-land" for many Cambodians becomes a hyphenated notion, problematized by physical and psychic dislocation, by memories too painful to relive and even more painful to let go. The country that is exalted in the exilic imaginary is also one stigmatized by a bloody history and an equally unsettling present, a country, as one Cambodian American bemoaned, "advertised in disgrace."[74] A young poet exposes the complex, ambivalent, and conflictual positions that Cambodia occupies in the imagination of many of his generation: "I hear people speak of Khmer pride—the same people who kill and die."[75] The hyphen that marks the duality of diasporic identity connotes both separation and connection between Cambodia and America. It is in the interstices of disdain and longing, of the desire to forget and the inability to do so, that many of the 1.5 generation,[76] born in the conflagration, too young to engage but old enough to remember, confront their liminality: "I am very much a lost Khmer generation during the day . . . and the Khmer Rouge nightmares still haunted [me] in my dream during the night."[77] Bound only by memory and imagination, they nonetheless intuitively feel the nation's collective pain: "I've never been to the Mekong but I've heard its cries."[78] Unable to avert their gaze either from the ancestral source or the consuming present, they are a "bifocal of oneness,"[79] tugging and being tugged at simultaneously by the bond and the disconnect:

> I love my land to death,
> A child of the Killing Fields.[80]

Transnationalizing Home

It is this need to confront and navigate multiple hegemonic contexts that obliges diasporas "to live within a transnational space" and engage "in a kind of lifelong psychological balancing act."[81] The dream of the return to the ancestral land presents for many "a pragmatic solution to the dilemma of being part of two contexts, two countries and two sets of norms and values, which may not only be different, but in most cases contradictory."[82] Straddling between the "here" and the "there," the dislocated become "skilled exponents of a cultural bifocality that defies reduction to a singular order."[83] Thus, as Homi Bhabha points out, rather than speaking of locality in "some utopian sense of liberation or return," "the place to speak from [is] through those incommensurable contradictions within which people survive, are politically active and change."[84]

In the process of moving from the destruction of all that is familiar toward integration into everything that is new, Cambodian refugees have had to learn to make sense of their world, which has, in essence, been turned upside down. Their lives have been torn in many places, and in those many places they seek to reconnect, finding refuge in the familiar in the face of discontinuity and disorientation. Diasporic nostalgia is essentially rooted in that desire to erase the disjunction between the forcefully sundered past and the present, hence to deny the rupture. For Cambodians, the process of reassembling the archives of memories began almost immediately in the refugee camps, made even more noteworthy by the trying conditions. Monks were ordained and music and dance repertoires retrieved, often through faulty memory, with instruments and costumes adapted from whatever materials were available.[85]

This reparative process continues in resettlement. Names emblazoned on neighborhood storefronts hark back to familiar sounds and places of belonging—Pailin, Tonle Sap, Battambang—etching into the ethnoscape of urban America an imprint of home that refugees carry with them in their exilic imagination. They stake the presence of the community with a certain vitality and permanence that belie the disconcerting reality of dilapidated apartments and flux of a population in constant search of elusive security.

Inside ethnic stores crammed with material markers of home, pirated reproductions of remastered music favorites and popular films of the 1960s—Cambodia's "golden era"—fill the shelves. Popular singers and actors of the Sangkum period, once on the social margin of a class-conscious prewar Cambodia, are resurrected and recentered in diasporic imagination; for young Cambodian Americans, bands such as Dengue Fever provide a venue for accessing the stolen times of their parents. In Long Beach's Cambodia Town, restaurants with names of old Phnom Penh's popular eateries serve traditional fare such as "Phnom Penh noodles" to the crooning of singers and musical bands from Cambodia, all designed to seduce the clientele with a sense of uninterrupted continuity. In the same vein, reproductions of 1960s paintings depict idyllic scenes of Cambodian folklife, imbuing permanency to a land convulsed by turmoil, with the realities of minefields, bomb craters, and mass graves strategically edited out. Images of a verdant countryside, dotted with palm trees, evoke sentimentalism even in urbanites and youths whose life experiences are framed more by the rhythm of America's inner cities and suburbia than they are by the bucolic agrarianism of Cambodia.

Against the backdrop of fragmentation and uncertainty, the memory of the homeland, though filtered and refracted by time and distance, presents itself as the sinew of an otherwise dispersed community in diaspora. Community events are opportunities for Cambodian Americans to immerse themselves in momentary reprieve in the reconstituted world of familiar sights, sounds, and smells, in the adornment of traditional dress, in the partaking of traditional foods, religious chants, and music. Though weddings are now abridged and ceremonies charted not always in accordance with cosmology but with the practicality of postmodern life in the West, they remain important cementing forces for a community that can be fractionalized along class, gender, generational, and political lines. Rituals, food, music, and art as cultural markers of the prewar era constitute what Clifford Geertz refers to as the "web of significance" that weaves continuity, structure, and meaning through fragmented lives, defying the fissures borne of the violence and conflict of the last four decades, imparting a "security of sameness" in a context, however fleeting, where traditional norms regarding social status and relations of obligation are still valid and legitimated.

These reassemblages make it possible for diasporas to "live out the tension embedded in the 'experiences of separation and entanglement,' of living here and remembering/desiring another place."[86] As loci for the articulation and reaffirmation of ethnic identity and homeland culture, they serve as an anchor to an otherwise highly fluid context. In the face of whirlwind change, there is coherence and solace in the re-created world of the past, one protected by beliefs and faith, and ordered by the sanction of traditions. Within the confines of Buddhist temples and other cultural spaces, the community is brought together in affirmation of their cultural and ethnic identity and of a sense of continuum despite the dislocations. There, wedged betwixt past and future, memory flows from the realm of private remembrance to an anchored *lieu de mémoire*.[87] In earlier years, when the Khmer nation was kept bifurcated by a geographical and political divide, the cultural memory of home was incubated and nurtured within these enclaves, moored to that insistent call of the home/land to drown out the discordance of displacement and rupture. Ultimately, as Homi Bhabha points out, it is in this ability to "work their anxieties and alienations towards a life that may be radically incomplete but continues to be intricately communitarian, busy with activity, noisy with stories, garrulous with grotesquerie, gossip, humor, aspirations, fantasies" that resilience emerges from the shadows of history.[88]

Exile and Return

In essence, what is attempted is the recovery of an uninterrupted past that transcends the fracturing of politics, geography, and temporality. In fundamental ways, Cambodian diasporas' struggle to free themselves from a tormenting past and an unsettling present is a struggle to break free of temporal boundaries through imagined return. Paradoxically, more than the actual referent, it is the *denied* possibility of return that makes for the poignancy of longing. In the reconstruction of myth and memory it is, as Said argues, "fragmentation [that] makes it even more real."[89] Throughout the late 1970s and 1980s, the communist regime's disavowal of the diasporas not only bifurcated the nation ideologically and geographically, but further widened the psychic distance from the homeland. Against the unsubjugated memory of territorial loss, Vietnam's decade-long occupation evoked deeply held anxiety about national survival and, for refugees, the permanency of exile.

Memory and remembering thus became an integral part of the Khmer struggle to survive as a nation, which infuses nostalgia with a moral purpose. Exile and nationalism dialectically inform and constitute each other. With the country under occupation, refugees saw themselves as a depository of a culture and traditions threatened by ethnocide. Whether done through family narratives, the arts, or politics, the struggle was to recollect, preserve, and proclaim the "other" Cambodia, an act of "redescribing" that Rushdie defines as political.[90] A former pilot who taught himself to carve traditional violins out of American baseball bats spoke of the moral obligation to remember and memorialize:

> I started to make these instruments because there was no Cambodian instrument available at that time. I wanted the younger generation, my kids, to know what is the real, traditional music, the way I had seen the elders do it. Now if you listen to the music from Cambodia today, . . . there is a lot of Vietnamese and Thai influence. Look at the musical repertoire of the classical ballet. First the Hun Sen regime disallowed the usage of royal words in the songs, so they replaced them with revolutionary language. And now, after reconciliation, the royal terms are brought back. But since everything is committed to memory, sometimes we forget. We cannot bring everything back, and they are lost forever.

Pointing to the intricate tableau of epic battle scenes from the Ramayana etched onto cardboard, hanging as if frozen in time on the garage wall among rusted tools, he said,

> As a child, I used to go to the ancient temples, and run my fingers over the bas-reliefs. Now I just let my fingers remember. I am not an artist and these are not really arts. They are just memories. My children have never seen Cambodia. This may be the closest to their roots they will ever get. That's all that is left of Cambodia that I have to give them.

Nostalgia, in this sense, rather than pathology, is resistance against the erasure of time and distance, a nationalist act, a weapon of the dispossessed.

Threads of Memory, Pillars of Home

Underscoring both the subjectivity and agency embedded in the refugee experience, Richmond argues that refugees must be considered not "as helpless victims of forces beyond their control but 'survivors' who create something out of their crisis."[91] For Cambodian diasporas, reconnection with the homeland is not only through the imaginary but takes on different forms—from the actual to the virtual, from the political to the cultural, from the formal to the informal, and from the personal to the collective. For the refugees, politics inform the context of both disconnection and reconnection. Politics defines their condition of statelessness, and for many, their identity, as well as shapes the vision and actions aimed at bringing an end to that condition: "It is because of politics that I ended up a refugee, and it is because of politics that I have returned."[92] In the late 1970s through late 1980s, with Cambodia under occupation, many diasporas viewed themselves, and are viewed by their external supporters, as the alternative voice of the Cambodian nation that has been silenced by a colonized and oppressive state. Mobilization for national independence galvanized Cambodian diasporas, scattered throughout refugee camps and in third-country resettlement. With former elites coming out of their Western exile to assume leadership positions in the movement, resistance waged and sustained as much from Long Beach, Washington, DC, New York, Paris, and Bangkok as inside Cambodia, acquired a transnational feature. Financial and human capital needed to sustain the politico-military struggle flowed through the multiple nodes of the diaspora. In numerous cities with large Cambodian communities, political meetings and fund-raising activities, often held in local Buddhist temples or community organizations, became part of the texture of diasporic life.

Others find hope for national salvation in cultural artifacts. An English translation of the *Puth Tomney*, replete with interpretation and adaptation to contemporary Cambodian politics, circulated on the Internet, while political myths and spiritual cults, particularly those centering on rebirth of the Khmer nation, were revived in diaspora. References to Preah Bat Thommoeuk,[93] whose arrival will herald the return to stability and prosperity for the Khmer people, is frequently evoked in political discourse both in Cambodia and in exile. Likewise, the revival and transnational following of the cult of Neak Ta Khleang Muang,[94] a sixteenth-century martyred nationalist who sacrificed himself to save the country, underscores the vitality of diasporic nationalism.

Technology greatly assists in the promotion of transnational ties and the cultivation of long-distance nationalism. Phones, fax machines, and the Internet have made communication possible in ways and at a speed previously unimaginable. In the same way that printed media fostered the Andersonian "imagined community," technology and the relative ease of information flow between the homeland and the diaspora allow diasporic Cambodians to affirm their ethnic, cultural, and political identities, hence a sense of community. The relative affordability of long-distance calls makes it possible for families and friends to keep in touch and to cultivate the sense of familial obligation transnationally, with video recordings providing another practical tool of accountability for the less literate members of the community.

Among diasporic Cambodians, Internet nationalism also finds expression in online discussion groups that proliferate, enlivened and embittered by heated political discourse. During the coup of 1997, as it was with the 2014 mass protests, websites frequented by Cambodia watchers were blanketed with graphic and virtually instantaneous pictures of the violence, while electronic mail kept friends and families apprised of the latest developments. In anticipation of the 2013 national elections, hopes (and fear) of the Arab Spring spread over the Internet amongst Cambodians in Cambodia and in the diaspora. While politics was once the purview of a small, "older-generation" intelligentsia, the virtual, anonymous space afforded by the Internet to some extent has "democratized" political access, especially in the West. Young students and professionals alike now have an accessible forum for exploring and articulating their Khmer-ness, however tentatively, and to be able to do so behind the anonymity and safety of the virtual community. Even those with limited or no written Khmer-language competency can and often do resort to Romanization to dialogue with their peers. Where civil society remains incipient, the power of the Internet to strengthen vertical and horizontal networks transcends and challenges the sovereignty of the state and elevates public accountability beyond the traditional, and often oppressive, confines of the nation-state.

For many Cambodian diasporas, it is "survivor's guilt" that animates the desire to reengage the homeland. For Mr. Vinuth, who had dedicated the last three decades to homeland political activism, reengagement is a moral obligation: "Many died; we lived. Those who are in Cambodia do not have the freedoms that we have. They cannot speak. How can we abandon them?" The decimation of the educated class and the enormity of Cambodia's needs exert pressure especially on the surviving educated class in the diaspora. Dr. Pen Dareth, who traded an established position in Holland for a return home, reflected, "The country has helped me a lot by sending me abroad on a scholarship, now it's payback time. . . . I must help rebuild my country."[95] Like many of his educated peers, Sothy rests the imperative of participating in national reconstruction on the simple fact that "we had the opportunity [for education, for jobs] which people in Cambodia did not have. . . . Without Cambodia, I wouldn't be who I am; I need to put something back."

Those unable or unwilling to access the political arena turn to alternate venues for transnational engagement. As Cambodia emerged from war and isolation, its dire need of services and skilled human resources also meant opportunities for returnees that may not be afforded to them in the West. Especially in the early years of the political thaw, many leveraged their social and financial capital and experiences acquired in the West to access positions in both public and private sectors. Especially since 1993, trading companies, travel and entertainment industry, restaurants, and educational enterprises have mushroomed in response to market demands, many building on expertise and capital from overseas Cambodians. Cambodian American women, still marginalized by patriarchy in diasporic politics, found a ready niche in Cambodia, where women make up 52 to 58 percent of the population and where nongovernmental organizations have proliferated. Some, like Sochua Mu from California, a minister of Parliament and once secretary of state for women's and veterans' affairs, became an important political voice in a country where gender-based violence and other human rights concerns continue to dominate the advocacy agenda.

Similarly for some of the younger-generation Cambodians who returned, Cambodia presented unmatched opportunities, especially in the early years, when English-language mastery and a Western education commanded a premium. For many, such as those who participated in the CANDO program (often referred to as the "Cambodian Peace Corps"), return is not about the opportunity to advance professionally but to make "real" that which has always lived in the imaginary, a way of legitimating their claim over that history that has so informed their identity: "I have a lot of dreams, like the dream I had of working at Angkor Wat, when I was in the United States. I even told my friends then of the magnificence of Angkor monuments without having been there. But now, I live and work there."[96]

While the preoccupation with homeland and return threads through class and generations, it is also true that actual return has been a confined privilege of the few. With the exception of retirees and recent college graduates, not many have the economic freedom for long-term stay in Cambodia, or the financial security necessary to maintain multiple households. For those who repatriated, return often fails to yield the desired outcomes. Many had looked to Cambodia out of unfulfilled aspirations in the diaspora, only to find opportunities there equally elusive, as lucrative opportunities remain largely inaccessible except to those with connections and political currency. Political portfolios, one of the avenues for self-enrichment, are reserved for the party loyal, while the more readily dispensed advisory positions confer titles desired by the downwardly mobile diasporas but not monetary compensation. Over time, with the new wealth and increased cosmopolitanism of Cambodia's new elites, power shifts away from the diasporic North. The notion of *Khmer dach yai* (down-and-out Cambodians) that has circulated in Phnom Penh debunked the image of the rich and highly skilled returnees, reflecting unmet expectations of both parties.

In the private sector, lack of capital available in the refugee communities, weak legal institutions, and lack of systemic transparency in Cambodia continue to test the entrepreneurial resolve of the diaspora. Nevertheless, transnational economic activities remain robust especially at the micro and more informal levels. As people travel back and forth, goods are brought in and sold, which not only help defray travel expenses but potentially garner handsome profits for the purveyors. Of similar practices among Dominican diasporas, Portes observes, "To the untrained eye, these travelers may appear as common migrants visiting and bearing gifts for their relatives back home, when they are actually engaged in trade."[97] In a community of high English-language illiteracy, particularly among the elderly population who constitute a significant proportion of returnees, "professional travelers" found an important business niche coordinating and escorting group visits. Before the establishment of a reliable and trustworthy banking system in Cambodia, facilitating remittances through personal delivery, at a surcharge ranging from 10 to 25 percent (depending on the destination), was a lucrative undertaking, especially in the years prior to reconciliation.

For most Cambodians, engagement with the homeland was not through physical return but through these remittances, transmitted not only to support families but for social and cultural projects. Since the political thaw of the early 1990s, individuals and organizations in the diaspora have actively fund-raised for various causes, from well digging to scholarships and other educational projects. Hometown associations and alumni groups have also contributed to the building, renovation, and expansion of schools and clinics in Cambodia. The Boeung Trabek High School Association, for instance, once raised $50,000 for the rehabilitation of its alma mater.[98] Other contributions are in the form of individual or family sponsorship of development projects. With potable water accessible to only 31 percent of rural Cambodians, water projects are among the most needed and the most undertaken. For Mr. Ouch, the motivation is the simple gratification of knowing that one's simple actions are bettering lives: "At night I go to bed and think about people drinking my water, cooking food with it and bathing from the clean water of my well." Given the relative affordability of development projects, especially in the earlier years, even the economically marginalized can become benefactors. Where else, as that proud sponsor of a well-digging project once pointed out, "can one get that level of satisfaction for a mere $200!" For a people so inculcated with an accrued sense of helplessness, the ability to undertake positive actions is indeed empowering. For Vinnath, an established Cambodian American professional who funded the construction of a clinic in his family's native province, the development project is also a way of re-rooting one's presence: "My family is from that area. It is a way of keeping the family name in that place." This echoes the spirit of Mexican American transnational communalism, "the Absent Ones, Always Present."[99] In that sense, contributions to the establishment of family micro-enterprises and real estate purchases, which are now on the increase with the aging of the first and 1.5 generations seeking alternate retirement options than in the West, are not just the fulfillment of family obligations, but essentially a purchase of future security. What is returned from this investment is, in essence, an assurance of home and belonging.

Resources within the diasporic communities were also mobilized for religious and cultural projects. Given the destruction, renovation of monasteries and *stupas*[100] in Cambodia is one of the most-undertaken fund-raising activities. With families dispersed, merit-making activities such as *kathen* (temple fund-raising), once geographically bound, now acquire a transnational dimension, underscoring the multilocality of a dispersed "community." Principally the initiatives of elders, most living on economic margins, the success of these initiatives is empowering and assuring. They impart a sense of connection and continuity with the ancestral homeland and with the ancestors, and through accrued merits, hope of betterment. The younger generation participates if not for themselves, at least for their parents and their departed relatives: "We should all do it [participate in merit-making] so that we can avoid such hardship in the next life. Hopefully, it will get to the ancestors." Many survivors also conduct village ceremonies for the disappeared in hope that the wandering souls would ultimately find their familial resting place. With the passing of the older generation, some families have repatriated the ashes of their loved ones from the diaspora back to the ancestral home. In death, the return that was denied to them in life could finally be achieved.

In her work *Insistence of Memory*, Marina Tsvetaeva spoke of the homeland not as "a geographical convention but an insistence of memory and blood."[101] Be it through contributions to the political process, development projects, or ceremonies and rituals, these initiatives reflect the fundamental desire of the forcibly dislocated to reconnect across multiple domains. For many first-generation Cambodians, nation and identity are territorially rooted, and there can be no wholeness without the reconnection between place and being: "Let me live on the dirt on which I stand. Bury me smiling in the rich soil of my homeland."[102] The land, however, signifies not just place but also belonging, and not just to a living nation but also to a longer genealogy.

While a rallying force, homeland politics also fractionalize, and to some extent, even intensify intrinsic cleavages among dispersed Cambodians. As hopes for durable peace and reconciliation dim with persisting volatility, the line drawn between regime-opposing and regime-accommodating forces deepened. Those advocating constructive engagement deem it a "patriotic duty" of all Cambodians, at home and abroad, to contribute to the process of national development, arguing for the imperative of keeping the *nation* separate from the *state*, and of not transforming resistance to the state into a callous disregard for the nation. For others, genuine reform in Cambodia could be achieved only through unrelenting pressure from the outside. Hence, the utmost nationalist act is to withstand the temptation toward regime accommodation.

With transnational circulation, the "here" and the "there" are not demarcated locales. In many aspects, return reinforces the vicious cycle of longing and deracination. Marginalization accentuates the longing for return, which in turn impedes the process of planting a firmer, more permanent foundation in the adopted country. The orientation toward the homeland also deflects critical human and financial resources and psychic attention away from the diasporic community. While the leadership vacuum may present opportunities for new talent to emerge, many organizations in the diaspora are unable to survive the succession crisis, leaving many communities without a much-needed support structure at a time when the sociopolitical climate of the United States presents unrelenting challenges.

Efforts to sustain transnational relations also have profound impact on family and gender relations. With most of the returnees being unaccompanied males, the formation of new relationships (or in some cases multiple and simultaneous "marriages") and spousal abandonment further destabilize the family institution. Women and children once again are left to negotiate the absence of husbands and fathers. Rather than the enviable opportunity that was envisioned, return can also present additional economic hardship for many families who now need to provide support to their spouses overseas while shouldering the burden of being a single wage earner and parent. In the same vein, rather than strengthening transnational familial ties, remittances can also adversely impact relational dynamics. For many refugee families already stretched economically, the obligation to remit adds to the financial strain, exacerbating the resentment engendered by the inability to reconcile between obligation and accountability: "Relatives in Cambodia are abusing the money we send them. They do not use the money as we intended. They use the money for eating out, . . . for Seiko watches, expensive jeans."[103] What is often perceived by relatives in Cambodia as condescension is, for their relatives overseas, a matter of accountability: "We work hard in America; I don't have money for them to squander." In some instances, efforts to manage these relationships risk transforming that which was once extended without the articulated expectation of return into "contractual" arrangements.

The Myth of Return

The only true paradise is the paradise we have lost.
—*Marcel Proust*

Where the land has been rendered synonymous with the killing fields and with compromised sovereignty, the image of "home," for many Cambodians, was reduced to one constructed of treasured fragments of prewar memory:

> I wade through solitude
> To the cottage where we used to
> Gather to drink rice wine
> Enjoying false peace.[104]

In essence, what most diasporas desire is not simply return but a reinsertion into a specific temporal frame, affixed in the exilic memory at the moment of rupture. For Ronnie, a child survivor, the physical return to the site of the family home was essentially a metaphysical journey to all that it represents, a return to "the last place where good memories still exist in my cluttered mind,"[105] to "a time when all my family members and my youth were still intact."[106] For those forcibly and prematurely aged by the Khmer Rouge experience, return that is sought is, therefore, not just to the "homeland" but to the ways that it is remembered, and to a childhood and innocence that were stolen from them:

> I want to feel my dark Cambodian skin crack from playing with the earth, my boyish brown eyes to stare again at the green bamboo, leaning to soak in the fragrance of the yellow, flowered hills. I want the serenity of the blue ponds and the white river of childhood and to feel the winds wiping away the dewdrops, still clinging to my naked body.
>
> I want my peasant home, to still be in that village among the surviving people on that laboring earth where I was born into my Cambodia.[107]

Preserved in memory, the desired return is essentially to a place accessible only to the imagination. Longing and nostalgia involve an imagined and desired return to moments, places, histories that are frozen in time: "The past continued to speak to us. But it no longer addresses us as a simple factual 'past.' . . . It is always constructed through memory, fantasy, narrative and myth."[108] Of the temporal dis/continuity engendered by exile, Józef Wittlin wrote, "In Spanish, there exists for describing an exile the word destierro, a man deprived of his land. I take the liberty to forge another term, destiempo, a man deprived of his time, meaning deprived of the time that now passes in his country. The time of exile is different."[109] At some fundamental level, "return" can never be fully achieved, for the rupture created by war, genocide, exile, and simply the steady march of time is irreversible. For Vann Vorn, the nation unveiled and exposed in the stark present bears no resemblance to the deeply cherished memories:

> Cambodians will never be the same
> Innocent souls screaming in pain
> The Cambodian soil soaked in puddles of blood left behind by our
>   Khmer people.[110]

Against the assumed permanency of nature, genocide has indelibly stained the land, that signifier of nationhood, leaving traces and spatial remains that cannot be masked by the return of life; a pond transformed from a mass grave, from which villagers draw water for their fields, maintains an unnatural hue that betrays its genesis, registering its unrelinquished material intimacy with death. Even nature could not return to itself. The loss of the familiar is fundamentally irretrievable, for the changes experienced are simultaneously external in the environment and internal to the diasporas. The disconcerting contrast between the actual and the imagined was felt by Chath pierSath, a young Cambodian American poet, for whom return brought no solace, only a harsh encounter with post-genocide realities of broken families, poverty, AIDS, and stifling corruption—afflictions that wreck both the body and the body politic.

The Politics of Belonging

The tension between the "actual" and the "imagined" is underscored for the younger returnees. For Ti, a returning volunteer who left Cambodia at the age of six, the anticipation of a heartwarming reception was marred by the cultural and ideological distancing conveyed through the label *anech kachun*, ascribed to overseas Cambodians. Instead of being embraced as prodigal children returning to the ancestral fold, many feel once again relegated to the margin, distinct and apart, this time not by the racial politics of the West but by their own people. In her poem "Visiting Loss," Anida Ali evokes a notion of return not to the maternal embrace of the motherland but into the fold of Loss, enveloped not in the uncertainty of anticipation but in the anticipation of uncertainty. For Kanika, the sense of alienation that she experienced upon her return of "just observing but not participating" is also shared by a fellow returnee who commented, "It was like I was in my country but not my home." For some of these youths, the long-cherished anticipation of the return ended not with a re-rooting but with a final severance. Disillusioned by what confronted him in his native land, a young Cambodian American professional reflected, "Cambodia is behind me now. I have to concentrate on building a life here in America." For others, there is a fatalistic resignation to the liminality of their exilic condition: "In America, I don't feel that I am an American; but in Cambodia, I am not really Cambodian either. I am not sure what I am, what to feel, where to belong. Maybe I will never know."

The rejection felt by some of the younger generation speaks to a larger question about the possibility of return and reunification. It is a tension felt in multiple realms—in daily interactions, in the way repatriated refugees from the Thai border camps were received by local communities, in the highly politicized discourse about nation and nationalism, and in the political and constitutional question about dual citizenship. Though often framed in terms of cultural authenticity, it is ultimately about the perception of betrayal and compromise. In delineating parameters of place and belonging, in legitimating regimes of representation, both self- and other-imposed,, politics continue to shape the discourse. As Clifford contends, "Self–other relations are matters of power and rhetoric rather than of essence."[111] While diasporic Cambodians see themselves just as much the victim of political circumstances as their compatriots who remained behind, the Hun Sen regime looked upon them as having "chosen" escape while others elected to stay. Flight, rather than seen as compelled by forces beyond one's control, hence an instinctual reaction for self-preservation, as Kuntz would describe it,[112] is imbued with volition. To the diaspora's contestation that exit is "not an alternative for voice but a necessary condition for the exercise of voice,"[113] the counter-claim is that because of exit, there can be no voice.

Nation and nationalism thus are made coterminous with geographical space, a notion that is problematized by the de-territorialization and bifurcation of the Cambodian nation engendered by mass dispersal. The imagined community of *Khmer Angkor* (Khmer of the Angkorian nation), once rooted in shared historical memories, is denied by the labeling of *Khmer chaol Angkor—Khmer chaol nokor* (Khmers who abandoned Angkor, Khmers who abandoned their country). Diasporas are regarded as divested of cultural authenticity by their removal from the ancestral source. In contrast, Cambodians who remained behind, rather than being tainted by foreign occupation, are "purer," hence more authentically Khmer. It is this sense of uncertainty and trepidation that constitutes a refrain of the return for Anida Ali when she writes of the motherland as Loss: "will she take me to the graves of the ancestors . . . or will I be asked to prove my belonging."[114]

Return and Healing

It is thus that return brings home, for many diasporas, the realization that even memory is stolen from them, erased, "swept away."[115] The exile's ultimate feeling of alienation within their originary place reverberates in Shevchenko's sobering description of Stalinist Russia: "This land of ours that is not ours."[116] Though perhaps never fully realizable, that journey—of return and of turning back—is necessary. While sociologists have described refugee migration in term of flight, diasporic return, be it literal or figurative, can be seen as an instinctual reaction *to* flight. In that sense, it is a process that is compelled more by the void carried into and heightened by exile than by concrete ideas of what awaits at the destination point. For many young survivors, even the unrequited reach for a lost childhood is a necessary gesture to break free from the temporal prison of a life abbreviated and punctuated by historical trauma:

> I remain a child in the body of a man
> In his yearning for monsoon's drops
> As I think of losses left unresolved
> For me to grow old because I keep wanting
> My childhood back as a gift I'd have to accompany my death.[117]

For other younger-generation diasporas, "return" is not just going back to the past but addressing the past in order to go beyond it, to pay homage to the painful history and the challenges of exile but also to the internal strengths of the diasporic communities. In his artistic-political project, Pete Pin uses photographs to illuminate what is present but invisible, not just the precarity and inherent contradictions of dislocated lives but also the resilience and vitality of the refugee family and community. Similarly, Bochan, a Cambodian American singer and songwriter, did not simply retrieve the popular 1960s song "I Am Sixteen" from what has been referred to as Cambodia's "golden era," but puts it in a historical continuum, juxtaposing the bucolic recollection of the era with the fracturing and triumphs of the ensuing decades. Infusing it with a new refrain, "I will survive, we will survive," she transforms the romantic idealization of Khmer women and feminized lightness by historicizing their resilience and agency: "I am a Khmer woman rising from Angkor, like an Apsara, I survived, we survived. . . . We are not victims, we are survivors." Similarly, her popular hit "Believe" acknowledges the painful history but also the strengths that refugees draw from their historical experiences. In so doing, these artists politically redefine the place and narratives of trauma and subjectivity from victims to survivors. Rather than a rupture, the past/end is read as the present/beginning, indexing the paradoxical cohabitation of loss and renewal as captured in another diasporic reflection: "When I think of this portrait of my grandparents in their last years, I always envision a beginning. To or toward what, I don't know, but always a beginning."[118] In that sense, memory, like identity, does not flow in linearity but in constantly evolving circularity.

In the attempt to pry open a space to "reflect on the good and bad memories," return, be it actual or imagined, is the first and perhaps the necessary step for many individuals, and possibly the nation in its bifurcation, to "heal and to reconcile."[119] As Arn Chorn, a returning social activist, points out, "How can we find healing if we don't even know who we are?"[120] Peace, in essence, "cannot return to a society when its members are unable to reconcile themselves with the past . . . because a society that does not assume responsibility for its dead can never entirely trust the living."[121] The famed Venerable Maha Ghosananda wrote of the need to achieve peace "step by step." Toward that end, return, be it actual or imagined, is a step toward recovery of the past and of the self, and hopefully of wholeness.

For many exiles, it is not the past but the present, not the "there" but the "here" that is ephemeral. As Rushdie puts it, "It's my present that is foreign, and that the past is home, albeit a lost home in a lost city in the mists of lost time."[122] Many carry within them the unflagging hope that they would awaken to find themselves in a mere dream state, and they do so with such intensity that it makes it difficult to distinguish, at times, between what is real and what is imagined: "Sometimes, I don't know what is real anymore, . . . the past, the present. . . . I used to say to myself, 'This can't be real; it must be a nightmare and I will wake up.' Except that nightmare never ends. I just got used to it." In my own youth, I remember sitting through the morning bulletin in the homeroom of my American public school, waiting for the news to come through the public announcement system that we can now go back home, that our exile is over. How long I waited for such news, I can't recall. I only know that it never came.

> Shall I walk with the ghosts of my two siblings and grandmother?
> Shall I walk with the ghosts of my beloved mother and father?
> Shall I walk with history, memory, and forgetfulness?
> Shall I walk with my own shadow?
> Shall I walk alone?
> I have arrived, I am home.[123]

Epilogue

Apology

His arrival in the courtroom on the opening day of his trial was almost imperceptible. Flanked by two security officers and exhibiting the self-confidence of someone accustomed to authority, he ignored the cameras and quietly took his seat behind his attorneys before being escorted subsequently to the defendant's dock. As he sat there in a simple white dress shirt, perusing the documents in front of him, he appeared almost like the schoolteacher that he once was. After more than three decades of waiting, there was but a murmured stirring of mild curiosity in the audience as the presence of the man who ran the notorious Tuol Sleng extermination center, S-21, was finally noted. A decade after his chance discovery in 1999 (by the British photographer Nic Dunlop) and subsequent arrest, Kaing Guek Eav, better known by his *nom de guerre*, Duch, stood in front of the mixed tribunal, charged with crimes against humanity. The trial was to last over a year. In the end, the initial verdict delivered was as unmomentous as his appearance in court—thirty-five years imprisonment for over twelve thousand lives brutally tortured and snuffed out. The search for justice tottered forward, amidst political haggling and scandals, with the trials of the surviving senior Khmer Rouge leaders. Beyond the walled compound of the ECCC, a wholly different world, of wrecking corruption, endemic violence, and impetuous disregard for human life, prevailed in smug defiance of the ideals and internationalist principles. Outside, a lone motorbike sped by, kicking up a trail of red dust, its rider fixed on the more pressing matter of daily survival. The contours of justice blurred in the parched tropical heat.

Many, like the Tuol Sleng survivor Vann Nath, who only wanted to confront the perpetrators with the question "Why?," never lived to see those closest to Pol Pot—namely, Ieng Sary and his wife, Ieng Thirith, Nuon Chea, and Khieu Samphan—brought to justice. His death on the eve of the start of their cluster trial as Case 002 was a resounding indictment of the process that had taken over three decades. Nor will they likely see those whose hands wielded the hoes that "smashed" their loved ones brought to account for their crimes, for they are immune to the limited mandate of this hybrid court. While survivors are still denied the explanations they desired, what they did get from Duch was an apology, not necessarily for his actions, but more for the failure of his leadership. While it drew a flurry of attention, especially from Western media, Cambodians attached a different meaning to this gesture. In Khmer, the word for apology, *som tos*, translates literally as "asking for punishment,"[1] not forgiveness, connoting the subjection of oneself to the punishment set by the aggrieved as he or she deems necessary. Though the ultimate power to cleanse lies beyond any individual's power, it is incumbent upon a Buddhist to break the karmic cycle by "lifting" or "negating" the punishment (*loeuk tos* or *ot tos*). Devoid of the liberatory connotation of the Christian concept of confession, familiar to the newly converted Duch, the Buddhist notion of atonement places importance, rather, on self-correction (*ker kloun*), hence on transformative effects rather than mere admission of guilt or articulation of remorse. In that sense, apologies and the asking for the "lifting of punishment" are necessary but not sufficient. It is thus not surprising that a public apology in and of itself was received with a certain disregard by Cambodians; only about 5 percent of respondents of the Berkeley survey considered apologies to be necessary for forgiveness, and only 1.2 percent considered the demonstration of remorse to be essential. This cultural footnote was not lost on Duch, who acknowledged that forgiveness may not be granted immediately, if ever. In fact, in his apology, he acknowledged praying first for forgiveness not from his victims but from his parents, whom he wanted to assure that his actions had not dishonored the family.

Though tribunals and other juridically based accountability are often seen as the necessary mechanisms for truth finding, the process of bearing witness itself may in fact contribute to the silencing of memories that are contested, edited out, or dismissed for failing to meet evidentiary standards. As Vann Nath recounts, "When I tell them the truth they doubt me, ask me a lot of questions. I don't feel the trust when I tell them, and that makes me feel bad. It seems like the accused person has more rights than the civil parties do."[2] What implications might that have for the legitimation of memory and remembrance and, more importantly, for the reparative process? Of his photographic installation *The Messengers*, Ly Daravuth spoke of "truth and its documentation,"[3] and how these notions are complicated and blurred by auto-genocide. It is indeed significant and ironic that S-21 has become emblematic of the Cambodian genocide, given that most of those tortured and killed were cadres who had been perpetrators of genocidal violence, which provokes the question as to whose truths are being documented and legitimated. In the same vein, while much attention has been placed on the Tuol Sleng documents, there is a virtual absence of discussion about the missing and "culled" S-21 archives.[4] What, if anything, might the missing picture, to evoke Rithy Panh, reveal? Equally important, what is then inscribed into the historical ellipsis? If it is imperative to gesture toward the possible impossibility of accessing any truth, as Ingrid Muan contends, what does this mean for the nation's ability to heal, and what in fact does healing mean?

Though imperfect, the pursuit of legal accountability makes possible an acknowledgment. For many of the civil parties, it is imperative that the crimes be named, and through the power of words, to be insured against oblivion as if they had never occurred. At the very least, it illuminates, and thus exposes, the system that thrives in secrecy and darkness. What Anne Anlin Cheng refers to as "transformation from grief to grievance"[5] is not only a transformation of the experience from "suffering injury to speaking out against that injury," but of the individual plaintiff that amounts to a reclaiming of agency and personhood.

But what of the histories that remain buried, or shadowed by new injurious encounters? What place do they have in the continuum of violence? If the politics of remembering entails, as Elizabeth Jelin argues, negotiations of power, a struggle "not only over the meaning of what took place in the past but over the meaning of memory itself,"[6] what memories are being suppressed, entombed, and peripheralized because they don't fit or threaten the dominant frames? Whose frames, in fact, are being privileged given that the power to document, interpret, represent, and legitimate rests in no small ways in non-Cambodian hands?

For many Cambodians, the hauntings, sometimes as registers of countermemories, are both real and metaphorical. Disturbances of ghostly revenants were such that decades into the aftermath, monks were brought to Tuol Sleng for spiritual cleansing. Whether they reflect the restlessness of the dead or of the living, they index the disquiet past in the present. For many survivors, the passage from trauma to mourning means living with loss, not just of things in the past but of a future that may have been but will never be. For the generation that follows, it is about living with a "double awareness," as Gerard Fromm puts it, a simultaneous sense of knowing and not knowing. For those dispersed from the ancestral fold, will the suitcase ever close, and if and when it does, does it signify the end of the road long traveled or a tacit resignation to exile?

For many survivors, living in the afterwards means reconciling with the imperfection of the justice that can be delivered in the here and now. As Vann Nath put it, "Pol Pot died unpunished, without ever having to answer for his deeds. And perhaps the surviving Khmer Rouge leaders will never be punished either. But one way or another, I believe there will be justice. A person harvests what he has sown."[7] This, however, does not necessarily imply forgetting. Of Indonesia's unsettling history, a Balinese survivor of the anticommunist massacres posits, "Forgetting has not been our problem. The problem is how to live together with what we still remember."[8] For many Buddhists, healing can be made possible by confronting and transcending the source of pain, by finding *sangvek*, compassion for that which injures. To echo Séra Ing, that which is unnameable—memory—is like smoke, "something you see but you won't be able to catch, . . . in constant evolution, changing, . . . disappearing"[9] and, I would add, often settling imperceptibly to envelop, when loss returns as a familiar presence, no longer an unrequited insistence to be acknowledged.

Healing, however, is necessarily dialectical and contingent, involving both personal and social acts of repair. It rests on the rebuilding of the system of meaning, of sociality, on a restored sense of orderliness, certainty, faith. As I penned these final words, the royal body of King Sihanouk lay in state as the nation mourned. Thus marks the end of a momentous chapter in the country's history that, in many fundamental aspects, bore the *snaam*—traces and stains—of his political rule. The national mourning overshadowed the individual and collective loss that is evoked daily in the ongoing Khmer Rouge tribunal. Even the call for the prince's shared accountability for Cambodia's tragedies that reverberated in some corners not too long ago was muted by momentary deference to propriety. The country seems to have come full circle from the Sangkum days, when few could imagine a Cambodia without a monarch, to a time when the future of the monarchy appears less certain than ever. If the Khmer Rouge experience marks a historic rupture, then Sihanouk's demise is one of the last threads in the frayed seam between pre- and post-genocide Cambodia.

For both those living in and outside Cambodia, the search for answers remains unfulfilled. To someone who wakes up one day and finds himself or herself in a strange country, struggling with a strange language and inhabiting a surreal reality, the question is almost immediate. It also never fades: "Why?" Like most refugees, what I was seeking through this painful undertaking was an answer, which I came to discover is both simple and complex. It was in essence an answer that lies in its own negation. For ultimately, what most survivors are searching for is not understanding but reason, which in this case may always be elusive. Perhaps this quest for the story to be told fully, and just right, would never end, perhaps because there is no one story, nor only one way of telling it. More importantly, it is perhaps that this exercise forces our gaze onto an abyss from which we can never truly see the light. Somewhere there is the story that is yet to be told.

This book, like the narratives, has no conclusion. Concluding remarks connote finality, and finality is what many survivor refugees resist, for much remains beyond the punctum. I started this project driven by an overwhelming need to understand the death and rupture that had consumed the Khmer nation, and our lives. What I gained was a deeper understanding not just about how and why people died, but perhaps even more importantly how they live. The story of the Khmer Rouge survivors is not just about the tragedies that befell them, but about the heroism in the daily acts of living, the ability to retain one's dignity and humanity in the moral abyss, to rediscover one's capacity to trust, to be affirmed of the importance and beauty of human relations after debasement, and to believe that tomorrow still matters. These were the things that the Khmer Rouge sought to destroy in us. These are what remind us that they have not won.

I have not found the missing picture. I looked for it, in vain. . . .
This missing picture I now hand over to you so that it never
ceases to seek us out.
—Rithy Panh

NOTES

INTRODUCTION

1 Foreword to Djaout, 2001: ix.

2 Khmer word for mythical dragons.

3 Author interview. Unless cited otherwise, all survivors' quotes are from my personal interviews. The names used in the text are aliases.

4 Ebihara, 1985: 133–34.

5 Term coined by Jean Lacouture to distinguish Khmer Rouge intra-ethnic killing from other genocides. *New York Times Book Review*, March 30, 1977.

6 Some writers, like Philip Short, and jurists have argued that the term "genocide" should not be applied to Cambodia because it did not involve interethnic killings. I have also used the term "autocide."

7 Vickery, 1984: 89.

8 Mbembe, 2001.

9 Girling, 1971.

10 Thion, 1990: 149.

11 Said, 1979.

12 Levene, 2000: 324.

13 In Tully, 2002: 485.

14 Stoler, 2008: 205.

15 Stoler, 2008.

16 Kuan-Hsing Chen, *Asia as Method: Toward Deimperialization* (Durham: Duke University Press, 2010).

17 Vickery, 1989: 90.

18 In Stoler, 2008: 191.

19 Ibid., 200.

20 Osborne, 1994: 57.

21 Ibid., 57.

22 In Stoler, 2008: 205.

23 Ibid., 201.

24 Chinua Achebe, *Things Fall Apart* (New York: Anchor, 1994), 215.

25 Chinua Achebe, "An African Voice," interview with Katie Bacon, *Atlantic Unbound*, August 2, 2000.

26 Wong, 1995: 10.

27 Agamben, 1998: 16.

28 Nguyen, 2012: 183.

29 Derrida, 1994: xix.

30 Aihwa Ong, 1999.

31 Kumar, 2000: 6.

32 Malkki, 1995: 8.

33 Dr. Kinzie of the Oregon Health and Science University had conducted longitudinal studies of Cambodian child survivors. For analysis of Cambodian American memory works, see Schlund-Vials, 2012.

34 Espiritu, 2006: 420.

35 The concept of generation is problematic especially in migration studies. I use "1.8" to refer to those who left Cambodia before adolescence or were born in the refugee camps with very tenuous connection to Cambodia.

36 Kiernan in Maguire, 2005: 52. Also Caldwell, 1979: 32.

37 Manz, 1988.

38 Shawcross, 1984: 14.

39 Stewart and May, 2002: 181.

40 Tony Kushner, "Holocaust Testimony, Ethics, and the Problem of Representation," *Poetics Today* 27, no. 2 (Summer 2006): 275.

41 Schama, 1990: xvii.

42 Zia, 2000: 43.

43 In Espiritu, 2006: 426.

44 De Alwis, 2009: 37.

45 Mbembe, 2003: 22.

46 Mbembe, 2003.

47 Todorov, 2009: 448.

THE PRISONER

1 "The Prisoner" is a composite of historical and autobiographical details compiled through my interviews, centered on the recounting of a then student-soldier, Prum, who in the early months of the fall of Phnom Penh was arrested and held in one of the detention centers in Phnom Penh that he claimed was at the "school at Tuol Sleng," although I have not been able to verify this detail. An uncle who was a high-ranking Khmer Rouge was able to vouch for him and secure his release. Unless cited otherwise, all survivors' quotes throughout the book are from my interviews.

2 An anti–French colonial movement that came to include the pro-Vietnam, communist Khmer Vietminh and a group more aligned with political elements in Thailand.

3 *Pak* means factions.

CHAPTER 1. VIOLENCE IN UTOPIA

1 The *Puth Tomney* are ancient oracles that are often referred to in discussions of political developments. Some attribute them to a man named Puth, while others claim that they were from Preah Puth (Buddha), while others still claim that *Puth Tomney* and *En Tomney* are the same messages from Indra. Though these sayings were part of

the recantations that I had grown up with, I am grateful to Professor Peter Gallay-Pap for reminding me of their cultural importance. Excerpts of the English translation were drawn from Pin Yathay's memoir.

2 Khmer use relational terms as a respect for age.

3 Common Khmer saying that inspired the title of Chanrithy Him's biography.

4 Maguire, 2005: 53. See also Becker, 1986.

5 The Cambodian refugee community in San Diego, California, turned up to protest the showing of a documentary promoting the success of the Khmer Rouge revolution in 1978. The author was present.

6 For a discussion of the discounting of survivor testimonies, see also Ana Douglass, "The Menchu Effect: Strategic Lies and Approximate Truths in Texts of Witness," in Douglass and Vogler, 2003.

7 Bizot, 2003: 4.

8 Des Pres, 1977: 46.

9 Levi, 1996: 82.

10 Maureen Katz, "Prisoners of Azkaban: Understanding Intergenerational Transmission of Trauma Due to War and State Terror (with Help from Harry Potter)," *Journal for the Psychoanalysis of Culture and Society* 8, no. 2 (Fall 2003): 200–207.

11 See Kiernan, 1985; and Vickery, 1984.

12 See www.yale.edu/cgp/maps/bigmap01.htm.

13 Airgram, U.S. Embassy, Bangkok, August 26, 1975, Indochina Archive, University of California–Berkeley.

14 Chhouk Rin, testimony, Cambodia Tribunal Monitor, April 23, 2013. See also Ian Harris, *Buddhism in a Dark Age: Cambodian Monks under Pol Pot* (Honolulu: University of Hawaii Press, 2013).

15 Um, interview. Unless cited otherwise, all quotes are my interviews.

16 The Party Center refers to the Pol Potist–controlled Standing Committee of the Communist Party of Kampuchea (CPK), the decision-making arena of Democratic Kampuchea. Its full-fledged members included Pol Pot as party secretary and prime minister, Nuon Chea as deputy secretary, and seven others. Though Khieu Samphan claimed that he was not a member of the Standing Committee, Heder noted that he regularly attended the committee meetings at least in 1975–1976. See Heder, 2004: 5, 9. The word has also been used to refer to the Standing Committee's Office 870 in Phnom Penh.

17 Summers, 1987.

18 Locard, 2004: 2. See also Vickery, 1984.

19 In some instances, survivors refer to base peasants as *neak phum* (local villagers).

20 Laura Summers identified six formal categories: feudal, capitalist, small entrepreneurs, workers, peasants, and a special class for Cambodians returning from abroad. Each sociopolitical category can be further broken down into different cohorts. Base peasants, for instance, are further categorized into the pre- and post-"March 18" people, with the implication that those who joined the revolution after the coup of

March 18, 1970, did so for reasons other than their ideological convictions, hence politically suspect.

21 Locard, 2004: 12.

22 Term used in ancient times to refer to slaves. In contemporary Khmer, it has come to mean people without manners or social grace.

23 Agamben, 1998.

24 Mbembe, 2003.

25 Nordstrom, 1998: 108.

26 Tony Barta, "Relations of Genocide: Land and Lives in the Colonization of Australia," in Wallimann and Dobkowski, 1987: 239.

27 Title of Lida Chan and Guillaume Suon's 2012 documentary.

28 Mbembe, 2003: 34.

29 *Tevada* means protective deities.

30 See also Kiernan, 1985; and Vickery, 1984.

31 Pin, 1987: 102.

32 Vickery, 1983: 129–30.

33 Literally means "cotton rice grains."

34 One refugee who passed through the area recalled that even cold beer was available in the early months, most likely taken from the province's ice factories.

35 Chandler, 1999: 69.

36 Um, interview. Commerce Ministry records showed a 5,000-ton shipment to China.

37 See Kenneth Quinn, 1982; and Debré, 1976.

38 Vickery, 1983: 91.

39 Ibid., 134.

40 Ea, 2005: 31.

41 Ibid., xi.

42 For more on detention centers, see Ea, 2005. Arn Chorn was told to play music nonstop while people were being executed.

43 Vickery, 1983: 133.

44 Closing Statement, Case 002, Cambodia Tribunal Monitor, October 18, 2013.

45 Various accounts, including those of Khmer Rouge officers, suggest that an initial order for mass liquidation of military personnel and urban evacuees was countermanded by new decrees prohibiting unsanctioned killings. Chandler, 1996: 45; Vickery, 1983: 96, 109.

46 Battambang had a long history of dissension. Under French colonialism, it was the hotbed of the Khmer Issarak. For more on the Issarak, see Bun Chan Mol, *1973*.

47 See also Osborne, 1979a.

48 Um, interview.

49 The word *mé* means leader and *phum* hamlet. In Democratic Kampuchea, *kang* refers to a work unit of fifty people and *krom*, a smaller group of ten.

50 Mbembe, 2003: 11.

51 Yum Probal decides whether a soul will go to paradise or purgatory.

52 Vickery, 1983. This was corroborated by refugee accounts.

53 Heder and Tittemore, 2004: 111.

54 Khmer Rouge Tribunal Closing Order, Case 002, September 15, 2010.

55 This customarily refers to a can of condensed milk that was commonly used to measure rice in Cambodia.

56 Vickery, 1983.

57 Traditional Khmer scarf.

58 Chandler and Kiernan: 143.

59 In Depaul, 1997: 52.

60 Mydans, 1997.

61 Chandler and Kiernan: 141.

62 Here the word *pouch* refers to genealogy. Since in Khmer society, an individual's social worth is measured according to his or her family background, genealogy matters greatly.

63 Agamben, 1998: 12.

64 Ieng Sary reinforced this claim at a meeting with returning intellectuals. Ong Thong Hoeung, 2003: 215.

65 Maguire, 2005: 2.

66 Dacil Q. Keo and Nean Yin, "Fact Sheet: Pol Pot and His Prisoners at Secret Prison S21," Documentation Center of Cambodia, January 7, 2011.

67 Ea, 2005: 27.

68 David Hawk, in Jackson, 1989.

69 His life history informed the writing of "The Prisoner" in the introduction. Though there was no independent verification of Prum's story, we do know that there were prisons and auxiliary detention centers set up as early as 1975 in and around Phnom Penh and linked to S-21. For more details, see Becker, 1986; and Vilim, 2010.

70 For more details, see Ong Thong Hoeung, 2003.

71 Mbembe, 2003: 40.

72 Ibid., 14.

73 Ibid.

74 *Katuok* is used mostly as animal feed, though in some impoverished villages it is used as a food supplement.

75 Chandler and Kiernan, 1983: 141.

76 Since power is assumed to be in the head, which is the highest corporeal realm, abuse targeting the head or conducted with one's feet or an impersonal object is a way of "diluting" or "neutralizing" (*ban-saab*).

77 See, for example, Hinton, 2005.

78 Because the liver and gallbladder are linked to blood production, they are believed to be sources of power and vitality. In Eastern medicine, animal gallbladder and liver are sought after for their curative properties. See Porée and Porée-Maspero, 1938.

79 There are earlier writings about ritualistic killing in Cambodia. See Bun, 1973. Accounts of this gruesome practice also appeared in popular narratives and in war reports in 1970–1975.

80 Ung, 2000: 156.

81 Depaul, 1997: 14.

CHAPTER 2. THE CHILDREN OF ANGKAR

1 As in other chapters, unless cited, all quotes are from my interviews.

2 Literally means "someone with good merits" and refers to someone who is powerful, a leader with legitimacy and charisma.

3 Depaul, 1997: 85.

4 Some of these dignitaries were described as Chinese visitors, others as *neak thom* (important people).

5 Panh, 2013.

6 Depaul, 1997: 79.

7 Ibid.

8 Picq, 1989: 46.

9 Tracy Manzer, "Psychologist Relives Past through His Patients," *Long Beach Press-Telegram*, December 6, 2001.

10 Thompson attributed this to the Chinese influence on Khmer juridical concepts; Thompson, 1937: 330.

11 Depaul, 1997: 25.

12 Feldman, 1991: 7.

13 Depaul, 1997: 78.

14 Vickery, 1984: 174.

15 Ung, 2000: 137.

16 Depaul, 1997: xii.

17 Ibid., 182.

18 Ibid., xvi.

19 Ibid., 158.

20 Todorov, 1996: 15.

21 *Mak Thoeung* is a Khmer literary piece depicting royal absolutism.

22 Bruno, 1990.

CHAPTER 3. PRELUDE TO TERROR

1 The high estimate of 3.3 million was provided by the PRK and the low estimate of 740,000 by Michael Vickery. Scholars have cited methodological problems with the PRK data, while a grave-mapping survey suggests that Vickery's estimate is far too low. Chandler cited a total of 1.5 to 2 million, and noted in his testimonial in Case 002 that most scholars agree on the estimate of 1.5 to 1.7 million dead. The Khmer Rouge Tribunal concluded that between 1.75 million and 2.2 million perished, of which between 800,000 and 1.3 million died violently. The U.S. government estimated that another 700,000 died after the Vietnamese invasion in 1978 ("Kampuchea:

Demographic Catastrophe," U.S. declassified document, February 12, 1980). Ysa Osman (2002) placed the number of deaths of Cham at around 500,000. Kiernan's estimate is 90,000. For analyses of the death toll under the Khmer Rouge, see Etcheson, 1999, 2000; and Kiernan, 2003.

2 Ben Kiernan placed executions at 31 percent, Steve Heder at 33 percent, and Marek Sliwinski at 40 percent. Heder placed the rate of execution among base peasants at 50 percent because of the intra-party purges; Ea, 2005: 14. An estimate of 500,000 to 1 million was cited in Laura Vilim's study. It is possible that the mass graves include those who had died during the war in 1970–1975 and from causes other than execution under the Khmer Rouge.

3 This is the number used by the Extraordinary Chambers in the Courts of Cambodia (ECCC) during the trials of Kaing Guek Eav, based on surviving records. It also projected that the number could be as high as 16,000, though other sources place it as high as 20,000.

4 Youk Chhang, "The Poisonous Hill That Is Tuol Sleng," Documentation Center of Cambodia online publication, www.dccam.org.

5 See Etcheson, 1999; and www.dccam.org/Projects/Maps/MappingKillingField.htm.

6 In Sharp, 2008.

7 Heder and Tittemore, 2004: 95.

8 Ponchaud, 1978: 214.

9 See Alex Hinton, Senglim Bit, and Francois Ponchaud, *American Experience*, PBS, March 29, 2005. Questions of Khieu Samphan's and Pol Pot's sexuality have been raised (see Short, 2006; and Barron and Paul, 1977). In an interview with Radio Free Asia, Keng Vannsak posited that the violence stemmed from Pol Pot's unrequited love. "Pol Pot's Broken Heart Influenced His Actions, Biographer Says," Radio Free Asia, Khmer Service, May 15, 2006.

10 Quoted in Shawcross, 1979: 127.

11 Bit, 1991.

12 See Hinton, 1998; and Haing, 1987: 9.

13 Short, 2006: 148, 284.

14 This is also the title of Debré's book (1976). See also Ponchaud, 1978.

15 Quinn in Jackson, 1989: 217.

16 Todorov, 2009: 452–53.

17 Hoffer, 1951.

18 See Khmer Rouge Tribunal Closing Order, Case 002, http://www.eccc.gov.kh/en/articles/evacuation-phnom-penh-case-002-closing-order.

19 Wallimann and Dobkowski, 1987: 126.

20 Gurr, 1971: 359.

21 Nuon Chea, Opening Statement, November 22, 2011. Heretofore cited as Nuon Chea, Statement.

22 Stoler, 2008: 193.

23 Girling, 1971.

24 See Khin, 2002: 361.

25 The debate about the U.S. role in this chapter of Khmer history is long-standing. Some had traced the U.S. desire for Sihanouk's removal to the early 1960s. See Corfield, 1994; and Norodom Sihanouk, 1973.

26 See Um, 2006b.

27 In Frederick Quinn, 2000: 142.

28 Martin, 1994: 32. The development of Siam's rail infrastructure that extended to the Cambodian border may have fueled French concern about its control over Cambodia and Laos and spurred the completion of the Battambang–Phnom Penh line in 1933.

29 Osborne, 1969: 289.

30 Martin, 1994: 36.

31 See Thompson, 1937.

32 Cited in Osborne, 1969: 203.

33 Tully, 2002: 122.

34 Cited in Osborne, 1969: 202.

35 Martin, 1994: 36.

36 Tully, 2002: 221.

37 Forest, 1980: 151. See also Clayton, 1995.

38 Clayton, 1995: 8. See also Delvert, 1961: 312. For more, see Um, 2013.

39 In Tully, 2002: 220.

40 Ibid.; Forest cited in Clayton, 1995: 3.

41 Roger Smith, 1970: 47. See also Osborne, 1994: 36. According to Tully, 390 students were enrolled in secondary schools in 1940. Tully, 2002: 222.

42 Kiernan, 1985: xiii.

43 Ibid.

44 See Frieson, 2000.

45 In Clayton, 1995: 3. See also Osborne,1969; and Ablin and Hood, 1990.

46 A School of Administration was established in 1917 in Cambodia but did not start to effectively function until 1922. Osborne, 1994.

47 Osborne, 1969: 167.

48 Osborne, 1969: 203.

49 Clayton, 1995: 3. See also Frieson, 2000; and Tully, 2002.

50 For discussion of this period, see Edwards, 2007.

51 Among the issues raised by the writers in the 1930s were the gross underrepresentation of Cambodians in colonial administration and the extraterritoriality extended to Vietnamese in Cambodia who did not have to be accountable to the Cambodian court. Goscha, 2008: 23.

52 In Tully, 2002: 244.

53 Thompson, 1937: 438.

54 Tully, 2002: 218. The French police subsequently raided the printing house. Martin, 1994: 53.

55 Kautsky, 1962: 67.

56 Vickery in Kiernan and Boua, 1982: 103.

57 Um, interview. Unless cited, all quotes are from my interviews.

58 Prince Chantaraingsey, one of the leaders of the Issarak, reportedly sold his protection services to Chinese gambling houses in Phnom Penh. Debré, 1976: 113. A palace insider also recalled that his foot soldiers were implicated in various incidents of urban banditry. Um, interview.

59 Many, such as Pen Sovann, became part of the post-1979 government in Phnom Penh. See Pen Sovann's autobiography, published by Khmer Vision Publishing in 2002.

60 In the Black Paper, Democratic Kampuchea stated that after the Geneva Accords, "those who fought against the French colonialists laid down their weapons and created a political association to participate in the elections." Ministry of Foreign Affairs of Democratic Kampuchea, 1979: 24, n 2.

61 Um, interview with a former Issarak sergeant.

62 Kiernan, 1985: 153.

63 Son Ngoc Thanh was prevented from returning from exile in 1952. He became head of the Khmer Serei (Free Khmer) movement, which became a persistent thorn in Sihanouk's side in the decades to follow.

64 Two packages containing explosives were delivered to the royal palace. The bomb killed the head of palace protocol. The royal couple narrowly missed the explosion when they were called away for another audience.

65 Dap Chhuon was an Issarak sergeant who rallied to the government and became the governor of Siemreap. Following Battambang and Siemreap's aborted plot to secede from Cambodia, Dap Chhuon was captured and killed.

66 Tou Samouth's death, in effect, opened the way for Pol Pot's political rise within the party. See also Chandler, 1999. See also Kiernan, 1985: 198.

67 See Kiernan, 1985; and Chandler, 1993.

68 Kiernan and Boua, 1982: 90.

69 The ICP was the Vietnam-led communist party, formed in 1930. In 1951 it gave way to the establishment of separate communist parties in Vietnam, Laos, and Cambodia.

70 Kiernan, 1985: 171.

71 Marie Martin noted that in the mid-1960s, students and faculty from the Sala Dek technical school used the cover of field excursions to conduct political discussions.

72 The 21 members consisted of "14 peasant representatives in charge of work in the rural areas, and seven representatives of the cities." Pol Pot, 1978: 9.

73 Um, interview.

74 See Kiernan, 1985.

75 Rothstein's description of "neutralist" foreign relations can also apply to Sihanouk's "domestic neutralism." Rothstein, 1968: 26.

76 Pol Pot, 1978: 13.

77 They accounted for approximately 50 percent of party affiliates, with at least two members in every district. This is based on an estimate of 822 returnees. Kiernan, 1985: 320. The Khmer Rouge tribunal placed the number at 3,000. Cambodia Tribunal Monitor, October 31, 2013.

78 Heder argues that the distinction between the pro-China and pro-Vietnam factions among the Khmer communists is overstated because none of the groups ever openly resisted Vietnam's political control. At whatever degree, it was clear that some Khmer communists deeply resented Vietnamese control. See also *Ieng Sary's Regime*, 1998: section 78.

79 Translation in Kiernan and Boua, 1982: 209. The titles of the Party's newspapers, *Voice of Neutrality* and *Cooperation*, reflected this moderated stance.

80 Pol Pot, 1978: 13.

81 See Chandler, 1993; and Kiernan, 1985.

82 Short, 2006: 177.

83 Kautsky, 1962: 34.

84 Brinton, 1965: 250.

85 Kalab, 1968: 533.

86 Osborne, 1994: 268–69.

87 Osborne, 1979b: 122.

88 Girling, 1971: 13.

89 Osborne, 1973: 80; and Osborne, 1994.

90 Many, such as the poet U Sam Oeur, came to the United States on U.S. government-sponsored programs. See SEARAC statistics, 2011.

91 Roger Smith, 1970: 347; see also Pomonti and Thion, 1971: 80; and Osborne, 1979b.

92 Osborne, 1979b: 39.

93 Girling, 1971: 9.

94 Some viewed the casino as the materialization of the reference in the Puth Tumney to "the palace of gold and silver" that will precede the turmoil, and as a harbinger of national catastrophe.

95 See Kirk, 1974.

96 These whispered concerns circulated in intimate circles in Phnom Penh on the eve of Sihanouk's deposition.

97 Justin Corfield noted that these involved formalized agreements. Corfield, 1994: 36. Allegations of high-level involvement in the sale of arms and rice to the Vietnamese communists were used to justify the coup against Sihanouk in 1970.

98 Jeldres, 2005: 68. Sihanouk acknowledged that he instructed Lon Nol to resume the transport of supplies when the Vietnamese registered their concerns about its interruption.

99 It was widely rumored that the transport company Hak Ly, with highly placed ties, ferried rice supplies via the port of Sihanoukville to the Vietnamese border.

100 Short, 2006: 182.

101 See Osborne, 1973; Kirk, 1974; Osborne, 1979b; Girling, 1971.

102 Pomonti and Thion, 1971: 41. See also Kiernan and Boua, 1982.

103 Girling, 1971: 12.

104 Ibid., 27.

105 Hu Nim confessions, May 3, 1977, Documentation Center of Cambodia; and Roger Smith in Gettleman, Gettleman, and Kaplan, 1970: 347.

106 Girling, 1971: 11.

107 Khieu, 2004: 13.

108 Kiernan and Boua, 1982: 102; and Osborne, 1979b: 114.

109 Kiernan, 1985. Among those implicated was Long Boreth, who later became minister of commerce. It has been argued that the experience of 1963 provided the impetus for his active involvement in Sihanouk's deposition in 1970.

110 Schama, 1990: 197.

111 Heder, 1979: 55.

112 Osborne, 1973: 67.

113 Um, interview.

114 Roger Smith, 1970: 75.

115 Osborne, 1979b: 39.

116 Chandler, in Engelbert and Goscha, 1995.

117 See Steinbach and Steinbach, 1976: 14.

118 In Kiernan, 1985: 169.

119 Pol Pot, 1978: 16.

120 Pol Pot, 1978: 16. Though this reflects a large percentage, it is important to note that the movement and the leadership were quite small.

121 As late as 1962, Pol Pot's appointment as deputy party secretary in 1961 appeared not to have been known to the Eastern Zone cadres. Kiernan, 1985: 193.

122 Kiernan, 1985: 204.

123 Delvert, 1961.

124 Steinberg, 1985: 24.

125 Thompson, 1937: 325.

126 Ibid., 340.

127 For details, see Migozzi, 1973; Kalab, 1968; and Delvert, 1983. Because 90 percent of the population was concentrated in about one-third of the total area, the actual national density reached from ninety to six hundred people per square kilometer.

128 See Migozzi, 1973; and Kalab, 1968: 521.

129 Steinberg, 1985: 25; Porée and Porée-Maspero, 1938: 193.

130 Thompson also captured that sense of abundance.

131 Um, interview.

132 Ibid.

133 Delvert reported that during the prewar years the average Cambodian consumed six hundred to seven hundred grams of rice and a hundred grams of fish daily. Delvert, 1983: 76.

134 Kiernan, 1985: xv.

135 Khieu Samphan in Kiernan, 1985: 267.

136 Kalab, 1968: 521.

137 Ibid., 522.

138 Many self-identified as being from the Northwest though many were not native of the region but had relocated there during the war or the Pol Pot period.

139 Kiernan noted that 10–15 percent of the peasantry perished under the Khmer Rouge. Kiernan, 2005.

140 Kalab described the Cambodian population as being "fairly mobile" in the 1960s.

141 Gurr, 1971.

142 Quoted in Ablin and Hood, 1990: 25.

143 Pol Pot, 1978: 12.

144 Um, interview.

145 Pomonti and Thion, 1971: 39.

146 Thompson, 1937: 356.

147 For more on the Chinese community in Cambodia, see Willmott, 1967.

148 Um, interview.

149 Hou Yuon in Kiernan and Boua, 1982: 60.

150 Ibid.

151 The term *doch nek sre* or *samrer* (like a peasant or peasant-like) is a pejorative term connoting crudeness.

152 Kuon, 1989: 43.

153 See Kiernan, 1985; and Meyer, 1971.

154 Kiernan, 1985.

155 Reportedly, military officers were given land concessions that encroached on indigenous land.

156 Corfield, 1994: 44.

157 Kiernan, 1982: 174. In her 1968 study, Kalab also noted the presence of new immigrant families moving into the area.

158 Debré, 1976: 109.

159 The allegations were that these initiatives favored officials and speculators at the expense of the local peasants.

160 As with other historical instances of peasant revolt in Cambodia, the Samlaut uprising was subsequently defused through royal intercession, accompanied by an appeal from the Buddhist patriarch, Samdech Iv Tuot, for an end to the rebellion. Sihanouk granted the protestors a royal audience and a promise for the construction of schools and clinics and amnesty for the protesters. See Kiernan, 1985; and Chandler, 1993.

161 Khieu, 2004: 29.

162 Kirk, 1974: 78.

163 Pol Pot, 1978: 11.

164 See Meyer, 1971. As in Vietnam, this promise was never realized in the post-victory period.

165 Toasted rice.

166 Um, interview.

167 Um, interview.

168 Survivors recalled that in 1970, students from the Chinese schools in Kompong Cham where Maoism had made deep inroads took to the *maquis*. Um, interview. See also Huang Shiming's memoir *On the Wave of Mekong*, cited in Lui, 2012.

169 Pomonti and Thion : 61. A renewed promise of noninterference prevented the withdrawing of embassies. On Chinese community in Cambodia, see also Huang Shiming.

170 "Unsigned Report of Base Area Meeting," April 19, 1970, 59, Indochina Archive, University of California–Berkeley. In 1970 these communities were considered strategic communication points, and essential "springboards" for support.

171 Corfield, 1994: 92.

172 Um, conversation with a Dega leader, Washington, DC, 2001.

173 Meyer, 1971: 197.

174 A contingent of Khmer Loeu soldiers, some of whom had joined the Khmer Rouge army since 1969, was among the last bastion of Khmer Rouge *ralliés*. The author was present during their transport back from the border to the Northeast in 1999.

175 Willmott, 1967: 224.

176 Johnson, 1962.

177 Pol Pot, 1977: 16. The disclosure of its limited role may have been the Party's attempt to divorce itself from the brutalizing consequences of the failed insurrection. See also Ministry of Foreign Affairs of Democratic Kampuchea, 1979: 25.

178 Kiernan, 1985: 287.

179 It was not an unfounded concern. In response to what he perceived to be Hanoi's unwillingness to control the Khmer Rouge, Sihanouk's denouncements of Vietnamese communist presence in Cambodia grew.

180 Nuon Chea also spoke of Vietnam's withholding of arms from the Khmer communists. Opening Statement, Case 002, November 22, 2011.

181 Heder, 1979: 20.

182 Osborne, 1994: 136.

183 Chandler, 1972: 84. See also Chandler, 2000.

184 Shawcross, 1979. See also Zasloff and Goodman, 1972; and Ablin and Hood, 1990.

185 See Starr, 1971.

186 Cambodians have interpreted this reference in the prophecy of *Puth* as the prince's exile in China and the brutal war that ensued.

187 Skocpol, 1979.

188 In Ablin and Hood, 1990: xxvi.

189 Um, interview.

CHAPTER 4. FROM PEASANTS TO REVOLUTIONARIES

1 President Richard Nixon, Address to the Nation on the Situation in Southeast Asia, video from the Richard Nixon Presidential Library and Museum, www.youtube.com, September 3, 2009.

2 Document no. CK3100607956, *Declassified Documents Reference System* (Farmington Hills, MI: Gale, 2013).

3 Nixon press conference, November 15, 1971, cited in Sydney Schanberg, "New York: Cambodia Forgotten (2)," op-ed, *New York Times*, April 9, 1985. http://www.nytimes.com/1985/04/09/opinion/new-york-cambodia-forgotten-2.html.

4 Corfield, 1994: 100. According to U.S. declassified documents, Lon Nol may have been informed shortly before that such operations were being planned but not provided with specifics. See cable from Rives in Phnom Penh after meeting with Lon Nol on May 1, 1970. Declassified cable from U.S. embassy in Phnom Penh, National Security Archive, George Washington University.

5 This was recounted in confidence by an official who was present during the meeting.

6 Um, interview.

7 Girling, 1971: 6. See also Paul Sweezy and Harry Magdoff in Gettleman, Gettleman, and Kaplan, 1970.

8 See also Doan, 1985: 176; Gettleman, Gettleman, and Kaplan, 1970: 439; and Shawcross, 1979: 415.

9 Unmarked captured document, Indochina Archive, University of California–Berkeley. See also Al Rockoff, testimony, Cambodia Tribunal Monitor, January 29, 2013.

10 See Short, 2006.

11 Kiernan and Boua, 1982: iv.

12 Document no. 10, April 29, 1970, and Document no. 9, Spring 1970, 66, Indochina Archive, University of California–Berkeley.

13 Kate Webb of UPI, Dudman, and Bizot all were initially taken prisoner by Vietnamese communist forces operating in Cambodia, not the Khmer Rouge. See Webb, 1972; Dudman, 1971; and Bizot, 2003.

14 Document no. 9, 72, Indochina Archive, University of California–Berkeley.

15 Short, 2006: 205.

16 Shawcross, 1979: 249.

17 Sak, 1980: 27.

18 CIA report, 1971, declassified document; see Shawcross, 1979: 249.

19 Sak, 1980: 91.

20 Skocpol, 1982.

21 Skocpol, 1979: 115.

22 See Johnson, 1962.

23 Shawcross, 1979: 420.

24 Grant Peck, "Accused Blames U.S. for Rise of Khmer Rouge," *Sydney Morning Herald*, April 8, 2009.

25 The United States had to rely on air campaigns to minimize American casualties and because of the Church-Cooper Amendment, which restricted the U.S. role in Cambodia. For a seminal work on this chapter of American policy, see Shawcross, 1979. See also Becker, 2004.

26 Shawcross, 1979: 297.

27 See Shawcross, 1979.

28 Ibid.

29 Conversation dated December 9, 1970, Nixon Presidential Materials Project, Henry A. Kissinger Telephone Conversations Transcripts, Home File, Box 29, File 2, 106–10, National Security Archive, George Washington University, Washington, DC.

30 Swain, 1996: 168.

31 Cambodia Tribunal Monitor, April 9, 2013.

32 Shawcross, 1979: 222.

33 Johnson, 1962: 19.

34 See Hoffer, 1951.

35 U Sam Oeur, 2005: 154.

36 Short, 2006: 249.

37 Map File, Indochina Archive, University of California–Berkeley.

38 Swain, 1996: 24.

39 Tilly, 1975: 520.

40 Debré, 1976: 180.

41 Case no. 002/19–09–2007-ECCC/TC, September 4, 2013.

42 Kiernan, 1985: 363.

43 Ibid., 336.

44 Chanda, 1986: 72.

45 In Zasloff and Goodman, 1972: 224.

46 Sak, 1980: 173.

47 Martin, 1994: 141. The cooperatives also did away with the *compradores* in the sale and distribution of key commodities, most of whom were Sino-Cambodian. Short, 2006: 257.

48 Kiernan, 1985: 382.

49 Khieu, 2004.

50 Pol Pot, 1978: 22.

51 Khieu, 2004: 61.

52 Debré, 1976: 180.

53 Short, 2006: 247.

54 Kiernan, 1985.

55 Um, interview. Also Short, 2006: 256.

56 Kirk, in Zasloff and Goodman, 1972: 223.

57 Heder, testimony, Cambodia Tribunal Monitor, July 10, 2013. On mass graves found in Kompong Thom and elsewhere, see Martin, 1994: 141; Short, 2006: 230.

58 This was supported by my refugee interviews.

59 In Bienen, 1968: 60.

60 See Chandler, 1999; and Shawcross, 1979.

61 Shawcross, 1979: 174.

62 Pomonti and Thion, 1971: 230.

63 Nuon, 1988: 19.

64 AP, July 17, 1971.

65 Um, interview.

66 Nuon, 1988: 15.

67 Shawcross, 1979: 185.

68 "National Security Adviser Henry Kissinger Updates President Richard M. Nixon on Deputy National Security Adviser Alexander Haig, Jr.'s 5/23/1970 Two-Hour Conversation with Cambodian Prime Minister Lon Nol," May 26, 1970, declassified document no. CK3100607956. Reproduced in Declassified Documents Reference System (Farmington Hills, MI: Gale, 2013).

69 *Christian Science Monitor*, September 18, 1971.

70 CIA report in Shawcross, 1979: 249.

71 See Khin, 2002. See also Harris, 2008.

72 See Chandler, 1996; Osborne, 1969; and Porée and Porée-Maspero, 1938: 131.

73 See Chandler, 1996 for this historical recounting.

74 Osborne, 1969: 251.

75 Ibid. The Chinese population also numbered nearly sixty thousand in 1908, with 41 percent of the population residing in the rural areas. See also Willmott, 1967.

76 Porée and Porée-Maspero, 1938: 20. Chinese presence in Cambodia's rural communities was more pronounced than anywhere else in Southeast Asia. Thompson, 1937: 330; and Steinberg, 1985: 175.

77 Short placed the population at one-third in 1928, while Thompson placed the ratio at 50 percent by 1936. Short, 2006: 24; and Thompson, 1937: 338.

78 Um, interview.

79 In Tully, 2002: 242.

80 Chandler, 1972.

81 Chanda, 1986: 53.

82 Yang, 1987: 35. For more discussion of the difference in national character between Vietnamese and Cambodians, see Chandler, 1996.

83 In his rebuttal, Nuon Chea argued that Khmers could not have committed genocide because they were Buddhist, and even communists light incense and pray.

84 In Marston and Guthrie, 2004: 51.

85 Thompson, 1937: 339.

86 These anxieties resurfaced in the late 1960s in light of the cross-border sanctuaries and again after Vietnam's invasion in 1979. Today, the issue of Vietnamese immigration is one of the most volatile in Cambodian politics.

87 Even though Chinese paid higher taxes, they were exempt from *corvée* and conscription, two of the most dreaded decrees for the average peasant. Thompson, 1937: 329.

88 Gregor Muller, 2006: 112, 113.

89 Nuon, 1988: 4.

90 It is noteworthy that many colonial administrative reports bore the signature of clerks with Vietnamese names. Archives d'Outre Mer in Aix-en Provence. There are

also numerous references to the challenges of court translation in Khmer jokes of that period.

91 Nuon, 1988: 5.

92 Cohn, 1961: 104.

93 Thion, 2000: 17.

94 Osborne, 1979a: 18. In the kingdom, the "ploughing ceremony" is performed annually.

95 Hansen, 2004: 47.

96 The rumor that the stroke had incapacitated Lon Nol's right arm, which he had used to sign the decree for Sihanouk's deposition, gained traction among superstitious Phnom Penh residents. Corfield, 1994: 110.

97 The notion of power here is not just physical or military, but moral and mystical.

98 Literally translated as "a star with a tail."

99 A woman who was part of the Queen Mother's entourage recounted this story to my parents. It was said that during King Sihanouk's coronation, the victory candle blew out on the second day, causing serious consternation within the royal court. See also Becker, 1986; and Harris, 2008.

100 Norodom, 1981.

101 Osborne, 1994: 18.

102 Cambodia Tribunal Monitor, April 24, 2013.

103 Norodom, 1986.

104 Hoffer, 1951.

105 Osborne, 1969: 221.

106 Um, interview. Pomonti and Thion wrote that some of the elderly Khmer peasants were brought to tears by these radio appeals. Pomonti and Thion, 1971: 176.

107 Um, interview. The term refers to Vietnamese, largely from North Vietnam, and to the traditional practice of lacquering the teeth.

108 Keng Vannsak claimed that Pol Pot may have taken his advice to heart when he suggested that the latter deal with his unrequited love by going to the forest like the character in the Ramayana.

109 Document no. 9, 1971, Indochina Archive, University of California–Berkeley.

110 Corfield, 1994: 92.

111 Citing a Western observer, Pomonti and Thion placed the number of armed cadres at 1,500–3,000. Pomonti and Thion, 1971: 285.

112 Dudman, 1971: 61.

113 Theth Sambath and Rob Lemkin, *Enemies of the People* (Old Street Films, 2012).

114 A *raa-mork* is a three-wheeled transport.

115 Ith Sarin, 1973: 39.

116 Osborne, 1970: 19.

117 Delvert, 1983: 94.

118 Women cannot be ordained monks, though they can become nuns or *doan chi*. They can accumulate this highest form of merit only if they have ordained sons.

119 Yang, 1987: 24.

120 It is noteworthy that a temple boy is not referred to as a servant but as a *koun soeus lok*, literally "a student of the monks," which speaks to the role of monks as educators.

121 See McAlister, 1973.

122 Jackson, 1985.

123 Many millenarian leaders were *achars* (religious leaders) or former monks. See Chandler, 1996; Hansen, 2004; and Yang, 1987.

124 One of the principal issues was the French attempt to romanize the Khmer script as they had successfully done in Vietnam, which some viewed as an attempt to destroy Khmer culture and undercut the power and influence of the Buddhist *sangha*.

125 Um, interview. See also Bun, 1971; and Lek, 2005. Penny Edwards (2004) noted that in 1931 preaching to Cambodian soldiers became part of the Buddhist institute's tours.

126 Kiernan, 1975.

127 Short, 2006: 166.

128 For more on the *sangha* during the war, see Thion, 2000: 13.

129 It is important to note that many of the leading Khmer communists, including Pol Pot, Ieng Sary, and Duch, were teachers.

130 Thion, 2000: 15.

131 In prewar Cambodia, private schools were not highly ranked.

132 Kuon, 1989: 34.

133 Ith Sarin, 1973: 48.

134 Kuon, 1989: 19.

135 Ith Sarin, 1973: 46.

136 Simon in Zasloff and Goodman, 1972: 207.

137 In Pailin, price restructuring was the first initiative undertaken by the Khmer Rouge upon their takeover of the city.

138 Um, interview.

139 Shawcross, 1979: 185.

140 Sak, 1980: 5.

141 Al Rockoff, testimony, Cambodia Tribunal Monitor, January 29, 2013.

142 Sak, 1980: 150.

143 Becker, 1986: 13.

144 Sak, 1980: 150.

145 Cohn, 1961.

146 Schama, 1989.

147 Shawcross, 1979: 358.

CHAPTER 5. INSTRUMENTALITY OF TERROR

1 Bienen, 1968: 23.

2 Johnson, 1982.

3 Tucker, 1975.

4 Lowenthal in Johnson, 1970.

5 Panh, 2013.

6 Wole Soyinka in Tahar, 2001: ix.

7 Leo Kuper in Melson, 1992: xii.

8 In Hoffer, 1951: 105.

9 Tim Carney, "The Unexpected Victory," in Jackson, 1989. See also *Far Eastern Economic Review*, July 25, 1975.

10 Levene, 2000: 325.

11 Jackson, 1989: 233.

12 Panh, 2013.

13 In Arendt, 1958: 311.

14 Shawcross, 1979. Elizabeth Becker puts the KR strength in 1973 at sixty-eight thousand soldiers. Becker, 1986: 179.

15 Chandler, Kiernan, and Boua, 1988: 17.

16 Ibid.

17 Becker, 1986: 179.

18 Ith Sarin, 1973: 26.

19 Nuon Chea (Brother Number 2) was a member of the Thai Communist Party and later, along with Ta Mok and Saloth Sar (Pol Pot), a member of the Indochinese Communist Party. Pol Pot and Ieng Sary belonged to the French Communist Party. In August 1951 they attended the youth festival in East Berlin. The Khmer student association to which they belonged also had ties to the International Union of Students, based in Bucharest. See Martin, 1994: 99–101.

20 Nate Thayer, "Forbidden City: New Strongman Ta Mok Reaches Out of Isolation," *Far Eastern Economic Review*, October 30, 1997.

21 Pol Pot, Ieng Sary, Khieu Ponnary, Khieu Thirith, Khieu Samphan, and Son Sen all studied in Paris. The Khieu sisters came from one of Phnom Penh's elite families. See Martin, 1994; and Norodom, 1979.

22 Heder, 2003: 72.

23 Conquest, 1990: 4.

24 Chandler, Kiernan, and Boua, 1988: 22.

25 Ibid., 19.

26 Ibid., 203.

27 Ibid., 202.

28 Ibid., 204.

29 Ibid., 329, n 17.

30 See Ong Thong Hoeung, 2003.

31 Chandler, Kiernan, and Boua, 1988: 204.

32 In Shub, 1948: 182.

33 Chandler, Kiernan, and Boua, 1988: 33.

34 Heder, *Reassessing the Roles of Senior Leaders and Local Officials in Democratic Kampuchea Crimes*, cited by David Chandler in his testimony at the Khmer Rouge Tribunal, Cambodia Tribunal Monitor, July 23, 2012.

35 In Chandler, 1992: 175. This came from a study session document dated 1986.

36 Barnett in Chandler and Kiernan, 1983: 215.

37 Pol Pot, 1977: 18.

38 Bizot, 2003: 175.

39 Martin, 1994: 159.

40 Szymusiak, 1984: 9.

41 Cambodia Tribunal Monitor, July 26, 2012.

42 Short, 2006: 224.

43 Cambodia Tribunal Monitor, April, 22, 2013.

44 Um, interview. The Khmer Rouge often lumped escapees with resistance forces and referred to them as *chaor prey* (forest bandits). Nuon Chea mentioned Chantaraingsey's forces near the Thai border and another group on the Vietnamese border. Nuon Chea, statement. See also U Sam Oeur, 2005. For more details on the resistance movement, see Um, 2006a.

45 See also Yimsut, 2011.

46 Ysa, 2002: 20.

47 This was mentioned in his confession, which was later found at S-21. Ysa, 2002: 103.

48 Heder and Tittemore, 2004: 117. Khmer Sar (White Khmer) was a term used generically for all anti–Khmer Rouge opposition, and in some instances specifically for Prince Chantaraingsey's forces. The reference to "liberation from the rice by the can" was a protest against food rationing in which a Nestlé milk can was a common measure.

49 Kiernan, 1985: 415.

50 See Heder, 1991b.

51 Hu Nim's confession suggested that there was criticism of the decision to evacuate the towns and of Pol Pot's call to intensify class struggle. Chou Chet, head of the Western Zone, confessed to having been lax with executions and having opted instead to "reeducate" former Republican soldiers. Heder, 1991a: 15. Testimonials by former cadres given to the Khmer Rouge tribunal reference differing opinions regarding de-urbanization and other critical decisions.

52 In Heder and Tittemore, 2004: 103.

53 Kiernan, 1985: 415. According to Martin, Hou Yuon purportedly referred to the evacuation of the capital city as "a pillage." Martin, 1994: 158. He reportedly "dare[d] to scold" Pol Pot, and accused the Party of making him a "puppet minister." Kiernan, 1985: 329.

54 Heder, 1991a: 19.

55 Ibid., 16.

56 Ibid., 21.

57 Heder and Tittemore, 2004: 117, n 456.

58 For this view, see also Chandler, 1993. Vorn Vet confessed to being galvanized into organizing opposition after Sao Phim's and Ruoh Nheum's deaths. Heder, 1991a: 21.

59 Martin referenced three attempts against Pol Pot, including one by his adopted son, Pang (Martin, 1994: 196). See also Ros Souy's testimony, Cambodia Tribunal Monitor, April 22, 2013.

60 Um, interview. See FEER, *Yearbook*, 1978: 154 on the reported uprising.

61 Martin, 1994: 207.

62 Chan Chakrey's unit exploded an ordinance near the Party headquarters in May 1976.

63 Heder, 1991a: 9.

64 Agamben, 1998: 16.

65 Mbembe, 2003: 30.

66 Kiernan, 1985: 267. There were suggestions that plans were made to unveil the existence and leadership of the Khmer Communist Party at the anniversary celebrations but that they were postponed. The Party remained secret for another year.

67 In Ponchaud, 1978: 20.

68 Um, interview.

69 Cambodia Tribunal Monitor, May 6, 2013, and October 18, 2013.

70 The first units to enter Phnom Penh were, in fact, Republican forces led by Keth Dara who were passing themselves off as the Khmer Rouge in a failed bid to snatch victory from the latter.

71 Cambodia Tribunal Monitor, July 11, 2013.

72 Cambodia Tribunal Monitor, May 2, 2013.

73 Cambodia Tribunal Monitor, May 6, 2013, and July 26, 2013.

74 Quoted in Brown and Zasloff, 1986 : 136. See also Closing Order, Case 002, http://www.eccc.gov.kh.

75 Bizot, 2003: 6.

76 *Ieng Sary's Regime*, 1998: section 58. This anonymous "diary" was initially attributed to Ieng Sary (deputy prime minister and foreign minister of Democratic Kampuchea) because it was found in a house that he had occupied in early 1979 by a Cambodian who had returned to Phnom Penh from the countryside after the collapse of the Khmer Rouge regime.

77 Quoted in Brown and Zasloff, 1986: 136.

78 Um, interview. See also U Sam Oeur, 2005; and Snepp, 1977: 148.

79 Cambodia Tribunal Monitor, October 18, 2013.

80 In Chandler, 1999: 43.

81 Levene, 2000: 325.

82 Becker in Chandler, 1999: 46.

83 See Neumann, 1965.

84 Chandler, 1992: 113.

85 Heder and Tittemore, 2004: 40.

86 Cambodia Tribunal Monitor, April 23, 2013.

87 Chandler and Kiernan, 1983: 118.

88 The phrase *kser tream* refers to the security cordon deployed around villages and cooperatives. Um, interview.

89 Akineth (Eyes of Fire) is a character in Khmer legend who can set someone on fire with his glance.

90 Maier, 1997: 81.

91 Black and Thornton, 1964: 4.

92 Sémelin, 2000.

93 Ong Thong Hoeung, 2003: 125.

94 Closing Order of the Extraordinary Chambers in the Courts of Cambodia (ECCC) indicting Kaing Guek Eav, August 8, 2008.

95 Foucault, 1977: 201.

96 Ibid.

97 In Todorov, 1996: 28.

98 Ong Thong Hoeung, 2003: 71.

99 Foucault, 1977: 201.

100 Arendt, 1969: 54.

101 Pol Pot, 1978: 25.

102 Schama, 1990: xv.

103 Johnson, 1982: 92.

104 In Hoffer, 1951: 79.

105 Ibid., 9.

106 Bizot, 2003: 7.

107 Word taken from the title of Francois Ponchaud's book and recontextualized.

108 In Tucker, 1975: 182.

109 Hoffer, 1951: 146.

110 In Osborne, 1994: 137.

111 Pol Pot, 1978: 8.

112 In Martin, 1994: 202.

113 Jackson, 1989: 4.

114 In Nate Thayer, "My Education: How Saloth Sar Became Pol Pot," *Far Eastern Economic Review*, October 30, 1997.

115 Ibid.

116 See Quinn in Jackson, 1989.

117 Khieu Samphan stated that he did not renew his membership in the French communist party after 1957 because, as he put it, "the party's activities were primarily geared towards France's interior problems." Khieu, 2004: 34.

118 In Martin, 1994: 99.

119 In Thayer, "My Education."

120 They involved student plays and newsletters. One bulletin, *Reasmey*, for which Pol Pot wrote articles under the pen name "The Original Khmer," lasted about five years.

121 In Jackson, 1989: 43.

122 Chomsky and Herman, 1979: 231.

123 The word "Angkor" is one of the most commonly used brand names for Cambodian enterprises, products, and services both in Cambodia and in the diaspora.

124 Chandler, 1993.

125 Pol Pot, 1978: 45.

126 Ibid., 24.

127 In Armstrong, 1964: 28.

128 Norodom, 1973: 80.

129 Ibid., 139.

130 Ibid., 140.

131 Roger Smith, 1965: 98.

132 Reportedly, Vietnam attempted to disrupt the flow of military supplies from China. Short, 2006: 202.

133 Ibid., 252.

134 This is also part of the title of Grant Evans's book.

135 Straus, 2007: 482.

136 See Ysa, 2006.

137 Ibid.

138 See Kiernan, 2008 for this line of argument.

139 Pol Pot, 1979: 31.

140 In Chandler and Kiernan, 1983: 30.

141 Ibid.

142 Khieu, 2004: 57.

143 Goscha, 2008: 1193.

144 Edwards, 2008: 157.

145 In Jackson, 1989: 44.

146 *Neak psar* means "people of the market" but refers generally to urbanites. Reference to the swollen knees refers to the effect of starvation, which implies that at least those cadres were fully aware of the famine, which makes the claim of ignorance of the Khmer Rouge leadership that much more difficult to accept. The tone also reflects the retributive nature of the deportation.

147 Barbu, 2003: 195.

148 The Steinbachs, who lived in Phnom Penh, reported that some cadres borrowed their car to go see the royal palace. Steinbach and Steinbach, 1976: 23.

149 Shawcross, 1979: 276.

150 In Wallimann and Dobkowski, 1987: 294.

151 For more discussion of the inverted cosmology, see Edwards, 2008.

152 Chandler and Kiernan, 1983: 187.

153 Pol Pot, 1978: 30.

154 Martin, 1994: 190. It was only in 1978 that the regime acknowledged that training requires seven years for high-level technicians and ten for engineers.

155 Martin, 1994: 202.

156 FBIS, May 19, 1975.

157 See Chandler, 1999, for discussion of the relationship between prominent personalities in the Chinese Cultural Revolution and the Pol Potist group.

158 Ea, 2005: 6.

159 FBIS, May 14, 1975.

160 Neumann, 1965: 60.

161 Ibid., 38.

162 In Chandler and Kiernan, 1983: 170.

163 Conquest, 1990: 6.

164 Khieu, 2004: 59.

165 *Ieng Sary's Regime*, 1998: section 67.

166 Ibid., section 58.

167 Nuon Chea, Statement.

168 Meisner, 1982: 43.

169 In Chandler, 1983: 34.

170 Rosenberg and Young, 1982: 250.

171 Pol Pot, 1978.

172 *Ieng Sary's Regime*, 1998: section 67.

173 Ong Thong Hoeung, 2003: 169.

174 In Chandler and Kiernan, 1983: 169.

175 Ibid., 24.

176 See Norodom, 1986.

177 In Chandler and Kiernan, 1983: 46.

178 Ibid.

179 Ibid.

180 Ibid.

181 Pol Pot, 1979.

182 In Chandler and Kiernan, 1983: 49.

183 In Chanda, 1986: 44.

184 In Short, 2006: 213.

185 FBIS, July 1, 1975.

186 In Chandler and Kiernan, 1983: 48.

187 In Jackson, 1989: 40.

188 FBIS, April 18, 1977.

189 Phnom-Penh Radio, May 10, 1978.

190 Martin, 1994: 190.

191 A commercial emporium was set up in Hong Kong in 1976 and another one in Singapore in 1978 to facilitate economic dealings with the West. Martin, 1994: 192; and Kiernan, 2008: 379. Refugees whom I interviewed recalled rice bags bearing Chinese writing being carted off in numerous transports from their villages during times of rampant starvation. It is not clear whether those writings reflect the destination or the manufactured origin of the bags.

192 Martin, 1994: 190.

193 Ponchaud, 1978: 15.

194 Jackson, 1989: 2.

195 Heder contends that some of the senior Party members saw this stance as too extreme and pointed to Vietnam as an example. This marked them as Vietnamese sympathizers. See Heder, 1991a and 2003.

196 FBIS, May 14, 1975.

197 Pol Pot, 1978: 11.

198 Ibid.

199 See Willmott, 1967; Thompson, 1937; Delvert, 1983.

200 Pol Pot, 1978: 12.

201 Chandler and Kiernan, 1983: 184.

202 Caldwell, 1979: 1.

203 See Chandler and Kiernan, 1983.

204 Pol Pot, 1979: 31.

205 In Chandler and Kiernan, 1983: 199.

206 Um, interview.

207 In Chandler and Kiernan, 1983: 195.

208 Cambodia Tribunal Monitor, July 23, 2012.

209 Khieu, 2004: 58.

210 Arendt, 1958: 457.

211 Pol Pot, 1978: 30.

212 Pol Pot, 1979: 19.

213 Pol Pot, 1978: 61.

214 Ibid., 58.

215 Aronson in Levene, 2000: 325.

216 Pol Pot, 1978: 31.

217 Hoffer, 1951: xiii.

218 Cohn, 1961.

219 Arendt, 1958: 420.

220 Panh, 2012: 29.

221 In Chandler and Kiernan, 1983: 188.

222 This was drawn from Chou Chet's confession, although Heder translates it as "if the teacher was vicious, the student would be vile." Heder, 1991a: 17.

223 On failure to report starvation, see Chuon Thy, testimony, Cambodia Tribunal Monitor, April 24, 2013. In 1978, five thousand tons of rice were sent to China. See Kiernan, 2005.

224 In Chandler and Kiernan, 1983: 183.

225 Ibid., 184–85, 189.

226 Ibid.

227 Ibid., 48.

228 Pol Pot, 1978: 28.

229 Ea, 2005: 5.

230 Ibid.

231 Heder and Tittemore, 2004: 41.

232 Ibid., 43.

233 Ibid.

234 Catalogue no. D06936, Documentation Center of Cambodia. Duch stated that Son Sen insisted on the confessions of the "important ones."

235 Chandler, 2000: 44.

236 In Panh and Bataille, 2012: 1.

237 Pol Pot, 1978: 48.

238 Pictures of prisoners at Tuol Sleng and remains unearthed at Choeung Ek mass graves included those of newborns.

239 Chandler and Kiernan, 1983: 184.

240 This practice is referenced in an epic poem, *Tum Teav*. For an analysis of the poem, see Hinton, 1998.

241 Hoffer, 1951: 145.

242 In Schama, 1990: 714.

243 Arendt, 1958: 457.

244 Solomon, 1971: 353.

245 Um, interview.

246 See Lifton, 1986.

247 Lifton, 1986: 59.

248 Um, interview.

249 Brinton, 1965: 146.

250 Duch stated that the order to kill the remaining prisoners at S-21 came from Nuon Chea.

251 Hoffer, 1951: 146.

252 In Skocpol, 1979: 18.

CHAPTER 6. FRAGMENTS

1 Robben and Suárez-Orozco, 2000b: 44.

2 Samphy Iep, "Dreaming in My Own Language," in Tenhula, 1991: 7.

3 In McLellan, 2004: 105.

4 In Ball, 2003: 271.

5 Ledgerwood, 2008: 204.

6 In Letsinger, 2004.

7 War and dislocation have destabilized the family institution and undermined socialization.

8 See U Sam Oeur, 2005; and Lefreniere, 2000.

9 Martin Buber in Alan Berger, "Bearing Witness: Second Generation Literature of the 'Shoah,'" *Modern Judaism* 10, no. 1 (1990): 43.

10 Arendt, 1978: 212.

11 Robben and Suárez-Orozco, 2000b: 43.

12 Um, interview. Unless cited, all quotes are from my interviews.

13 Giddens in McLellan, 2004: 111.

14 Panh and Bataille, 2012: 3."

15 Eyerman, 2002: 2.

16 Thida Butt Mam, in Depaul, 1997: 16.

17 In Lefreniere, 2000: 98.

18 Um, 1998.

19 Honorifics such as *Mrs.* and *Mr.* are sometimes used with individual interviewees' names when the interviewees are in their fifties or older. This is to reflect the Khmer cultural norm of never referring to an elder by first name.

20 Pielert, 2007.

21 In Leslie, 2001: 52.

22 Quoted in Sarah Stephens, "Legacies of Absence: Cambodian Artists Confront the Past," *Persimmon: Asian Literature, Arts, and Culture*, Summer 2000.

23 ECCC, May 29, 2013, http://www.eccc.gov.kh/en/witness-expert-civil-party/ms-thouch-phandara.

24 Eng and Kazanjian, 2002: 3.

25 Robben in Robben and Suárez-Orozco, 2000: 94.

26 Bou Meng, Case File no. 001/18–07–2007-ECCC/TC, 86.

27 Cambodia Tribunal Monitor, May 29, 2013.

28 See Dwyer, 2004.

29 Youk Chhang, "My Sister," *Camnews*, 1998.

30 Douglass and Vogler, 2003: 18.

31 Sontag, 2001: 16.

32 Wiesel, 1995: 107.

33 This is the subtitle of Francois Ponchaud's book.

34 In "Cambodia's Panh Awarded Asian Filmmaker of the Year at Busan," Agence France Press, October 4, 2013.

35 The Khmer word for kapok is *kor*, which is a homonym for "mute."

36 Interview with Nick Olivari, Reuters, September 27, 2012.

37 Stoler, 2008: 210.

38 Gampel, 2000: 50.

39 Eng and Kazanjian, 2002: 125.

40 I am indebted to Michel Antelme for his explanation of the Buddhist context.

41 Marc Nichanian in Eng and Kazanjian, 2002: 145.

42 It is important to note that the full nature of the Jewish Holocaust was not captured in language or notation until long after it was exposed.

43 Feitlowitz, 1998: 19.

44 Wiesel, 1990: 33.

45 Ibid., 27.

46 Young in Douglass and Vogler, 2003: 276.

47 In ibid., 31.

48 Socheata Poeuv, speech at the screening of *New Year Baby*, Oakland Cultural Center, 2008.

49 In Lefreniere, 2000: 78.

50 Green, 1994: 227.

51 Yimsut, n.d.

52 See Kidron, 2012.

53 Panh, 2013.

54 In Hinton and O'Neill, 2009: 114.

55 Maguire, 2005: 52.

56 The prospect of refugee resettlement in the United States in 1975 reportedly was an issue of contention even among Asian Americanists, many of whom felt that those

to be given asylum were politically tainted. Comments by Professor Ling-Chi Wang at "Changing Boundaries and Reshaping Itineraries: An International Conference on Asian American Expressive Culture," Beijing, 2012.

57 Schlund-Vials, 2012: 14.

58 Ibid., 45.

59 Chandler, 1999: 8.

60 Gordon, 2008: 115.

61 See Um, 2012.

62 Herbert Hirsch,1985: 32.

63 The only official textbook to examine the Khmer Rouge era to be compiled and disseminated to the high schools was produced by the Documentation Center of Cambodia in 2007.

64 Colonial Archive, Aix-en-Provence. See also Thompson, 1937: 348; and Chandler, 1996. The word *derachhaan* has been incorrectly translated as "cursed." Literally, it is used to refer to something that is less than human.

65 Dwyer in Hinton and O'Neill, 2009.

66 In Dwyer, 2006: 203.

67 Wiesel, 1995: 96.

68 Wiesel, 1990: 144.

69 In Afkhami, 1994: 188.

70 Pham et al., 2011.

71 In Tenhula, 1991: 157.

72 Wiesel, 1990: 142.

73 Caruth in Hamera, 2002: 65.

74 Panh, 2013.

75 Connerton, 1998: 14.

76 Steven Okazaki, *The Conscience of Nhem En*, documentary (Farallon Films, 2008).

77 Chan and Suon, 2012.

78 Dwyer, 2006: 209.

79 Pin, 1987: xiii.

80 Panh and Bataille, 2012: 4.

81 Connerton, 1998: 15.

82 In Douglass and Vogler, 2003: 18.

83 Levi, 1989: 174.

84 Panh and Bataille, 2012: 3.

85 Assumpta Mugiraneza, "Transmission of Children's Names and Postmemory in Rwanda" (paper presented at Creation and Postmemory Conference, Columbia University, April 2013).

86 Wiesel, 1990: 142.

87 Ibid., 143.

88 In Stewart and May, 2002: 16.

89 Ibid., 20.

90 Ibid.,16.

91 Emily Wight, "Sculptor Plans Genocide Memorial for Historic French Embassy Grounds," *Phnom Penh Post*, February 21, 2014.

92 Séra Ing, *The Cambodian Tragedy Memorial*, 2014, https://www.cambodiantragedymemorial.com.

93 Wiesel, 1995: 16.

94 Ibid.

95 Mardi Seng, "Hope," n.d., www.edwebproject.org.

96 Sémprun in Ferran, 2007: 72.

97 Nam Le, *The Boat* (New York: Knopf, 2008), 24.

98 Loung Ung, interview with Andy Brouwer, Cambodia Tales, January 2007, www.andybrouwer.co.uk.

99 LaCapra, 1998: 10.

100 Van Boemel and Rozée, 1992: 240. See also Alexandria Smith, "Cambodian Witnesses to Horror Cannot See," *New York Times*, September 8, 1989.

101 Trent Walker, "How Sophea Lost Her Sight," *Peace Review* 23, no. 4 (2011): 528.

102 In Joseph P. Kahn, "Cambodian Brings Story of Genocide to Younger Audience," *Boston Globe*, November 8, 2012.

103 U Sam Oeur, at the opening night of the play the *Krasang Tree*.

104 Sophal Leng, "Hear Me Now," n.d., www.edwebproject.org.

105 Marianne Hirsch, 1996: 661.

106 Marianne Hirsch, presentation at the Creation and Postmemory Conference, Columbia University, April 2013.

107 Séra Ing, presentation at the Creation and Postmemory Conference, Columbia University, April 2013.

108 Bourke, 2004: 481.

109 Sophal Leng, "Hear Me Now," n.d., www.edweb.org.

110 Stoler, 2008: 201.

111 Alessandro Portelli in Hesse Biber, "Oral History: A Collaborative (Auto) Biography Interview," http://www.sagepub.com/.

112 Leslie, 2001: 55.

113 In Ashley Cooper, "Responding to Genocide," February 13, 2011, http://dara-duong.blogspot.com/2011/02/.

114 In Elizabeth Becker, "For Cambodia, an Oscar Nod Means Much More Than Box-Office Gold," *Los Angeles Times*, op-ed, February 27, 2014.

115 In Said, 1994: 149.

116 Alexandra Seno, "A River View Reshapes a Sculptor's Work," *Wall Street Journal*, April 23, 2011.

117 "In Cambodia: A Tide of 'Change' Sweeps Some Lives Under," NPR, October 28. 2013.

118 In Laurent Le Gouanvic, "Emmanuelle Nhean: From Phnom Penh to Paris—The Celebration of Happiness through Khmer Art," *Ka-set*, December 29, 2008.

119 In Stewart and May, 2002: 82.

120 In Tenhula, 1991: 168.

121 In Okazaki, *The Conscience of Nhem En.*

122 This is particularly true of the involvement of Cambodian staff in the documentation project of the Documentation Center of Cambodia.

123 Pham et al., 2009.

124 See the 2006 report of the Economic Institute of Cambodia.

125 Pham et al., 2009.

126 Dwyer, 2004.

127 The Berkeley population-based survey found that some 58 percent of the respondents harbored this sentiment.

128 Vann Nath, 1998: 118.

129 In David Scheffer, Cambodia Tribunal Monitor, May 22, 2011.

130 In Sebastian Strangio, "Limited Liability for Khmer Rouge Tribunal," *Asia Times*, May 13, 2011.

131 Um, interview.

132 Levi, 1989: 75.

133 In Lefreniere, 2000: 134.

134 Stammel et al., 2010.

135 Levi in Herbert Hirsch, 1985: 50.

136 In Alexis Burling, interview, Bookreporter.com, August 9, 2012.

137 Witness to History, CD-ROM production.

138 I thank Jodi Kim for pointing out the etymology.

139 Stammel et al., 2010.

140 In Maguire, 2005: 28.

141 Cambodia Tribunal Monitor, May 29, 2013.

142 Ly, 2003: 81.

143 Cambodia Tribunal Monitor, November 23, 2009.

144 In U Sam Oeur, 2002: 194.

145 Ibid., 215.

146 Youk Chhang, public lecture, University of California–Berkeley, April 2010.

CHAPTER 7. HOMELAND, EXILE, AND RETURN

1 Um, personal communication. Unless cited, all quotes are from the author's interviews. For details on the fall of the Republic, see Sak, 1980.

2 Lawyers Committee for Human Rights, *Seeking Shelter: Cambodians in Thailand* (New York: Lawyers Committee for Human Rights, 1987); and Barbara Crossette, "Cambodian Refugee Abuse Reported," *New York Times*, February 19, 1987.

3 Freeman, 1989: 38.

4 In Stanley Harper, *Situation Zero*, documentary (1989).

5 Um, 2009.

6 U.S. Census, 1990; Pacific Rim Data Project, Berkeley.

7 Rumbaut and Ima, 1988.

8 Marshall et al., 2005: 572.

9 According to the 1990 census, approximately 38 percent of Cambodian workers are employed in manufacturing sectors, with machine operator/assembler and precision/craft accounting for 15.6 percent and 23.8 percent, respectively.

10 Um, 2009.

11 Rouse, 1991: 33.

12 In Becker, Beyene, and Ken, 2000: 330.

13 See Josephine Reynell, *Political Pawns: Refugees on the Thai-Kampuchean Border* (Oxford, UK: Refugee Studies Program, 1989).

14 See Kibria, 1995.

15 Bhuchung D. Sonam, "Tibet Writes," December 27, 2007, http://tibetwrites.org.

16 Commission on National Cambodian American Health Initiative, "Health Emergency in the Cambodian Community in the U.S.," report, 2007. For post-genocide trauma, see Van Schaak et al., 2011.

17 J. D. Kinzie, "'The Concentration Camp Syndrome' among Cambodian Refugees," in Ablin and Hood, 1990: 333.

18 L. Handelman and G. Yeo, "Using Explanatory Models to Understand Chronic Symptoms of Cambodian Refugees," *Family Medicine* 28 (1996): 271–76.

19 Report of the Transcultural Psychosocial Organization, Cambodia, 2005.

20 Dr. Sam Keo, interview, *Voice of America*, April 18, 2012.

21 In his autobiography, Ronnie Yimsut talks about domestic violence in the Cambodian refugee community in Seattle.

22 See Yoshioka and Dang, 2000.

23 Ibid.

24 *Pol Pot's Legacy*, documentary, Journeyman Pictures, uploaded online January 14, 2008.

25 Lifton in Herbert Hirsch, 1985: 84.

26 In Gampel, 2000.

27 Greg Mellen, "PTSD from Cambodia's Killing Fields Affects Kids Who Were Never There," *Long Beach Press-Telegram*, April 22, 2012.

28 See http://www.pbs.org/independentlens/newyearbaby/family.html.

29 Gobodo-Madikizela, 2003: 86.

30 Maru Elahi, "Ajun," in Karim, 2006: 111.

31 Schwab, 2010: 5.

32 Hirsch and Spitzer, 2003: 85.

33 Hirsch in Schwab, 2010: 33.

34 Pete Pin, "Displaced: The Cambodian Diaspora," *Time Lightbox*, February 6, 2012, http://lightbox.time.com/2012/02/06/displaced-the-cambodian-diaspora/. This is also evident from discussions that took place among Cambodian Americans, aged seventeen to twenty-five, who participated in three forums held in California, in the spring and fall of 2011.

35 Fresco in Goertz, 1998: 34.

36 Johannes Klabbers, "The Art of Indirect Witnessing," in Kennedy and Whitlock, 2009: 12.

37 In Marianne Hirsch, 2008: 105.

38 In Schwab, 2010: 15.

39 Hoffman in Goertz, 1998: 484.

40 Cambodia Tribunal Monitor, May 29, 2013.

41 David de Levita in Robben and Suárez-Orozco, 2000a: 150.

42 Hoffman in Goertz, 1998: 484.

43 Ung, 2005: 6.

44 Marianne Hirsch, 2008: 106.

45 Marina Kem, *Bonne Nuit, Papa*, trailer, Berlin 2014.

46 Sheraz Sadiq, "Cambodian Americans Speak: The Rapper, the Dancer and the Storyteller," *Frontline/World*, October 2002.

47 In May in Stewart and May, 2002: 82.

48 Finkelkraut in Goertz, 1998: 33.

49 Persis Karim, "Ode to the Eggplant," in Karim: 137.

50 Pin, "Displaced."

51 Lois P. Jones, 2011.

52 Said applied the concept of counterpoint used in music to refer to the relationship and negotiations between two or more voices, perspectives, histories that are simultaneously independent and interdependent. Said, 1993: 59–60.

53 Said, 1994: 140.

54 Ibid., 145.

55 Barudy, 1988: 141.

56 Kaminsky, 1999: 10.

57 Florence Simfukwe, "I Was Never Homesick at Home," in Afkhami, 1994: 121.

58 Jura Avizienis, "The Early Poetry of Kazys Bradunas: Infant, Mother and National *Jouissance*," *Lithuanian Quarterly Journal of Arts and Sciences* 43, no. 1 (Spring 1997): 70–78.

59 Said, 1984: 49.

60 Afkhami, 1994.

61 Arendt, 1973: 293.

62 Mario Benedetti in Kaminsky, 1999: 38.

63 Said, 1984: 51.

64 Ronnie Yimsut, "Twenty Five Years Later the Haunting Nightmares Continue," n.d., KhmerConnection.com.

65 Said, 1984: 51.

66 Nguyen, 2012: 169.

67 In ibid., 181.

68 Said, 1984: 55.

69 Rieff, 1993: 64.

70 Ibid., 63.

71 Said, in Rushdie, 1992: 180.

72 Said, 1984: 50.

73 Bhabha, 1994.

74 "My Khmerness," anonymous poem, 2004, post on Khmer Voice website (no longer available).

75 "Cambodia," anonymous poem, n.d., post on Khmer Voice website (no longer available)

76 I define the 1.5 cohort as those who migrate after adolescence.

77 Yimsut, "Twenty Five Years Later."

78 Chath pierSath, 1997a.

79 Chath pierSath, "I Am Bifocal of Oneness," *KhmerVoice*, February 18, 1999, www. khmervoice.com.

80 Sadiq, "Cambodian Americans Speak."

81 Wicker and Schoch, 1988: 17.

82 Al-Rasheed, 1994.

83 Rouse, 1991: 15.

84 In Gupta and Ferguson, 1992: 18.

85 Anita Amirrezvani, "Dancers Work to Revive Cambodian Traditions," *San Jose Mercury News*, September 8, 2001.

86 Clifford, 1997: 255.

87 See Nora, 1989.

88 Bhabha, 1994: xiii.

89 In Rushdie, 1992: 12.

90 Ibid.

91 Richmond, 1988: 18.

92 "Back to Help Rebuild Cambodia," *Cambodia Times*, July 1996.

93 The prophecies mentioned the return of peace with the arrival of Preah Bat Thommoeuk. Some in the diaspora have argued that this savior entity is in all Cambodians and that peace and progress can come about only through collective engagement.

94 Neak Ta Khleang Muang is the spirit of a nationalist general who sacrificed himself so that in death he can raise an army of the dead to fight Cambodia's enemies. About the transplantation of the spirit cult to the diaspora, see Yamada, 1998.

95 "Giving Up the Good Life to Return Home," *Cambodia Times*, July 15–21, 1996.

96 *Motherland*, November 15, 1994.

97 Portes, 1996: 74.

98 "Back to Help Rebuild Cambodia," *Cambodia Times*, July 15–21, 1996.

99 Portes, 1996: 74.

100 Buddhist commemorative structures to house relics and ashes of the dead.

101 In Marc Robinson, 1994: 99.

102 Vann Vorn, "Together We Stand," *KhmerVoice*, n.d.

103 See www.soc.culture.cambodia, February 5, 1997.

104 In Stewart and May, 2002: 195.

105 Yimsut, "Twenty Five Years Later."

106 Ibid.

107 Chath pierSath, 1997b.

108 Hall, 1993: 226.

109 Cited in Neubauer and Török, 2009: 400.

110 Vann Vorn, "A Dying Breed," *KhmerVoice*, n.d.

111 Clifford, in Basch, Schiller, and Szanton Blanc, 1994: 32.

112 Kuntz, 1973.

113 Birch and Barry in Shain, 1999: 24.

114 In Schlund-Vials, 2012: 184.

115 Kaminsky, 1999: 120.

116 Shevchenko in Marc Robinson, 1994.

117 Chath pierSath, "In the Womb of Life," *KhmerVoice*, October 20, 1999.

118 Lê, 2004: 79.

119 Yimsut, "Twenty Five Years Later."

120 Letsinger, 2004.

121 Robben and Suárez-Orozco, 2000: 96.

122 Rushdie, 1992: 9.

123 Ly, 2012: 283.

EPILOGUE

1 Special thanks to Michel Antelme for confirming this translation.

2 "Cambodia's Khmer Rouge Trial," PBS, May 14, 2010.

3 See http://www.legacy-project.org.

4 Chandler, 1999: 170 n42. See also his KRT testimony.

5 Anne Anlin Cheng, *The Melancholy of Race: Psychoanalysis, Assimilation, and Hidden Grief* (New York: Oxford University Press, 2001), 3.

6 Jelin and Godoy-Anativia, 2003: 19.

7 See http://www.legacy-project.org.

8 In Dwyer and Degung, 2006: 190.

9 See http://www.anvaya.info.

BIBLIOGRAPHY

ARCHIVES

Centre des archives nationales d'outre mer, Aix-en-Provence, France.

Declassified Documents Reference System, Gale Digital Collections, gdc.gale.com/ . . .
/declassified-documents-reference-system.

Documentation Center of Cambodia, online resources.

Indochina Archive, University of California, Berkeley.

National Archives, Washington, DC.

National Security Archive, George Washington University, Washington, DC.

PUBLISHED WORKS

Ablin, David, and Marlowe Hood, eds. *The Cambodian Agony*. Armonk, NY: M. E.
Sharpe, 1990.

Adelman, Jonathan R. *Terror and Communist Politics: The Role of the Secret Police in
Communist States*. London: Westview, 1984.

Afkhami, Mahnaz. *Women in Exile*. Charlottesville: University of Virginia Press, 1994.

Agamben, Giorgio. *Homo Sacer: Sovereign Power and Bare Life*. Palo Alto: Stanford
University Press, 1998.

Alphen, Ernst van. "Second-Generation Testimony, Transmission of Trauma, and
Postmemory." *Poetics Today* 27, no. 2 (2008): 473–88.

Al-Rasheed, Madawi. "The Myth of Return: Iraqi Arab and Assyrian Refugees in London." *Journal of Refugee Studies* 7, nos. 2–3 (1994): 200–219.

Anderson, Benedict. *Imagined Communities: Reflections on the Origin and Spread of
Nationalism*. Rev. ed. London: Verso, 1991.

Arad, Michael. "Reflecting Absence." *Places Journal* 21, no. 1 (2009): 42–51.

Arendt, Hannah. *The Life of the Mind*. New York: Harcourt, 1978.

———. *On Violence*. New York: Harcourt Brace Jovanovich, 1969.

———. *On Revolution*. New York: Viking, 1963.

———. *The Origins of Totalitarianism*. Cleveland: Meridian, 1958.

Armstrong, John. *Sihanouk Speaks*. New York: Walker, 1964.

Aymonier, Étienne. *Le Cambodge: Le royaume actuel*. Paris: Ernest Leroux, 1900.

Ball, Karyn. "Ex/propriating Survivor Experience, or Auschwitz 'after' Lyotard." In *Witness and Memory: The Discourse of Trauma*, edited by Ana Douglass and Thomas
Vogler. New York: Routledge, 2003.

Barbu, Zevedei. *Democracy and Dictatorship: Their Psychology and Patterns of Life*.
New York: Routledge, 2003.

Barron, John, and Anthony Paul. *Murder of a Gentle Land*. New York: Reader's Digest Press, 1977.

Barudy, Jorge. "The Therapeutic Value of Solidarity and Hope." In *Refugees—The Trauma of Exile: The Humanitarian Role of Red Cross and Red Crescent*, ed. D. Miserez. Dordrecht: Martinus Nijhoff, 1988.

Basch, Linda, Nina Glick Schiller, and Christina Szanton Blanc. *Nations Unbound: Transnational Projects, Postcolonial Predicaments, and Deterritorialized Nation-States*. Florence: Psychology Press, 1994.

Becker, Elizabeth. "Kissinger Tapes Describe Crises, War and Stark Photos of Abuse." *New York Times*, May 27, 2004.

———. *When the War Was Over*. New York: Touchstone, 1986.

Becker, Gay, Yewoubdar Beyene, and Pauline Ken. "Memory, Trauma, and Embodied Distress: The Management of Disruption in the Stories of Cambodians in Exile." *Ethos* 28, no. 3 (September 2000): 320–45.

Bertelsmann Stiftung. "BTI 2008: Cambodia Country Report." Gütersloh: Bertelsmann Stiftung, 2007.

Bhabha, Homi. *Location of Culture*. New York: Routledge, 1994.

Bhattacharyya, Jnanabrata. "An Examination of Leadership Entry in Bengal Peasant Revolts, 1937–1947." *Journal of Asian Studies* 37, no. 4 (August 1978): 611–35.

Bienen, Henry. *Violence and Social Change*. Chicago: University of Chicago Press, 1968.

Bit, Seanglim. *The Warrior Heritage: A Psychological Perspective of Cambodian Trauma*. El Cerrito, CA: Seanglim Bit, 1991.

Bizot, Francois. *The Gate*. Translated by Euan Cameron. New York: Knopf, 2003.

Black, Cyril, and Thomas Thornton, eds. *Communism and Revolution: The Strategic Use of Political Violence*. Princeton: Princeton University Press, 1964.

Bourke, Joanne. "'Remembering' War." In "Collective Memory," special issue, *Journal of Contemporary History* 39, no. 4 (October 2004): 473–85.

Brinton, Crane. *The Anatomy of Revolution*. New York: Vintage, 1965.

Brown, MacAlister, and Joseph Zasloff. *Apprentice Revolutionaries: The Communist Movement in Laos, 1930–1985*. Palo Alter: Hoover, 1986.

Bruno, Ellen, dir. *Samsara: Death and Rebirth in Cambodia*. Documentary film. EllenFilms, 1990.

Brzezinski, Zbigniew. *The Permanent Purge*. Cambridge: Harvard University Press, 1956.

Bun, Chan Mol. *Charit Khmer*. Phnom Penh, 1973.

———. *Kok Niyobay*. Phnom Penh, 1971.

Caldwell, Malcolm. *Kampuchea: Rationale for a Rural Policy*. Hyderabad: Janata Prachuranalu, 1979.

Carney, Timothy. *Communist Party Power in Kampuchea (Cambodia): Documents and Discussion*. Data paper 106. Ithaca: Cornell University, Southeast Asia Program, 1977.

Chakotin, Serge. *The Rape of the Masses*. London: Routledge and Kegan Paul, 1940.

Chan, Lida, and Guillaume Suon, dirs. *Red Wedding*. Bophana Production and Tipasa Production, 2012.

Chan, Sucheng. *Survivors: Cambodian Refugees in the United States*. Urbana: University of Illinois Press, 2004.

———, ed. *Not Just Victims: Conversations with Cambodian Community Leaders in the United States*. Interviews conducted by Audrey U Kim. Urbana: University of Illinois Press, 2003.

Chanda, Nayan. *Brother Enemy*. New York: Harcourt, Brace and Jovanovich, 1986.

Chandler, David. *A History of Cambodia*. 4th ed. Boulder: Westview, 2000.

———. *Voices from S-21: Terror and History in Pol Pot's Secret Prison*. Berkeley: University of California Press, 1999.

———. *Facing the Cambodian Past*. Sydney: Allen and Unwin, 1996.

———. *Tragedy of Cambodian History: Politics, War, and Revolution since 1945*. New Haven: Yale University Press, 1993.

———. *Brother Number One: A Political Biography of Pol Pot*. Boulder: Westview, 1992.

———. "Seeing Red: Perceptions of Cambodian History in Democratic Kampuchea." In *Revolution and Its Aftermath in Kampuchea: Eight Essays*, edited by David P. Chandler and Ben Kiernan, 34–56. New Haven: Yale University Southeast Asia Studies, 1983.

———. "Songs at the Edge of the Forest." In *Moral Order and the Question of Change: Essays on Southeast Asian Thought*, edited by D. K. Wyatt and A. Woodside, 53–77. Monograph Series, no. 24. New Haven: Yale University Southeast Asian Studies, 1982.

———. *The Land and People of Cambodia*. New York: Lippincott, 1972.

Chandler, David, and Ben Kiernan, eds. *Revolution and Its Aftermath in Kampuchea: Eight Essays*. New Haven: Yale University Southeast Asia Studies, 1983.

Chandler, David, Ben Kiernan, and Chanthou Boua, eds. *Pol Pot Plans the Future*. New Haven: Yale University Southeast Asia Studies, 1988.

Chath pierSath. "The Mekong River." *Bridge Review: Merrimack Valley Culture*, 1997a. www.ecommunity.uml.edu/bridge.

———. "The Way I Want to Remember My Cambodia." *Bridge Review: Merrimack Valley Culture*, 1997b. www.ecommunity.uml.edu/bridge.

Chatterjee, Partha. *The Nation and Its Fragments: Colonial and Post Colonial Histories*. Princeton: Princeton University Press, 1993.

Chomsky, Noam, and Edward S. Herman. *After the Cataclysm: Postwar Indochina and the Reconstruction of Imperial Ideology*. Cambridge, MA: South End, 1979.

Chorley, Katharine. *Armies and the Art of Revolution*. Boston: Beacon, 1973.

Clayton, Thomas. "Restriction or Resistance? French Colonial Educational Development in Cambodia." *Education Policy Analysis Archives* 3, no. 19 (December 1995): 1–14.

Clifford, James. *Routes: Travels and Translation in the Late Twentieth Century*. Cambridge: Harvard University Press, 1997.

Cohen, Leonard, and Jane Shapiro, eds. *Communist Systems in Comparative Perspective*. New York: Anchor, 1974.

Cohn, Norman. *The Pursuit of the Millennium: Revolutionary Millenarians and Mystical Anarchists of the Middle Ages*. Oxford: Oxford University Press, 1961.

Colm, Sara, and Sorya Sim. "Anatomy of an Interrogation: The Torture of Comrade Ya at S-21." *Phnom Penh Post*, November 2, 2007.

Connerton, Paul. *How Societies Remember*. Cambridge: Cambridge University Press, 1998.

Conquest, Robert. *The Great Terror: A Reassessment*. Oxford: Oxford University Press, 1990.

———. *Harvest of Sorrow: Soviet Collectivization and the Terror-Famine*. New York: Oxford University Press, 1986.

Corfield, Justin. *Khmers Stand Up: A History of the Cambodian Government, 1970–1975*. Clayton: Monash Asia Institute, 1994.

D'Avanzo, Carolyn, Barbara Frye, and Robin Froman. "Culture, Stress, and Substance Use in Cambodian Refugee Women." *Journal of Studies on Alcohol* 55, no. 4 (1994): 420–26.

De Alwis, Malathi. "'Disappearance' and 'Displacement' in Sri Lanka." *Journal of Refugee Studies* 22, no. 3 (2009): 378–91.

Debré, Francois. *Cambodge: La revolution de la foret*. Paris: Flammarion, 1976.

De Certeau, Michel. *The Practice of Everyday Life*. Translated by Steven Rendall. Berkeley: University of California Press, 1984.

Degung, Santikarma. "Exploring the Meaning of Reconciliation." *Jakarta Post*, June 22, 2000.

De Levita, David. "Child Psychotherapy as an Instrument in Cultural Research: Treating War-Traumatized Children in the Former Yugoslavia." In *Cultures under Siege: Collective Violence and Trauma*, edited by Antonius C. G. M. Robben and Marcelo M. Suárez-Orozco. Cambridge: Cambridge University Press, 2000.

Delvert, Jean. *Le Cambodge*. Paris: Presses Universitaires de France, 1983.

———. *Le paysan cambodgien*. Paris: Mouton, 1961.

Depaul, Kim, ed. *Children of Cambodia's Killing Fields: Memoirs by Survivors*. Compiled by Dith Pran. New Haven: Yale University Press, 1997.

Derrida, Jacques. *Spectres of Marx: The State of the Debt, the Work of Mourning, and the New International*. Translated by Peggy Kamuf. New York: Routledge, 1994.

Des Pres, Terrence. *The Survivor*. New York: Pocket Books, 1977.

Djaout, Tahar. *The Last Summer of Reason*. St. Paul: Ruminator, 2001.

Doan, Van Toai. *A Vietcong Memoir*. San Diego: Harcourt Brace Jovanovich, 1985.

Douglass, Ana, and Thomas Vogler, eds. *Witness and Memory: The Discourse of Trauma*. New York: Routledge, 2003.

Dudman, Richard. *Forty Days with the Enemy*. New York: Liveright, 1971.

Dwyer, Leslie. "The Intimacy of Terror: Gender and the Violence of 1965–1966 in Bali." *Intersections: Gender, History and Culture in the Asia Contexts* 10 (August 2004): 1–18.

Dwyer, Leslie, and Degung Santikarma. "Speaking from the Shadows: Memory and Mass Violence in Bali." In *After Mass Crime: Rebuilding States and Communities*, edited by Beatrice Pouligny. Tokyo: United Nations University Press, 2006.

Ea, Meng-Try. *The Chain of Terror: The Khmer Rouge Southwest Zone Security System.* Phnom Penh: Documentation Center of Cambodia, 2005.

Ebihara, May. "Khmer." In *Refugees in the United States: A Reference Handbook*, edited by David Haines, 127–47. Westport: Greenwood, 1985.

Ebihara, May, and Judy Ledgerwood. "Aftermaths of Genocide: Cambodian Villagers." In *Annihilating Difference: The Anthropology of Genocide*, edited by Alexander Hinton. Berkeley: University of California Press, 2002.

Ebihara, May M., Carol Mortland, and Judy Ledgerwood, eds. *Cambodian Culture since 1975: Homeland and Exile.* Ithaca: Cornell University Press, 1994.

Edwards, Penny. "Between a Song and a Prei." In *At the Edge of the Forest: Essays on Cambodia, History and Narrative in Honor of David Chandler*, edited by Anne R. Hansen and Judy Ledgerwood. Ithaca: Cornell Southeast Asia Program, 2008.

———. *Cambodge: The Cultivation of a Nation, 1860–1945.* Honolulu: University of Hawaii Press, 2007.

———. "Making a Religion of the Nation and Its Language." In *History, Buddhism, and New Religious Movements in Cambodia*, edited by John Marston and Elizabeth Guthrie. Honolulu: University of Hawaii Press, 2004.

Eng, David, and David Kazanjian, eds. *Loss: The Politics of Mourning.* Berkeley: University of California Press, 2002.

Engelbert, Thomas, and Christopher Goscha. *Falling Out of Touch: A Study on Vietnamese Communist Policy towards an Emerging Cambodian Communist Movement, 1930–1975.* Clayton: Monash Asia Institute, Monash University, 1995.

Espiritu, Yên Lê. "Toward a Critical Refugee Study: The Vietnamese Refugee Subject in U.S. Scholarship." *Journal of Vietnamese Studies* 1, nos. 1–2 (2006): 410–33.

———. "Thirty Years afterWARd: The Endings That Are Not Over." *Amerasia Journal* 31, no. 2 (2005): xiii-xxiii.

Etcheson, Craig. "3.3 Million Dead and Still Counting." *Phnom Penh Post*, April 14, 2000.

———. *"The Number": Quantifying Crimes against Humanity in Cambodia.* Phnom Penh: Documentation Center of Cambodia, 1999.

Eyerman, Ron. *Cultural Trauma: Slavery and the Formation of African American Identity.* Cambridge: Cambridge University Press, 2002.

Fanon, Frantz. *The Wretched of the Earth.* New York: Grove, 1966.

Far Eastern Economic Review (FEER), Yearbook, 1975, 1978, 1997.

Feitlowitz, Margaret. *A Lexicon of Terror: Argentina and the Legacies of Torture.* Oxford: Oxford University Press, 1998.

Feldman, Allen. *Formations of Violence: The Narrative of the Body and Political Terror in Northern Ireland.* Chicago, University of Chicago Press, 1991.

Ferran, Ofelia. *Working through Memory: Writing and Remembrance in Contemporary Spanish Narrative.* Lewisburg: Bucknell University Press, 2007.

Forest, Alain. *Le Cambodge et la colonisation francaise: Histoire d'une colonisation sans heurts (1897–1920).* Paris: L'Harmattan, 1980.

Foucault, Michel. *Discipline and Punish: The Birth of the Prison.* New York: Pantheon, 1977.

Freeman, James. *Hearts of Sorrow: Vietnamese-American Lives*. Palo Alto: Stanford University Press, 1989.

Frieson, Kate. "Sentimental Education: Les Sages Femmes and Colonial Cambodia." *Journal of Colonialism and Colonial History* 1, no. 1 (2000): 1–27.

Gampel, Yolanda. "Reflections on the Prevalence of the Uncanny in Social Violence." In *Cultures under Siege: Collective Violence and Trauma*, edited by Antonius C. G. M. Robben and Marcelo M. Suárez-Orozco. Cambridge: Cambridge University Press, 2000.

Gellately, Robert, and Ben Kiernan, eds. *The Specter of Genocide: Mass Murder in Historical Perspective*. Cambridge: Cambridge University Press, 2003.

Gellner, Ernest. *Nations and Nationalism*. Ithaca: Cornell University Press, 1983.

Gettleman, Marvin, Susan Gettleman, and Carol Kaplan, eds. *Conflict in Indochina: A Reader on the Widening War in Laos and Cambodia*. New York: Random House, 1970.

Girling, J. L. S. "Cambodia and the Sihanouk Myths." Occasional Paper 7, Institute of Southeast Asian Studies, Singapore, 1971.

Gobodo-Madikizela, Pumla. *A Human Being Died That Night: A South African Story of Forgiveness*. Boston: Houghton Mifflin, 2003.

Goertz, Karen. "Transgenerational Representation of the Holocaust: From Memory to Post Memory." *World Literature Today* 72, no. 1 (Winter 1998): 33–38.

Goldhagen, Erich. "The Glorious Future: Realities and Chimeras." In *Russia under Khrushchev: An Anthology from Problems of Communism*, ed. Abraham Brumberg. New York: Praeger, 1963.

Gordon, Avery. *Ghostly Matters*. Minneapolis: University of Minnesota Press, 2008.

Gordon, Bernard K., and Kathryn Young. "The Khmer Republic: That Was the Cambodia That Was." *Asian Survey* 11, no. 1 (January 1971): 26–40.

Goscha, Christopher. "Widening the Colonial Encounter: Asian Connections inside French Indochina during the Interwar Period." *Modern Asian Studies* 43, no. 5 (2008): 1189–228.

Green, Linda. "Fear as a Way of Life." *Cultural Anthropology* 9, no. 2 (1994): 227–56.

Gupta, Akhil, and James Ferguson. "Beyond 'Culture': Space, Identity, and the Politics of Difference." *Cultural Anthropology* 7, no. 1 (1992): 6–23.

Gurr, Ted. "Why Men Rebel Redux: How Valid Are Its Arguments 40 Years On?" November 17, 2011. http://www.e-ir.info/2011/11/17/why-men-rebel-redux-how-valid-are-its-arguments-40-years-on/.

———. *Why Men Rebel*. Princeton: Princeton University Press, 1971.

Haing Ngor. *A Cambodian Odyssey*. New York: Warner Books, 1987.

Halbwachs, Maurice. *On Collective Memory*. Translated by Lewis A. Coser. Chicago: University of Chicago Press, 1992.

Hall, Stuart. "Cultural Identity and Diaspora." In *Colonial Discourse and Post-colonial Theory: A Reader*, edited by Patrick Williams and Laura Chrisman. London: Harvester Wheatsheaf, 1993.

Hamera, Judith. "Answerability of Memory: 'Saving' Khmer Classical Dance." *TDR* 46, no. 4 (Winter 2002): 65–85.

Hansen, Anne. "Khmer Identity and Theravada Buddhism." In *History, Buddhism, and New Religious Movements in Cambodia*, edited by John Marston and Elizabeth Guthrie. Honolulu: University of Hawaii Press, 2004.

Hansen, Anne R., and Judy Ledgerwood, eds. *At the Edge of the Forest: Essays on Cambodia, History and Narrative in Honor of David Chandler*. Ithaca: Cornell Southeast Asia Program, 2008.

Harris, Ian. *Cambodian Buddhism*. Honolulu: University of Hawaii Press, 2008.

Hawk, David. "Tuol Sleng Extermination Center (Cambodia)." *Index on Censorship* 15, no. 1 (January 1986): 25–31.

Heder, Stephen. *Cambodian Communism and Vietnamese Model: Imitation and Independence, 1930–1975*. Bangkok: White Lotus, 2003.

———. *Pol Pot and Khieu Samphan*. Clayton: Centre of Southeast Asian Studies, Monash University, 1991a.

———. "Reflections on Cambodian Political History: Backgrounder to Recent Developments." Working paper 239, Strategic and Defense Studies Centre, Australian National University, Canberra, 1991b.

———. "From Pol Pot to Pen Savan to the Village." *International Conference on Indochina and Problems of Security in Southeast Asia*. Conference Publications. Bangkok: Chulalongkorn University, 1980.

———. "Kampuchea's Armed Struggle: The Origin of an Independent Revolution." *Bulletin of Concerned Asian Scholars* 11, no. 1 (1979): 2–23.

Heder, Stephen, and Brian Tittemore. *Seven Candidates for Prosecution: Accountability for the Crimes of the Khmer Rouge*. Phnom Penh: Documentation Center of Cambodia, 2004.

Heeger, G. A. *The Politics of Underdevelopment*. New York: St. Martin's, 1974.

Hefner, Nancy Smith. *Khmer American: Identity and Moral Education in a Diasporic Community*. Berkeley: University of California Press, 1999.

Hein, Jeremy. *Ethnic Origins: The Adaptation of Cambodian and Hmong Refugees in Four American Cities*. New York: American Sociological Association Rose Monographs, 2006.

———. *From Vietnam, Laos and Cambodia: A Refugee Experience in the United States*. Woodbridge CT: Twayne, 1995.

Hinton, Alexander L. *Why Did They Kill? Cambodia in the Shadow of Genocide*. Berkeley: University of California Press, 2005.

———. "A Head for an Eye: Revenge in the Cambodian Genocide." *American Ethnologist* 25, no. 3 (1998): 352–77.

Hinton, Alexander L., and Kevin Lewis O'Neill, eds. *Genocide: Truth, Memory, and Representation*. Durham: Duke University Press, 2009.

Hirsch, Herbert. *Genocide and the Politics of Memory*. Chapel Hill: University of North Carolina Press, 1985.

Hirsch, Herbert, and David Perry, eds. *Violence as Politics*. New York: Harper and Row, 1969.

Hirsch, Marianne. "The Generation of Postmemory." *Poetics Today* 29, no. 1 (2008): 103–28.

——. "Past Lives: Postmemories in Exile." *Poetics Today* 17, no. 4 (1996): 659–86.

Hirsch, Marianne, and Leo Spitzer. "'We Would Never Have Come without You': Generations of Nostalgia." In *Contested Pasts: The Politics of Memory*, edited by Katharine Hodgkin and Susannah Radstone. London: Routledge, 2003.

Hoffer, Eric. *The True Believer*. New York: Harper and Row, 1951.

Hron, Madelaine. "The Czech Émigré Experience of Return after 1989." *Slavonic and East European Review* 85, no. 1 (2007): 47–78.

Huntington, Samuel. *Political Order in Changing Societies*. New Haven: Yale University Press, 1968.

Ieng Sary's Regime: A Diary of the Khmer Rouge Foreign Ministry, 1976–79. Translated by Phat Kosal and Ben Kiernan with Sorya Sim. New Haven: Yale Center for International and Area Studies, 1998.

Ith Sarin. *Sranos Proloeung Khmer* [Regrets for the Khmer soul]. Phnom Penh: n.p., 1973.

Jackson, Karl, ed. *Cambodia, 1975–78: Rendezvous with Death*. Princeton: Princeton University Press, 1989.

——. "Post-Colonial Rebellion and Counter-Insurgency in Southeast Asia." In *Governments and Rebellion in Southeast Asia*. Singapore: Institute of Southeast Asian Studies, 1985.

Jeldres, Julio. *Shadow over Angkor: Memoirs of His Majesty King Norodom Sihanouk of Cambodia*. Phnom Penh: Monument Books, 2005.

Jelin, Elizabeth. *State Repression and the Labors of Memory*. Translated by Marcial Godoy-Anativia. Minneapolis: University of Minnesota Press, 2003.

Johnson, Chalmers. *Revolutionary Change*. Palo Alto: Stanford University Press, 1982.

——. *Change in Communist Systems*. Palo Alto: Stanford University Press, 1970.

——. *Peasant Nationalism and Communist Power: The Emergence of Revolutionary China, 1937–45*. Palo Alto: Stanford University Press, 1962.

Jones, Adam. "Gendercide and Genocide." *Journal of Genocide Research* 2, no. 2 (2000): 185–211.

Jones, Lois P. "Exile." InterBoard Poetry Competition, February 2011.

Kalab, Milada. "Study of a Cambodian Village." *Geographical Journal* 134, no. 4 (1968): 521–37.

Kaminsky, Amy. *After Exile: Writing the Latin American Diaspora*. Minneapolis: University of Minnesota Press, 1999.

Karim, Persis. *Let Me Tell You Where I Have Been*. Fayetteville: University of Arkansas Press, 2006.

Kautsky, John, ed. *Political Change in Underdeveloped Countries*. New York: John Wiley, 1962.

Kelly, G. P. "Colonial Schools in Vietnam: Policy and Practice." In *Education and Colonialism*, edited by Philip G. Altbach and Gail P. Kelly, 96–121. New York: Longman, 1978.

Kennedy, Rosanne, and Gillian Witlock, eds. "Testimony, Trauma and Social Suffering: New Framings/Directions." Conference proceedings, Australian National University, Canberra, 2009.

Khieu, Samphan. *Cambodia's Recent History and the Reasons behind the Decisions I Made*. Phnom Penh: Ponleu Khmer Publishing, 2004.

Khin, Sok. *L'annexion du Cambodge par les Vietnamiens au XIX siècle d'après les deux poèmes du Vénérable Batum Baramey Pich*. Paris: Editions You-Feng, 2002.

Kibria, Nazli. *Family Tightrope*. Princeton: Princeton University Press, 1995.

Kidron, Carol. "Alterity and the Particular Limits of Universalism: Comparing Jewish-Israeli Holocaust and Canadian-Cambodian Genocide Legacies." *Current Anthropology* 53, no. 6 (December 2012): 723–54.

Kiernan, Ben. *The Pol Pot Regime: Race, Power, and Genocide in Cambodia under the Khmer Rouge, 1975–1979*. New Haven: Yale University Press, 2008.

———. "Barbaric Crimes of a Mystical Communism Seen through Its Own Eyes." *Times Higher Education Supplement*, February 25, 2005.

———. "The Demography of Genocide in Southeast Asia: The Death Tolls in Cambodia, 1975–79, and East Timor, 1975–80." *Critical Asian Studies* 35, no. 4 (2003): 585–97.

———. *Cambodia: The Eastern Zone Massacres; A Report on Social Conditions and Human Rights Violation in the Eastern Zone of Democratic Kampuchea under the Rule of Pol Pot*. New York: Center for the Studies of Human Rights at Columbia University, 1986.

———. *How Pol Pot Came to Power*. London: Verso, 1985.

———. "Wild Chickens, Farm Chickens and Cormorants: Kampuchea's Eastern Zone under Pol Pot." In *Revolution and Its Aftermath in Kampuchea: Eight Essays*, edited by David Chandler and Ben Kiernan, 153–54. New Haven: Yale University Southeast Asia Studies, 1983.

———. *The Samlaut Rebellion and Its Aftermath, 1967–1970: The Origins of Cambodia's Liberation Movement*. Working Papers. Clayton: Centre of Southeast Asian Studies, Monash University, 1975.

Kiernan, Ben, and Chanthou Boua, eds. *Peasants and Politics in Kampuchea, 1942–1981*. London: Zed Press, 1982.

King, Elisabeth. "Memory Controversies in Post-Genocide Rwanda: Implications for Peacebuilding." *Genocide Studies and Prevention* 5, no. 3 (2010): 293–309.

Kirk, Donald. "Cambodia 1973: Year of the 'Bomb Halt.'" *Asian Survey* 14, no. 1 (January 1974): 89–100.

Kissi, Edward. *Revolution and Genocide in Ethiopia and Cambodia*. Lanham, MD: Lexington Books, 2006.

Kissinger, Henry. *The White House Years*. New York: Simon and Schuster, 1979.

Kumar, Amitava. *Passport Photos*. Berkeley: University of California Press, 2000.

Kuntz, E. F. "The Refugee in Flight: Kinetic Models and Forms of Displacement." *International Migration Review* 7, no. 2 (1973): 125–46.

Kuon, Lumphuon. Typescript. Indochina Archive, University of California–Berkeley, 1989.

Kushner, Tony. "Holocaust Testimony, Ethics, and the Problem of Representation." *Poetics Today* 27, no. 2 (2006): 275–95.

Kwon, Heonik. "To Hunt the Black Shaman: Memory of the Great Purge in East Siberia." *Etnofoor* 13, no. 1 (2000): 33–50.

LaCapra, Dominick. *History and Memory after Auschwitz*. Ithaca: Cornell University Press, 1998.

Lê, T. *The Gangster We Are All Looking For*. New York: Anchor, 2004.

Ledgerwood, Judy. "Ritual in 1990 Cambodian Political Theatre: New Songs at the Edge of the Forest," in *At the Edge of the Forest: Essays on Cambodia, History and Narrative in Honor of David Chandler*, edited by Anne R. Hansen and Judy Ledgerwood. Ithaca: Cornell Southeast Asia Program, 2008.

Lee, Hong Yung. *The Politics of the Chinese Cultural Revolution*. Berkeley: University of California Press, 1978.

Lefreniere, Bree. *Music through the Dark*. Honolulu: University of Hawaii Press, 2000.

Lek, Sam Oeun. *A Khmer Nationalist*. Lowell, MA: n.p., 2005.

Leslie, Helen. "Healing the Psychological Wounds of Gender-Related Violence in Latin America: A Model for Gender-Sensitive Work in Post-Conflict Contexts." *Gender and Development* 9, no. 3 (2001): 50–59.

Letsinger, Miranda. "Cambodian Musicians Sing Centuries-Old Tunes to Save a Dying Tradition." *Asian Reporter*, January 13, 2004.

Levene, Mark. "Why Is the Twentieth Century the Century of Genocide?" *Journal of World History* 11, no. 2 (Fall 2000): 305–36.

Levi, Primo. *Survival in Auschwitz*. New York: Touchstone, 1996.

———. *The Re-Awakening*. New York: Touchstone, 1995.

———. *The Drowned and the Saved*. New York: Vintage, 1989.

Lifton, Robert Jay. *The Nazi Doctors: Medical Killing and the Psychology of Genocide*. New York: Basic Books, 1986.

Locard, Henri. *Pol Pot's Little Red Book: The Sayings of Angkar*. Chiang Mai: Silkworm Books, 2004.

Lui, Michael Yiqiang. *Seeing the Khmer Rouge from a Retired Chinese Spy*. Phnom Penh: Documentation Center of Cambodia, 2012.

Ly, Boreth. "Buddhist Walking Meditations." *Positions* 20, no. 1 (2012): 267–85.

———. "Devastated Vision(s): The Khmer Rouge Scopic Regime in Cambodia." *Art Journal* 62, no. 1 (Spring 2003): 66–81.

Maguire, Peter. *Facing Death in Cambodia*. New York: Columbia University Press, 2005.

Maier, Charles S. *The Unmasterable Past: History, Holocaust, and German National Identity*. Cambridge: Harvard University Press, 1997.

Malkki, Liisa. *Purity and Exile: Violence, Memory, and National Cosmology among Hutu Refugees in Tanzania*. Chicago: University of Chicago Press, 1995.

Mannheim, Karl. *Ideology and Utopia*. Boston: Houghton Mifflin Harcourt, 1955.

Manz, Beatriz. *Refugees of a Hidden War: The Aftermath of Counterinsurgency in Guatemala*. Albany: State University of New York Press, 1988.

Marshall, G. N., Terry Schell, Marc Elliott, Megan Berthold, and Chi-Ah Chun. "Mental Health of Cambodian Refugees 2 Decades after Resettlement in the United States." *Journal of the American Medical Association* 294, no. 5 (2005): 571–79.

Marston, John, and Elizabeth Guthrie, eds. *History, Buddhism, and New Religious Movements in Cambodia*. Honolulu: University of Hawaii Press, 2004.

Martin, Marie A. *Cambodia: A Shattered Society*. Translated by Mark McLeod. Berkeley: University of California Press, 1994.

Mbembe, Achille. "Necropolitics." *Public Culture* 15, no. 1 (2003): 11–40.

———. *On the Postcolony*. Berkeley: University of California Press, 2001.

McAlister, John T. Jr., ed. *Southeast Asia: The Politics of National Integration*. New York: Random House, 1973.

McCormick, Patricia. *Never Fall Down*. New York: Balzer and Bray, 2012.

McLellan, Janet. "Cambodian Refugees in Ontario: Religious Identities, Social Cohesion and Transnational Linkages." *Canadian Ethnic Studies* 36, no. 2 (2004): 101–18.

Meisner, Maurice. *Marxism, Maoism, Utopianism*. Madison: University of Wisconsin Press, 1982.

Melson, Robert. *Revolution and Genocide: On the Origins of the Armenian Genocide and the Holocaust*. Chicago: University of Chicago Press, 1992.

———. "A Theoretical Inquiry into the Armenian Massacres of 1894–1896." *Comparative Studies in Society and History* 24, no. 3 (July 1982): 481–509.

Men, Chan Rithy. "The Changing Religious Beliefs and Ritual Practices among Cambodians in Diaspora." *Journal of Refugee Studies* 15, no. 2 (2002): 222–33.

Meyer, Charles. *La vie quotidienne des francais en Indochine, 1860–1910*. Paris: Hachette, 1985.

———. *Derrière le sourire khmer*. Paris: Librairie Plon, 1971.

Migdal, J. S. *Peasants, Politics and Revolution: Pressures toward Political and Social Change in the Third World*. Princeton: Princeton University Press, 1974.

Migozzi, Jacques. *Cambodge: Faits et problemes de population*. Paris: Centre National de la Recherche Scientifique, 1973.

Ministry of Foreign Affairs of Democratic Kampuchea. *Black Paper: Facts and Evidences of the Acts of Aggression and Annexation of Vietnam against Kampuchea*. Department of Press and Information of the Ministry of Foreign Affairs of Democratic Kampuchea. Reprinted by Group of Kampuchean Residents in America (G. K. Ram), 1979.

Mollica, Richard. *Healing Invisible Wounds: Paths to Hope and Recovery in a Violent World*. Nashville: Vanderbilt University Press, 2008.

Muan, Ingrid. "Reflections on Ly Daravuth's Photographic and Sound Exhibit, *The Messengers.*" The Legacies of Absence Project, Reyum, Cambodia, 2000. http://www.genocidewatch.org/images/Cambodia_Mar_06_The_Messengers.pdf.

Mugiraneza, Assumpta. "Transmission of Children's Names and Postmemory in Rwanda." Paper presented at Creation and Postmemory Conference, Columbia University, April 2013.

Muller, Beate. "Trauma, Historiography and Polyphony: Adult Voices in the CJHC's Early Postwar Child Holocaust Testimonies." *History & Memory* 24, no. 2 (2012): 157–95.

Muller, Gregor. *Colonial Cambodia's Bad Frenchmen: The Rise of French Rule and Life of Thomas Caraman, 1840–1887.* New York: Routledge, 2006.

Mydans, Seth. "Cambodian Aesop Tells a Fable of Forgiveness." *New York Times*, June 28, 1997. http://www.nytimes.com/1997/06/28/world/cambodian-aesop-tells-a-fable-of-forgiveness.html.

Needham Susan, and Karen Quintiliani. *Cambodians in Long Beach.* Chicago: Arcadia, 2008.

Neubauer, John, and Borbála Zsuzsanna Török, eds. *Exile and Return of Writers from East-Central Europe: A Compendium.* Berlin: Walter de Gruyter, 2009.

Neumann, Sigmund. *Permanent Revolution.* New York: Praeger, 1965.

Nguyen, Mimi. *The Gift of Freedom: War, Debt and Other Refugee Passages.* Durham: Duke University Press, 2012.

Nguyen-Vo, T. H. *Khmer-Vietnamese Relations and the Third Indochina Conflict.* Jefferson, NC: McFarland, 1992.

Nixon, Richard. "Address to the Nation on the Situation in Southeast Asia." April 30, 1970. http://www.mekong.net/cambodia/nixon430.htm.

Nora, Pierre. "Between Memory and History: Les lieux de mémoire." Translated by Marc Roudebush. *Representations* 26 (1989): 7–24.

Nordstrom, Carolyn. "Terror Warfare and the Medicine of Peace." *Medical Anthropology Quarterly* 12, no. 1 (1998): 1–19.

Norodom Sihanouk. *Prisonnier des Khmer Rouges.* Paris: Hachette, 1986.

———. *Souvenirs doux et amers.* Paris: Hachette, 1981.

———. *Chroniques de guerre . . . et d'espoir.* Hachette, 1979.

———. *My War with the CIA: The Memories of Prince Norodom Sihanouk.* New York: Pantheon, 1973.

Nuon, Siphy. *Understanding How to Live with the Communists through the Events in Cambodia.* Cleveland: Variety Printing and Publishing, 1988.

Nuselovici, Alexis. "Exiliance: Condition et conscience." February 7, 2013. Archives Ouvertes HAL-SHS.

Ong, Aihwa. *Buddha Is Hiding: Refugees, Citizenship, the New America.* Berkeley: University of California Press, 2003.

———. *Flexible Citizenship: The Cultural Logics of Transnationality.* Durham: Duke University Press, 1999.

Ong, Thong Hoeung. *J'ai cru aux Khmers Rouge.* Paris: Buchet-Chastel, 2003.

Osborne, Milton. *Sihanouk: Prince of Light, Prince of Darkness*. Chiang Mai: Silkworm Books, 1994.

———. *Southeast Asia: An Introductory Handbook*. London: Allen and Unwin, 1979a.

———. *Before Kampuchea*. London: Allen and Unwin, 1979b.

———. *Politics and Power in Cambodia: The Sihanouk Years*. London: Longman, 1973.

———. *Region of Revolt: Focus on Southeast Asia*. Adelaide: Pergamon, 1970.

———. *The French Presence of Cochinchina and Cambodia: Rules and Response (1859–1905)*. Ithaca: Cornell University Press, 1969.

Panh, Rithy. *The Missing Picture*. Documentary film. CDP and Bophana Productions, 2013.

Panh, Rithy, and Christophe Bataille. *The Elimination*. Translated by John Cullen. New York: Other Press, 2012.

Pham Phuong, Patrick Vincik, Mychelle Balthazard, and Hean Sokhom. "After the First Trial: A Population-Based Survey on Knowledge and Perception of Justice and the Extraordinary Chambers in the Courts of Cambodia." Berkeley Human Rights Center, Berkeley, CA, 2011.

Pham Phuong, Patrick Vincik, Mychelle Balthazard, Hean Sokhom, and Eric Stover. "So We Will Never Forget: A Population-Based Survey on Attitudes about Social Reconstruction and the Extraordinary Chambers in the Courts of Cambodia." Berkeley Human Rights Center, Berkeley, CA, 2009.

Phat, Rachana. *The Khmer Rouge Rice Fields: The Story of Rape Survivor Tang Kim*. Phnom Penh: Documentation Center of Cambodia, 2005.

Picq, Laurence. *Beyond the Horizons: Five Years under the Khmer Rouge*. New York: St. Martin's, 1989.

Pielert, Beth. *Out of the Poison Tree*. Good Filmworks, 2007.

Pin Yathay. *Stay Alive, My Son*. New York: Simon and Schuster, 1987.

Pol Pot. "Speech Given on the 18th Anniversary of the Communist Party of Kampuchea, 1978." Red Flag Publications, Quebec, 1979.

———. "Speech Given on the 17th Anniversary of the Communist Party of Kampuchea, 1977." Red Flag Publications, Quebec, 1978.

———. "Speech Given on the 17th Anniversary of the Communist Party of Kampuchea, 1977." Red Flag Publications, Quebec, 1977.

Pomonti, Jean-Claude, and Serge Thion. *Des courtisans aux partisans: Essai sur la crise cambodgienne*. Paris: Gallimard, 1971.

Ponchaud, Francois. *Cambodia: Year Zero*. New York: Holt, Rinehart and Winston, 1978.

Poole, Peter. *Expansion of the Vietnam War into Cambodia*. Ann Arbor: University of Michigan Press, 1978.

Porée, Guy, and Porée-Maspero, Eveline. *Moeurs et coutumes des Khmers*. Paris: Payot, 1938.

Porée-Maspero, Eveline. *Etude sur les rites agraires des cambodgiens*. Paris: Mouton, 1962.

Portes, Alejandro. "Transnational Communities: Their Emergence and Significance in the Contemporary World-System." In *Latin America in the World-Economy*, edited by Roberto Patricio Korzeniewicz and William C. Smith. Westport: Greenwood, 1996.

Pouligny, Beatrice, ed. *After Mass Crime: Rebuilding States and Communities*. Tokyo: United Nations University Press, 2006.

Quinn, Frederick. *The French Overseas Empire*. Westport: Praeger, 2000.

Quinn, Kenneth M. "The Origins and Development of Radical Cambodian Communism." PhD diss., University of Maryland, 1982.

Richmond, A. "Sociological Theories of International Migration: The Case of Refugees." *Current Sociology* 36, no. 2 (1988): 7–25.

Rieff, David. *The Exile: Cuba in the Heart of Miami*. New York: Simon and Schuster, 1993.

Robben, Antonius C. G. M. "How Traumatized Societies Remember: The Aftermath of Argentina's Dirty War." *Cultural Critique*, no. 59 (2005): 120–64.

———. "The Assault on Basic Trust: Disappearance, Protest and Reburial in Argentina." In *Cultures under Siege: Collective Violence and Trauma*, edited by Antonius C. G. M. Robben and Marcelo M. Suárez-Orozco. Cambridge: Cambridge University Press, 2000.

Robben, Antonius C. G. M., and Marcelo M. Suárez-Orozco, eds. *Cultures under Siege: Collective Violence and Trauma*. Cambridge: Cambridge University Press, 2000a.

———. "The Management of Collective Trauma." In *Cultures under Siege: Collective Violence and Trauma*, edited by Antonius C. G. M. Robben and Marcelo M. Suárez-Orozco. Cambridge: Cambridge University Press, 2000b.

Robinson, Court. *Terms of Refuge: The Indochinese Exodus and the International Response*. New York: Zed, 1998.

Robinson, Marc, ed. *Altogether Elsewhere: Writers on Exile*. London: Faber and Faber, 1994.

Rosenberg, William G., and Marilyn B. Young. *Transforming Russia and China: Revolutionary Struggle in the Twentieth Century*. New York: Oxford University Press, 1982.

Rothstein, Robert. *Alliances and Small Powers*. New York: Columbia University Press, 1968.

Rouse, Roger. "Mexican Migration and the Social Space of Postmodernism." *Diaspora* 1, no. 1 (1991): 8–23.

Rumbaut, Ruben and Ima, Kenji. *The Adaptation of Southeast Asian Refugee Youth: A Comparative Study*. Final Report to the Office of Refugee Resettlement. Washington, DC, 1988.

Rushdie, Salman. *Imaginary Homelands: Essays and Criticism, 1981–1991*. New York: Penguin, 1992.

Said, Edward. "Reflections on Exile." In *Altogether Elsewhere: Writers on Exile*, edited by Marc Robinson. London: Faber and Faber, 1994.

———. *Culture and Imperialism*. New York: Vintage, 1993.

———. "The Mind of Winter: Reflections on Life in Exile." *Harper's Magazine*, September 1984, 49–55.

————. *Orientalism*. New York: Vintage, 1979.

Sak, Sutsakhan. *The Khmer Republic at War and the Final Collapse*. Indochina Monographs. Washington, DC: US Army Center of Military History, 1980.

Schama, Simon. *Citizens: A Chronicle of the French Revolution*. New York: Vintage, 1989.

Schlund-Vials, Cathy J. *War, Genocide and Justice: Cambodian American Memory Work*. Minneapolis: University of Minnesota Press, 2012.

Schurmann, Franz. *Ideology and Organization in Communist China*. Berkeley: University of California Press, 1966.

Schwab, Gabriele. *Haunting Legacies: Violent Histories and Generational Trauma*. New York: Columbia University Press, 2010.

Scott, James. *Domination and the Arts of Resistance: Hidden Transcripts*. New Haven: Yale University Press, 1992.

SEARAC. *Southeast Asian Americans at a Glance: Statistics on Southeast Asians Adapted from the American Community Survey*. Washington, DC: Southeast Asia Resource and Action Center, 2011.

Sémelin, Jacques. *Purify and Destroy: The Political Uses of Massacre and Genocide*. Translated by Cynthia Schoch. New York: Columbia University Press, 2009.

————. "Analysis of Mass Crime: Ethnic Cleansing in the Former Yugoslavia, 1991–1999." Montreal Institute for Genocide and Human Rights Studies Occasional Papers Series, October 2000.

Shafer, Boyd. *Nationalism, Myth and Reality*. New York: Harvest Books, 1955.

Shain, Yossi. *Marketing the American Creed Abroad: Diasporas in the U.S. and Their Homelands*. Cambridge: Cambridge University Press, 1999.

Sharp, Bruce. "Counting Hell." 2008. http://www.mekong.net/cambodia/deaths.htm.

Shawcross, William. *The Quality of Mercy: Cambodia, Holocaust, and Modern Conscience*. New York: Simon and Schuster, 1984.

————. *Sideshow*. New York: Simon and Schuster, 1979.

Short, Philip. *Pol Pot: Anatomy of a Nightmare*. New York: Holt, 2006.

Shub, David. *Lenin*. New York: Mentor, 1948.

Skocpol, Theda. "What Makes Peasants Revolutionary? A Review." *Comparative Politics* 14, no. 3 (April 1982): 351–75.

————. *States and Social Revolutions*. Cambridge: Cambridge University Press, 1979.

Smith, Linda Tuhiwai. *Decolonizing Methodologies: Research and Indigenous Peoples*. London: Zed, 1999.

Smith, Roger. "Cambodia: Social and Historical Background." In *Conflict in Indochina: A Reader on the Widening War in Laos and Cambodia*, edited by Marvin Gettleman, Susan Gettleman, and Carol Kaplan. New York: Random House, 1970.

————. *Cambodia's Foreign Policy*. Ithaca: Cornell University Press, 1965.

Smith-Hefner, Nancy. *Khmer American Identity and Moral Education in a Diasporic Community*. Berkeley: University of California Press, 1999.

Snepp, Frank. *Decent Interval: An Insider's Account of Saigon's Indecent End*. New York: Random House, 1977.

So, Farina. *The Hijab of Cambodia: Memory of Cham Muslim Women after the Khmer Rouge*. Documentation Series, no. 16. Phnom Penh: Documentation Center of Cambodia, 2011.

Solomon, Richard H. *Mao's Revolution and the Chinese Political Culture*. Berkeley: University of California Press, 1971.

Sontag, Susan. *On Photography*. New York: Picador, 2001.

Stammel, Nadine, Sebastian Burchert, Sopheap Taing, Estelle Bockers, and Christine Knaevelsrud. "The Survivors' Voices: Attitudes on the ECCC, the Former Khmer Rouge and Civil Party Participation." Berlin Center for the Treatment of Torture Victims, Berlin, December 2010.

Starr, Richard. *Yearbook on International Communist Affairs, 1970*. Palo Alto: Hoover Institutions, 1971.

Steinbach, Jerome, and Jocelyn Steinbach. *Phnom-Penh libérée: Cambodge l'autre sourire*. Paris: Editions Sociales, 1976.

Steinberg, David Joel, ed. *In Search of Southeast Asia: A Modern History*. Honolulu: University of Hawaii Press, 1985.

Stern, Jacques. *The French Colonies: Past and Future*. Translated by Norbert Guberman. New York: Didier, 1944.

Stewart, Frank, and Sharon May, eds. *In The Shadow of Angkor*. Honolulu: University of Hawaii Press, 2002.

Stoler, Ann. "Imperial Debris: Reflections on Ruins and Ruination." *Cultural Anthropology* 23, no. 2 (2008): 191–219.

Straus, Scott. "Second-Generation Comparative Research on Genocide." *World Politics* 59, no 3 (April 2007): 476–501.

Stuart-Fox, Martin. *The Murderous Revolution: Life and Death in Pol Pot's Kampuchea*. Chippendale, New South Wales: Alternative Publishing Cooperative, 1985.

Summers, Laura. "The Secret Vanguard of Pol Pot's Revolution." *Journal of Communist Studies* 3, no. 1 (March 1987): 5–18.

Swain, Jon. *River of Time*. London: Minerva Edition, 1996.

Szymusiak, Molyda. *Les pierres crieront: Une enfance cambodgienne, 1975–1980*. Paris: Editions La Decouverte, 1984.

Tchou Ta-Kuan. *The Customs of Cambodia*. Bangkok: Siam Society, 1929.

Tenhula, John. *Voices from Southeast Asia: The Refugee Experience in the United States*. New York: Holmes and Meier, 1991.

Thion, Serge. *Watching Cambodia*. Bangkok: White Lotus, 2000.

———. "The Pattern of Cambodian Politics." In *The Cambodian Agony*, edited by David Ablin and Marlowe Hood, 149–64. Armonk, NY: M. E. Sharpe, 1990.

———. "The Cambodian Idea of Revolution." In *Revolution and Its Aftermath in Kampuchea: Eight Essays*, edited by David Chandler and Ben Kiernan, 10–33. New Haven: Yale University Southeast Asia Studies, 1983.

———. "The Ingratitude of the Crocodiles: The 1978 Cambodian Black Paper." *Bulletin of Concerned Asian Scholars* 12, no. 4 (1980): 38–54.

Thion, Serge, and Ben Kiernan. *Khmer Rouges!* Paris: J. E. Hallier, 1981.

Thompson, Virginia. *French Indochina*. New York: Macmillan, 1937.

Thomson, R. S. "The Establishment of the French Protectorate over Cambodia." *Far Eastern Quarterly* 4, no. 4 (1945): 313–40.

Tilly, Charles. "Revolutions and Collective Violence." In *Handbook of Political Science*, edited by Fred I. Greenstein and Nelson Polsby. Boston: Addison-Wesley Educational, 1975.

Todorov, Tzvetan. "Memory as Remedy for Evil." *Journal of International Criminal Justice* 7 (2009): 447–62.

———. *Facing the Extreme: Moral Life in the Concentration Camps*. New York: Henry Holt, 1996.

Tooze, Ruth. *Cambodia: Land of Contrasts*. New York: Viking, 1962.

Tucker, Robert C., ed. *The Lenin Anthology*. New York: Norton, 1975.

Tully, John. *France on the Mekong*. New York: University Press of America, 2002.

U Sam Oeur. *Crossing Three Wildernesses*. Minneapolis: Coffee House Press, 2005.

———. "Interview with U Sam Oeur." By Sharon May. In *In the Shadow of Angkor*, edited by Frank Stewart and Sharon May. Honolulu: University of Hawaii Press, 2002.

———. *Sacred Vows*. Translated by Ken McCullough. Minneapolis: Coffee House Press, 1998.

Um, Khatharya. "Education in Colonial and Post-Colonial Cambodia: Technology of Dominance, Technology of Liberation." In *Equity, Opportunity and Education in Postcolonial Southeast Asia*, edited by Cynthia Joseph. New York: Routledge, 2014.

———. "History, Postmemory, and Second Generation Cambodians." Paper presented at Creation and Postmemory Conference, Columbia University, New York, April 9–10, 2013.

———. "Exiled Memory: History, Identity and Remembering in the South East Asian Diaspora." In "Southeast Asians in the Diaspora," edited by Mimi Nguyen, Fiona Ngo, and Miriam Lam. Special issue, *Positions* 20, no. 3 (2012): 831–50.

———. "Southeast Asians in the U.S.: Communities in Transition." In *Encyclopedia of Asian American Issues Today*, edited by Edith Chen and Grace Yoo. Santa Barbara, CA: Greenwood, 2009.

———. "Political Remittances." In *Diasporas: Peace Builders or Peace Wreckers?*, edited by Hazel Smith and Paul Starr, 253–79. Tokyo: United Nations University Press, 2006a.

———. "The Vietnam War: What's in a Name?" *Amerasia* 31, no. 2 (2006b): 134–39.

———. "Diasporic Nationalism and Citizenship." *Refuge* 23, no. 2 (2005): 8–19.

———. "The Broken Chain: Genocide in the Re-Construction and De-Struction of Cambodian Society." *Social Identities* 4, no. 1 (1998): 131–54.

Ung, Loung. *Lucky Child: A Daughter of Cambodia Reunited with the Sister She Left Behind*. New York: Harper Collins, 2005.

———. *First They Killed My Father: A Daughter of Cambodia Remembers*. New York: Harper Collins, 2000.

Van Boemel, Gretchen B., and Patricia D. Rozée. "Treatment for Psychosomatic Blindness among Cambodian Refugee Women." *Women and Therapy* 13, no. 3 (1992): 239–66.

Van Schaak, Beth, Daryn Reicherter, Youk Chhang, and Autumn Talbot, eds. *Cambodia's Hidden Scars: Trauma Psychology in the Wake of the Khmer Rouge, an Edited Volume on Cambodia's Mental Health*. Phnom Penh: Documentation Center of Cambodia, 2011.

Vann Nath. *A Cambodian Prison Portrait: One Year in the Khmer Rouge's S-21*. Bangkok: White Lotus, 1998.

Vickery, Michael. *Cambodia: 1975–1982*. Boston: South End, 1984.

———. "Democratic Kampuchea: Themes and Variations." In *Revolution and Its Aftermath in Kampuchea: Eight Essays*, edited by David Chandler and Ben Kiernan, 99–135. New Haven: Yale University Southeast Asia Studies, 1983.

Vilim, Laura. "Keeping Them Alive, One Gets Nothing; Killing Them, One Loses Nothing: Prosecuting Khmer Rouge Medical Practices as Crimes against Humanity." Documentation Center of Cambodia, Phnom Penh, 2010.

Wakeman, Frederick, Jr. "Rebellion and Revolution: The Study of Popular Movements in Chinese History." *Journal of Asian Studies* 31, no. 2 (February 1977): 201–37.

Wallimann, Isidor, and Michael N. Dobkowski, eds. *Genocide and the Modern Age: Etiology and Case Studies of Mass Death*. Syracuse: Syracuse University Press, 1987.

Webb, Kate. *On the Other Side: 23 Days with the Viet Cong*. New York: Quadrangle, 1972.

Weil, Jennifer M., and Hwayun H. Lee. "Cultural Considerations in Understanding Family Violence among Asian American Pacific Islander Families." *Journal of Community Health Nursing* 21, no. 4 (2004): 217–27.

Wicker, Hans-Rudolf, and Hans-Karl Schoch. "Refugees and Mental Health: Southeast Asian Refugees in Switzerland." In *Refugees—The Trauma of Exile: The Humanitarian Role of Red Cross and Red Crescent*, ed. D. Miserez. Dordrecht: Martinus Nijhoff, 1988.

Wiesel, Elie. *All Rivers Run to the Sea: A Memoir*. New York: Knopf, 1995.

———. *From the Kingdom of Memory: Reminiscences*. New York: Summit, 1990.

Willmott, William E. *The Chinese in Cambodia*. Toronto: University of British Columbia, 1967.

Wong, Sau-ling. "Denationalization Reconsidered: Asian American Cultural Criticism at a Theoretical Crossroads." *Amerasia Journal* 21, nos. 1–2 (1995): 1–27.

Yamada, Terri. "The Spirit Cult of Klang Moeung in Long Beach California." Paper presented at the Association of Asian Studies, Washington, DC, 1998.

Yang Sam. *Khmer Buddhism and Politics, 1954–1984*. Newington, CT: Khmer Studies Institute, 1987.

Yimsut, Ronnie. *Facing the Khmer Rouge: A Cambodian Journey*. New Jersey: Rutgers University Press, 2011.

———. "The Tonle Sap Lake Massacre." *Khmer Voice*, n.d. http://www.edwebproject.org/sideshow/stories/ronnieyimsut.html.

Yin, Luoth. *The Land of Tears*. Seattle: Hara, 1998.

Yoshioka, M. R., and Q. Dang. "Asian Family Violence Report: A Study of the Cambodian, Chinese, Korean, South Asian, and Vietnamese Communities in Massachusetts." Asian Task Force against Domestic Violence, Boston, 2000.

Young, James. "Between History And Memory." In *Witness and Memory: The Discourse of Trauma*, edited by Ana Douglass and Thomas Vogler, 275–84. New York: Routledge, 2003.

Ysa, Osman. *The Cham Rebellion: Survivors' Stories from the Villages*. Phnom Penh: Documentation Center of Cambodia, 2006.

———. *Oukoubah*. Phnom Penh: Documentation Center of Cambodia, 2002.

Zasloff, J. J., and A. E. Goodman. *Indochina in Conflict*. Lexington, MA: Lexington, 1972.

Zeleza, Paul Tiyambe. "The Politics of Poetics of Exile: Edward Said in Africa." *Research in African Literatures* 36, no. 3 (2005): 1–22.

Zia, Helen. *Asian American Dreams: The Emergence of an American People*. New York: Farrar, Strauss, and Giroux, 2000.

INDEX

Absence, 5, 83, 185, 187, 188, 197, 204, 227, 246

Absolutism (*pdach kar niyum*), 171

Accountability, 206–7, 209–11, 256–58, 290n127

Achar (laymen with religious training), 129

Agamben, Giorgio, 29, 38, 45, 66

Agrarian society, 87, 91; abundance of land and natural resources of, 94–96; objective conditions of, 94–96, 271n133, 272n140

Agricultural proletariats, 99

Agriculture: education relating to, 63; under Khmer Rouge, 158, 165; under Sihanouk, 103

Aid to Families with Dependent Children (AFDC), 221

Akineth, 149, 281n89

Algos (pain), 235

Ali, Anida, 249, 250

Altruism, 37; consideration (*yok-yul khnear*), 37

Ambivalence, 154–57

American aid, 91, 108

American Dream, 234

Anech kachun (overseas Cambodians), 249

Angkar (the Organization), 26, 28, 41, 155, 282n122

Angkar, children of: abandonment of, 66; abject conditions of, 55–57; citizen-soldier, 62–69; education and social engineering, 62–69; hope of, 68–69; living conditions of, 51–55; in prison, 50–51; reconstruction of, 61; shame and guilt of, 60; solidarity, 67; stain, 69–71; starvation of, 50, 55–59, 60, 68; survival of, 58–59, 71; terror of, 60, 62, 66, 70; work assignments of, 54–55, 266n4

Angkar Loeu, 45

Ang-kor daem, 138, 170

Ang-kor sraley (cotton rice grains), 32, 264n33

Annihilation, 177–78

Anti-imperialist platform, 88

Apology: from Kaing Guek Eav, 253; significance of, 255–56

Arendt, Hannah, 29, 118, 135, 150, 151, 169, 182, 279n13

Art, 10, 204, 205–6, 237, 239, 251, 252

Asian American studies, 8, 17

Asian studies, 8

Assassination attempt, 281n62; on monarchy, 85–86, 269n64; on Pol Pot, 280n59

Atrocities. *See* Mass atrocities

Authenticity, 8, 15, 155, 160, 250

Auto-genocide, 5, 19, 70, 183, 184, 210, 261n5

Bad karma (*kam*), 97

Bam bak sbat (breaking of inner fortitude), 66

Barb (sins), 130

Bare life, 29, 38

Bartering, 32, 37, 38

Base Areas, 110, 116, 130, 146

Base peasants (*mulathan*), 29, 32, 36, 39, 40–41, 43, 263n19

ABOUT THE AUTHOR

Khatharya Um is a political scientist and Associate Professor in the Department of Ethnic Studies at the University of California–Berkeley. She has written extensively on Southeast Asia and Southeast Asian American issues, and is widely recognized for her community leadership, advocacy, and service. She is the first Cambodian American woman to receive a PhD.

CPSIA information can be obtained at www.ICGtesting.com
Printed in the USA
BVOW08s0240130816

458674BV00002B/2/P